AMERICA UNRIVALED

A volume in the series

CORNELL STUDIES IN SECURITY AFFAIRS

edited by Robert J. Art, Robert Jervis, and Stephen M. Walt

A full list of titles in the series appears at the end of the book.

Published under the auspices of the
  Woodrow Wilson International Center for Scholars

AMERICA UNRIVALED

The Future of
the Balance of Power

EDITED BY

G. John Ikenberry

CORNELL UNIVERSITY PRESS

Ithaca and London

First published 2002 by Cornell University Press
First printing, Cornell Paperbacks, 2002

Printed in the United States of America

Library of Congress Cataloging-in-Publication Data

America unrivaled : the future of the balance of power / edited by G. John Ikenberry.

       p. cm. — (Cornell studies in security affairs)
  ISBN 0-8014-4063-7 (cloth : alk. paper) — ISBN 0-8014-8802-8 (pbk. : alk. paper)
    1. United States—Foreign relations—2001–   2. Balance of power.   3. National security—United States.   I. Ikenberry, G. John.   II. Series.
  E895 .A44 2002
  327.73—dc21

                     2002004120

Cloth printing   10   9   8   7   6   5   4   3   2   1

Paperback printing   10   9   8   7   6   5   4   3   2

Contents

v

Contributors

G. JOHN IKENBERRY is the Peter F. Krogh Professor of Geopolitics and Global Justice in the School of Foreign Service and Government Department at Georgetown University.

JOSEF JOFFE is publisher and editor of the German weekly *Die Zeit* and associate of the Olin Center for Strategic Studies at Harvard University.

CHARLES A. KUPCHAN is associate professor in the School of Foreign Service and Government Department at Georgetown University and senior fellow at the Council on Foreign Relations.

MICHAEL MASTANDUNO is professor of government and director of the John Sloan Dickey Center for International Understanding at Dartmouth College.

JOHN M. OWEN IV is assistant professor of government and foreign affairs at the University of Virginia.

THOMAS RISSE is professor and chair of international politics at the Department of Political and Social Science, Free University of Berlin, Germany.

STEPHEN M. WALT is the Robert and Renee Belfer Professor of International Affairs at the John F. Kennedy School of Government at Harvard University and Faculty Chair of the International Security Program of the Belfer Center for Science and International Affairs.

KENNETH N. WALTZ is Ford Professor Emeritus of the University of California, Berkeley, and is now an adjunct professor and research associate of the Institute of War and Peace Studies at Columbia University.

WILLIAM C. WOHLFORTH is associate professor of government at Dartmouth College.

Acknowledgments

The idea for this book began when I spent a year as a visiting fellow at the Woodrow Wilson International Center for Scholars in Washington, D.C., during the 1998–99 academic year. I thank the Woodrow Wilson Center—and particularly its director of international studies, Robert Litwak—for supporting this project and for hosting a conference in May 2000 where the chapters in this book were first presented. I am also grateful to Robert Lieber, Geir Lundestad, and Tony Smith for their participation in this conference. Jessica Wolfe and Thomas Wright provided helpful research and editorial assistance. I also thank Robert Art and Stephen Krasner for comments on earlier drafts of the chapters and overall editorial suggestions. Finally, I thank Roger Haydon for his keen editorial eye and help in moving the project to publication.

G. J. I.

Washington, D.C.

AMERICA UNRIVALED

Introduction

G. John Ikenberry

The preeminence of American power today is unprecedented in modern history. No other great power has enjoyed such formidable advantages in military, economic, technological, cultural, or political capabilities. We live in a one-superpower world, and there is no serious competitor in sight. Other states rival the United States in one area or another, but it is the multifaceted character of American power that makes it so commanding, far reaching, and provocative. The sudden collapse of the Soviet Union, the decline in rival ideologies, and the successful restructuring of the American economy all intensified these power asymmetries during the 1990s.

Disparities in economic and military power between the United States and the other major states widened during the 1990s. Between 1990 and 1998, United States economy grew by 27 percent, almost twice that of the European Union (15 percent) and three times that of Japan (9 percent). The weakness of the Euro today is ultimately a result of these divergent European and American economic trends. While Europe and Japan have struggled with economic restructuring, the United States has ridden the wave of the "new economy" and rising productivity. The United States also reduced defense spending at a slower rate after the Cold War than the other major powers, resulting in greater relative military capabilities by the end of the 1990s. In fact, it has come close in recent years to monopolizing military-related research and development, spending roughly 80 percent of the world's total. The twentieth century may have ended, but the American century gives every indication of becoming a long-running phenomenon.[1]

The world has taken note of America's commanding position. "The United States of America today predominates on the economic level, the monetary level, on the technological level, and in the cultural area in the broadest sense of the word," the French foreign minister, Hubert Védrine, observed in a speech in Paris in early 1999. "It is not comparable, in terms of power and influence, to anything known in modern history."[2] The American-led air campaign in Kosovo intensified perceptions of unchecked American hegemony—or what some European diplomats call American "hyperpower." During the Cold War, the Soviet Union and the United States restrained each other. Today the restraints are less evident, and this has made American power increasingly controversial. In May 1999, the Oxford Union debated the proposition: "Resolved, the United States is a rogue state." The resolution was ultimately voted down, but the debate continues.

The rise of a unipolar American order after the Cold War has not yet triggered a global backlash but it has unsettled relationships worldwide. Europeans worry about the steadiness of American leadership. Other governments and peoples around the world resent the omnipotence and intrusiveness of American power, markets, and culture. Some intellectuals in the West even suggest that an arrogant and overbearing America brought the terrorism of September 11, 2001, on itself.[3] Aside from diffuse hatreds and resentments, the practical reality for many states around the world is that they need the United States more than it needs them—or so it would seem. In the early months of the Bush administration the political consequences of being the sole superpower seemed all too obvious. It could walk away from treaties and agreements with other countries—including the Kyoto Protocol, the International Criminal Court, the Germ

---

[1] Calculated from OECD statistics (July 1999 web edition). GDP measures are figured at 1990 prices and exchange rates. See International Institute for Strategic Studies, *The Military Balance 1999/2000* (London: Oxford University Press, 1999).

[2] Quoted in Craig R. Whitney, "NATO at 50: With Nations at Odds, Is It a Misalliance?" *New York Times*, February 15, 1999, A7. See also, Roger Cohen, "Shifts in Europe Pose Prickly Challenge to U.S.," *New York Times*, February 11, 2001, A4.

[3] See for example, Steven Erlanger, "In Europe, Some Say the Attacks Stemmed from American Failings," *The New York Times*, September 22, 2001; and Elaine Sciolino, "Who Hates the U.S.? Who Loves It?" *The New York Times*, September 23, 2001. For imperial views of American power, see Chalmers Johnson, *Blowback: The Costs and Consequences of American Empire* (New York: Henry Holt, 2000); and Michael Hardt and Antonio Negri, *Empire* (Cambridge, Mass.: Harvard University Press, 2000).

Weapons Ban, and the Trade in Light Arms Treaty—and suffer fewer consequences than its partners.

American unipolar power raises important theoretical and policy issues. Rapid shifts in the distribution of power are interesting to scholars because they allow more acute assessment of competing theories about the sources of international order. International relations theories advance very different views about the character and durability of order built on such an extraordinary concentration of power. During the Cold War, both realist and liberal theories posited similar patterns of order among the Western industrial democracies. Both expected high levels of cooperation and alliance cohesion. But the end of this Cold War threat—combined with the recent intensification of American power—lead these theories to expect very different outcomes.

One debate that comes clearly into focus with these changing circumstances concerns the realist theory of balance of power. This is the most elegant and time-honored theory of international order: order is the result of balancing by states under conditions of anarchy to counter opposing power concentrations or threats. In this view, American preponderance is unsustainable: it poses a basic threat to other states and balancing reactions are inevitable. "There is one ideology left standing, liberal democratic capitalism, and one institution with universal reach, the United States," observes Fareed Zakaria. "If the past is any guide, America's primacy will provoke growing resistance."[4] Resistance has in fact appeared and may be growing. But it is remarkable that despite the sharp shifts in the distribution of power, the other great powers have not yet responded in a way anticipated by balance-of-power theory.

The central puzzle that this book addresses is: why? Why, despite the widening power gulf between the United States and the other major states, has a counterbalancing reaction not yet taken place? Despite the disappearance of the Soviet threat, it is difficult to discern a significant decline in alliance solidarity between the United States and its European and Asian partners. Both NATO and the U.S.–Japan alliance have recently reaffirmed and deepened their ties. Nor have wider realms of political and economic cooperation or accompanying multilateral relations declined in serious ways. Trade and investment has expanded across the Atlantic and Pacific and an increasingly dense web of intergovernmental and transnational relations connect these countries. "Rather than edging away

---

[4] Fareed Zakaria, "The Empire Strikes Out," *New York Times Magazine*, April 18, 1999, 99. For views along these lines, see Peter W. Rodman, "The World's Resentment: Anti-Americanism as a Global Phenomenon," *The National Interest* 60 (summer 2000): 33–41; and Samuel Huntington, "The Lonely Superpower," *Foreign Affairs* 78, no. 2 (March/April 1999): 35–49.

from the United States, much less balancing against it, Germany and Japan have been determined to maintain the pattern of engagement that characterized the Cold War," argues Michael Mastanduno. "Neither China nor Russia, despite having some differences with the United States, has sought to organize a balancing coalition against it. Indeed, the main security concern for many countries in Europe and Asia is not how to distance from an all-too-powerful United States, but how to prevent the United States from drifting away."[5] Despite the most radical shifts in international power in half a century, the relations among the major states have remained remarkably stable and continuous. This is surprising: according to the traditional realist account there should be fewer reasons to ally with and more reasons to resist American power.

For some, the realist expectation of a return to a global balance of power will eventually be realized. Kenneth Waltz argues in this volume that realist theory clearly expects that "balances disturbed will one day be restored," but it cannot predict when national governments will respond to these structural pressures. In Waltz's structural realist view, unipolarity is the least durable of international configurations and inevitably will provoke actions and responses by the dominant and weaker states that will ultimately return the system to a more traditional balance-of-power order. A unipolar state is fundamentally unrestrained, and this makes its foreign policy less disciplined and more dangerous to other states. Resistance and counterbalancing will follow. Indeed, Waltz claims that one can observe "balancing tendencies already taking place." But full-scale balancing has not yet been manifest. When Russian and Chinese leaders meet they inevitably complain about the dangers of American hegemony, but serious counterbalancing steps—such as a formal alliance or joint military mobilization—have not occurred. As Stephen Walt notes, it is "striking how half-hearted and ineffective these efforts are" to counter American power. The puzzle is to explain the dog that has not yet barked. Or as the question is posed in this book: is a balance-of-power order—triggered by a backlash against American unipolar power—just around the corner, or have some characteristics of today's international order altered or even eliminated the logic of power balancing?

The chapters that follow provide widely divergent answers to this question but most agree that nuclear weapons, the spread of capitalism and democracy, and novel features of American hegemony complicate or render unlikely the automatic return to a traditional balance-of-power order.

---

[5] Michael Mastanduno, "Preserving the Unipolar Moment: Realist Theories and U.S. Grand Strategy after the Cold War," *International Security* 21, no. 4 (spring 1997): 58.

Beyond this, the arguments offered by the authors tend to hinge on their response to three questions about the character of American unipolarity.

First, is American power different and less threatening to other states than that envisaged in theoretical and historical claims about the balance of power? Charles V, Louis XIV, Napoleon I, Wilhelm II, and Nazi Germany all inspired massive counterbalancing responses. Is the United States simply the most recent in a long line of powerful states, and like these earlier states soon to encounter the same response, or is the United States a new type of powerful state whose singularity carries implications for how other states respond to its hegemonic capacities? These unique features of American power might stem from geography, technology, ideology, democracy, or its institutional and policy commitments. If there are features of American power that mute or restrain it, the risk calculations of weaker and secondary states will be altered. It also matters whether these restraining characteristics are deeply rooted in the American polity—and therefore not easily compromised by the vagaries of specific state leaders or actions—or whether restraint is a more delicate, day-to-day matter fundamentally in the hands of foreign policy officials. Is it the American polity or its policy—or both—that is at work?

Second, does American unipolar power solve problems for other states in ways that serve to diminish the incentives for weaker states to resort to counterbalancing? Some authors argue that there is a demand for American power. For example, its security commitments help overcome regional security dilemmas in Europe, Asia, and the Middle East, and its domestic economy provides an essential market for exports. The security and economic costs and benefits of the current unipolar order must be compared with the costs and benefits of whatever order might emerge from a return to a balance of power. It also matters if these American commitments—such as extended overseas security cooperation and an open domestic economy—are affordable to the United States. If the costs to the United States of its hegemonic services are modest and sustainable and other states prefer the situation to any conceivable alternative, the unipolar order might well be stable. But if the domestic costs of hegemony are high, growing, and ultimately unsustainable regardless of the costs and benefits for other states, unipolar order is doomed.

Finally, what does balancing really mean in today's global system? American power today is not just expressed in its military capabilities. It is also manifest in its expansive culture and economy. If the complaint about American power has to do with the spread of its popular culture, there are policy responses available—such as trade protectionism—but this has little to do with the balance of power. If it is the dominance of America's so-called New Economy, the response might entail policy and institutional reforms at home but the reconfiguration of global military alliances is again not responsive to the underlying problem. Muslim fundamentalism may be threatened by the economic, social, and military reach of American power but will terrorism—even of the horrific sort inflicted on New York and Washington in September 2001—alter that long-run stability? Specifying the precise threat posed by American power and the likely responses is critical to understanding the coming politics of unipolarity. Even if the threats are of the more traditional sort—that is, highly asymmetrical military capabilities—the practical question still arises: can counterbalancing alliances alter the risks inherent in sharp power disparities? If traditional military balancing responses to American power are not available or not responsive to the specific threat that American power poses to other states, are there other types of pre- or neobalancing steps that these states might pursue in specific policy realms?

Besides the theoretical questions that are at stake in this unipolarity debate, there are also important policy implications for American foreign policy makers. If we are moving into an era of strategic rivalry—and an eventual end to the postwar alliance system—a radically new American grand strategy will be necessary.[6] If an incipient balancing order is emerging, the United States must prepare to operate within it. If the current order is stable, we need to know what policies reinforce stability and what policies weaken it. Liberal theories argue that institutional strategies can mitigate power disparities and security dilemmas and therefore have an impact on the incentives that states have to balance against concentrated power. American hegemonic power is rendered more acceptable to others because of the dense institutional structures in which it is situated. This argument leads to a very different foreign policy agenda. As the global controversy over American power increases in the years ahead, answers to these questions about the sources of order and the logic of power balancing become especially critical. By focusing on the theoretical controversy, this book yields answers to the policy questions as well.

---

[6] A large and growing literature has emerged on American grand strategy. For a survey, see Barry R. Posen and Andrew L. Ross, "Competing Visions for U.S. Grand Strategy," *International Security* 21, no. 3 (winter 1996/97): 5–53. Other works, in addition to those cited elsewhere in this introduction, include Robert Art, "Geopolitics Updated: The Strategy of Selective Engagement," *International Security* 23, no. 3 (winter 1998–99): 79–113; Christopher Layne, "From Preponderance to Offshore Balancing: America's Future Grand Strategy," *International Security* 22, no. 1 (summer 1997): 86–124; Layne, "Rethinking American Grand Strategy," *World Policy Journal* 15, no. 2 (summer 1998): 8–28; Eugene Gholz, Daryl G. Press, and Harvey M. Sapolsky, "Come Home, America: A Strategy of Restraint in the Face of Temptation," *International Security* 21, no. 4 (spring 1997): 5–48; and Charles A. Kupchan, "Life after Pax Americana," *World Policy Journal* 16, no. 3 (fall 1999): 20–27.

The debate about the future of American unipolarity hinges on answers to the questions posed above. This book does not propose to do the impossible—to settle this debate. It does attempt to sharpen the alternative positions and illuminate the theoretical and policy questions that are at stake. This is a debate both within the realist tradition and between realists and nonrealists. Many authors use the Waltzian structural realist position as a starting point and advance their own theoretical position by exploring the current post–Cold War pattern of relations among the major states—both the relations among the industrial democracies and between them and the other (non-Western) great powers. Others advance liberal and identity-based theories that diminish the importance of asymmetrical power relations and the balancing logic, arguing in one way or another that the United States and the other advanced democratic countries have created a liberal political order largely inexplicable in realist theory. We can look more closely at this theoretical debate and the contending views of American unipolarity advanced in this book.

Balance of Power and Hegemony

The debate about the future of American unipolarity is really a debate about the sources of international order. The realist tradition advances the most clearly defined answers to the basic question of how order is created among states. The fundamental realist claim is that order is created and maintained by state power and shifts in order are ultimately driven by shifts in the distribution of state power. Built on this view, realism—and its neorealist advancements—offers two images of order in world politics: balance of power and hegemony.[7]

Balance-of-power theory explains order and the pattern of relations among major states as the result of balancing to counter opposing power concentrations or threats.[8] Order is the product of an ongoing process of balancing and adjustment among states under conditions of anarchy. Bal-

[7] For a survey of realist theories and their expectations about the post–Cold War international order, see Michael Mastanduno, "A Realist View: Three Images of the Coming International Order," in *International Order and the Future of World Politics,* ed. T. V. Paul and John A. Hall (London: Cambridge University Press, 1999), 19–40; and Michael Mastanduno and Ethan B. Kapstein, "Realism and State Strategies after the Cold War," in *Unipolar Politics: Realism and State Strategies after the Cold War,* ed. Mastanduno and Kapstein (New York: Columbia University Press, 1999). See also Dale Copeland, *The Origins of Great Power Wars* (Ithaca, N.Y.: Cornell University Press, 2000).

[8] See Kenneth Waltz, *Theory of International Politics* (Reading, Mass.: Addison-Wesley, 1979). For extensions and debates, see Robert O. Keohane, ed., *Neorealism and Its Critics* (New York: Columbia University Press, 1986).

ancing can be pursued both internally and externally—through domestic mobilization and through the formation of temporary alliances among threatened states to resist and counterbalance a looming or threatening concentration of power. Under conditions of anarchy, alliances will come and go as temporary expedients, states will guard their autonomy, and entangling institutions will be resisted. Balance-of-power theories vary over how explicit and self-conscious the rules of balance are.[9]

In a unipolar distribution of power, balance-of-power realism makes a clear prediction: weaker states will resist and balance against the predominant state. Security—indeed survival—is the fundamental goal of states, and because states cannot ultimately rely on the commitments or guarantees of other states to ensure their security, states will be very sensitive to their relative power position. When powerful states emerge, secondary states will seek protection in countervailing coalitions of weaker states. Alternative strategies put states at risk of domination. As Kenneth Waltz argues: "Secondary states, if they are free to choose, flock to the weaker side; for it is the stronger side that threatens them. On the weaker side they are both more appreciated and safer, provided, of course, that the coalition they join achieves enough defensive or deterrent strength to dissuade adversaries from attacking."[10] Alliances emerge as temporary coalitions of states formed to counter the concentration of power. As the distribution of power shifts, coalitions will also shift.

Waltz contrasts balancing with "bandwagoning." In domestic politics, losers in a leadership election have an incentive to jump on the bandwagon of the winning candidate. But in international politics to do so would allow the emergence of a "world hegemony," which would leave weaker states at the mercy of the strong. In anarchy, the only effective check on the rising power of another state is to increase your own power or combine with other states to resist domination.[11] The character of the

[9] The order that emerges is either the unintended outcome of balancing pressures or a reflection of learned and formalized rules of equilibrium and balance. For discussions of balance-of-power politics, see Martin Wight, "The Balance of Power," in *Diplomatic Investigations*, ed. Butterfield and Wight (Cambridge, Mass.: Harvard University Press, 1966), 149–76; Edward V. Gulick, *Europe's Classical Balance of Power* (New York: Norton, 1967); Inis L. Claude Jr., *Power and International Relations* (New York: Random House, 1962), 3–93; Claude, "The Balance of Power Revisited," *Review of International Studies* 15 (April 1989): 77–86; Ernst Haas, "The Balance of Power: Prescription, Concept, or Propaganda," *World Politics* 15, no. 3 (1953): 370–98; Stephen M. Walt, *The Origins of Alliances* (Ithaca, N.Y.: Cornell University Press, 1987); Glenn H. Snyder, *Alliance Politics* (Ithaca, N.Y.: Cornell University Press, 1997); Michael W. Doyle, *Ways of War and Peace* (New York: Norton, 1997), chap. 5; and John A. Vasquez and Colin Elman, eds., *Realism and the Balancing of Power: A New Debate* (Cambridge, Mass.: MIT Press, 2000).

[10] Waltz, *Theory of International Politics*, 127.

[11] Ibid., 126.

dominant state—its ideology, regime type, leadership, or history—is ultimately not sufficiently reliable as guides or guarantees to future state action. Only power can check power and this is precisely what balancing entails.

Aside from balance-of-power theory, a second neorealist theory holds that order is created and maintained by a hegemonic state that uses power capabilities to organize relations among states.[12] The preponderance of power by a state allows it to offer positive and negative incentives to the other states to agree to ongoing participation within the hegemonic order. According to Robert Gilpin, an international order is, at any particular moment in history, the reflection of the underlying distribution of power of states within the system. Over time, this distribution of power shifts, leading to conflicts and ruptures in the system, hegemonic war, and the eventual reorganization of order so as to reflect the new distribution of power capabilities. It is the rising hegemonic state or group of states, whose power position has been ratified by war, that defines the terms of the postwar settlement and the character of the new order.

The strong version of hegemonic order is built around direct and coercive domination of weaker and secondary states by the hegemon. But hegemonic orders can also be more benevolent and less coercive—organized around more reciprocal, consensual, and institutionalized relations. The order is still organized around asymmetrical power relations, but the most overtly malign character of domination is muted.[13]

Following this observation, it is possible to posit three types of mechanisms that explain the persistence of a hegemonic order. The first is coercive domination. Weaker and secondary states are not happy about their subordinate position and would actively seek to overturn the order if they were capable of doing so. But the prevailing power distribution provides insufficient capabilities for these states to challenge the dominant state. This political formation is in effect an informal imperial order.[14] Power—

[12] See Robert Gilpin, *War and Change in World Politics* (New York: Cambridge University Press, 1981). For other theoretical perspectives, see David Rapkin, ed., *World Leadership and Hegemony* (Boulder, Colo.: Lynne Rienner Publishers, 1990); and William R. Thompson, *On Global War: Historical-Structural Approaches to World Politics* (Columbia: University of South Carolina Press, 1988).

[13] The distinction between benevolent and coercive hegemony is made by Duncan Snidal, "The Limits of Hegemonic Stability Theory," *International Organization* 35 (1985): 579–614; Bruce Russett, "The Mysterious Case of Vanishing Hegemony: Or Is Mark Twain Really Dead?" *International Organization* 39 (1985): 207–31; and Joseph Lepgold, *The Declining Hegemon: The United States and European Defense, 1960–1990* (New York: Praeger, 1990).

[14] For discussion of empires—their sources of order and variation—see Michael Doyle, *Empires* (Ithaca, N.Y.: Cornell University Press, 1986); Alexander Motyl, *Revolutions, Nations, Empires: Conceptual Limits and Theoretical Possibilities* (New York: Columbia University Press, 1999); S. N. Eisenstadt, *The Political Systems of Empires: The Rise and Fall of the Historical Bureau-*

and in the final instance coercive power—keeps the order together. A second type of hegemonic order is held together by some minimal convergence of interests. The dominant state might provide "services" to subordinate states that these states find sufficiently useful to prevent them from actively seeking to overturn the order. As Michael Mastanduno and several other authors in this volume suggest, America's extended military commitment to Asia and Europe is useful to these partner states by solving regional security dilemmas. The alternatives to an American security presence would be more costly and dangerous for these allies and even to nonallies in Europe and Asia. The demand for American hegemony is high. The fact that the United States is geographically remote from these regional problem areas reduces the worry about American domination.

Finally, hegemonic order might be even more thoroughly institutionalized and infused with mutual consent and reciprocal processes of political interaction—so much so that the hierarchy of the order is all but obscured. In effect, it is a liberal hegemony. Where hegemony takes a more benevolent form, with real restraints on the exercise of power, the resulting order begins to reflect less faithfully the underlying distribution of power.[15] As we shall see, the chapters by Ikenberry, Owen, and Risse point in the direction of this sort of explanation. These differences in the character of hegemony lead to differences in why weaker and secondary states do not attempt to balance against the lead state in a hegemonic order. In a highly coercive hegemonic order, weaker and secondary states are simply unable to counterbalance. Domination itself prevents the escape to a balance-of-power system. In more benign and consensual hegemonic orders, where restraints on hegemonic power are sufficiently developed, it is the expected value of balancing that is lowered. Balancing is a choice for weaker and secondary states, but the benign character and institutional limits on hegemonic power reduce the incentives to do so.

---

cratic Societies (New York: Free Press, 1969); and Karen Dawisha and Bruce Parrott, *The Disintegration and Reconstruction of Empires* (Armonk, N.Y.: M. E. Sharpe, 1966). For a broad historical survey of types of international orders in historical and comparative perspective, see Barry Buzan and Richard Little, *International Systems in World History: Remaking the Study of International Relations* (New York: Oxford University Press, 2000).

[15] This conception of hegemonic order is developed in G. John Ikenberry, *After Victory: Institutions, Strategic Restraint, and the Building of Order after Major Wars* (Princeton: Princeton University Press, 2001). These categories of hegemony do not include neo-Marxist conceptions that see domination manifest in the deep structures of capitalist imperialism. The diffuse rules and logic of the American-centered world order inflict "oppression and domination" but through false-consciousness and imperial alliances, the order remains uncontested and even legitimate. See Hardt and Negri, *Empire.*

The Durability of Unipolarity

Structural realism provides an elegant vision of international order and predicts a bleak future for unipolarity. This perspective expects the Cold War political and security relations between the United States and its allies to loosen and move toward more traditional great-power balancing relations. Waltz argues that with the end of bipolarity, "the United States as the strongest power will often find other states edging away from it: Germany moving toward Eastern Europe and Russia, and Russia moving toward Germany and Japan." Nor is NATO likely to remain an effective organization. "We know from balance-of-power theory as well as from history that war-winning coalitions collapse on the morrow of victory, the more surely if it is a decisive victory." Germany will soon find its feet as a great power and resist the historical shackles of the Atlantic alliance. For this reason, "NATO's days are not numbered, but its years are."[16]

With the end of the Soviet threat, balance-of-power theory predicts a decline in alliance cohesion, a reassertion of German and Japanese great-power status, and a return to strategic rivalry among the major states.[17] The intensification of American preponderance during the 1990s adds additional incentives for counterbalancing reactions by Asian and European allies—contributing to a loosening of the political and security ties that marked the Cold War era.[18] Unipolar power is not stable. The problems of anarchy will be exacerbated in the years ahead: economic rivalry, security dilemmas, alliance decay, and balance-of-power politics among the major states.

Waltz acknowledges that balance-of-power dynamics can be suppressed by hegemony. European acceptance of American hegemonic leadership, for example, has helped prevent the return of a balance of power on the continent. But from a structural realist perspective, unipolarity is nonetheless likely to be the least durable of the various types of international order. Two reasons are offered for this view. First, the dominant

---

[16] Waltz, "The Emerging Structure of International Politics," *International Security* 18, no. 2 (fall 1993): 75, 76.

[17] John J. Mearsheimer, "Back to the Future: Instability of Europe after the Cold War," *International Security* 15 (summer 1990): 5–57; Mearsheimer, "Why We Will Soon Miss the Cold War," *The Atlantic* 266 (August 1990), 35–50; Mearsheimer, *The Tragedy of Great Power Politics* (New York: W. W. Norton, 2001); Conor Cruise O'Brien, "The Future of the West," *The National Interest* 30 (winter 1992–93): 3–10.

[18] See, for example, Christopher Layne, "The Unipolar Illusion: Why New Great Powers Will Arise," *International Security* 17, no. 4 (spring 1993): 5–51; and Layne, "From Preponderance to Offshore Balancing: America's Future Grand Strategy," *International Security* 22, no. 1 (summer 1997): 86–124.

state will tend to take on more tasks and responsibilities, which over the long term will weaken the state. The argument echoes the thesis made famous by Paul Kennedy that the United States would eventually go the way of all powers—down. Dominant states tend to make mistakes in the exercise of their power, a problem that emerges directly from its concentration.[19] The other reason why unipolar order is unstable follows directly from the underlying condition of anarchy: even if the dominant state acts with moderation, other states will still fear the insecurities of unchecked concentrated power. During the Cold War, the United States and the Soviet Union restrained each other, but today the United States is largely unrestrained. As Waltz argues, "Faced with unbalanced power, some states try to increase their own strength or they ally with others to bring the international distribution of power into balance." Regardless of its good intentions or eagerness of please, the United States will experience the same fate of other dominant states in history.

Charles Kupchan also presents an argument that casts doubt on the stability of unipolarity but sees the sources of transition residing inside the United States and in the specific challenge of a rising Western Europe. The United States may have successfully established a stable and legitimate international order, centered around American power, but that order rests on a fragile foundation: the American political system and the parochialism of its domestic politics. The hegemonic structure is only as stable as the policies pursued by United States politicians—and their steady embrace of internationalism and an ethic of global leadership is increasingly problematic. The United States may be "indispensable" to the stable operation of global order but American voters are not really aware of this or much impressed by its imperatives. The result is the possibility of a sort of "hollowing out" of American hegemony.[20] The external support for American hegemony is not the threat to order—the demand it still there—but the willingness of the American polity to act accordingly is in some doubt.

Charles Kupchan argues that a "shrinking American willingness to be the global protector of last resort will be the primary engine of a changing global landscape." Today's hegemonic order will crack from a growing mismatch between domestic support and external commitments. The demand for American leadership draws the United States further outward

[19] Paul Kennedy, *The Rise and Fall of Great Powers: Economic Change and Military Conflict from 1500 to 2000* (New York: Random House, 1987).

[20] See Fareed Zakaria, "The New American Consensus: Our Hollow Hegemony," *New York Times Magazine*, November 1, 1998.

into commitments and interventions near and far—but the expansion of these commitments triggers domestic backlash. The NATO air campaign in Kosovo is illustrative: the structure of the Atlantic order made American involvement a logical and perhaps inevitable step in the chain of events. Only the United States has the military power and NATO command capacity to project force into the Balkans. But this external super-structure of commitments and leadership still rests on American public opinion. The viability of the operation—and the functioning of the ordering mechanisms of the hegemonic system—depends on whether American politicians can convince middle America that the costs are worth it. "The United States is thus taking the lead in building a larger European edifice covering the continent's new and aspiring democracies. But the foundation is shaky, because America has a dwindling interest in paying for the construction and upkeep. . . . Rather than pursue a hollow hegemony that misleads and creates unmet expectations, it is better for the United States to give advance notice that its days as a guarantor of last resort may be numbered."[21] The big oak tree of American hegemony has grown steadily over the decades—others still want it and benefit from it and the fact of its existence makes alternative ordering systems less viable—but it still depends on a subterranean water supply that seems to be drying up. The world needs to begin preparing for life after the American century.

The coming retraction of American hegemonic leadership could result in either a hard or soft landing for international order. One view is that a shift in the system toward multipolarity and an international order built around regional power centers provides the most hopeful and constructive alternative. If these regional powers are sufficiently benign in their exercise of power, the result could be a stable and cooperative system with a more decentralized leadership structure.[22] Alternatively, it might be that an abrupt and radical retrenchment of American power will trigger more convulsive responses in Europe and Asia. If American alliance commitments to Europe and Japan were to buckle, the response could be rapid upgrades in German and Japanese military capabilities, which in turn could trigger security dilemmas, arms races, and balancing actions in both regions.

Although not strictly a theory of hegemonic domination, the argument

[21] See Charles Kupchan, "Fractured U.S. Resolve," *The Washington Post*, Outlook Section, June 13, 1999, B1, B4.

[22] Charles A. Kupchan, "After Pax Americana: Benign Power, Regional Integration, and the Sources of Stable Multipolarity," *International Security* 23, no. 3 (fall 1998): 40–79.

advanced by William Wohlforth emphasizes that the sheer preponderance of American power prevents a return to a balance of power. American power is so overwhelming that a countervailing coalition is not possible. Weaker and secondary states are bandwagoning not because they want to do so but because they have no alternative. "No other major power is in a position to follow any policy that depends for its success on prevailing against the United States in a war or an extended rivalry," Wohlforth argues. "None is likely to take any step that might invite the focused enmity of the United States."[23] The costs to balancing are simply too high. Moreover, even if potential rivals attempted to aggregate power to counter the United States—either alone or in coalition—these states are likely to spark regional counterbalancing reactions that will resist such efforts. The preponderance and geopolitical configuration of American power explains the peacefulness and stability of the unipolar order.

The insight that Wohlforth puts forward is that balancing—even in the most likely circumstances of modern Europe—is hard. One problem is collective action. As Stephen Walt argues, states ideally would like to have others do the costly work of power balancing. There is an incentive for "buck passing." But Wohlforth also notes that states often think of their security in very local terms and therefore system-wide balancing imperatives are not likely to be as intensely felt by state leaders. The loss of policy autonomy in such coalitions also make balancing coalitions costly. These inherent constraints on balancing are even more severe given the extreme asymmetry of American power. The great powers that might seek to balance American power represent a smaller share of world capabilities than in previous international systems. It is not clear how a coalition could be mustered that would actually aggregate sufficient power capability to bring the world into balance. Beyond this, a closer look at the actual character of American power—most importantly, its geographical isolation—and the regional security dilemmas of the other great powers—where mustering power by one state will trigger a counterreaction by a regional neighbor—further reduce the incentives to balance. While Stephen Walt argues that American foreign policy self-restraint is critical to the stability of unipolarity, Wohlforth sees stability locked into the system by the deep structure of unipolar power, which generates a clear and durable array of costs, benefits, and constraints that reinforce the existing order. This is an argument that is offered as a realist solution to the puzzle of nonbalanced power.

[23] William Wohlforth, "The Stability of a Unipolar World," *International Security* 24, no. 1 (summer 1999): 5–41.

The Management of Unipolarity

For those realists who move beyond the simple balance-of-power model, the durability of American unipolarity hinges on the array of threats, costs, and benefits that American power offers. The strategy that the United States pursues and the way in which American power is connected to specific regional political and security situations are key to an assessment of the larger unipolar order. Stephen Walt advances a modification of balance-of-power theory focusing on threats and the way they can be manipulated to alter the incentives states have to power balance. In their chapters, Michael Mastanduno and Josef Joffe provide insights into the way in which American power operates in Europe and Asia where unipolarity is actually manifest and where stability or instability is at stake.

Stephen Walt has adapted the power-balancing logic by introducing considerations of threats into state calculations.[24] The intentions and foreign policy behavior of major states—including the most powerful state—matter in whether weaker and secondary states resist or cooperate. Alliances are responses to security threats. With the collapse of the Soviet threat, the major source of alliance cohesion among the Western states has disappeared, resulting in a fraying of American and European ties.[25] But while the disappearance of the Soviet threat leads Walt to expect looser or less cooperative security relations between Europe and the United States, the threat perspective also can help explain why balancing against the United States has not occurred. The United States is hugely powerful but it is not threatening—at least not enough to trigger counteralliance formation.

Walt identifies four components of threat. Power itself matters, of course, and when a state's power is increasing the likelihood that other states will balance against it increases. But changing power disparities are not enough to explain why and how states act. Proximity to concentrated power also effects the degree of threat. In this sense, America's isolated geographical position makes it less threatening to other great powers. The offensive capacities of the dominant state also matter. Nuclear deterrence, for example, makes American power less offensive to other states, although the Bush administration's push for a national missile defense might undercut that security. Finally, the offensive intentions of the dom-

[24] Stephen Walt, *The Origins of Alliances* (Ithaca, N.Y.: Cornell University Press, 1987). For critiques of balance-of-threat theory as it relates to unipolarity, see Layne, "The Unipolar Illusion," 11–15, and Mastanduno, "Preserving the Unipolar Moment," 59–73.

[25] Stephen Walt, "The Ties That Fray: Why Europe and America Are Drifting Apart," *The National Interest* 54 (winter 1998/99): 3–11.

inant state also help shape the degree of threat. As Walt points out, the fact that the United States has no aggressive territorial ambitions and generally pursues a cooperative and reassuring foreign policy matters in the way other states decide to react to American power.

A focus on threats in addition to capabilities shifts the analysis to more differentiated patterns of power. Preponderant states are not ipso facto dangerous to weaker or secondary states. Powerful states will pose different types and levels of threats and so the responses by other states will also vary. American unipolar power, in this formulation, may or may not pose the type of threat to other states that requires a balancing reaction. In Walt's view, the United States is a remarkably nonthreatening state defined in terms of power proximity and offensive capabilities and intentions. But unlike other writers in this book, he does not think this power benignity is deeply rooted in domestic or international structures. It is conceivable for the United States to stumble into self-encirclement if it pursues policies that threaten other states or force them to rethink their risk and reward calculations. Foreign policy matters. An unbalanced world order—that is, an order where other states are not actively seeking to ally against or undermine the United States—is deeply in the American interest. There is nothing in Walt's neorealist threat theory that suggests that a return to balance is inevitable. But the United States is most likely to act in a way that diminishes such a possibility if it clearly sees the interests it has at stake in unipolarity and is self-conscious about how its policies can reinforce or undermine it.

Threat analysis is a modification of balance-of-power realism that can be more or less harmful to the original theory. If threats and intentions only slightly modify the balancing implications of the prevailing distribution of power, the basic framework remains decidedly realist. Walt's specification of what determines threat levels is rooted in a realist understanding of power and security. But where threats and intentions are modified more fully by domestic structures and international institutions, the resulting explanation for nonbalancing anomalies requires reaching beyond realism. For example, one type of explanation for continuity and stability in Atlantic alliance relations despite shifting and highly asymmetrical power distributions is that prevailing domestic structures, ideology, and military doctrine tend to dampen security dilemmas and other sources of instability.[26] Some authors in this volume move even further away for realism, focusing on structures of democracy and international

---

[26] See Stephen Van Evera, "Primed for Peace: Europe after the Cold War," in *The Cold War and After: Prospects for Peace*, ed. Sean M. Lynn-Jones and Steven E. Miller, rev. ed. (Cambridge, Mass.: MIT Press, 1993), 193–43.

liberal community. These authors also argue that American power is unusually unthreatening but their explanation for why and how differs markedly.

Joffe looks for historical comparisons to explain the absence of balancing against the United States. While the list of powerful states that have inspired counterbalancing alliances is long, Britain and Bismarckian Germany were able to hold off such responses for a relatively long stretch of time. But they did so with different grand strategies. Britain's strategy was to use its geographical insularity and maritime supremacy to remain aloof from the rivalries of the continental European great powers. This remote geopolitical position reduced the incentives for the other states to ally against Britain but it also allowed Britain to selectively intervene in continental struggles to break up threatening power formations. The Bismarckian strategy was to pursue strategic entanglement with neighboring great powers, creating an array of partnerships that made a counter-German coalition unlikely. Joffe argues that the United States has pursued a grand strategy that draws on aspects of both approaches. In the current era, the United States is not able to be as removed as nineteenth-century Britain from the other great powers but its geographical remoteness and eschewing of territorial conquest nonetheless make it a less threatening hegemon. Joffe sees the real genius of American strategy in its neo-Bismarckian "hub and spoke" orientation. The United States has built a network of allies across the major regions of the world, providing security and markets in exchange for stable partnership. A realist calculation lies at the heart of this sprawling American order: the United States provides public goods and solves regional security dilemmas for other states and thereby removes the incentives for a challenger coalition.

The Bismarckian engagement strategy ultimately broke down and the catastrophes of German history ensued. So the question is: can the United States avoid a similar fate? Joffe does see important differences. One is that the United States has been an "institution-builder"—launching after World War II an unprecedented array of regional and global multilateral institutions and continuing to sponsor and expand these institutions over the decades—which has both made American power and leadership more durable but also more acceptable to others. The character of American power itself is also different. In the final analysis, American "hard" power is what puts the United States in an advantaged position, but its "soft"

[27] The term was coined by Joseph S. Nye in his *Bound to Lead: The Changing Nature of American Power* (New York: Basic Books, 1990).

power also is at work.[27] The appeal of its ideas and popular culture frustrates the power-balancing game. How do you balance against soft power?

Michael Mastanduno looks at American unipolarity as it is positioned within East Asia. This region—with its complex array of rising and transforming states, historical estrangements, and divergent political and economic traditions—is a particularly important geographical location to explore the stability of American hegemonic power. Mastanduno observes that there are several different pathways toward a transformed political order in East Asia. It is possible to envisage a concert of great powers in the region or the rise of a balance-of-power regional order—either with the United States and China balancing each other or a more multipolar balance among the major regional states. Mastanduno finds that American hegemony is at the core of the existing regional order driven by the push and pull of American power and regional politics. The reasons why American hegemony has "worked" in the region has implications for a wider understanding of how American hegemony is manifest around the world and the sources of its durability.

Mastanduno's understanding of what hegemony is and how it operates draws on Robert Gilpin's original theory. Hegemony is not just material power capabilities, and hegemonic order cannot be assured simply by a preponderance of such capabilities. A leader needs followers and the acquiescence of these followers is only achieved if the leader is seen as legitimate—and useful. Seen in this light, Mastanduno argues that the United States has succeeded in establishing at least a partial hegemonic order in East Asia. American power in the region has served to restrain traditional rivals in the region from engaging in major conflict and helped to reassure the smaller states in the region that their security and interests will be protected. In promoting liberal economic reform and the expansion of trade, the United States has also diffused nationalist movements and fostered greater regional integration. Japan's embrace of the American security umbrella, of course, is the critical axis of this regional hegemonic system and the U.S.–Japan alliance is perhaps the purest expression of the hegemonic logic.

In this view, the durability of American unipolar order rests on the usefulness of its military and political presence in dampening regional security dilemmas and defusing potential conflicts. The offshore character of American power makes involvement in the region less threatening. The alternatives to this American-centered order are perceived by key states in the region to be more costly and dangerous. The inability of the regional states to compose their differences also makes the American-led option more desirable. It also matters that the United States is willing and able to commit its power in this and other regional settings—even when immediate threats to its security are not evident. In Mastanduno's view, the durability of this order will hinge on cost and benefit calculations that are made in Beijing and Washington. Bejing is profoundly ambivalent about the American hegemonic presence in the region: that presence keeps Japanese military power contained but the American-led alliance system nonetheless leaves them surrounded and worried. The stability of the order depends a great deal on how Washington manages the partial hegemonic order. Can it find ways to entice China to more fully accept the American presence or even integrate into the existing regional security order? And will the United States be able to avoid either too much military presence in the region—thereby triggering a backlash by China and perhaps other states—or too little presence—thereby triggering renewed regional conflict, arms racing, and instability?

The Institutions and Ideology of Unipolarity

Other factors that potentially render concentrated power less threatening move further away from the realist tradition. The democratic peace thesis is a potential explanation for the absence of balancing against American power: open democratic polities are less able or willing to use power in an arbitrary and indiscriminate manner against other democracies.[28] Power asymmetries are less threatening when they are manifest between democracies. This might be so for several reasons. Open polities make the exercise of power more visible and easy to anticipate. Accountable governments make the exercise of power more predictable and institutionalized. Democracies are more accessible from the outside than nondemocracies—so alliance partners have more opportunities to actively shape security policies. Leaders who rise through the ranks within democratic countries are more inclined to participate in "give and take" with other democratic leaders than those who rise up in autocratic and authoritarian states.[29] European and Asian governments are willing to bandwagon with

[28] The democratic peace literature is huge. See Michael W. Doyle, "Kant, Liberal Legacies, and Foreign Affairs," *Philosophy and Public Affairs* 12, no. 3 (summer 1983): 205–35, and no. 4 (fall 1983): 323–53; Bruce Russett et al., *Grasping the Democratic Peace* (Princeton, N.J.: Princeton University Press, 1993); and Michael Brown, Sean Lynn-Jones, and Steven Miller, eds., *Debating the Democratic Peace* (Cambridge, Mass.: MIT Press, 1996).

[29] This facet of democratic politics is stressed by John Lewis Gaddis as a factor: "Negotiation, compromise, and consensus-building came naturally to statesmen steeped in the uses of such practices at home: in this sense, the American political tradition served the country better than its realist critics—Kennan definitely among them—believed it did." Gaddis, *We Now Know: Rethinking Cold War History* (New York: Oxford University Press, 1997), 50.

American power because that power is wielded by a democracy that makes the United States unusually able to co-opt and reassure.

I argue in my chapter that it is possible to spell out the logic of this stable pattern of order by looking more closely at the specific institutional character of American hegemony. The incentives to balance against the United States are low not because the costs of balancing are high but because the demand to do so is low. American hegemony is distinctive: it can be characterized as reluctant, open, and highly institutionalized.[30] The reluctance is seen in the absence of a strong impulse to directly dominate or manage weaker and secondary states within the American order. In the early postwar years, the United States resisted making binding political and military commitments, and although the Cold War drew the United States into security alliances in Asia and Europe, the resulting political order was in many respects shaped by its junior partners as much as by the hegemon. The remarkable global reach of American postwar hegemony has been at least in part driven by the efforts of European and Asian governments to harness American power, render that power more predictable, and use it to overcome their own regional insecurities.

The liberal character of the American polity has shaped the way American power is exercised. America's open, decentralized, and transparent democracy provides opportunities for other states to exercise their voice in the operation of the hegemonic order, thereby reassuring these states that their interests could be actively advanced and that processes exist to reconcile conflicts. The pluralistic and regularized way in which American foreign and security policy is made reduces surprises and allows other states to build long-term, mutually beneficial relations. The governmental separation of powers creates a shared decision-making system that opens up the process and reduces the ability of any one leader to make abrupt or aggressive moves toward other states. An active press and competitive party system also provide a service to outside states by generating information about United States policy and determining its seriousness of purpose. The messiness of democracy can frustrate American diplomats and confuse foreign observers. But over the long term, democratic institutions produce more consistent and credible policies than autocratic or authoritarian states.

This American-led system of alliances and multilateral institutions are the core of today's world order. American power both undergirds this system and is transformed by it. By enmeshing itself in a postwar web of alliances and multilateral commitments, the United States is able to project its influence outward and create a relatively secure environment in which to pursue its interests. But that order also shapes and restrains American

---

[30] See Ikenberry, *After Victory.*

power and makes the United States a more genial partner for other states. Likewise, the array of institutions and cooperative security ties that link Europe, the United States, Japan, and the rest of the democratic world creates a complex and stable order that in sheer size overwhelms any alternative global order. Russia, China, or any other combination of states or movements are structurally too small to mount a fundamental challenge to the American system.

Other authors make the related argument that the existing international order—at least within the advanced democratic world—has largely transcended the traditional dynamics of balance of power. Drawing in various ways on liberal and constructivist insights, the claim is that American unipolarity is embedded in a wider and more complex order than is grasped by realist theory—structural realist or otherwise. In effect, the deeper ideational structures of political order among the Western democracies lower the risks of asymmetrical power. The social purposes of power matter and, at least within the advanced industrial world, shared values and norms make power balancing less necessary. It is the fundamental "unthinkableness" of the use of force between these countries that erases the threats that otherwise trigger security dilemmas and strategic rivalry.

John Owen argues that the inner workings of this stable liberal order can be seen in the shared values and interests of elites in democratic countries. The benign character of American hegemony is seen in the eyes of liberal elites. Where these elites are not present or widespread—such as in China and segments of Russia—the perception of American power is less sanguine. The focus on elite perceptions is useful in illuminating both the underlying structures of the order and the variation across countries in the willingness to accept American hegemony. Owen also shows that the elite support and opposition to American liberal hegemony is also tied to internal struggles for supremacy. Russian liberals, for example, welcome American predominance because it strengthens their position at home and so they seek to prevent their country from balancing against the United States.

Elite views ultimately reflect the socioeconomic values that are dominant in their society. In this sense, Owen agrees that the post–World War II movement toward liberal democracy has been a critical precondition for the stable acceptance or support for American power. For the countries within the industrial democratic world, American values are essentially their values and this congruence in elite opinion prevents states from acting on realist-style incentives to balance against the dominant state. Owen presents a theory of elite identity. Groups within society identify with others who share their ideological commitments, including other elites outside their national borders. Once in power these elites seek to implement their ideas and value commitments and align themselves with likeminded states and against states governed by ideological opponents. Owen argues that this dynamic helps explain why American unipolarity persists: potential challenger states—aside from China—are dominated by liberal elites who share American values and who therefore find American hegemony acceptable.

While Owen sees this transnational liberal elite rooted in a democratic world that is in part an outgrowth of American hegemony, Thomas Risse argues that a Western security community is at the core of contemporary stable order. The claim is sweeping: the rise of capitalist democratic societies has transformed the basic structure of international politics within the West. Anarchy as the deep organizing principle of state relations has disappeared and a new "social structure" of state relations has emerged. The result is a security community where power configurations such as unipolarity and balancing alliances are irrelevant. In realist theory, anarchy provides the deep structure out of which states are constituted as actors and the logic of their interaction is determined. In the same way today, according to Risse, the social structure of the Western security community shapes the basic character and identities of the actors who operate within it.[31] This Western security community does not vanquish conflict but it does radically reduce security dilemma dynamics and makes great-power war impossible. In this view, it is not a benign America or the web of international institutions that reduce the incentives for great powers to balance against the United States. The roots of stable peace are deeper.

Risse identifies three features of the Western security community that produce the observed political outcomes: collective identities and shared values; transnational political, economic, and cultural interdependence; and governance structures regulating the social order. Karl Deutsch originally defined a security community as an group of like-minded peoples who were economically and politically integrated, linked together by common institutions and practices, and united by a shared "sense of community."[32] Democracy, economic interdependence, and institutionalized governance relations are characteristics of Western political order that work together to produce shared values and collective identities.[33] Peoples in

[31] This argument draws on Alexander Wendt's constructivist arguments about anarchy. See Wendt, "Anarchy Is What States Make of It: The Social Construction of Power Politics," *International Organization* 88, no. 2 (1992): 384–96; and *Social Theory of International Politics* (Cambridge: Cambridge University Press, 1999).

[32] Karl Deutsch et al., *Political Community and the North Atlantic Area* (Princeton, N.J.: Princeton University Press, 1957). See also Emanuel Adler and Michael Barnett, eds., *Security Communities* (New York: Cambridge University Press, 1998).

[33] These three characteristics of liberal order are explored in Bruce Russet and John Oneal, *Triangulating Peace: Democracy, Interdependence, and International Organizations* (New York: Norton, 2001).

Western states have attained a sufficient level of shared loyalty to each other and trust that the structure of interstate relations has changed. Risse argues that as a result of this shared sense of community and collective identity, countries within the Western order do not regard as threatening state actions that would be seen as highly threatening if they came from states outside the community. Disputes over trade, defense, and other issues do not disappear—indeed because these democratic societies are becoming more interdependent such conflicts may actually increase—but they are contained within shared political institutions and stable expectations that their resolution can be achieved short of result to armed violence. Because security threats and insecurity are circumscribed within the security community, the puzzle of unipolarity and the dog that has not barked disappear.

Conclusion

Why has the unprecedented concentration of American power today not triggered balancing responses from other major states? One answer is to be patient: the slow distancing of allies and other states from the American imperium is only a matter of time. Perhaps the NATO campaign in Kosovo will be seen in retrospect as a watershed moment when European allies begin to develop more independent military capabilities, setting the stage for future strategic rivalry.[34] The American campaign against terrorism launched after September 11, 2001, could ultimately trigger a backlash if it takes the shape of a unilateral military crusade. But one of the insights that emerges from these chapters is that balancing is not an automatic or inevitable process. In an era of peace among the great powers, it is not clear what the triggering circumstances for the formation of a counterhegemonic coalition might be. As Josef Joffe argues, even when Europeans faced the likes of Napoleon I or Wilhelm II, countercoalitions did not instantly spring to life. But the chapters to follow also show that the distinctive complexity of great-power politics today makes it even more unclear how the logic of balance can or will reassert itself.

This book shows that the future of the balance of power in the age of American unipolarity hinges on three major factors. The first relates to the character of the United States itself. There is general agreement among the authors that American power is indeed unprecedented but it is also fundamentally different than the power manifest by past would-be

---

[34] See Roger Cohen, "Crisis in the Balkans: The Continent; Europe Aims: Arms Parity," *The New York Times*, June 15, 1999, A1.

hegemons. America's geographical remoteness, its democratic institutions and liberal political orientation, its commitment after World War II to build a remarkable array of multilateral institutions—these and other features of American power make it less threatening and more useable to other states. But there is less agreement about how deeply rooted these features are. For some, such as Stephen Walt, the conduct of American foreign policy matters. It might take a great deal of foolish and self-destructive American behavior to return the world to balance. But an imperial and domineering foreign policy—for example, a unilateral move toward full-scale national missile defense—might trigger countermeasures that eventually make it easier for the other great powers to disengage strategically from the United States. Others, particularly Charles Kupchan, see American domestic pressure for strategic retreat as the threat to unipolar order. The political constituency for maintaining America's far-flung security commitments will wither and the unipolar order will crumble. Both these views—one warning of a too assertive foreign policy and the other of too little—suggest that the stability of unipolarity is in the uncertain hands of American foreign policymakers.

Other authors see a much more durable structure within which American hegemony can thrive. Risse also sees the deep logic of a Western security community muting the implications of power asymmetries. If the use of force between these countries is "unthinkable"—which is the claim of security community theory—American military power is also unusable and confers few if any advantages on the United States in its dealings with the other democratic states. In this view, there is little that the United States can do to undermine the existing order. The liberal democratic social structure of international relations has sunk its roots deeply and eliminated the realist logic of power balancing.

The second factor that contributes to unipolar stability is the array of practical, everyday benefits that the American unipolar presence spreads around the world. A clear theme that emerges from several chapters is the usefulness of the American-led alliance system—which is perhaps the global spinal cord of unipolarity—to various regions. The United States security commitment reduces regional security dilemmas. Even Russia and China indirectly have indicated that the American military presence in East Asia and Europe has had a stabilizing impact by reducing the incentives for Japan and Germany to acquire nuclear weapons and pursue more independent military roles in their respective regions. Wohlforth adds the interesting insight that efforts by any of the great powers to pursue a counterbalancing strategy against the United States through military mobilization would trigger a regional reaction thereby raising the costs of such a strategy. This array of costs and benefits in comparing the unipolar order to global and regional alternatives gives the status quo a stabilizing advantage.

As mentioned earlier, the weak link in this logic is the American domestic support for a unipolar foreign policy. If Charles Kupchan is correct, the costs of maintaining the status quo are rising while the willingness of the American public to accept these costs is declining. These costs will be felt most intensely in the maintenance of troops and a security commitment to Europe. The rising capacity of Europe to provide for its own security compounds the problem. This analysis opens an important line of questions about the costs and benefits of unipolarity for the United States. Some authors, such as Mastanduno and Joffe, see the advantages of a unified American-led strategic bloc too overwhelming to fall victim to budget battles and declining public support of internationalism. Some argue, for example, that the economic benefits of America's global alliance structure are underappreciated and if they are added to the balance sheet, the costs would pale in comparison to the political and economic returns on America's security commitment.[35] If the Untied States were to withdraw from Asia, the arms race and political instability that would follow might increase American security costs in the long run and its economic interests would also be jeopardized. What these costs and benefits are, how they are calculated and by whom, how they are perceived and experienced within the United States government and society-at-large are critical questions that shape assessments of unipolar stability.

Finally, there is the question of what balancing actually means in the twenty-first century. In an era of nuclear deterrence, the massing of counterbalancing military power is less relevant than countering other aspects of American power. Military alliances and the mustering of power may be inconsequential when the advantages that the United States brings to the table are rooted in its economy, technological achievements, and the diffuse elements of "soft power." On a wide range of policy questions that engage the world community today, it is differential costs of noncooperation that determine relative power.[36] Because of the sheer size of the United States economy, it is much easier for it to walk away from agreements than other countries. If nuclear weapons level the security playing field—reducing the incentives to engage in old-style balancing—what is the new

[35] Robert Gilpin argues that today's open world economy has been possible because of the Cold War security alliances that reduced relative gains competition and gave the United States security interests in the economic growth and trade expansion of Western Europe and non-Communist Asia. See Gilpin, *The Challenge of Global Capitalism: The World Economy in the Twenty-First Century* (Princeton, N.J.: Princeton University Press, 2000), chap. 2.

[36] The classic statement of this notion of power is Albert O. Hirschman, *National Power and the Structure of Foreign Trade* (1945; Berkeley: University of California Press, 1969).

logic of power balancing? Joffe argues that balancing itself is called into question. The way to deal with American cultural or economic hegemony is to either engage in selective trade protectionism or to try to compete through emulating American economic practices. Economic regionalism may also be pursued today as an element of postmodern power balancing. But it is far from clear that these neo- or proto-styles of balancing have system-level consequences for unipolarity. Unless other states are willing to risk the return to the dangerous and mutually destructive bloc politics of the 1930s, great power strategies in the age of unipolarity are just as likely to reinforce as they are to undermine the existing world order.

PART I

The Durability
of Unipolarity

1

Structural Realism after the Cold War

Kenneth N. Waltz

Some students of international politics believe that realism is obsolete.[1] They argue that, although realism's concepts of anarchy, self-help, and power balancing may have been appropriate to a bygone era, they have been displaced by changed conditions and eclipsed by better ideas. New times call for new thinking. Changing conditions require revised theories or entirely different ones.

True, if the conditions that a theory contemplated have changed, the theory no longer applies. But what sorts of changes would alter the international political system so profoundly that old ways of thinking would no longer be relevant? Changes *of* the system would do it; changes *in* the system

I am indebted to Karen Adams and Robert Rauchhaus for help on this article from its conception to its completion. For insightful and constructive criticisms I wish to thank Robert Art, Richard Betts, Barbara Farnham, Anne Fox, Robert Jervis, Warner Schilling, and Mark Sheetz. An earlier version of this chapter appeared in *International Security* 25, no. 1 (summer 2000): 5–41. Reprinted by the permission of the president and fellows of Harvard College and the Massachusetts Institute of Technology.

[1] For example, Richard Ned Lebow, "The Long Peace, the End of the Cold War, and the Failure of Realism," *International Organization* 48, no. 2 (spring 1994): 249–77; Jeffrey W. Legro and Andrew Moravcsik, "Is Anybody Still a Realist?" *International Security* 24, no. 2 (fall 1999): 5–55; Bruce Russett, *Grasping the Democratic Peace: Principles for a Post–Cold War Peace* (Princeton, N.J.: Princeton University Press, 1993); Paul Schroeder, "Historical Reality vs. Neo-realist Theory," *International Security* 19, no. 1 (summer 1994): 108–48; and John A. Vasquez, "The Realist Paradigm and Degenerative vs. Progressive Research Programs: An All Appraisal of Neotraditional Research on Waltz's Balancing Proposition," *American Political Science Review* 91, no. 4 (December 1997): 899–912.

would not. Within-system changes take place all the time, some important, some not. Big changes in the means of transportation, communication, and war fighting, for example, strongly affect how states and other agents interact. Such changes occur at the unit level. In modern history, or perhaps in all of history, the introduction of nuclear weaponry was the greatest of such changes. Yet in the nuclear era, international politics remains a self-help arena. Nuclear weapons decisively change how some states provide for their own and possibly for others' security; but nuclear weapons have not altered the anarchic structure of the international political system.

Changes in the structure of the system are distinct from changes at the unit level. Thus, changes in polarity also affect how states provide for their security. Significant changes take place when the number of great powers reduces to two or one. With more than two, states rely for their security both on their own internal efforts and on alliances they may make with others. Competition in multipolar systems is more complicated than competition in bipolar ones because uncertainties about the comparative capabilities of states multiply as numbers grow, and because estimates of the cohesiveness and strength of coalitions are hard to make.

Both changes of weaponry and changes of polarity were big ones with ramifications that spread through the system, yet they did not transform it. If the system were transformed, international politics would no longer be international politics, and the past would no longer serve as a guide to the future. We would begin to call international politics by another name, as some do. The terms "world politics" or "global politics," for example, suggest that politics among self-interested states concerned with their security has been replaced by some other kind of politics or perhaps by no politics at all.

What changes, one may wonder, would turn international politics into something distinctly different? The answer commonly given is that international politics is being transformed and realism is being rendered obsolete as democracy extends its sway, as interdependence tightens its grip, and as institutions smooth the way to peace. I consider these points in successive sections. A fourth section explains why realist theory retains its explanatory power after the Cold War.

Democracy and Peace

The end of the Cold War coincided with what many took to be a new democratic wave. The trend toward democracy combined with Michael Doyle's rediscovery of the peaceful behavior of liberal democratic states inter se contributes strongly to the belief that war is obsolescent, if not obsolete, among the advanced industrial states of the world.[2]

The democratic peace thesis holds that democracies do not fight democracies. Notice that I say "thesis," not "theory." The belief that democracies constitute a zone of peace rests on a perceived high correlation between governmental form and international outcome. Francis Fukuyama thinks that the correlation is perfect: Never once has a democracy fought another democracy. Jack Levy says that it is "the closest thing we have to an empirical law in the study of international relations."[3] But, if it is true that democracies rest reliably at peace among themselves, we have not a theory but a purported fact begging for an explanation, as facts do. The explanation given generally runs this way: Democracies of the right kind (i.e., liberal ones) are peaceful in relation to one another. This was Immanuel Kant's point. The term he used was *Rechtsstaat* or republic, and his definition of a republic was so restrictive that it was hard to believe that even one of them could come into existence, let alone two or more.[4] And if they did, who can say that they would continue to be of the right sort or continue to be democracies at all? The short and sad life of the Weimar Republic is a reminder. And how does one define what the right sort of democracy is? Some American scholars thought that Wilhelmine Germany was the very model of a modern democratic state with a wide suffrage, honest elections, a legislature that controlled the purse, competitive parties, a free press, and a highly competent bureaucracy.[5] But in the French, British, and American view after August of 1914, Germany turned out not to be a democracy of the right kind. John Owen tried to finesse the problem of definition by arguing that democracies that perceive one another to be liberal democracies will not fight.[6] That rather gives the game away.

[2] Michael W. Doyle, "Kant, Liberal Legacies, and Foreign Affairs, Parts 1 and 2," *Philosophy and Public Affairs* 12, no. 3 (summer 1983): 205–35, and no. 4 (autumn 1983): 323–53. and Doyle, "Kant: Liberalism and World Politics," *American Political Science Review* 80, no. 4 (December 1986): 1151–69.

[3] Francis Fukuyama, "Liberal Democracy as a Global Phenomenon," *Political Science and Politics* 24, no. 4 (1991): 662. Jack S. Levy, "Domestic Politics and War," in *The Origin and Prevention of Major Wars*, ed. Robert I. Rotberg and Theodore K. Rabb (Cambridge: Cambridge University Press, 1989), 88.

[4] Kenneth N. Waltz, "Kant, Liberalism, and War," *American Political Science Review* 56, no. 2 (June 1962): 331–40. Subsequent Kant references are found in this work.

[5] Ido Oren, "The Subjectivity of the 'Democratic' Peace: Changing U.S. Perceptions of Imperial Germany," *International Security* 20, no. 2 (fall 1995): 157ff.; Christopher Layne, in the second half of Layne and Sean M. Lynn-Jones, *Should America Spread Democracy? A Debate* (Cambridge, Mass.: MIT Press, forthcoming), argues convincingly that Germany's democratic control of foreign and military policy was no weaker than France's or Britain's.

[6] John M. Owen IV, "How Liberalism Produces Democratic Peace," *International Security* 19, no. 2 (fall 1994): 87–125. Cf. his *Liberal Peace, Liberal War: American Politics and International Security* (Ithaca, N.Y.: Cornell University Press, 1997).

Liberal democracies have at times prepared for wars against other liberal democracies and have sometimes come close to fighting them. Christopher Layne shows that some wars between democracies were averted not because of the reluctance of democracies to fight each other but for fear of a third party—a good realist reason. How, for example, could Britain and France fight each other over Fashoda in 1898 when Germany lurked in the background? In emphasizing the international political reasons for democracies not fighting each other, Layne gets to the heart of the matter.[7] Conformity of countries to a prescribed political form may eliminate some of the causes of war; it cannot eliminate all of them. The democratic peace thesis will hold only if all of the causes of war lie inside of states.

The Causes of War

To explain war is easier than to understand the conditions of peace. If one asks what may cause war, the simple answer is "anything." That is Kant's answer: The natural state is the state of war. Under the conditions of international politics, war recurs; the sure way to abolish war, then, is to abolish international politics.

Over the centuries, liberals have shown a strong desire to get the politics out of politics. The ideal of nineteenth-century liberals was the police state, that is, the state that would confine its activities to catching criminals and enforcing contracts. The ideal of the laissez-faire state finds many counterparts among students of international politics with their yen to get the power out of power politics, the national out of international politics, the dependence out of interdependence, the relative out of relative gains, the politics out of international politics, and the structure out of structural theory.

Proponents of the democratic peace thesis write as though the spread of democracy will negate the effects of anarchy. No causes of conflict and war will any longer be found at the structural level. Francis Fukuyama finds it "perfectly possible to imagine anarchic state systems that are nonetheless peaceful." He sees no reason to associate anarchy with war. Bruce Russett believes that, with enough democracies in the world, it "may be possible in part to supersede the 'realist' principles (anarchy, the security dilemma of states) that have dominated practice . . . since at least the seventeenth century."[8] Thus the structure is removed from structural

---

[7] Christopher Layne, "Kant or Cant: The Myth of the Democratic Peace," *International Security* 19, no. 2 (fall 1994), 5–49.

[8] Francis Fukuyama, *The End of History and the Last Man* (New York: Free Press, 1992), 254–56. Bruce Russett, *Grasping the Democratic Peace*, 24.

theory. Democratic states would be so confident of the peace-preserving effects of democracy that they would no longer fear that another state, so long as it remained democratic, would do it wrong. The guarantee of the state's proper external behavior would derive from its admirable internal qualities.

This is a conclusion that Kant would not sustain. German historians at the turn of the nineteenth century wondered whether peacefully inclined states could be planted and expected to grow where dangers from outside pressed daily upon them.[9] Kant a century earlier entertained the same worry. The seventh proposition of his "Principles of the Political Order" avers that establishment of the proper constitution internally requires the proper ordering of the external relations of states. The first duty of the state is to defend itself, and outside of a juridical order none but the state itself can define the action required. "Lesion of a less powerful country," Kant writes, "may be involved merely in the condition of a more powerful neighbor prior to any action at all; and in the State of Nature an attack under such circumstances would be warrantable."[10] In the state of nature, there is no such thing as an unjust war.

Every student of international politics is aware of the statistical data supporting the democratic peace thesis. Everyone has also known at least since David Hume that we have no reason to believe that the association of events provides a basis for inferring the presence of a causal relation. John Mueller properly speculates that it is not democracy that causes peace but that other conditions cause both democracy and peace.[11] Some of the major democracies—Britain in the nineteenth century and the United States in the twentieth century—have been among the most powerful states of their eras. Powerful states often gain their ends by peaceful means where weaker states either fail or have to resort to war.[12] Thus, the American government deemed the democratically elected Juan Bosch of the Dominican Republic too weak to bring order to his country. The United States toppled his government by sending twenty-three thousand troops within a week, troops whose mere presence made fighting a war unnecessary. Salvador Allende, democratically elected ruler of Chile, was

[9] For example, Leopold von Ranke, Gerhard Ritter, and Otto Hintze. The American William Graham Sumner and many others shared their doubts.

[10] Immanuel Kant, *The Philosophy of Law*, trans. W. Hastie (Edinburgh: T. and T. Clark, 1887), 218.

[11] John Mueller, "Is War Still Becoming Obsolete?" paper presented at the annual meeting of the American Political Science Association, Washington, D.C., August–September 1991, 55ff; cf. his *Quiet Cataclysm: Reflections on the Recent Transformation of World Politics* (New York: HarperCollins, 1995).

[12] Edward Hallett Carr, *Twenty Years' Crisis: An Introduction to the Study of International Relations*, 2d ed. (New York: Harper and Row, 1946), 129–32.

systematically and effectively undermined by the United States, without the open use of force, because its leaders thought that his government was taking a wrong turn. As Henry Kissinger put it: "I don't see why we need to stand by and watch a country go Communist due to the irresponsibility of its own people."[13] That is the way it is with democracies—their people may show bad judgment. "Wayward" democracies are especially tempting objects of intervention by other democracies that wish to save them. American policy may have been wise in both cases, but its actions surely cast doubt on the democratic peace thesis. So do the instances when a democracy did fight another democracy.[14] So do the instances in which democratically elected legislatures have clamored for war, as has happened for example in Pakistan and Jordan.

One can of course say, yes, but the Dominican Republic and Chile were not liberal democracies nor perceived as such by the United States. Once one begins to go down that road, there is no place to stop. The problem is heightened because liberal democracies, as they prepare for a war they may fear, begin to look less liberal and will look less liberal still if they begin to fight one. I am tempted to say that the democratic peace thesis in the form in which its proponents cast it is irrefutable. A liberal democracy at war with another country is unlikely to call it a liberal democracy.

Democracies may live at peace with democracies, but even if all states became democratic, the structure of international politics would remain anarchic. The structure of international politics is not transformed by changes internal to states, however widespread the changes may be. In the absence of an external authority, a state cannot be sure that today's friend will not be tomorrow's enemy. Indeed, democracies have at times behaved as though today's democracy is today's enemy and a present threat to them. In Federalist Paper number six, Alexander Hamilton asked whether the thirteen states of the Confederacy might live peacefully with one another as freely constituted republics. He answered that there have been "almost as many popular as royal wars." He cited the many wars fought by republican Sparta, Athens, Rome, Carthage, Venice, Holland, and Britain. John Quincy Adams, in response to James Monroe's contrary claim, averred "that the government of a Republic was as capable of intriguing with the leaders of a free people as neighboring monarchs."[15] In the latter half of

---

[13] Quoted in Anthony Lewis, "The Kissinger Doctrine," *New York Times*, February 27, 1975, 35, and see Henry Kissinger, *The White House Years* (Boston: Little, Brown, 1979), chap. 17.

[14] See, for example, Kenneth N. Waltz, "America as Model for the World? A Foreign Policy Perspective," *PS: Political Science and Politics* 24, no. 4 (December 1991): 667–70; and Mueller, "Is War Still Becoming Obsolete?" 5.

[15] Quoted in Walter A. McDougall, *Promised Land, Crusader State* (Boston: Houghton Mifflin, 1997), 28 and n. 36.

the nineteenth century, as the United States and Britain became more democratic, bitterness grew between them, and the possibility of war was at times seriously entertained on both sides of the Atlantic. France and Britain were among the principal adversaries in the great-power politics of the nineteenth century, as they were earlier. Their becoming democracies did not change their behavior toward each other. In 1914, democratic England and France fought democratic Germany, and doubts about the latter's democratic standing merely illustrate the problem of definition. Indeed, the democratic pluralism of Germany was an underlying cause of the war. In response to domestic interests, Germany followed policies bound to frighten both Britain and Russia. And today if a war that few have feared were fought by the United States and Japan, many Americans would say that Japan was not a democracy after all, but merely a one-party state.

What can we conclude? Democracies rarely fight democracies, we might say, and then add as a word of essential caution that the internal excellence of states is a brittle basis of peace.

Democratic Wars

Democracies coexist with undemocratic states. Although democracies seldom fight democracies, they do, as Michael Doyle has noted, fight at least their share of wars against others.[16] Citizens of democratic states tend to think of their countries as good, aside from what they do, simply because they are democratic. Thus former secretary of state Warren Christopher claimed that "democratic nations rarely start wars or threaten their neighbors."[17] One might suggest that he try his proposition out in Central or South America. Citizens of democratic states also tend to think of undemocratic states as bad, aside from what they do, simply because they are undemocratic. Democracies promote war because they at times decide that the way to preserve peace is to defeat nondemocratic states and make them democratic.

During World War I, Walter Hines Page, American ambassador to England, claimed that there "is no security in any part of the world where people cannot think of a government without a king and never will be." During the Vietnam War, Secretary of State Dean Rusk claimed that the

---

[16] Doyle, "Kant, Liberal Legacies, and Foreign Affairs, Part 2," 337.

[17] Warren Christopher, "The U.S.–Japan Relationship: The Responsibility to Change," address to the Japan Association of Corporate Executives, Tokyo, Japan, March 11, 1994 (U.S. Department of State, Bureau of Public Affairs, Office of Public Communication), 3.

"United States cannot be secure until the total international environment is ideologically safe."[18] Policies aside, the very existence of undemocratic states is a danger to others. American political and intellectual leaders have often taken this view. Liberal interventionism is again on the march. President Bill Clinton and his national security adviser, Anthony Lake, urged the United States to take measures to enhance democracy around the world. The task, one fears, will be taken up by the American military with some enthusiasm. Former army chief of staff, General Gordon Sullivan, for example, favored a new military "model," replacing the negative aim of containment with a positive one: "To promote democracy, regional stability, and economic prosperity."[19] Other voices urge us to enter into a "struggle to ensure that people are governed well." Having apparently solved the problem of justice at home, "the struggle for liberal government becomes a struggle not simply for justice but for survival."[20] As R. H. Tawney said: "Either war is a crusade, or it is a crime."[21] Crusades are frightening because crusaders go to war for righteous causes, which they define for themselves and try to impose on others. One might have hoped that Americans would have learned that they are not very good at causing democracy abroad. But, alas, if the world can be made safe for democracy only by making it democratic, then all means are permitted and to use them becomes a duty. The war fervor of people and their representatives is at times hard to contain. Thus Hans Morgenthau believed that "the democratic selection and responsibility of government officials destroyed international morality as an effective system of restraint."[22]

Since, as Kant believed, war among self-directed states will occasionally break out, peace has to be contrived. For any government, doing so is a difficult task, and all states are at times deficient in accomplishing it, even if they wish to. Democratic leaders may respond to the fervor for war that their citizens sometimes display, or even try to arouse it, and governments are sometimes constrained by electoral calculations to defer preventive measures. Thus British prime minister Stanley Baldwin said that if he had called in 1935 for British rearmament against the German threat, his

[18] Page quoted in Waltz, *Man, the State, and War: A Theoretical Analysis* (New York: Columbia University Press, 1959), 121. Rusk quoted in Layne, "Kant or Cant," 46.
[19] Quoted in Clemson G. Turregano and Ricky Lynn Waddell, "From Paradigm to Paradigm Shift: The Military and Operations Other than War," *Journal of Political Science* 22 (1994): 15.
[20] Peter Beinart, "The Return of the Bomb," *New Republic*, August 3, 1998, 27.
[21] Quoted in Michael Straight, *Make This the Last War* (New York: G. P. Putnam's Sons, 1945), 1.
[22] Hans J. Morgenthau, *Politics among Nations: The Struggle for Power and Peace*, 5th ed. (New York: Knopf, 1973), 248.

party would have lost the next election.[23] Democratic governments may respond to internal political imperatives when they should be responding to external ones. All governments have their faults, democracies no doubt fewer than others, but that is not good enough to sustain the democratic peace thesis. That peace may prevail among democratic states is a comforting thought. The obverse of the proposition—that democracy may promote war against undemocratic states—is disturbing. If the latter holds, we cannot even say for sure that the spread of democracy will bring a net decrease in the amount of war in the world.

With a republic established in a strong state, Kant hoped the republican form would gradually take hold in the world. In 1795, America provided the hope. Two hundred years later, remarkably, it still does. Ever since liberals first expressed their views, they have been divided. Some have urged liberal states to work to uplift benighted peoples and bring the benefits of liberty, justice, and prosperity to them. John Stuart Mill, Giuseppe Mazzini, Woodrow Wilson, and Bill Clinton are all interventionist liberals. Other liberals, Kant and Richard Cobden, for example, while agreeing on the benefits that democracy can bring to the world, have emphasized the difficulties and the dangers of actively seeking its propagation.

If the world is now safe for democracy, one has to wonder whether democracy is safe for the world. When democracy is ascendant, a condition that in the twentieth century attended the winning of hot wars and cold ones, the interventionist spirit flourishes. The effect is heightened when one democratic state becomes dominant, as the United States is now. Peace is the noblest cause of war. If the conditions of peace are lacking, then the country with a capability of creating them may be tempted to do so, whether or not by force. The end is noble, but as a matter of *right*, Kant insists, no state can intervene in the internal arrangements of another. As a matter of *fact*, one may notice that intervention, even for worthy ends, often brings more harm than good. The vice to which great powers easily succumb in a multipolar world is inattention; in a bipolar world, overreaction; in a unipolar world, overextension.

Peace is maintained by a delicate balance of internal and external restraints. States having a surplus of power are tempted to use it, and weaker states fear their doing so. The laws of voluntary federations, to use Kant's language, are disregarded at the whim of the stronger, as the United States demonstrated a decade ago by mining Nicaraguan waters and by invading Panama. In both cases, the United States blatantly violated inter-

---

[23] Gordon Craig and Alexander George, *Force and Statecraft: Diplomatic Problems of Our Time*, 2d ed. (New York: Oxford University Press, 1990), 64.

national law. In the first, it denied the jurisdiction of the International Court of Justice, which it had previously accepted. In the second, it flaunted the law embodied in the Charter of the Organization of American States, of which it was a principal sponsor.

If the democratic peace thesis is right, structural realist theory is wrong. One may believe, with Kant, that republics are by and large good states *and* that unbalanced power is a danger no matter who wields it. Inside of, as well as outside of, the circle of democratic states, peace depends on a precarious balance of forces. The causes of war lie not simply in states or in the state system; they are found in both. Kant understood this. Devotees of the democratic peace thesis overlook it.

The Weak Effects of Interdependence

If not democracy alone, may not the spread of democracy combined with the tightening of national interdependence fulfill the prescription for peace offered by nineteenth-century liberals and so often repeated today?[24] To the supposedly peaceful inclination of democracies, interdependence adds the propulsive power of the profit motive. Democratic states may increasingly devote themselves to the pursuit of peace and profits. The trading state is replacing the political-military state, and the power of the market now rivals or surpasses the power of the state, or so some believe.[25]

Before World War I, Norman Angell believed that wars would not be fought because they would not pay, yet Germany and Britain, each other's second-best customers, fought a long and bloody war.[26] Interdependence in some ways promotes peace by multiplying contacts among states and contributing to mutual understanding. It also multiplies the occasions for conflicts that may promote resentment and even war.[27] Close interde-

[24] Strongly affirmative answers are given by John R. Oneal and Bruce Russett, "Assessing the Liberal Peace with Alternative Specifications: Trade Still Reduces Conflict," *Journal of Peace Research* 36, no. 4 (July 1999): 423–42; and Russett, Oneal, and David R. Davis, "The Third Leg of the Kantian Tripod for Peace: International Organizations and Militarized Disputes, 1950–85," *International Organization* 52, no. 3 (summer 1998): 441–67.

[25] Richard Rosecrance, *The Rise of the Trading State: Commerce and Coalitions in the Modern World* (New York: Basic Books, 1986); and at times Susan Strange, *The Retreat of the State: The Diffusion of Power in the World Economy* (New York: Cambridge University Press, 1996).

[26] Norman Angell, *The Great Illusion*, 4th rev. and enlarged ed. (New York: Putnam's, 1913).

[27] Katherine Barbieri, "Economic Interdependence: A Path to Peace or a Source of Interstate Conflict?" *Journal of Peace Research* 33, no. 1 (February 1996): 29–49. Lawrence Keely, *War before Civilization: The Myth of the Peaceful Savage* (New York: Oxford University Press, 1996), 196, shows that with increases of trade and intermarriage among tribes, war became more frequent.

pendence is a condition in which one party can scarcely move without jostling others; a small push ripples through society. The closer the social bonds, the more extreme the effect becomes, and one cannot sensibly pursue all interest without taking others' interests into account. One country is then inclined to treat another country's acts as events within its own polity and to attempt to control them.

That interdependence promotes war as well as peace has been said often enough. What requires emphasis is that, either way, among the forces that shape international politics, interdependence is a weak one. Interdependence within modern states is much closer than it is across states. The Soviet economy was planned so that its far-flung parts would be not just interdependent but integrated. Huge factories depended for their output on products exchanged with others. Despite the tight integration of the Soviet economy, the state fell apart. Yugoslavia provides another stark illustration. Once external political pressure lessened, internal economic interests were too weak to hold the country together. One must wonder whether economic interdependence is more effect than cause. Internally, interdependence becomes so close that integration is the proper word to describe it. Interdependence becomes integration because internally the expectation that peace will prevail and order will be preserved is high. Externally, goods and capital flow freely where peace among countries appears to be reliably established. Interdependence, like integration, depends on other conditions. It is more a dependent than an independent variable. States, if they can afford to, shy away from becoming excessively dependent on goods and resources that may be denied them in crises and wars. States take measures, such as Japan's managed trade, to avoid excessive dependence on others.[28]

The impulse to protect one's identity—cultural and political as well as economic—from encroachment by others is strong. When it seems that "we will sink or swim together," swimming separately looks attractive to those able to do it. From Plato onward, utopias were set in isolation from neighbors so that people could construct their collective life uncontaminated by contact with others. With zero interdependence, neither conflict nor war is possible. With integration, international becomes national politics.[29] The zone in between is a gray one with the effects of interdependence sometimes good, providing the benefits of divided labor, mutual un-

[28] On states managing to avoid excessive dependence, see especially Robert Gilpin, *The Political Economy of International Relations* (Princeton, N.J.: Princeton University Press, 1987), chap. 10; and Suzanne Berger and Ronald Dore, eds., *National Diversity and Global Capitalism* (Ithaca, N.Y.: Cornell University Press, 1996).

[29] Cf. Kenneth N. Waltz, "Conflict in World Politics," in *Conflict in World Politics,* ed. Steven L. Spiegel and Waltz (Cambridge, Mass.: Winthrop, 1971), chap. 13.

derstanding, and cultural enrichment, and sometimes bad, leading to protectionism, mutual resentment, conflict, and war.

The uneven effects of interdependence, with some parties to it gaining more, others gaining less, are obscured by the substitution of Robert Keohane's and Joseph Nye's term "asymmetric interdependence" for relations of dependence and independence among states."[30] Relatively independent states are in a stronger position than relatively dependent ones. If I depend more on you than you depend on me, you have more ways of influencing me and affecting my fate than I have of affecting yours. Interdependence suggests a condition of roughly equal dependence of parties on one another. Omitting the word "dependence" blunts the inequalities that mark the relations of states and makes them all seem to be on the same footing. Much of international, as of national, politics is about inequalities. Separating one "issue area" from others and emphasizing that weak states have advantages in some of them reduces the sense of inequality. Emphasizing the low fungibility of power furthers the effect. If power is not very fungible, weak states may have decisive advantages on some issues. Again, the effects of inequality are blunted. But power, not very fungible for weak states, is very fungible for strong ones. The history of American foreign policy since World War II is replete with examples of how the United States used its superior economic capability to promote its political and security interests.[31]

In a 1970 essay, I described interdependence as an ideology used by Americans to camouflage the great leverage the United States enjoys in international politics by making it seem that strong and weak, rich and poor nations are similarly entangled in a thick web of interdependence.[32] In her recent book, *The Retreat of the State*, Susan Strange reached the same conclusion, but by an odd route. Her argument is that "the progressive integration of the world economy, through international production, has shifted the balance of power away from states and toward world markets." She advances three propositions in support of her argument: (1) power has "shifted upward from weak states to stronger ones" having global or regional reach; (2) power has "shifted sideways from states to markets and

[30] Robert O. Keohane and Joseph S. Nye, *Power and Interdependence*, 2d ed. (New York: HarperCollins, 1989).

[31] Keohane and Nye are on both sides of the issue. See, for example, ibid., 28. Keohane emphasized that power is not very fungible in "Theory of World Politics," in *Neorealism and Its Critics*, ed. Keohane (New York: Columbia University Press, 1986); and see Kenneth N. Waltz, "Reflection on Theory of International Politics: A Response to My Critics," ibid. Robert J. Art analyzes the fungibility of power in detail. See Art, "American Foreign Policy and the Fungibility of Force," *Security Studies* 5, no. 4 (summer 1996): 7–42.

[32] Kenneth N. Waltz, "The Myth of National Interdependence," in *The International Corporation*, ed. Charles P. Kindleberger (Cambridge, Mass.: MIT Press, 1970).

thus to non-state authorities deriving power from their market shares"; and (3) some power has "evaporated" with no one exercising it.[33] In international politics, with no central authority, power does sometimes slip away and sometimes moves sideways to markets. When serious slippage occurs, however, stronger states step in to reverse it, and firms of the stronger states control the largest market shares anyway. One may doubt whether markets any more escape the control of major states now than they did in the nineteenth century or earlier—perhaps less so since the competence of states has increased at least in proportion to increases in the size and complications of markets. Anyone, realist or not, might think Strange's first proposition is the important one. Never since the Roman Empire has power been so concentrated in one state. Despite believing that power has moved from states to markets, Strange recognized reality. She observed near the beginning of her book that the "authority—the 'power over' global outcomes enjoyed by American society, and therefore indirectly by the United States government—is still superior to that of any other society or any other government." And near the end, she remarked that the "authority of governments tends to over-rule the caution of markets." If one wondered which government she had in mind, she answered immediately: "The fate of Mexico is decided in Washington more than Wall Street. And the International Monetary Fund (IMF) is obliged to follow the American lead, despite the misgivings of Germany or Japan."[34]

The history of the past two centuries has been one of central government acquiring more and more power. Alexis de Tocqueville observed during his visit to the United States in 1831 that "the Federal Government scarcely ever interferes in any but foreign affairs; and the governments of the states in reality direct society in America."[35] After World War II, governments in Western Europe disposed of about a quarter of their peoples' income. The proportion now is more than half. At a time when Americans, Britons, Russians, and Chinese were decrying the control of the state over their lives, it was puzzling to be told that states were losing control over their external affairs. Losing control, one wonders, as compared to when? Weak states have lost some of their influence and control over external matters, but strong states have not lost theirs. The patterns are hardly new ones. In the eighteenth and nineteenth centuries, the strongest state with the longest reach intervened all over the globe and built history's most extensive empire. In the twentieth century, the

---

[33] Strange, *Retreat of the State*, 46, 189.
[34] Ibid., 25, 192.
[35] Alexis de Tocqueville, *Democracy in America*, ed. J. P. Mayer, trans. George Lawrence (New York: Harper Perennial, 1988), 446, n. 1.

strongest state with the longest reach repeated Britain's interventionist behavior and, since the end of the Cold War, on an ever widening scale, without building an empire. The absence of empire hardly means, however, that the extent of America's influence and control over the actions of others is of lesser moment. The withering away of the power of the state, whether internally or externally, is more of a wish and an illusion than a reality in most of the world.

Under the Pax Britannica, the interdependence of states became unusually close, which to many portended a peaceful and prosperous future. Instead, a prolonged period of war, autarky, and more war followed. The international economic system, constructed under American auspices after World War II and later amended to suit its purposes, may last longer, but then again it may not. The character of international politics changes as national interdependence tightens or loosens. Yet even as relations vary, states have to take care of themselves as best they can in an anarchic environment. Internationally, the twentieth century for the most part was an unhappy one. In its last quarter, the clouds lifted a little, but twenty-five years is a slight base on which to ground optimistic conclusions. Not only are the effects of close interdependence problematic, but so also is its durability.

The Limited Role of International Institutions

One of the charges hurled at realist theory is that it depreciates the importance of institutions. The charge is justified, and the strange case of NATO's (the North Atlantic Treaty Organization's) outliving its purpose shows why realists believe that international institutions are shaped and limited by the states that found and sustain them and have little independent effect. Liberal institutionalists paid scant attention to organizations designed to buttress the security of states until, contrary to expectations inferred from realist theories, NATO not only survived the end of the Cold War but went on to add new members and to promise to embrace still more. Far from invalidating realist theory or casting doubt on it, however, the recent history of NATO illustrates the subordination of international institutions to national purposes.

Explaining International Institutions

The nature and purposes of institutions change as structures vary. In the old multipolar world, the core of an alliance consisted of a small number of states of comparable capability. Their contributions to one another's security were of crucial importance because they were of similar size. Because major allies were closely interdependent militarily, the defection of one would have made its partners vulnerable to a competing alliance. The members of opposing alliances before World War I were tightly knit because of their mutual dependence. In the new bipolar world, the word "alliance" took on a different meaning. One country, the United States or the Soviet Union, provided most of the security for its bloc. The withdrawal of France from NATO's command structure and the defection of China from the Soviet bloc failed even to tilt the central balance. Early in the Cold War, Americans spoke with alarm about the threat of monolithic communism arising from the combined strength of the Soviet Union and China, yet the bloc's disintegration caused scarcely a ripple. American officials did not proclaim that with China's defection, America's defense budget could safely be reduced by 20 or 10 percent or even be reduced at all. Similarly, when France stopped playing its part in NATO's military plans, American officials did not proclaim that defense spending had to be increased for that reason. Properly speaking, NATO and the WTO (Warsaw Treaty Organization) were treaties of guarantee rather than old-style military alliances.[36]

Glenn Snyder has remarked that "alliances have no meaning apart from the adversary threat to which they are a response."[37] I expected NATO to dwindle at the Cold War's end and ultimately to disappear.[38] In a basic sense, the expectation has been borne out. NATO is no longer even a treaty of guarantee because one cannot answer the question, guarantee against whom? Functions vary as structures change, as does the behavior of units. Thus the end of the Cold War quickly changed the behavior of allied countries. In early July 1990, NATO announced that the alliance would "elaborate new force plans consistent with the revolutionary changes in Europe."[39] By the end of July, without waiting for any such plans, the major European members of NATO unilaterally announced large reductions in their force levels. Even the pretense of continuing to act as an alliance in setting military policy disappeared.

With its old purpose dead, and the individual and collective behavior of

[36] See Kenneth N. Waltz, "International Structure, National Force, and the Balance of World Power," *Journal of International Affairs* 21, no. 2 (1967): 219.

[37] Glenn H. Snyder, *Alliance Politics* (Ithaca, N.Y.: Cornell University Press, 1997), 192.

[38] Kenneth N. Waltz, "The Emerging Structure of International Politics," *International Security* 18, no. 2 (fall 1993): 75–76.

[39] John Roper, "Shaping Strategy without the Threat," Adephi Paper no. 257 (London: International Institute for Strategic Studies, winter 1990/91), 80–81.

its members altered accordingly, how does one explain NATO's survival and expansion? Institutions are hard to create and set in motion, but once created, institutionalists claim, they may take on something of a life of their own; they may begin to act with a measure of autonomy, becoming less dependent on the wills of their sponsors and members. NATO supposedly validates these thoughts.

Organizations, especially big ones with strong traditions, have long lives. The March of Dimes is an example sometimes cited. Having won the war against polio, its mission was accomplished. Nevertheless, it cast about for a new malady to cure or contain. Even though the most appealing ones—cancer, diseases of the heart and lungs, multiple sclerosis, and cystic fibrosis—were already taken, it did find a worthy cause to pursue, the amelioration of birth defects. One can fairly claim that the March of Dimes enjoys continuity as an organization, pursuing an end consonant with its original purpose. How can one make such a claim for NATO?

The question of purpose may not be a very important one; create an organization and it will find something to do.[40] Once created, and the more so once it has become well established, an organization becomes hard to get rid of. A big organization is managed by large numbers of bureaucrats who develop a strong interest in its perpetuation. According to Gunther Hellmann and Reinhard Wolf, in 1993 NATO headquarters was manned by 2,640 officials, most of whom presumably wanted to keep their jobs.[41] The durability of NATO even as the structure of international politics has changed, and the old purpose of the organization has disappeared, is interpreted by institutionalists as evidence strongly arguing for the autonomy and vitality of institutions.

The institutionalist interpretation misses the point. NATO is first of all a treaty made by states. A deeply entrenched international bureaucracy can help to sustain the organization, but states determine its fate. Liberal institutionalists take NATO's seeming vigor as confirmation of the importance of international institutions and as evidence of their resilience. Realists, noticing that as an alliance NATO has lost its major function, see it mainly as a means of maintaining and lengthening America's grip on the foreign and military policies of European states. John Kornblum, U.S. senior deputy to the undersecretary of state for European affairs, neatly described NATO's new role. "The Alliance," he wrote, "provides a vehicle for the application of American power and vision to the security order in Eu-

---

[40] Joseph A. Schumpeter, writing of armies, put it this way: *"created by wars that required it, the machine now created the wars it required."* "The Sociology of Imperialism," in Schumpeter, *Imperialism and Social Classes* (New York: Meridian Books, 1955), 25 (emphasis in original).

[41] Gunther Hellmann and Reinhard Wolf, "Neorealism, Neoliberal Institutionalism, and the Future of NATO," *Security Studies* 3, no. 1 (autumn 1993): 20.

rope."[42] The survival and expansion of NATO tell us much about American power and influence and little about institutions as multilateral entities. The ability of the United States to extend the life of a moribund institution nicely illustrates how international institutions are created and maintained by stronger states to serve their perceived or misperceived interests.

The Bush administration saw, and the Clinton administration continued to see, NATO as the instrument for maintaining America's domination of the foreign and military policies of European states. In 1991, U.S. undersecretary of state Reginald Bartholomew's letter to the governments of European members of NATO warned against Europe's formulating independent positions on defense. France and Germany had thought that a European security and defense identity might be developed within the EU and that the Western European Union, formed in 1954, could be revived as the instrument for its realization. The Bush administration quickly squelched these ideas. The day after the signing of the Maastricht Treaty in December 1991, President George Bush could say with satisfaction that "we are pleased that our Allies in the Western European Union ... decided to strengthen that institution as both NATO's European pillar and the defense component of the European Union."[43]

The European pillar was to be contained within NATO, and its policies were to be made in Washington. Weaker states have trouble fashioning institutions to serve their own ends in their own ways, especially in the security realm. Think of the defeat of the European Defense Community in 1954, despite America's support of it, and the inability of the Western European Union in the more than four decades of its existence to find a significant role independent of the United States. Realism reveals what liberal institutionalist "theory" obscures: namely, that international institutions serve primarily national rather than international interests.[44] Robert Keohane and Lisa Martin, replying to John Mearsheimer's criticism of liberal institutionalism, ask: How are we "to account for the willingness of major states to invest resources in expanding international institutions if such institutions are lacking in significance?"[45] If the answer

[42] John Kornblum, "NATO's Second Half Century—Tasks for an Alliance," *NATO on Track for the 21st Century*, Conference Report (The Hague: Netherlands Atlantic Commission, 1994), 14.

[43] Mark S. Sheetz, "Correspondence: Debating the Unipolar Moment," *International Security* 22, no. 3 (winter 1997/98): 170; and Mike Winnerstig, "Rethinking Alliance Dynamics," paper presented at the annual meeting of the International Studies Association, Washington, D.C., March, 18–22, 1997, 23.

[44] Cf. Alan S. Milward, *The European Rescue of the Nation-State* (Berkeley: University of California Press, 1992).

[45] Robert O. Keohane and Lisa L. Martin, "The Promise of Institutionalist Theory," *International Security* 20, no. 1 (summer 1995): 40.

were not already obvious, the expansion of NATO would make it so: to serve what powerful states believe to be their interests.

With the administration's Bosnian policy in trouble, Clinton needed to show himself an effective foreign policy leader. With the national heroes Lech Walesa and Vaclav Havel clamoring for their countries' inclusion, foreclosing NATO membership would have handed another issue to the Republican party in the congressional elections of 1994. To tout NATO's eastward march, President Clinton gave major speeches in Milwaukee, Cleveland, and Detroit, cities with significant numbers of East European voters.[46] Votes and dollars are the lifeblood of American politics. New members of NATO will be required to improve their military infrastructure and to buy modern weapons. The American arms industry, expecting to capture its usual large share of a new market, has lobbied heavily in favor of NATO's expansion.[47]

The reasons for expanding NATO are weak. The reasons for opposing expansion are strong.[48] It draws new lines of division in Europe, alienates those left out, and can find no logical stopping place west of Russia. It weakens those Russians most inclined toward liberal democracy and a market economy. It strengthens Russians of the opposite inclination. It reduces hope for further large reductions of nuclear weaponry. It pushes Russia toward China instead of drawing Russia toward Europe and America. NATO, led by America, scarcely considered the plight of its defeated adversary. Throughout modern history, Russia has been rebuffed by the West, isolated and at times surrounded. Many Russians believe that, by expanding, NATO brazenly broke promises it made in 1990 and 1991 that former WTO members would not be allowed to join NATO. With good reason, Russians fear that NATO will not only admit additional old members of the WTO but also former republics of the Soviet Union. In 1997, NATO held naval exercises with Ukraine in the Black Sea, with more joint exercises to come, and announced plans to use a military testing ground in western Ukraine. In June 1998, Zbigniew Brzezinski went to Kiev with the message that Ukraine should prepare itself to join NATO by the year

---

[46] James M. Goldgeier, "NATO Expansion: The Anatomy of a Decision," *Washington Quarterly* 21, no. 1 (winter 1998): 94–95. And see his *Not Whether but When: The U.S. Decision to Enlarge NATO* (Washington, D.C.: Brookings, 1999).

[47] William D. Hartung, *Welfare for Weapons Dealers 1998: The Hidden Costs of NATO Expansion* (New York: New School for Social Research, World Policy Institute, 1998); and Jeff Gerth and Tim Weiner, "Arms Makers See Bonanza in Selling NATO Expansion," *New York Times*, June 29, 1997, 1, 8.

[48] See Michael E. Brown, "The Flawed Logic of Expansion," *Survival* 37, no. 1 (spring 1995): 34–52. Michael Mandelbaum, *The Dawn of Peace in Europe* (New York: Twentieth Century Fund Press, 1996). Philip Zelikow, "The Masque of Institutions," *Survival* 38, no. 1 (spring 1996): 77–89.

2010.[49] The farther NATO intrudes into the Soviet Union's old arena, the more Russia is forced to look to the east rather than to the west.

The expansion of NATO extends its military interests, enlarges its responsibilities, and increases its burdens. Not only do new members require NATO's protection, they also heighten its concern over destabilizing events near their borders. Thus Balkan eruptions become a NATO and not just a European concern. In the absence of European initiative, Americans believe they must lead the way because the credibility of NATO is at stake. Balkan operations in the air and even more so on the ground exacerbate differences of interest among NATO members and strain the alliance. European members marvel at the surveillance and communications capabilities of the United States and stand in awe of the modern military forces at its command. Aware of their weaknesses, Europeans express determination to modernize their forces and to develop their ability to deploy them independently. Europe's reaction to America's Balkan operations duplicates its determination to remedy deficiencies revealed in 1991 during the Gulf War, a determination that produced few results.

Will it be different this time? Perhaps, yet if European states do achieve their goals of creating a sixty-thousand strong rapid reaction force and enlarging the role of the WEU, the tension between a NATO controlled by the United States and a NATO allowing for independent European action will again be bothersome. In any event, the prospect of militarily bogging down in the Balkans tests the alliance and may indefinitely delay its further expansion. Expansion buys trouble, and mounting troubles may bring expansion to a halt.

European conditions and Russian opposition work against the eastward extension of NATO. Pressing in the opposite direction is the momentum of American expansion. The momentum of expansion has often been hard to break, a thought borne out by the empires of Republican Rome, of Czarist Russia, and of Liberal Britain.

One is often reminded that the United States is not just the dominant power in the world but that it is a liberal dominant power. True, the motivations of the artificers of expansion—President Clinton, National Security Adviser Anthony Lake, and others—were to nurture democracy in young, fragile, long-suffering countries. One may wonder, however, why this should be an American rather than a European task and why a military rather than a political-economic organization should be seen as the appropriate means for carrying it out. The task of building democracy is not a military one. The military security of new NATO members is not in

---

[49] J. L. Black, *Russia Faces NATO Expansion: Bearing Gifts or Bearing Arms?* (Lanham, Md.: Rowman and Littlefield, 2000), 5–35, 175–201.

jeopardy; their political development and economic well-being are. In 1997, U.S. assistant secretary of defense Franklin D. Kramer told the Czech defense ministry that it was spending too little on defense.[50] Yet investing in defense slows economic growth. By common calculation, defense spending stimulates economic growth about half as much as direct investment in the economy. In Eastern Europe, economic not military security is the problem and entering a military alliance compounds it.

Using the example of NATO to reflect on the relevance of realism after the Cold War leads to some important conclusions. The winner of the Cold War and the sole remaining great power has behaved as unchecked powers have usually done. In the absence of counterweights, a country's internal impulses prevail, whether fueled by liberal or by other urges. The error of realist predictions that the end of the Cold War would mean the end of NATO arose not from a failure of realist theory to comprehend international politics, but from an underestimation of America's folly. The survival and expansion of NATO illustrate not the defects but the limitations of structural explanations. Structures shape and shove; they do not determine the actions of states. A state that is stronger than any other can decide for itself whether to conform its policies to structural pressures and whether to avail itself of the opportunities that structural change offers, with little fear of adverse affects in the short run.

Do liberal institutionalists provide better leverage for explaining NATO's survival and expansion? According to Keohane and Martin, realists insist "that institutions have only marginal effects."[51] On the contrary, realists have noticed that whether institutions have strong or weak effects depends on what states intend. Strong states use institutions, as they interpret laws, in ways that suit them. Thus Susan Strange, in pondering the state's retreat, observes that "international organization is above all a tool of national government, an instrument for the pursuit of national interest by other means."[52]

Interestingly, Keohane and Martin, in their effort to refute Mearsheimer's trenchant criticism of institutional theory, in effect agree with him. Having claimed that his realism is "not well specified," they note that "institutional theory conceptualizes institutions both as independent and dependent variables."[53] Dependent on what?—on "the realities of power and interest." Institutions, it turns out, "make a significant

---

[50] Ibid., 72.
[51] Keohane and Martin, "The Promise of Institutionalist Theory," 42, 46.
[52] Strange, *Retreat of the State*, xiv; and see 192–93. Cf. Carr, *The Twenty Years' Crisis*, 107: "International government is, in effect, government by that state which supplies the power necessary for the purpose of governing."
[53] Keohane and Marlin, "The Promise of Institutionalist Theory," 46.

difference in conjunction with power realities."[54] Yes! Liberal institution-alism, as Mearsheimer says, "is no longer a clear alternative to realism, but has, in fact, been swallowed up by it."[55] Indeed, it never was an alter-native to realism. Institutionalist theory, as Keohane has stressed, has as its core structural realism, which Keohane and Nye sought "to broaden."[56] The institutional approach starts with structural theory, applies it to the origins and operations of institutions, and unsurprisingly ends with realist conclusions.

Alliances illustrate the weaknesses of institutionalism with special clar-ity. Institutional theory attributes to institutions causal effects that mostly originate within states. The case of NATO nicely illustrates this shortcom-ing. Keohane has remarked that "alliances are institutions, and both their durability and strength . . . may depend in part on their institutional char-acteristics."[57] In part, I suppose, but one must wonder in how large a part. The Triple Alliance and the Triple Entente were quite durable. They lasted not because of alliance institutions, there hardly being any, but be-cause the core members of each alliance looked outward and saw a press-ing threat to their security. Previous alliances did not lack institutions be-cause states had failed to figure out how to construct bureaucracies. Previous alliances lacked institutions because in the absence of a hege-monic leader, balancing continued within as well as across alliances. NATO lasted as a military alliance as long as the Soviet Union appeared to be a direct threat to its members. It survives and expands now because of its institutions but mainly because the United States wants it to.

NATO's survival also exposes an interesting aspect of balance-of-power theory. Robert Art has argued forcefully that without NATO and without American troops in Europe, European states will lapse into a "security competition" among themselves.[58] As he emphasizes, this is a realist ex-pectation. In his view, preserving NATO, and maintaining America's lead-ing role in it, are required in order to prevent a security competition that would promote conflict within, and impair the institutions of, the Euro-pean Union. NATO now is an anomaly; the dampening of intraalliance tension is the main task left, and it is a task not for the alliance but for its leader. The secondary task of an alliance, intraalliance management, con-

[54] Ibid., 42.

[55] John J. Mearsheimer, "A Realist Reply," *International Security* 20, no. 1 (summer 1995): 85.

[56] Keohane and Nye, *Power and Interdependence*, 251; cf. Keohane, "Theory of World Poli-tics," in Keohane, *Neorealism and Its Critics*, 193, where he describes his approach as a "modi-fied structural research program."

[57] Robert O. Keohane, *International Institutions and State Power: Essays in International Rela-tions Theory* (Boulder, Colo.: Westview Press, 1989), 15.

[58] Robert J. Art, "Why Western Europe Needs the United States and NATO," *Political Sci-ence Quarterly* 111, no. 1 (spring 1996): 1–39.

tinues to he performed by the United States even though the primary task, defense against an external enemy, has disappeared. The point is worth pondering, but I need to say here only that it further illustrates the dependence of international institutions on national decisions. Balancing among states is not inevitable. As in Europe, a hegemonic power may suppress it. As a high-level European diplomat put it, "It is not acceptable that the lead nation be European. A European power broker is a hegemonic power. We can agree on U.S. leadership, but not on one of our own."[59] Accepting the leadership of a hegemonic power prevents a balance of power from emerging in Europe, and better the hegemonic power should be at a distance than next door.

Keohane believes that "avoiding military conflict in Europe after the Cold War depends greatly on whether the next decade is characterized by a continuous pattern of institutionalized cooperation."[60] If one accepts the conclusion, the question remains: What or who sustains the "pattern of institutionalized cooperation"? Realists know the answer.

International Institutions and National Aims

What is true of NATO holds for international institutions generally. The effects that international institutions may have on national decisions are but one step removed from the capabilities and intentions of the major state or states that gave them birth and sustain them. The Bretton Woods system strongly affected individual states and the conduct of international affairs. But when the United States found that the system no longer served its interests, the Nixon shocks of 1971 were administered. International institutions are created by the more powerful states, and the institutions survive in their original form as long as they serve the major interests of their creators, or are thought to do so. "The nature of institutional arrangements," as Stephen Krasner put it, "is better explained by the distribution of national power capabilities than by efforts to solve problems of market failure"[61]—or, I would add, by anything else.

Either international conventions, treaties, and institutions remain close to the underlying distribution of national capabilities or they court fail-

[59] Quoted ibid., 36.
[60] Robert O. Keohane, "The Diplomacy of Structural Change: Multilateral Institutions and State Strategies," in *America and Europe in an Era of Change*, ed. Helga Haftendorn and Christian Tuschhoff (Boulder, Colo.: Westview Press, 1993), 53.
[61] Stephen D. Krasner, "Global Communications and National Power: Life on the Pareto Frontier," *World Politics* 43, no. 1 (April 1991): 234.

ure.[62] Citing examples from the past 350 years, Krasner found that in all of the instances "it was the value of strong states that dictated rules that were applied in a discriminating fashion only to the weak."[63] The sovereignty of nations, a universally recognized international institution, hardly stands in the way of a strong nation that decides to intervene in a weak one. Thus, according to a senior official, the Reagan administration "debated whether we had the right to dictate the form of another country's government. The bottom line was yes, that some rights are more fundamental than the right of nations to nonintervention. . . . We don't have the right to subvert a democracy but we do have the right against an undemocratic one."[64] Most international law is obeyed most of the time, but strong states bend or break laws when they choose to.

Balancing Power: Not Today but Tomorrow

With so many of the expectations that realist theory gives rise to confirmed by what happened at and after the end of the Cold War, one may wonder why realism is in bad repute.[65] A key proposition derived from realist theory is that international politics reflects the distribution of national capabilities, a proposition daily borne out. Another key proposition is that the balancing of power by some states against others recurs. Realist theory predicts that balance disrupted will one day he restored. A limitation of the theory, a limitation common to social science theories, is that it cannot say when. William Wohlforth argues that though restoration will take place, it will be a long time coming.[66] Of necessity, realist theory is better at saying what will happen than in saying when it will happen. Theory cannot say when "tomorrow" will come because international political theory deals with the pressures of structure on states and not with how states will respond to the pressures. The latter is a task for theories about how national governments respond to pressures on them and take advan-

[62] Stephen D. Krasner, *Structural Conflict: The Third World against Global Liberalism* (Berkeley: University of California, 1985), 263 and passim.
[63] Stephen D. Krasner, "International Political Economy: Abiding Discord," *Review of International Political Economy* 1, no. 1 (spring 1999): 16.
[64] Quoted in Robert Tucker, *Intervention and the Reagan Doctrine* (New York: Council on Religious and International Affairs, 1985), 5.
[65] Robert Gilpin explains the oddity. See Gilpin, "No One Loves a Political Realist," *Security Studies* 5, no. 3 (spring 1996): 3–28.
[66] William C. Wohlforth, "The Stability of a Unipolar World," *International Security* 29, no. 1 (summer 1999): 5–41.

tage of opportunities that may be present. One does, however, observe balancing tendencies already taking place.

On the demise of the Soviet Union, the international political system became unipolar. In the light of structural theory, unipolarity appears as the least durable of international configurations. This is so for two main reasons. One is that dominant powers take on too many tasks beyond their own borders, thus weakening themselves in the long run. Ted Robert Gurr, after examining 336 polities, reached the same conclusion that Robert Wesson had reached earlier: "Imperial decay is . . . primarily a result of the misuse of power which follows inevitably from its concentration."[67] The other reason for the short duration of unipolarity is that even if a dominant power behaves with moderation, restraint, and forbearance, weaker states will worry about its future behavior. America's founding fathers warned against the perils of power in the absence of checks and balances. Is unbalanced power less of a danger in international than in national politics? Throughout the Cold War, what the United States and the Soviet Union did, and how they interacted, were dominant factors in international politics. The two countries, however, constrained each other. Now the United States is alone in the world. As nature abhors a vacuum, so international politics abhors unbalanced power. Faced with unbalanced power, some states try to increase their own strength or they ally with others to bring the international distribution of power into balance. The reactions of other states to the drive for dominance of Charles V, Hapsburg ruler of Spain; of Louis XIV and Napoleon I of France; of Wilhelm II and Adolph Hitler of Germany illustrate the point.

The Behavior of Dominant Powers

Will the preponderant power of the United States elicit similar reactions? Unbalanced power, whoever wields it, is a potential danger to others. The powerful state may, and the United States does, think of itself as acting for the sake of peace, justice, and well-being in the world. These terms, however, are defined to the liking of the powerful, which may conflict with the preferences and interests of others. In international politics, overwhelming power repels and leads others to try to balance against it. With benign

[67] Quoted in Ted Robert Gurr, "Persistence and Change in Political Systems 1800–1971," *American Political Science Review* 68, no. 4 (December 1974): 1504, from Robert G. Wesson, *The Imperial Order* (Berkeley: University of California Press, 1967), unpaginated preface. Cf. Paul Kennedy, *The Rise and Fall of Great Powers: Economic Change and Military Conflict from 1500 to 2000* (New York: Random House, 1987).

intent, the United States has behaved and, until its power is brought into balance, will continue to behave in ways that sometimes frighten others.

For almost half a century, the constancy of the Soviet threat produced a constancy of American policy. Other countries could rely on the United States for protection because protecting them seemed to serve American security interests. Even so, beginning in the 1950s, Western European countries and, beginning in the 1970s, Japan had increasing doubts about the reliability of the American nuclear deterrent. As Soviet strength increased, Western European countries began to wonder whether the United States could be counted on to use its deterrent on their behalf, thus risking its own cities. When President Jimmy Carter moved to reduce American troops in South Korea, and later when the Soviet Union invaded Afghanistan and strengthened its forces in the Far East, Japan developed similar worries.

With the disappearance of the Soviet Union, the United States no longer faces a major threat to its security. As General Colin Powell said when he was chairman of the Joint Chiefs of Staff: "I'm running out of demons. I'm running out of enemies. I'm down to Castro and Kim Il Sung."[68] Constancy of threat produces constancy of policy; absence of threat permits policy to become capricious. When few if any vital interests are endangered, a country's policy becomes sporadic and self-willed.

The absence of serious threats to American security gives the United States wide latitude in making foreign policy choices. A dominant power acts internationally truly when the spirit moves it. One example is enough to show this. When Yugoslavia's collapse was followed by genocidal war in successor states, the United States failed to respond until Senator Robert Dole moved to make Bosnia's peril an issue in the forthcoming presidential election; and it acted not for the sake of its own security but to maintain its leadership position in Europe. American policy was generated not by external security interests, but by internal political pressure and national ambition.

Aside from specific threats it may pose, unbalanced power leaves weaker states feeling uneasy and gives them reason to strengthen their positions. The United States has a long history of intervening in weak states, often with the intention of bringing democracy to them. American behavior over the past century in Central America provides little evidence of self-restraint in the absence of countervailing power. Contemplating the history of the United States and measuring its capabilities, other countries may well wish for ways to fend off its benign ministrations. Concentrated power invites

---

[68] "Cover Story: Communism's Collapse Poses a Challenge to America's Military," *U.S. News and World Report*, October 14, 1991, 28.

distrust because it is so easily misused. To understand why some states want to bring power into a semblance of balance is easy, but with power so sharply skewed what country or group of countries has the material capability and the political will to bring the "unipolar moment" to an end?

Balancing Power in a Unipolar World

The expectation that following victory in a great war a new balance of power will form is firmly grounded in both history and theory. The last four grand coalitions (two against Napoleon and one in each of the world wars of the twentieth century) collapsed once victory was achieved. Victories in major wars leave the balance of power badly skewed. The winning side emerges as a dominant coalition. The international equilibrium is broken; theory leads one to expect its restoration.

Clearly something has changed. Some believe that the United States is so nice that, despite the dangers of unbalanced power, others do not feel the fear that would spur them to action. Michael Mastanduno, among others, believes this to be so, although he ends his article with the thought that "eventually, power will check power."[69] Others believe that the leaders of states have learned that playing the game of power politics is costly and unnecessary. In fact, the explanation for sluggish balancing is a simple one. In the aftermath of earlier great wars, the materials for constructing a new balance were readily at hand. Previous wars left a sufficient number of great powers standing to permit a new balance to be rather easily constructed. Theory enables one to say that a new balance of power will form but not to say how long it will take. National and international conditions determine that. Those who refer to the unipolar moment are right. In our perspective, the new balance is emerging slowly; in historical perspectives, it will come in the blink of an eye.

I ended a 1993 article this way: "One may hope that America's internal preoccupations will produce not an isolationist policy, which has become impossible, but a forbearance that will give other countries at long last the chance to deal with their own problems and make their own mistakes. But I would not bet on it."[70] I should think that few would do so now. Charles Kegley has said, sensibly, that if the world becomes multipolar once again,

---

[69] Michael Mastanduno, "Preserving the Unipolar Moment: Realist Theories and U.S. Grand Strategy after the Cold War," *International Security* 21, no. 4 (spring 1997): 88. See Josef Joffe's interesting analysis of America's role, " 'Bismarck' or 'Britain'? Toward an American Grand Strategy after Bipolarity," *International Security* 19, no. 4 (spring 1995): 94–117.

[70] Waltz, "The Emerging Structure of International Politics," 79.

realists will be vindicated.[71] Seldom do signs of vindication appear so promptly.

The candidates for becoming the next great powers, and thus restoring a balance, are the European Union or Germany leading a coalition, China, Japan, and in a more distant future, Russia. The countries of the European Union have been remarkably successful in integrating their national economics. The achievement of a large measure of economic integration without a corresponding political unity is an accomplishment without historical precedent. On questions of foreign and military policy, however, the European Union can act only with the consent of its members, making bold or risky action impossible. The European Union has all the tools—population, resources, technology, and military capabilities—but lacks the organizational ability and the collective will to use them. As Jacques Delors said when he was president of the European Commission: "It will be for the European Council, consisting of heads of state and government . . . , to agree on the essential interests they share and which they will agree to defend and promote together."[72] Policies that must be arrived at by consensus can be carried out only when they are fairly inconsequential. Inaction as Yugoslavia sank into chaos and war signaled that Europe will not act to stop wars even among near neighbors. Western Europe was unable to make its own foreign and military policies when it was an organization of six or nine states living in fear of the Soviet Union. With less pressure and more members, it has even less hope of doing so now. Only when the United States decides on a policy have European countries been able to follow it.

Europe may not remain in its supine position forever, yet signs of fundamental change in matters of foreign and military policy are faint. Now as earlier, European leaders express discontent with Europe's secondary position, chafe at America's making most of the important decisions, and show a desire to direct their own destiny. French leaders often vent their frustration and pine for a world, as Foreign Minister Hubert Védrine recently put it, "of several poles, not just a single one." President Jacques Chirac and Prime Minister Lionel Jospin call for a strengthening of such multilateral institutions as the International Monetary Fund and the United Nations, although how this would diminish America's influence is not explained. More to the point, Védrine complains that since president

---

[71] Charles W. Kegley Jr., "The Neoidealist Moment in International Studies? Realist Myths and the New International Realities," *International Studies Quarterly* 37, no. 2 (June 1993): 149.

[72] Jacques Delors, "European Integration and Security," *Survival* 33, no. 1 (March/April 1991): 106.

John Kennedy, Americans have talked of a European pillar for the alliance, a pillar that is never built.[73] German and British leaders now more often express similar discontent. Europe, however, will not be able to claim a louder voice in alliance affairs unless it builds a platform for giving it expression. If Europeans ever mean to write a tune to go with their libretto, they will have to develop the unity in foreign and military affairs that they are achieving in economic matters. If French and British leaders decided to merge their nuclear forces to form the nucleus of a European military organization, the United States and the world will begin to treat Europe as a major force.

The European Economic Community was formed in 1957 and has grown incrementally to its present proportions. But where is the incremental route to a European foreign and military policy to be found? European leaders have not been able to find it or even tried very hard to do so. In the absence of radical change, Europe will count for little in international politics for as far ahead as the eye can see, unless Germany, becoming impatient, decides to lead a coalition.

International Structure and National Responses

Throughout modern history, international politics centered on Europe. Two world wars ended Europe's dominance. Whether Europe will somehow, someday emerge as a great power is a matter for speculation. In the meantime, the all-but-inevitable movement from unipolarity to multipolarity is taking place not in Europe but in Asia. The internal development and the external reaction of China and Japan are steadily raising both countries to the great-power level.[74] China will emerge as a great power even without trying very hard so long as it remains politically united and competent. Strategically, China can easily raise its nuclear forces to a level of parity with the United States if it has not already done so.[75] China has five to seven intercontinental missiles (DF-5s) able to hit almost any American target and a dozen or more missiles able to reach the west coast of the United States (DF-4s).[76] Liquid fueled, immobile missiles are

[73] Craig R. Whitney, "NATO at 50: With Nations at Odds, Is It a Misalliance?" *New York Times*, February 15, 1999, A1.

[74] The following four pages are adapted from Waltz, "The Emerging Structure of International Politics."

[75] Nuclear parity is reached when countries have second-strike forces. It does not require quantitative or qualitative equality of forces. See Waltz, "Nuclear Myths and Political Realities," *American Political Science Review* 84, no. 3 (September 1990): 731–45.

[76] David E. Sanger and Erik Eckholm, "Will Beijing's Nuclear Arsenal Stay Small or Will It Mushroom?" *New York Times*, March 15, 1999, A1.

vulnerable, but would the United States risk the destruction of, say Seattle, San Francisco, and San Diego if China happens to have a few more DF-4s than the United States thinks or if it should fail to destroy all of them on the ground? Deterrence is much easier to contrive than most Americans have surmised.

If it is possible to be extremely moderate, Chinese nuclear programs have been that. The Bush administration's zeal for national missile defense can, however, be counted on to spark the building of strategic arms in Asia and beyond. A light American defense with about one hundred interceptors is expected to knock down twenty-five warheads. Impartial observers may not believe that defenses will do that well, but China will assume that they may do even better and arm itself accordingly. Where China leads, India and Pakistan will follow. The result, President Putin fears, may be "a hectic uncontrolled arms race on the borders of our country."[77] The only effective response to a nuclear threat, or to a conventional threat that one cannot meet, lies in the ability to retaliate. In the nuclear world, defense looks like offense; SDI should have been labeled SOI, strategic offense initiative. The shield makes the sword usable. Reagan understood the offensive implications of nuclear defenses, but played them down. With a lack of political sensibility that would be astonishing in other administrations, the present Bush administration plays them up. As Bush has said: "They seek weapons of mass destruction . . . to keep the United States and other responsible nations from helping allies and friends in strategic parts of the world."[78] In short, we want to be able to intervene militarily when and where we choose to. Our nuclear defenses would presumably make that possible even against countries lightly armed with nuclear weapons.

The first effect of developing defenses is to cause other states to multiply the number of their nuclear weapons and to think of sneaky ways of delivering them. President Putin has said that if the ABM Treaty is abrogated, then other arms-control treaties of the past thirty years will be nullified. The 1993 treaty providing for the eventual elimination of missiles with multiple warheads was a proud achievement of the first Bush administration. It was confirmed in the Start II agreement ratified by Russia in the year 2000. The cheapest way for Russia to overcome fears that American defenses will diminish their deterrent, however, is to place more warheads on their land-based missiles, one of the most dangerous forms of nuclear weaponry. The new Bush administration surpasses Clinton's in

---

[77] Patrick E. Tyler, "Putin Says Russia Would Add Arms to Counter Shield," *New York Times*, June 19, 2001, A1.

[78] Excerpts from President Bush's speech, *New York Times*, May 2, 2001, A10.

foolishness. An official of the latter's administration told Russian officials that if our potential defenses should make Russia uneasy, it could simply keep a thousand missiles on full alert.[79] To implement Bush's and Rumsfeld's dreams of defense is more dangerous for us and the world than a small number of nuclear weapons in the hands of India and Pakistan, or for that matter in the hands of North Korea or Iraq. Nuclear defenses destroy arms-control agreements. Agreements to control and reduce nuclear weapons are more useful than attempts to defend against them.

Some countries want us to be able to intervene militarily on their behalf; others do not. Given American nuclear and conventional dominance, what are the latter countries to do? Our dominance presses them to find ways of blocking our interventionist moves. As ever, dominance coupled with immoderate behavior by one country causes others to look for ways to protect their interests. China wants to incorporate Taiwan if only in loose form. Even if China has no intention of using force, and clearly it prefers not to, it believes that the prospect of American military protection of Taiwan removes the threat of force from China's set of diplomatic tools. Taiwan will have less incentive to compromise. China reacts as one would expect it to. Acquiring Russian Oscar II class submarines, capable of disabling our aircraft carriers, is one response. Another is maintaining a minimal nuclear deterrent against the United States. American intelligence reports that our defenses may prompt China to multiply its nuclear arsenal by ten and to place multiple warheads on its missiles.[80]

The mere prospect of American missile defense promotes the vertical proliferation of nuclear weapons. It also encourages the horizontal spread of nuclear weapons from one country to another. Japan, already made uneasy by China's increasing economic and military capabilities, will become uneasier still as China acts to counter America's prospective defenses. Since the new Bush administration is rending the fabric of agreements that brought nuclear weapons under a modicum of control, and since we offer nothing to replace it, other countries try harder to take care of themselves. North Korea, Iraq, Iran, and others know that America can be held at bay only by deterrence. Weapons of mass destruction are the only means by which they can hope to deter the United States. They cannot hope to do so by relying on conventional weapons.

Unlike China, Japan is obviously reluctant to assume the mantle of a great power. Its reluctance, however, is steadily though slowly waning.

---

[79] FitzGerald, "The Poseurs of Missile Defense," *New York Times,* June 4, 2000, sec. 4, 19.
[80] Steven Lee Myers, "Study Said to Find U.S. Missile Shield Might Incite China," *New York Times,* August 10, 2000, A1.

Economically, Japan's power has grown and spread remarkably. The growth of a country's economic capability to the great-power level places it at the center of regional and global affairs. It widens the range of a state's interests and increases their importance. The high volume of a country's external business thrusts it ever more deeply into world affairs. In a self-help system, the possession of most but not all of the capabilities of a great power leaves a state vulnerable to others that have the instruments that the lesser state lacks. Even though one may believe that fears of nuclear blackmail are misplaced, one must wonder whether Japan will remain immune to them.

Countries have always competed for wealth and security, and the competition has often led to conflict. Historically states have been sensitive to changing relations of power among them. Japan is made uneasy now by the steady growth of China's military budget. Its nearly 3-million-strong army, undergoing modernization, and the gradual growth of its sea- and air-power projection capabilities, produce apprehension in all of China's neighbors and add to the sense of instability in a region where issues of sovereignty and disputes over territory abound. The Korean peninsula has more military forces per square kilometer than any other portion of the globe. Taiwan is an unending source of tension. Disputes exist between Japan and Russia over the Kurile Islands, and between Japan and China over the Senkaku or Diaoyu Islands. Cambodia is a troublesome problem for both Vietnam and China. Half a dozen countries lay claim to all or some of the Spratly Islands, strategically located and supposedly rich in oil. The presence of China's ample nuclear forces, combined with the drawdown of American military forces, can hardly be ignored by Japan, the less so because economic conflicts with the United States cast doubt on the reliability of American military guarantees. Reminders of Japan's dependence and vulnerability multiply in large and small ways. For example, as rumors about North Korea's developing nuclear capabilities gained credence, Japan became acutely aware of its lack of observation satellites. Uncomfortable dependencies and perceived vulnerabilities have led Japan to acquire greater military capabilities, even though many Japanese may prefer not to.

Given the expectation of conflict, and the necessity of taking care of one's interests, one may wonder how any state with the economic capability of a great power can refrain from arming itself with the weapons that have served so well as the great deterrent. For a country to choose not to become a great power is a structural anomaly. For that reason, the choice is a difficult one to sustain. Sooner or later, usually sooner, the international status of countries has risen in step with their material resources. Countries with great-power economies have become great powers, whether or not reluctantly. Some countries may strive to become great powers; others may wish to avoid doing so. The choice, however, is a constrained one. Because of the extent of their interests, larger units existing in a contentious arena tend to take on system-wide tasks. Profound change in a country's international situation produces radical change in its external behavior. After World War II, the United States broke with its centuries-long tradition of acting unilaterally and refusing to make long-term commitments. Japan's behavior in the past half century reflects the abrupt change in its international standing suffered because of its defeat in war. In the previous half century, after victory over China in 1894–95, Japan pressed for preeminence in Asia, if not beyond. Does Japan once again aspire to a larger role internationally? Its concerted regional activity, its seeking and gaining prominence in such bodies as the IMF and the World Bank, and its obvious pride in economic and technological achievements indicate that it does. The behavior of states responds more to external conditions than to internal habit if external change is profound.

When external conditions press firmly enough, they shape the behavior of states. Increasingly Japan is being pressed to enlarge its conventional forces and to add nuclear ones to protect its interests. India, Pakistan, China, and perhaps North Korea have nuclear weapons capable of deterring others from threatening their vital interests. How long can Japan live alongside other nuclear states while denying itself similar capabilities? Conflicts and crises are certain to make Japan aware of the disadvantages of being without the military instruments that other powers command. Japanese nuclear inhibitions arising from World War II will not last indefinitely; one may expect them to expire as generational memories fade.

Japanese officials have indicated that when the protection of America's extended deterrent is no longer thought to be sufficiently reliable, Japan will equip itself with a nuclear force, whether or not openly. Japan has put itself politically and technologically in a position to do so. Consistently since the mid-1950s, the government has defined all of its Self-Defense Forces as conforming to constitutional requirements. Nuclear weapons purely for defense would be deemed constitutional should Japan decide to build some.[81] As a secret report of the Ministry of Foreign Affairs put it in 1969: "For the time being, we will maintain the policy of not possessing nuclear weapons. However, regardless of joining the NPT [Non-Proliferation Treaty] or not, we will keep the economic and technical potential for the production of nuclear weapons, while seeing to it that Japan will not

---

[81] Norman D. Levin, "Japan's Defense Policy: The Internal Debate," in *Japan, ASEAN, and the United States,* ed. Harry H. Kendall and Clara Joewono (Berkeley: Institute of East Asian Studies, University of California, 1990).

be interfered with in this regard."[82] In March 1988, Prime Minister Noboru Takeshita called for a defensive capability matching Japan's economic power.[83] Only a balanced conventional-nuclear military capability would meet this requirement. In June 1994, Prime Minister Tsutumu Hata mentioned in parliament that Japan had the ability to make nuclear weapons.[84]

Where some see Japan as a "global civilian power" and believe it likely to remain one, others see a country that has skillfully used the protection the United States has afforded and adroitly adopted the means of maintaining its security to its regional environment.[85] Prime Minister Shigeru Yoshida in the early 1950s suggested that Japan should rely on American protection until it had rebuilt its economy as it gradually prepared to stand on its own feet.[86] Japan has laid a firm foundation for doing so by developing much of its own weaponry instead of relying on cheaper imports. Remaining months or moments away from having a nuclear military capability is well designed to protect the country's security without unduly alarming its neighbors.

The hostility of China, of both Koreas, and of Russia combines with inevitable doubts about the extent to which Japan can rely on the United States to protect its security.[87] In the opinion of Masanori Nishi, a defense official, the main cause of Japan's greater "interest in enhanced defense capabilities" is its belief that America's interest in "maintaining regional stability is shaky."[88] Whether reluctantly or not, Japan and China will follow each other on the route to becoming great powers. China has the greater long-term potential. Japan, with the world's second or third largest defense budget and the ability to produce the most technologically advanced weaponry, is closer to great power status at the moment.

[82] "The Capability to Develop Nuclear Weapons Should Be Kept: Ministry of Foreign Affairs Secret Document in 1969," *Mainichi*, August 1, 1994, 41, quoted in Selig S. Harrison, "Japan and Nuclear Weapons," in *Japan's Nuclear Future*, ed. Harrison (Washington, D.C.: Carnegie Endowment for International Peace, 1996), 9.

[83] David Arase, "U.S. and ASEAN Perceptions of Japan's Role in the Asian-Pacific Region," in *Japan, ASEAN, and the United States*, 276.

[84] David E. Sanger, "In Face-Saving Reverse, Japan Disavows Any Nuclear-Arms Expertise," *New York Times*, June 22, 1994, 10.

[85] Michael J. Green, "State of the Field Report: Research on Japanese Security Policy," *Access Asia Review* 2, no. 2 (September 1998), judiciously summarized different interpretations of Japan's security policy.

[86] Kenneth B. Pyle, *The Japanese Question: Power and Purpose in a New Era* (Washington, D.C.: AEI Press, 1992), 26.

[87] Andrew Hanami, for example, points out that Japan wonders whether the United States would help defend Hokkaido. Hanami, "Japan and the Military Balance of Power in Northeast Asia," *Journal of East Asian Affairs* 7, no. 2 (summer/fall 1994): 364.

[88] Stephanie Strom, "Japan Beginning to Flex Its Military Muscles," *New York Times*, April 8, 1999, A4.

When Americans speak of preserving the balance of power in East Asia through their military presence,[89] the Chinese understandably take this to mean that they intend to maintain the strategic hegemony they now enjoy in the absence of such a balance. When China makes steady but modest efforts to improve the quality of its inferior forces, Americans see a future threat to their and others' interests. Whatever worries the United States has and whatever threats it feels, Japan has them earlier and feels them more intensely. Japan has gradually reacted to them. China then worries as Japan improves its airlift and sealift capabilities and as the United States raises its support level for forces in South Korea.[90] The actions and reactions of China, Japan, and South Korea, with or without American participation, are creating a new balance of power in East Asia, which is becoming part of the new balance of power in the world.

Historically, encounters of East and West have often ended in tragedy. Yet, as we know from happy experience, nuclear weapons moderate the behavior of their possessors and render them cautious whenever crises threaten to spin out of control. Fortunately, the changing relations of East to West, and the changing relations of countries within the East and the West, are taking place in a nuclear context. The tensions and conflicts that intensify when profound changes in world politics take place will continue to mar the relations of nations, while nuclear weapons keep the peace among those who enjoy their protection.

America's policy of containing China by keeping 100,000 troops in East Asia and by providing security guarantees to Japan and South Korea is intended to keep a new balance of power from forming in Asia. By continuing to keep 100,000 troops in Western Europe, where no military threat is in sight, and by extending NATO eastward, the United States pursues the same goal in Europe. The American aspiration to freeze historical development by working to keep the world unipolar is doomed. In the not very long run, the task will exceed America's economic, military, demographic, and political resources; and the very effort to maintain a hegemonic position is the surest way to undermine it. The effort to maintain dominance stimulates some countries to work to overcome it. As theory shows and history confirms, that is how balances of power are made. Multipolarity is developing before our eyes. Moreover, it is emerging in accordance with the balancing imperative.

American leaders seem to believe that America's preeminent position

---

[89] Richard Bernstein and Ross H. Munro, *The Coming Conflict with China* (New York: Alfred A. Knopf, 1997); and Andrew J. Nathan and Robert S. Ross, *The Great Wall and the Empty Fortress: China's Search for Security* (New York: W. W. Norton, 1997).

[90] Michael J. Green and Benjamin L. Self, "Japan's Changing China Policy: From Commercial Liberalism to Reluctant Realism," *Survival* 38, no. 2 (summer 1996): 43.

will last indefinitely. The United States would then remain the dominant power without rivals rising to challenge it—a position without precedent in modern history. Balancing, of course, is not universal and omnipresent. A dominant power may suppress balancing as the United States has done in Europe. Whether or not balancing takes place also depends on the decisions of governments. Stephanie Neuman's book, *International Relations Theory and the Third World*, abounds in examples of states that failed to mind their own security interests through internal efforts or external arrangements, and as one would expect, suffered invasion, loss of autonomy, and dismemberment.[91] States are free to disregard the imperatives of power, but they must expect to pay a price for doing so. Moreover, relatively weak and divided states may find it impossible to concert their efforts to counter a hegemonic state despite ample provocation. This has long been the condition of the Western Hemisphere.

In the Cold War, the United States won a telling victory. Victory in war, however, often brings lasting enmities. Magnanimity in victory is rare. Winners of wars, facing few impediments to the exercise of their wills, often act in ways that create future enemies. Thus Germany, by taking Alsace and most of Lorraine from France in 1871, earned its lasting enmity; and the Allies' harsh treatment of Germany after World War I produced a similar effect. In contrast, Bismarck persuaded the Kaiser not to march his armies along the road to Vienna after the great victory at Königgärtz in 1866. In the Treaty of Prague, Prussia took no Austrian territory. Thus Austria, having become Austria-Hungary, was available as an alliance partner for Germany in 1879. Rather than learning from history, the United States is repeating past errors by extending its influence over what used to be the province of the vanquished.[92] This alienates Russia and nudges it toward China instead of drawing it toward Europe and the United States. Despite much talk about the "globalization" of international politics, American political leaders to a dismaying extent think of East *or* West rather than of their interaction. With a history of conflict along a 2,600 mile border, with ethnic minorities sprawling across it, with a mineral-rich and sparsely populated Siberia facing China's teeming millions, Russia and China will find it difficult to cooperate effectively, but the United States is doing its best to help them do so. Indeed, the United States has provided the key to Russian-Chinese relations over the past half century. Feeling American antagonism and fearing American power, China drew

[91] Stephanie Neuman, ed., *International Relations Theory and the Third World* (New York: St. Martin's, 1998).

[92] Tellingly, John Lewis Gaddis comments that he has never known a time when there was less support among historians for an announced policy. Gaddis, "History, Grand Strategy, and NATO Enlargement," *Survival* 40, no. 1 (spring 1998): 147.

close to Russia after World War II and remained so until the United States seemed less, and the Soviet Union more, of a threat to China. The relatively harmonious relations the United States and China enjoyed during the 1970s began to sour in the late 1980s when Russian power visibly declined and American hegemony became imminent. To alienate Russia by expanding NATO, and to alienate China by lecturing its leaders on how to rule their country, are policies that only an overwhelmingly powerful country could afford, and only a foolish one be tempted, to follow. The United States cannot prevent a new balance of power from forming. It can hasten its coming as it has been earnestly doing.

American conventional and strategic military dominance spurs other countries to act. Arrogance is the partner of dominance. "One reads about the world's desire for American leadership only in the United States," a British diplomat has observed. "Everywhere else one reads about American arrogance and unilateralism."[93] Recent history richly illustrates the effects of unbalanced power. George W. Bush has often emphasized our readiness to consult other countries. In his lexicon "consult" has meant that we explain our policies and then implement them whether or not other countries like them.

When even overwhelming power is insufficient, and the strongest country needs help, however, unilateralism gives way to multilateralism, and arrogance wanes. The terrorist attacks on the World Trade Center and the Pentagon changed the international as well as the domestic behavior of the United States. Terrorists did not tilt the balance of power. They did change some of the effects of the gross imbalance of power.

In this section, the discussion of balancing has been more empirical and speculative than theoretical. I therefore end with some reflections on balancing theory. Structural theory, and the theory of balance of power that follows from it do not lead one to expect that states will always or even usually engage balancing behavior. Balancing is a strategy for survival, a way of attempting to maintain a state's autonomous way of life. To argue that bandwagoning represents a behavior more common to states than balancing has become a bit of a fad. Whether states bandwagon more often than they balance is an interesting question. To believe that an affirmative answer would refute balance-of-power theory is, however, to misinterpret the theory and to commit what one might call "the numerical fallacy"—to draw a qualitative conclusion from a quantitative result. States try various strategies for survival. Balancing is one of them; bandwagoning is another. The latter may sometimes seem a less demanding and a more

---

[93] Quoted in Samuel Huntington, "The Lonely Superpower," *Foreign Affairs* 78, no. 2 (March/April 1999): 42.

rewarding strategy than balancing, requiring less effort and extracting lower costs while promising concrete rewards. Amid the uncertainties of international politics and the shifting pressures of domestic politics, states have to make perilous choices. They may hope to avoid war by appeasing adversaries, a weak form of bandwagoning, rather than by rearming and realigning to thwart them. Moreover, many states have insufficient resources for balancing and little room for maneuver. They have to jump on the wagon only later to wish they could fall off.

Balancing theory does not predict uniformity of behavior but rather the strong tendency of major states in the system, or in regional subsystems, to resort to balancing when they have to. That states try different strategies of survival is hardly surprising. The recurrent emergence of balancing behavior, and the appearance of the patterns the behavior produces, should all the more be seen as impressive evidence supporting the theory.

Conclusion

Every time peace breaks out, people pop up to proclaim that realism is dead. That is another way of saying that international politics has been transformed. The world, however, has not been transformed; the structure of international politics has simply been remade by the disappearance of the Soviet Union, and for a time we will live with unipolarity. Moreover, international politics was not remade by the forces and factors that some believe are creating a new world order. Those who set the Soviet Union on the path of reform were old Soviet apparatchiks trying to right the Soviet economy in order to preserve its position in the world. The revolution in Soviet affairs and the end of the Cold War were not brought by democracy, interdependence, or international institutions. Instead the Cold War ended exactly as structural realism led one to expect. As I wrote some years ago, the Cold War "is firmly rooted in the structure of postwar international politics and will last as long as that structure endures."[94] So it did, and the Cold War ended only when the bipolar structure of the world disappeared.

Structural change affects the behavior of states and the outcomes their interactions produce. It does not break the essential continuity of international politics. The transformation of international politics alone could do that. Transformation, however, awaits the day when the international system is no longer populated by states that have to help themselves. If the

[94] Kenneth N. Waltz, "The Origins of War in Neorealist Theory," *Journal of Interdisciplinary History* 18, no. 4 (spring 1988): 628.

day were here, one would be able to say who could be relied on to help the disadvantaged or endangered. Instead, the ominous shadow of the future continues to cast its pall over interacting states. States' perennial uncertainty about their fates presses governments to prefer relative over absolute gains. Without the shadow, the leaders of states would no longer have to ask themselves how they will get along tomorrow as well as today. States could combine their efforts cheerfully and work to maximize collective gain without worrying about how each might fare in comparison to others.

Occasionally, one finds the statement that governments in their natural, anarchic condition act myopically—that is, on calculations of immediate interest—while hoping that the future will take care of itself. Realists are said to suffer from this optical defect.[95] Political leaders may be astigmatic, but responsible ones who behave realistically do not suffer from myopia. Robert Axelrod and Robert Keohane believe that World War I might have been averted if certain states had been able to see how long the future's shadow was.[96] Yet, as their own discussion shows, the future was what the major states were obsessively worried about. The war was prompted less by considerations of present security and more by worries about how the balance might change later. The problems of governments do not arise from their short time horizons. They see the long shadow of the future, but they have trouble reading its contours, perhaps because they try to look too far ahead and see imaginary dangers. In 1914, Germany feared Russia's rapid industrial and population growth. France and Britain suffered from the same fear about Germany, and in addition Britain worried about the rapid growth of Germany's navy. In an important sense, World War I was a preventive war all around. Future fears dominated hopes for short-term gains. States do not live in the happiest of conditions that Horace in one of his odes imagined for man:

> Happy the man, and happy he alone, who can say,
> Tomorrow do thy worst, for I have lived today.[97]

---

[95] The point is made by Robert O. Keohane, *After Hegemony: Cooperation and Discord in the World Political Economy* (Princeton, N.J.: Princeton University Press, 1984), 99, 103, 108.

[96] Robert Axelrod and Robert O. Keohane, "Achieving Cooperation under Anarchy: Strategies and Institutions," in *Neorealism and Neoliberalism: The Contemporary Debate,* ed. David Baldwin (New York: Columbia University Press, 1993). For German leaders, they say, "the shadow of the future seemed so small" (92). Robert Powell shows that "a longer shadow . . . leads to greater military allocations." See Powell, "Guns, Butter, and Anarchy," *American Political Science Review* 87, no. 1 (March 1993): 116; see also p. 117 on the question of the compatibility of liberal institutionalism and structural realism.

[97] My revision.

Robert Axelrod has shown that the "tit-for-tat" tactic, and no other, maximizes collective gain over time. The one condition for success is that the game be played under the shadow of the future.[98] Because states coexist in a self-help system, they may, however, have to concern themselves not with maximizing collective gain but with lessening, preserving, or widening the gap in welfare and strength between themselves and others. The contours of the future's shadow look different in hierarchic and anarchic systems. The shadow may facilitate cooperation in the former; it works against it in the latter. Worries about the future do not make cooperation and institution building among nations impossible; they do strongly condition their operation and limit their accomplishment. Liberal institutionalists were right to start their investigations with structural realism. Until and unless a transformation occurs, it remains the basic theory of international politics.

[98] Robert Axelrod, *The Evolution of Cooperation* (New York: Basic Books, 1984).

2

Hollow Hegemony or Stable Multipolarity?

Charles A. Kupchan

The first post–Cold War decade was a relatively easy one for American strategists. America's preponderant economic and military might produced a unipolar international structure, which in turn provided a ready foundation for global stability. Hierarchy and order devolved naturally from power asymmetries, making less urgent the mapping of a new international landscape and the formulation of a new grand strategy. The elder Bush and Clinton administrations do deserve considerable credit for presiding over the end of the Cold War and responding sensibly to isolated crises around the globe. But America's uncontested hegemony spared them the task of managing competition among multiple poles of power—a challenge that has consistently bedeviled statesmen throughout history.

This new decade will be a far less tractable one for the architects of U.S. foreign policy. Combating terrorism and enhancing homeland security represent new and demanding challenges. And although the United States will remain atop the international hierarchy for some time to come, a global landscape in which power and influence are more equally distributed looms ahead. With this more equal distribution of power will come a more traditional geopolitics and the return of the competitive balancing that has been held in abeyance by America's uncontested preponderance. Economic globalization, nuclear weapons, new information technologies, and the spread of democracy may well tame geopolitics and dampen the rivalries likely to accompany a more diffuse distribution of power. But history provides sobering lessons in this respect. Time and again, postwar lulls in international competition and pronouncements of the obsolescence of major war have given way to the return of power balancing and great-power conflict.

The individuals who will shape U.S. foreign policy during the coming years will therefore face the onerous task of piecing together a grand strategy for managing the return to multipolarity. The challenge will be as demanding politically as it is intellectually. Recognizing that new power centers are emerging and adjusting to their rise will meet political resistance after fifty years of American primacy. Politicians and strategists alike will also have to engage in long-term planning and pursue policies that respond to underlying trends rather than immediate challenges. But American elites must rise to the occasion. The coming decade represents a unique window of opportunity; the United States should plan for the future while it still enjoys preponderance and not wait until the diffusion of power has already made international politics more competitive and unpredictable.

I begin by explaining how and why a transition to a multipolar world is likely to come about in the near term. I focus on two sources of international change—the rise of Europe as an emerging center of power and the decline of America's willingness to be the global protector of last resort. An ascending Europe and an America tiring of the burdens of hegemony are unlikely to clash head-on. On the contrary, America is likely to retreat from an expansive range of international commitments before the rest of the world is ready. In this sense, the key challenge for the United States is not preparing for battle with the next contender for hegemony, but weaning Europe and East Asia of their excessive dependence on U.S. power. Europeans and East Asians alike have found it both comfortable and cheap to rely on American power and diplomacy to provide their security. Americans have gone along with the deal for decades because of the importance of containing the Soviet Union and the profitability of being at the center of global politics. But now that communist regimes are a dying breed and the United States faces no peer competitor, America's protective umbrella will slowly retract. If this retrenchment in the scope of America's engagement abroad is not to result in the return of destructive power balancing to Europe and East Asia, the United States and its main regional partners must begin to prepare for life after *Pax Americana*.[1]

---

[1] This essay draws heavily on material presented in Charles A. Kupchan, *The End of the America Era: U.S. Foreign Policy and the Geopolitics of the 21st Century* (New York: Alfred A. Knopf, 2002).

The Sources of the Return to Multipolarity

Most analysts of international politics trace change in the distribution of power to two sources: the secular diffusion over time and space of productive capabilities and material resources; and balancing against concentrations of power motivated by the search for security and prestige. Today's great powers will become tomorrow's has-beens as nodes of innovation and efficiency move from the core to the periphery of the international system. In addition, reigning hegemons threaten rising secondary states and thereby provoke the formation of countervailing coalitions. Taken together, these dynamics drive the cyclical pattern of the rise and fall of great powers.[2]

The contemporary era departs from this historical pattern; neither the diffusion of power nor balancing against the United States will be important factors driving the coming transition in the international system. It will be decades before any single state can match the United States in terms of either military or economic capability. Current power asymmetries are by historical standards extreme. The United States spends more on defense than all other great powers combined and more on defense R&D than the rest of the world combined. Its gross economic output dwarfs that of most other countries and its expenditure on R&D points to a growing qualitative edge in a global economy increasingly dominated by high-technology sectors. As William Wohlforth sums up the prevailing wisdom emerging from these data, "The current unipolarity is not only peaceful but durable. . . . For many decades, no state is likely to be in a position to take on the United States in any of the underlying elements of power."[3]

Nor is balancing against American power likely to provoke a countervailing coalition. The United States is separated from both Europe and Asia by large expanses of water, making American power less threatening. Anti-American sentiment may run strong in the Middle East and other parts of the developing world. But it is hard to imagine that the United States would engage in behavior sufficiently aggressive to provoke an opposing alliance of industrialized countries. Local powers in Europe and East Asia for the most part welcome U.S. forces. Despite complaints from French, Russian, and Chinese officials about America's overbearing be-

[2] See Robert Gilpin, *War and Change in World Politics* (Cambridge: Cambridge University Press, 1981); Paul Kennedy, *The Rise and Fall of the Great Powers* (New York: Random House, 1987); and Christopher Layne, "The Unipolar Illusion: Why New Great Powers Will Rise," *International Security* 17, no. 4 (spring 1993): 5–51.

[3] William C. Wohlforth, "The Stability of a Unipolar World," *International Security* 24, no. 1 (summer 1999): 8, 10–22.

havior, the United States is generally viewed as more of a benign power than a predatory hegemon.[4]

The Rise of Europe

In contrast to the past, the waning of today's unipolarity will be driven by two unusual suspects: regional amalgamation in Europe and shrinking internationalism in the United States. Europe is in the midst of a long-term process of political and economic integration that is gradually eliminating the importance of borders and centralizing authority and resources. To be sure, the EU is not an amalgamated polity with a single center of authority. Nor does Europe have a military capability commensurate with its economic resources. But trend lines do indicate that Europe is heading in the direction of becoming a new center of power. Now that its single market has been accompanied by a single currency, Europe has a collective weight on matters of trade and finance rivaling that of the United States. The aggregate wealth of the EU's fifteen members is already approaching that of America, and the coming entry of a host of new members will tilt the balance in Europe's favor.

In addition, Europe has recently embarked on efforts to forge a common defense policy and to acquire the military wherewithal to operate independently of U.S. forces. The EU has set a goal of being able, by 2003, to deploy a force of roughly 60,000 troops within 60 days of notification and to sustain the deployment for one year. The union has also appointed a high representative for foreign and security policy, created the bodies necessary to provide political oversight, and started to revamp its forces. The EU's military capability will certainly remain quite limited compared to that of the United States. And it will be decades, if ever, before the EU becomes a unitary state, especially in light of its impending enlargement to the east. But as its resources grow and its decision making becomes more centralized, power and influence will become more equally distributed between the two sides of the Atlantic.

Skeptics of Europe counter that the EU has poor prospects of cohering as an effective actor in the global arena; the national states remain too strong and the union too decentralized and divided by cultural and linguistic boundaries. But Europe has repeatedly defied the skeptics as it has successfully moved from a free trade area, to a single market, to a single

---

[4] On the concept of benign power, see Charles Kupchan, "After Pax Americana: Benign Power, Regional Integration, and the Sources of a Stable Multipolarity," *International Security* 23, no. 2 (fall 1998): 40–79.

currency. Eastward enlargement does risk the dilution of the union, threatening to make its decision-making bodies more unwieldy. But precisely because of this risk, it is also likely to trigger institutional reform, inducing a core group of states to pursue deeper integration. Indeed, the German government is actively promoting proposals that would succeed in deepening the federal character of the EU. Important in both practical and symbolic terms, EU member states are now considering the drafting and ratification of a constitution.

A changing political discourse within Europe is also likely to fuel the EU's geopolitical ambition. For most of its history, national leaders have justified European integration to their electorates by arguing that it is needed to help Europe escape its past. Union was the only way out of great-power rivalry. This justification is now losing its political salience. World War II has receded sufficiently far into history that escaping the past no longer resonates as a pressing cause for many Europeans. The younger generations who lived through neither the war nor Europe's rebuilding have no past from which they seek escape. The dominant political discourse that has for decades given the EU its meaning and momentum is rapidly running out of steam.

In its place is emerging a new discourse. This new discourse emphasizes Europe's future rather than its past. And instead of justifying integration as a way to check the power and geopolitical ambition of the national state, it portrays integration as a way to acquire power and project geopolitical ambition for Europe as a whole. French President Jacques Chirac, in a speech delivered in Paris in November 1999, could hardly have been clearer: "The European Union itself [must] become a major pole of international equilibrium, endowing itself with the instruments of a true power."[5] Even the British, who for decades kept their distance from the EU, have changed their minds. In the words of Prime Minister Tony Blair, "Europe's citizens need Europe to be strong and united. They need it to be a power in the world. Whatever its origin, Europe today is no longer just about peace. It is about projecting collective power."[6]

Integration is thus being relegitimated among European electorates, but paradoxically through a new brand of European nationalism. Europe's states may have rid themselves for good of their individual claims to great power status, but such aspirations are returning at the level of a col-

[5] Speech on the occasion of the twentieth anniversary of the Institute Français des Relations Internationales, Elysee Palace, November 4, 1999. Text distributed by the French Embassy in Washington, D.C.

[6] Speech to the Polish Stock Exchange, October 6, 2000, available at http://www.number-10. gov.uk/news.asp?NewsId=1341&SectionId=32.

lective Europe. As these new political currents gather momentum, so will Europe's geopolitical ambition.

Europe need not emerge as a superpower, with a global range of interests and commitments, if its rise is to alter the effective polarity of the international system. As Europe's wealth, military capacity, and collective character increase, so will its appetite for greater international influence. Just as America's will to extend its primacy stems not just from self-interest, but also from an emotional satisfaction derived from its leadership position—call it nationalism—so will Europe's rise provoke a yearning for greater status. As the United States currently sits atop the international pecking order, the EU's search for greater autonomy will, at least initially, take the form of resisting U.S. influence and ending its long decades of deference to Washington.

An EU that becomes less dependent on the United States for its security and more often stands its ground on the major issues of the day will be sufficient to alter the structural dynamics of Europe's relationship with the United States. Increasing rivalry between the United States and Europe promises to deal a serious blow to the effectiveness of international organizations. Most multilateral institutions currently rely on a combination of U.S. leadership and European back-stopping to produce consensus and joint action. The United States and Europe often vote as a bloc, leading to a winning coalition in the UN, the IMF, the World Bank, and many other bodies. When Europe resists rather than back-stops American leadership in multilateral institutions, those institutions are likely to become far less effective instruments.

Early signs of such resistance have already been quite visible. In May 2001, the EU took the lead in voting the United States off the UN Commission on Human Rights, the first time Washington has been absent from the body since its formation in 1947. The apparent rationale was to deliver a payback for America's increasing unilateralism and to express disapproval of America's death penalty. The same day, in a separate vote of the UN's Economic and Social Council, the United States lost its seat on the International Narcotics Control Board.

The United States and Europe are also likely to engage in more intense competition over trade and finance. America and Europe today enjoy a remarkably healthy economic relationship, with both parties benefiting from strong flows of trade and investment. A more assertive Europe and a less competitive American economy does, however, increase the likelihood that trade disputes will become more politicized. America's protection of its steel industry and Europe's restriction on imports of genetically modified foods, a ban that could cost U.S. companies $4 billion per year, have particular potential to trigger a major dispute and stand in the way of a new round of global trade talks. The emergence of the euro as an alternative reserve currency also creates the potential for diverging views about management of the international financial system. The competitive devaluations and monetary instability of the interwar period made amply clear that the absence of a dominant economic power can provoke considerable financial turmoil and go-it-alone foreign policies—even among like-minded allies.

Looking beyond the coming decade, economic growth in East Asia will further the onset of a new distribution of global power. Japan already has a world-class economy and will eventually climb out of recession. During the last decade, China enjoyed an economic growth rate of about 10 percent per year. The World Bank estimates that by 2020, "China could be the world's second largest exporter and importer. Its consumers may have purchasing power larger than all of Europe's. China's involvement with world financial markets, as a user and supplier of capital, will rival that of most industrialized countries."[7] The rise of Japan and China will ultimately contribute to the return of a multipolar global landscape.

The Decline of American Internationalism

The continuing amalgamation of Europe, the eventual rise of Asia, and their leveling effect on the global distribution of power will occur gradually. Of more immediate impact will be a diminishing appetite for robust internationalism in the United States. Today's unipolar landscape is a function not just of America's preponderant resources, but also of its willingness to use them to underwrite international order. Accordingly, should the will of the body politic to bear the costs and risks of international leadership decline, so too will America's position of global primacy.

On the face of it, the appetite of the American polity for internationalism has diminished little, if at all, since the collapse of the Soviet Union. Both the elder Bush and Clinton administrations pursued ambitious and activist foreign policies. The George W. Bush administration initially took a different course, scaling back American involvement in regional disputes and distancing itself from the liberal multilateralism of its predecessors. But the Bush team then responded with alacrity and resolve to the terror attacks of September 11, 2001, exhibiting a return to an activist multilateralism. Since the end of the Cold War, the United States has thus taken the lead in building an open international economy and promoting

---

[7] World Bank, *China 2020: Development Challenges in the New Century* (Washington, D.C.: World Bank, 1997), 103.

financial stability, and it has repeatedly deployed its forces to trouble spots around the globe.

American internationalism, however, has reached a high-water mark and will be dissipating in the years ahead. I base this claim on three considerations: 1) a theoretically grounded position on the circumstances under which great powers extend commitments; 2) analysis of the underlying domestic trends that are leading to a decline in internationalism in the United States; 3) examination of the empirical evidence, including public opinion, congressional behavior, and the policies of the Clinton and George W. Bush administrations.

The Sources of Internationalism: Threat or Opportunity?

Most work on the rise and decline of great powers attributes systemic change to shifts in the distribution of material power. Robert Gilpin identifies uneven economic growth rates and the transfer of leading technologies from core to periphery as the main variables driving international change. Paul Kennedy argues that leading powers tend to lose their positions of primacy because the defense costs associated with maintaining extensive international commitments ultimately undermine their economic base. Both take for granted the external ambition that comes with material preponderance and therefore present an account of systemic change that largely ignores strategic choice.[8]

Other scholars have attempted to incorporate strategic choice into their accounts of international change, distinguishing among different types of great powers. Randall Schweller, for example, differentiates revisionist states from status quo states.[9] A revisionist state is a rising power that seeks to overturn the existing international system in favor of one more conducive to its interests. A status quo state is a power already at the top of the hierarchy; it is interested primarily in preserving and meeting threats to the existing international system. In similar fashion, offensive realists and defensive realists disagree about whether states pursue external ambition to acquire power or to acquire security. Offensive realists assume that great powers always behave like rising states, constantly seeking to increase their power. In contrast, defensive realists assume that great powers can and do behave like status quo states, constantly seeking to en-

---

[8] See note 1.

[9] Randall L. Schweller, "Tripolarity and the Second World War," *International Studies Quarterly* 37, no. 1 (March 1993): 73–103. Randall L. Schweller, *Deadly Imbalances: Tripolarity and Hitler's Strategy of World Conquest* (New York: Columbia University Press, 1998).

hance their security, but not always to enhance their power.[10] Stephen Walt's work on alliances draws a similar distinction. His claim that states balance against threats rather than power per se incorporates strategic choice and assessment of intentions into an account of the relationship between structure and the behavior of poles.[11]

The analysis in this essay follows logically from this effort to incorporate strategic choice into structural realism. I maintain that internationalism among status quo powers is primarily a product of threat, not opportunity. Whereas rising states regularly seek to alter the international system to their advantage when they have the chance to do so, status quo powers are motivated principally by threats to the existing system. After all, they are status quo powers precisely because they are satisfied with the status quo. They are therefore willing to expend blood and treasure in matters of foreign affairs only when the system they find so conducive to their interests is threatened.

The logical consequence of this analytic starting point is that status quo powers become less willing to shoulder onerous international responsibilities when the threats to international order diminish in severity. A decline in perceived threats, after a reasonable time lag, produces a decline in the domestic appetite for robust internationalism and the willingness to uphold or take on costly external commitments. Clear exceptions to this generalization do exist. During the 1920s, for example, Britain and France both pursued quite ambitious imperial policies despite the relatively quiescent strategic environment. They were, however, motivated in large part by the sense of vulnerability that was the legacy of World War I and the effort to mask their weakness by rebuilding imperial prestige.[12] The restrained behavior of nonthreatened status quo states is likely to be even more pronounced in the current era because of the lower benefits and increased costs of military conquest. With state power now much more dependent on technology and productivity rather than land and labor, conquest pays much less handsomely than it used to.

The claim that status quo powers extend external commitments when they must (in response to threat), rather than when they can (in response to opportunity), is the foundation for my claim that U.S. internationalism is now at a high-water mark and will soon be diminishing. To be sure, the United States has remained deeply engaged in all quarters of the globe since the end of the Cold War and the collapse of the Soviet Union. But

---

[10] For a good summary of this debate, see Fareed Zakaria, "Realism and Domestic Politics: A Review Essay," *International Security* 17, no. 1 (summer 1992): 90–96.

[11] See Stephen Walt, *The Origins of Alliances* (Ithaca, N.Y.: Cornell University Press, 1987).

[12] Charles Kupchan, *The Vulnerability of Empire* (Ithaca, N.Y.: Cornell University Press, 1994).

that is the essence of the problem. The scope of America's global commitments (and particularly its commitments in Europe) is becoming increasingly divorced from the new strategic landscape. The demise of the Soviet Union and the disappearance of a peer competitor should have induced America to lighten its load. Instead, America's strategic commitments have increased markedly over the course of the past decade.[13] The result is an increasing gap between the scope of America's external ambition and the American polity's appetite for internationalism.

The terror attacks of September 2001 certainly made clear that America is far from invulnerable and continues to face major external threats to its security. For many, the attacks ensured that America will remain fiercely internationalist. As Andrew Sullivan, the former editor of *The New Republic*, wrote only a few days after the attack, "We have been put on notice that every major Western city is now vulnerable." "For the United States itself," Sullivan continued, "this means one central thing. Isolationism is dead."[14]

It is by no means clear, however, that terrorism inoculates the United States against the allure of turning inward and lightening the burdens of hegemony. In the long run, America's leaders may well find the country's security better served by reducing its overseas commitments and raising protective barriers than by chasing terrorists through the mountains of Afghanistan. The United States has a strong tradition dating back to the founding fathers of seeking to cordon itself off from foreign troubles, an impulse that could well be reawakened by the rising costs of global engagement. America's initial response to the attacks of September 11, after all, was to close its borders with Mexico and Canada, ground the nation's air traffic, and patrol the country's coasts with warships and jet fighters.

If I am right that threat, not opportunity, induces status quo powers to extend external commitments, then the absence of a peer competitor will erode America's willingness to serve as the global protector of last resort. Europe will be America's competitor, but not the sort of adversary that evokes sacrifice and vigilance. From this perspective, the robust internationalism of the 1990s promises to be an aberration, not a precedent for the future.

Bringing American exceptionalism into the picture considerably

---

[13] NATO admitted Poland, Hungary, and the Czech Republic in 1999, extending American defense guarantees into Central Europe. In addition, Serbia, Bosnia, Kosovo, Macedonia, and Albania have effectively become NATO protectorates, and Slovenia, Croatia, Romania, Bulgaria, Slovakia, Estonia, Latvia, and Lithuania are now readying themselves to qualify for NATO membership. American forces remain deeply engaged in the Middle East, where U.S. aircraft regularly engage in combat missions over Iraq. And America's strategic posture in East Asia remains as ambitious as it was during the Cold War.

[14] "Why Did It Have to be a Perfect Morning?" *Sunday Times* (London), September 15, 2001.

strengthens this basic claim. Compared to other great powers, America has from the outset been remarkably ambivalent about taking on the responsibilities that accompany great-power status. The founding fathers were quite explicit in their conviction that the security of the United States would be best served by reining in its external ambition and avoiding entangling alliances. As a rising power during the nineteenth century, the United States waited decades before translating its world-class economic power into military strength and external ambition. And even then, it attempted to avoid major strategic commitments abroad until World War II and the Cold War left it with little choice.[15]

This potent strain of ambivalence in American internationalism appears to be the product of two main factors. First, the United States is blessed with wide oceans to its east and west and small, nonthreatening countries to its north and south. Because of its enviable geopolitical location, America is justified in calculating that its security is at certain times and under certain circumstances best served by less, rather than more, engagement abroad. International terrorism, the ballistic missile, and fiber optics no doubt diminish the extent to which America can afford to cordon itself off from threats in distant quarters. But proximity still matters, and the distance of the United States from other areas continues to afford it a natural security.

Second, the constitutional structure of the United States and the deliberate struggle it set up among the different branches of government have from the outset checked the scope of the country's external ambition. During the early years of the republic, the individual states were loath to give up their rights to maintain independent militias and armed forces. They were also fearful of giving too much coercive capacity to the federal government.[16] Times have obviously changed, but such internal checking mechanisms continue to constrain the conduct of U.S. foreign policy. The Senate's rejection of U.S. participation in the League of Nations, congressional adoption of the War Powers Act, the more recent efforts of Congress to mandate the withdrawal of U.S. troops from the Balkans—these are all manifestations of the continuing institutional constraints on American internationalism. Furthermore, these institutional constraints con-

---

[15] On the rise of the United States as a great power, see Fareed Zakaria, *From Wealth to Power* (Princeton, N.J.: Princeton University Press, 1998). On America's ambivalent internationalism during World War I and the interwar period, see Thomas J. Knock, *To End All Wars: Woodrow Wilson and the Quest for a New World Order* (New York: Oxford University Press, 1992); and Walter LaFeber, *The American Age* (New York: W.W. Norton, 1989), chaps. 9–12.

[16] See Daniel Deudney, "The Philadelphian System: Sovereignty, Arms Control, and Balance of Power in the American States-Union, circa 1787–1861," *International Organization* 49, no. 2 (spring 1995): 191–228.

tinue to have powerful ideological roots in what Walter Russell Mead has called the Jacksonian legacy.[17] Avoiding entangling alliances and restricting the power of the federal government are enterprises that hit a populist chord and run deep within the American creed.

Incorporating strategic choice and U.S. exceptionalism into analysis of the forces driving systemic change has profound implications for forecasting how and when America's unipolar moment is likely to end. In purely material terms, no single country is likely to catch the United States for decades—as Wohlforth convincingly argues in his chapter. But Wohlforth, like many other scholars, makes a critical analytic error in assuming that polarity emerges solely from the distribution of power. The willingness of states to deploy their resources and the ends to which they deploy their resources also play a role in shaping polarity. The decline of American internationalism, even if U.S. preponderance remains uncontested, has the potential to alter the global landscape.

Consider the degree to which strategic choice affected Europe's geopolitical landscape during the operation of the Concert of Europe (1815–1853). In material terms, the European landscape was effectively bipolar after the defeat of Napoleonic France, with Britain and Russia much stronger than the other powers. Nonetheless, the Concert of Europe was predicated on a rough equivalence of power among five states— Austria, Prussia, and France, as well as Britain and Russia. The effective influence and status of Austria, Prussia, and France were deliberately elevated beyond their material power in order to establish a cooperative mechanism for preserving peace.[18] In addition, the strongest power in Europe, Britain, was looking to limit its direct strategic engagement on the continent, thereby enabling greater focus on its overseas empire. Although bipolar in material terms, strategic choice and diplomatic practice meant that Europe's landscape was effectively multipolar.

In similar fashion, the choices that America makes in the years ahead about when and how it will use its material power will have a direct impact on the effective polarity of the global landscape. As America's appetite for robust internationalism wanes, the hierarchy that has naturally devolved from its preponderance will diminish as well. Add to this picture Europe's amalgamation and its rise as an alternative center of power, and America's unipolar moment is just that—a passing moment.

---

[17] Walter Russell Meade, "The Jacksonian Tradition," *The National Interest* 58 (winter 1999/2000): 5–29.
[18] On the operation of the Concert and formation of a great power club, see Bruce Cronin, *Community under Anarchy: Transnational Identity and the Evolution of Cooperation* (New York: Columbia University Press, 1999). See also Paul Shroeder, "The 19th-Century International System—Changes in the Structure," *World Politics* 39, no. 1 (October 1986): 1–26.

American Internationalism—the Trends

It may seem odd to presage a consequential decline in America's external ambition at a time when the United States is deeply engaged in virtually every quarter of the globe. America is the dominant strategic actor in
Europe and Asia and the main diplomatic broker in many of the world's
main regional disputes. I maintain, however, that this current level of activism and engagement will not be sustained. It is a legacy of the Cold War
and a product of America's unchallenged primacy. It takes time for
change in the external environment to filter through the polity and affect
both elite and popular attitudes—and ultimately policy. Furthermore, the
robust internationalism of the 1990s was made possible by three extraordinary trends. As these three trends dissipate, America's robust internationalism will diminish as well.

First, the internationalism of the 1990s was sustained by a period of unprecedented economic growth in the United States. A booming stock
market, an expanding economy, and substantial budget surpluses created
a political atmosphere conducive to trade liberalization, expenditure on
the military, and repeated engagement in solving problems in less fortunate parts of the globe. And even under these auspicious conditions, the
internationalist agenda showed signs of faltering. Congress, for example,
mustered only a fickle enthusiasm for free trade, approving NAFTA in
1993 and the Uruguay Round in 1994, but then denying President Clinton
fast-track negotiating authority when he sought it in 1997. Congress was
also skeptical of America's interventions in Bosnia and Kosovo, tolerating
them, but little more. Now that the stock market boom has ended and the
U.S. economy slowed, these inward-looking currents will grow much
stronger. Support for free trade will be even harder to come by. And such
stinginess is likely to spread into the security realm, intensifying the domestic debate over burden-sharing and calls within Congress for America's regional partners to shoulder increased defense responsibilities.

Second, although the United States pursued a very activist defense policy during the 1990s, it did so in a way that did not directly test the public's
willingness to tolerate considerable sacrifice.[19] Clinton repeatedly author-
ized the use of force in the Balkans and in the Middle East. But he relied
almost exclusively on air power, successfully avoiding the casualties likely
to accompany the introduction of ground troops. In the one operation in
which U.S. troops suffered casualties in combat—Somalia—the United

---

[19] On the potential sources of this aversion to take casualties, see Edward Luttwak, "Where
Are the Great Powers?" *Foreign Affairs* 73, no. 4 (July/August 1994): 23–29.

States promptly withdrew its forces from the mission. In laying the groundwork for the military component of the battle against terrorism, President Bush did go out of his way to warn Americans that U.S. casualties were likely. Nonetheless, the attack against Afghanistan was conducted largely from the air, with the United States sending into the country only a limited number of its own forces, instead relying heavily on local opponents of the Taliban to carry out the bulk of the ground operations.

However professional and well-prepared, U.S. forces are not likely always to be so fortunate. Americans will sooner or later die in combat, probably in significant numbers. It may be a suicide bomber targeting an American barracks, as in Lebanon in 1983. It may simply be that America finds itself in battle against an adversary more formidable than Iraq, Yugoslavia, or the Taliban. When a mission eventually goes awry or American units suffer considerable losses, the illusion that military interventions can be carried out with no or minimal casualties will likely come back to haunt the United States, contributing to a rapidly diminishing appetite for a robust internationalism.

Third, the internationalism of the 1990s was sustained in part by an older generation of politicians that brought to the table guiding assumptions and perspectives forged as a result of World War II and the Cold War. The younger Americans already rising to positions of influence in the public and private sectors have not lived through these formative experiences that have been serving as historical anchors of U.S. internationalism. Individuals coming of age after 1990 will have tasted the fear of terrorism, but they will not have known geopolitical urgency firsthand. Rising generations are unlikely to be isolationist; they face more opportunities for travel than their elders and many of them are partaking of the globalized economy with gusto. But being cosmopolitan and worldly is not the same thing as being internationalist. As these individuals rise to positions of prominence, the reflexive internationalism of the 1990s is likely to dissipate.

Generational change is thus likely to take a toll on the character and scope of U.S. engagement abroad. As detailed in the next section, congressional behavior has already begun to reflect this turnover and the diminishing appetite for internationalism that is accompanying it. In the absence of the manifest threat to American national security posed by a peer competitor, making the case for engagement and sacrifice abroad promises to grow increasingly difficult with time. These trend lines reinforce the theoretical argument spelled out above and strengthen the credibility of the claim that America's willingness to carry the burdens of global leadership will diminish in the years ahead.

American Internationalism—the Evidence

I have thus far built what is primarily a deductive case for the proposition that the United States will soon gravitate toward a more constrained internationalism. I now provide empirical evidence that this turning inward is in fact already taking place. I examine briefly public opinion, congressional behavior, U.S. policy during the war over Kosovo, and the foreign policy of George W. Bush—including the likely long-term impact of the war against terrorism.

Numerous indicators suggest that U.S. internationalism is already in retreat; America's domestic politics have begun catching up with the world's changed geopolitics. The terror attacks on New York and Washington did evoke national unity and an outpouring of enthusiasm for military action. But this was only a temporary spike in bipartisan support for robust internationalism and should not be allowed to mask the broader trends. Here is the picture that was emerging prior to the events of September 2001—and the picture that will reemerge as those events slowly recede into the past.

America's diplomatic corps, once a magnet for the country's most talented, lost much of its professional allure over the course of the 1990s. The few high-flyers that the State Department did succeed in attracting often left in frustration after only a few years. According to a front-page story in *The New York Times*, "The State Department, the institution responsible for American diplomacy around the world, is finding it hard to adjust to an era in which financial markets pack more punch than a Washington-Moscow summit meeting. It is losing recruits to investment banks, dot-com companies and the Treasury and Commerce Departments, which have magnified their foreign policy roles."[20]

Public opinion surveys paint a similar picture. Regular surveys by the Chicago Council on Foreign Relations and other bodies indicate that Americans remained generally internationalist throughout the 1990s.[21] However, the public's interest in foreign affairs did decline sharply. Dur-

---

[20] Jane Perlez, "As Diplomacy Loses Luster, Young Stars Flee State Department," *The New York Times*, September 5, 2000. In 2001, the State Department launched a publicity campaign to reverse its recruiting woes. The campaign was an apparent success, with the number of applicants for the 2001 Foreign Service entrance exam substantially larger than for the 2000 exam. See David Stout, "Sign-Ups for Foreign Service Test Nearly Double after 10–Year Ebb," *The New York Times*, August 31, 2001.

[21] The Chicago Council on Foreign Relations carries out a public opinion survey every four years. The 1998 survey indicated that 96% of U.S. leaders and 61% of the public "favor an active part for the US in world affairs." The figures for 1994 were 98% and 65% respectively, indicating only a slight drop. In general, public opinion surveys show only a minor decrease in internationalism since the end of the Cold War. See John E. Reilly, ed., *American Public Opinion and U.S. Foreign Policy* (Chicago: Chicago Council on Foreign Relations, 1999). Available at: http://www.ccfr.org/publications/opinion/AmPuOp99.pdf.

ing the Cold War, some pressing geopolitical issue of the day usually ranked near the top of the public's concerns. By the end of the 1990s, only 2 to 3 percent of Americans viewed foreign policy as a primary concern. When Americans were asked to name the "two or three biggest foreign-policy problems facing the United States today," the most popular response was "don't know." A solid majority of Americans indicated that events in other parts of the world have "very little" impact on the United States. As James Lindsay of the Brookings Institution summed up the situation in an article in *Foreign Affairs*, "Americans endorse internationalism in theory but seldom do anything about it in practice."[22] At the opening of the twenty-first century, Americans thus did not oppose their country's engagement in the world. They had just become profoundly apathetic about it.

It is precisely because of this attention deficit that newspapers, magazines, and the television networks dramatically cut back foreign coverage. In a competitive industry driven by market-share and advertisement fees per second, the media gave America what it wanted. Coverage of foreign affairs on television and in newspapers and magazines dropped precipitously. The time allocated to international news by the main television networks fell by almost 50 percent between the late 1980s and the mid-1990s.[23] Between 1985 and 1995 the space devoted to international stories declined from 24 to 14 percent in *Time* and from 22 to 12 percent in *Newsweek*.[24]

The spillover into the political arena was all too apparent. With foreign policy getting so little traction among the public, it had all but fallen off the political radar screen. Virtually every foreign matter that came before Congress, including questions of war and peace, turned into a partisan sparring match. Peter Trubowitz has documented that partisan conflict over foreign policy increased dramatically in the recent past.[25] Clinton's scandals and his repeated standoffs with an alienated Republican leadership no doubt played a role in pushing relations between the two parties to the boiling point. But the fact that even foreign policy was held hostage made clear that America's politics and priorities had entered a new era.

[22] James Lindsay, "The New Apathy," *Foreign Affairs* 79, no. 5 (September/October 2000): 2–8. The public opinion data in this paragraph are also from the Lindsay article.

[23] Andrew Tyndall, "Decline of International Network News Coverage since the End of the Cold War (in Minutes)," The Tyndall Report, cited in Media Studies Center, "The Decline of International News Coverage," available at: http://www.mediastudies.org/international/international.html.

[24] Hall's Magazine Editorial Reports cited in James F. Hoge Jr., "Foreign News: Who Gives a Damn?" *Columbia Journalism Review* (November/December 1997): 48–52.

[25] Peter Trubowitz (University of Texas at Austin), draft paper presented at the Autonomous National University of Mexico, Mexico City, August 20, 2000.

Partisan politics with worrisome regularity trumped the demands of international leadership. Important ambassadorial posts remained empty throughout the Clinton years because Republicans on the Senate Foreign Relations Committee, purely out of spite, refused to confirm the president's nominees. In August 2000, Peter Burleigh resigned from the State Department after waiting nine months for the Senate to confirm his appointment as ambassador to the Philippines.[26] Burleigh was widely recognized as one of America's most accomplished diplomats. America's dues to the United Nations went unpaid for most of the decade to keep happy the antiabortion wing of the Republican Party, which thought the UN's approach to family planning too aggressive. The Senate in 1999 rejected the treaty banning the testing of nuclear weapons despite the administration's willingness to shelve it. Better to embarrass Clinton than to behave responsibly on matters of war and peace. Senator Chuck Hagel, a Republican from Nebraska, even admitted as much on the record. Reflecting on the apparent Republican assault on internationalism, Hagel commented that "what this is about on the Republican side is a deep dislike and distrust for President Clinton."[27] It is hard to imagine a more potent indicator of the direction of American internationalism than the defeat of a major treaty because of political animosities on the Senate floor.

The battle for Kosovo provides perhaps the best window into these new attitudes, largely because it entailed putting U.S. forces into combat. Posturing and positioning are all too easy when debating NATO expansion, treaty commitments in East Asia, or defense spending—issues that in the near term entail primarily paper commitments, pledges of good faith, and budget authorization. It is when lives are on the lines that true colors start to appear.

On the surface, NATO's battle for Kosovo appeared to confirm that American leadership was alive and well. The United States led NATO into battle, Washington effectively ran the air campaign, and Clinton held course until Slobodan Milosevic capitulated and withdrew his forces from Kosovo. On a closer reading, however, the war was anything but a resounding confirmation of U.S. internationalism.

America's effort in the Balkans was at best half-hearted and enjoyed only razor-thin political support. From the outset, President Clinton blocked the use of ground forces, severely constraining the military operation and weakening NATO's hand in coercive diplomacy. The Clinton team expected Yugoslav president Slobodan Milosevic to capitulate after a

---

[26] "Stymied by Senate, Would-Be Envoy Quits," *The New York Times*, September 1, 2000.

[27] Alison Mitchell, "Bush and the G.O.P. Congress: Do the Candidate's Internationalist Leanings Mean Trouble?" *New York Times*, May 19, 2000.

few days of air strikes; when he did not, the administration was shell-shocked and in a state of virtual paralysis.[28] Even after weeks of an air war that only exacerbated the humanitarian crisis NATO was supposed to resolve and increased the probability of a southward spread of the war, President Clinton maintained his veto. Moreover, he insisted that allied aircraft bomb from no lower than 15,000 feet to avoid being shot down.

Congressional opposition to the conflict only made matters worse. A month into a war that had not produced a single U.S. casualty, the House nevertheless expressed grave misgivings, voting 290–139 to refuse funding for sending U.S. ground troops to Yugoslavia without congressional approval. The House was not even willing to pass a resolution endorsing the bombing campaign (the vote was 213–213). Congress's behavior hardly represented a resounding confirmation of America's commitment to stability in the heart of Europe.

American behavior after the end of the conflict over Kosovo gave further indication of Washington's clear intent to limit the scope of U.S. commitments in the Balkans. European forces picked up the bulk of peace-keeping responsibilities in Kosovo and the EU took the lead on economic reconstruction. Even before the end of the fighting, President Clinton promised Americans in his Memorial Day address that "when the peace-keeping force goes in there [Kosovo], the overwhelming majority of people will be European; and that when the reconstruction begins, the overwhelming amount of investment will be European."[29] When KFOR was deployed, American troops (which represent less than 15 percent of the total force) were sent to the east of Kosovo, where the likelihood of violence was presumed to be lower. In February 2000, a small contingent of U.S. troops was dispatched to the northern city of Mitrovica to help quell ethnic violence. When the troops were stoned by angry Serbs, the Pentagon responded by ordering U.S. forces back to their sector, making clear that Washington was prepared to undercut the KFOR commander on the ground and put U.S. forces under special restrictions.[30]

Despite the unusual protections afforded U.S. troops, American law-

---

[28] Brookings Institution scholars Ivo Daalder and Michael O'Hanlon offer a damning critique of the alliance's strategy: "The allies viewed force simply as a tool of diplomacy, intended to push negotiations one way or another. They were unprepared for the possibility that they might need to directly achieve a battlefield result. . . . NATO's war against Serbia was a vivid reminder that when using military power, one must be prepared for things to go wrong and to escalate." Ivo H. Daalder and Michael E. O'Hanlon, *Winning Ugly: NATO's War to Save Kosovo* (Washington, D.C.: Brookings Institution Press, 2000), 105.

[29] Remarks by the president at Memorial Day service, May 31, 1999, the White House, Office of the Press Secretary.

[30] Carlotta Gall, "Serbs Stone U.S. Troops in Divided Kosovo Town," *New York Times*, February 21, 2000.

makers continued to complain about the need for Europe to do more. Republican Senator John Warner, chairman of the Senate Armed Services Committee, in March 2000 pledged to seek to withhold half of the $2 billion appropriation for American troops in Kosovo unless European nations increased their financial contributions to the UN efforts there.[31] And Democratic Senator Robert Byrd proposed that the United States should turn over to the EU the peacekeeping and reconstruction effort in Kosovo and withdraw U.S. troops from the region in a timely fashion.[32]

Despite the facade of unity within NATO, America's deep ambivalence about the war and its aversion to casualties did not go unnoticed in Europe. It is no coincidence that in the aftermath of Kosovo, the European Union redoubled its efforts to forge a collective defense policy and a military force capable of operating independently of the United States. Europeans were acting on the recognition that they may well be on their own when the next military crisis emerges on the continent. As British prime minister Tony Blair asserted in justifying the initiative, "We Europeans should not expect the United States to have to play a part in every disorder in our own back yard."[33] As Europeans clearly noticed, the war over Kosovo made plain America's dissipating willingness to be Europe's chief peacemaker and its protector of last resort.

Signs of a diminishing appetite for internationalism only intensified after George W. Bush succeeded Clinton. As a candidate, Bush promised to pursue a more "humble" foreign policy, scale back America's international commitments, be more selective in picking the country's fights, and focus more attention on its own hemisphere. After taking the helm, Bush generally adhered to these promises. During his first months in office, he drew down U.S. troop levels in Bosnia and kept U.S. troops in Kosovo on a tight leash despite the spread of fighting to Macedonia. He reduced America's role as a mediator in many different regional conflicts. Secretary of State Colin Powell followed suit by dropping from the State Department's roster more than one-third of the fifty-five special envoys that the Clinton administration had appointed to deal with trouble spots around the world. The *Washington Post* summed up the thrust of these moves in its headline, "Bush Retreats from U.S. Role as Peace Broker."[34]

In similar fashion, Bush made good on his promise to focus U.S. foreign policy on the Americas. President Bush's first two meetings with for-

[31] Jane Perlez, "Kosovo's Unquenched Violence Dividing U.S. and NATO Allies," *New York Times*, March 12, 2000.
[32] Robert Byrd, "Europe's Turn to Keep the Peace," *New York Times*, March 20, 2000.
[33] Speech at the Royal United Services Institute, March 8, 1999.
[34] Alan Sipress, "Bush Retreats from U.S. Role as Peace Broker," *The Washington Post*, March 17, 2001.

eigner leaders were with Canadian prime minister Jean Chretien and Mexican president Vicente Fox. His first foreign trip was to Mexico. His first major international meeting was a Summit of the Americas in Quebec, at which he announced that he would host his first state dinner later in the year—for Vicente Fox.

The Bush administration also stepped away from a host of multilateral commitments, preferring the autonomy that comes with unilateral initiative. Within six months of taking office, Bush had pulled out of the Kyoto Protocol on global warming, made clear his intention to withdraw from the Anti-Ballistic Missile Treaty, stated his opposition to the Comprehensive Test Ban Treaty and the treaty establishing the International Criminal Court (both signed by Clinton but not ratified by the Senate), backed away from establishing a body to verify the 1972 Biological Weapons Convention, and watered down a UN pact aimed at controlling the proliferation of small arms.

The terror attacks of September 2001 were widely interpreted as an antidote to these unilateralist and isolationist trends. And they were, at least in the short run. Far from acting unilaterally, the Bush administration went out of its way to build a broad coalition, enlisting the support of not just NATO allies, but also Russia, China, and moderate Arab regimes. Far from reining in America's commitments, Bush declared a war on terrorism, sending large numbers of ground troops, aircraft, and warships to the Middle East. And Congress and the American people were fully engaged, with the Senate, the House, and the public overwhelmingly behind Bush's decision to use military force to combat the Al Qaeda network and its supporters.[35]

In the long run, however, the struggle against terror is unlikely to serve as a solid basis for ensuring either multilateral engagement or a robust brand of American internationalism. Despite the statements of support from abroad, U.S. forces were accompanied only by the British when the bombing campaign against Afghanistan began. A host of other countries offered logistical and intelligence support, but Americans did almost all the fighting. And that is exactly how both the United States and its allies wanted it.

America was loath to give up the autonomy that would have been compromised by a broader coalition. Other states were meanwhile happy to

[35] On September 14, 2001, both the Senate and the House voted on a resolution authorizing the president "to use all necessary and appropriate force" to respond to the attacks. The resolution passed 98–0 in the Senate and 420–1 in the House. In a poll conducted between September 20 and 23, 2001, 92% of the public supported military action against whoever was responsible for the attacks. See "Poll Finds Support for War and Fear on Economy," *The New York Times*, September 25, 2001.

let America take the lead, thereby distancing themselves from the operation. Many countries in the theater of conflict, such as Saudi Arabia and
Pakistan, were jittery about offering U.S. forces access to their bases, justi-
fiably fearful that they might suffer a domestic backlash for supporting attacks against another Muslim country. And America's NATO allies were
cautioning restraint, concerned that they too could face retribution from
a radicalized Islamic world. After all, although terrorists pose a collective
threat, they are quite careful to single out their actual targets. That is why
the apparent solidarity did not run deep. That is why terrorism is unlikely
to make of America an avowed multilateralist.

It is also by no means clear that terrorism will eradicate, rather than
fuel, isolationist strains within American society. The United States responded with alacrity and resolve to the attacks on New York and Washington. But the call for increased engagement in the global battle against
terror was accompanied by an alternative logic, one that gained currency
over time. A basic dictum of the country's founding fathers was that America should stay out of the affairs of other countries so that they stay out of
America's affairs. The United States is a formidable adversary and is unlikely to let any attack on its own go unpunished. But should the price of
hegemony mount and Americans come to believe that their commitments
abroad are compromising their security at home, they will legitimately
question whether the benefits of global engagement are worth the costs.

The potential allure of the founding fathers' admonition against foreign entanglement explains why, as one scholar put it, the attacks made
"Israelis worry that Americans may now think that supporting Israel is too
costly."[36] This logic also explains why Francois Heisbourg, one of France's
leading analysts, commented in *Le Monde* the day after the attacks that "it
is to be feared that the same temptation [that led America to withdraw
from the world after World War I] could again shape the conduct of the
United States once the barbarians of September 11 have been punished.
In this respect, the Pearl Harbor of 2001 could come to close the era
opened by the Pearl Harbor of 1941."[37]

The long-term consequences of the events of September 2001 could
thus be an America that devotes much more attention and energy to the
security of its homeland and much less attention to resolving problems far
from its borders. The more time U.S. forces spend defending American
territory, the less time they will spend defending the territory of others.
The Bush administration admittedly showed no lack of enthusiasm for

[36] Shibley Telhami, "The Mideast Is Also Changed," *The New York Times*, September 19,
2001.
[37] "De l'après guerre froide à l'hyperterrorisme," *Le Monde*, September 12, 2001.

waging a comprehensive and resolute war against terrorism. But prior to the events of September 2001, the initial instincts of Bush and his advisers were to scale back, not to deepen, America's involvement in distant disputes. In combination with the new focus on homeland defense and the political appeal of seeking to cordon off the country from foreign dangers, these instincts are a better indication of long-term trends than are actions taken amidst shock and anger.

It is equally doubtful that the threat of terror will over the long run ensure a more responsible Congress and a more engaged and attentive public. Bipartisan rancor did disappear instantly on September 11, 2001, and the U.S. public stood firmly behind military retaliation. But these were temporary phenomena arising from the grief of the moment; after a few months, partisan wrangling returned to Capitol Hill and the public mind again began to wander.

The relatively rapid return to business as usual stemmed from the fact that the United States proceeded to embark on a long march, not a war. After Pearl Harbor, American leaders had in Imperial Japan and Nazi Germany formidable and identifiable enemies against which to mobilize the nation and evoke continued sacrifice. The threat posed by the Soviet Union similarly kept America focused and determined during the long decades of the Cold War.

In contrast, terrorism represents a far more elusive enemy. Instead of facing a tangible adversary with armored columns and aircraft carriers, America confronts an enemy schooled in guerilla tactics—a type of warfare that, as the Vietnam War demonstrated, plays to the strengths of neither America's armed forces nor its citizens. In this battle, patience and tact are more useful weapons than military force. With much of the struggle against terrorism occurring quietly beyond the public eye—through intelligence, surveillance, and covert operations—this new challenge will not be accompanied by the evocative images that help rally the country around the flag. And far from inducing Americans to join the army or the production line to contribute to the war effort, terrorism's main impact on the average citizen is to induce him to stay at home. In the wake of the attacks on New York and Washington and the anthrax scare that followed, President Bush asked of Americans not that they make a special sacrifice, but that they return to normal life by shopping in malls and traveling by air. As before September 2001, keeping the U.S. public engaged in international affairs promises to be an uphill battle.

America is a status quo power. It faces no peer competitor. Ambivalence toward international engagement, stemming from both its geographic location and political culture, is very much a part of America's creed. The new threat of terror attacks against the U.S. homeland may well hasten rather than forestall a turning inward and efforts to distance the country from external threats. America's waning internationalism promises to play a major role in bringing about the onset of a multipolar world.

Managing the Return to Multipolarity

The bad news is that the global stability that unipolarity has engendered will be jeopardized as power becomes more equally distributed in the international system. The good news is that this structural change will occur through different mechanisms than in the past, and therefore *may be* easier to manage peacefully.

The near-term challenger is Europe, not a unitary state with hegemonic ambition. Europe will seek a voice commensurate with its station, but will not develop predatory intentions. Europe's aspirations will be moderated by the self-checking mechanisms inherent in the EU and by cultural and linguistic barriers to centralization. In addition, the United States may well react to a more independent Europe by stepping back and making room for an EU that appears ready to be more self-reliant and more muscular. Unlike reigning hegemons in the past, the United States will not fight to the finish to maintain its primacy and prevent its eclipse by a rising challenger. On the contrary, the United States is likely to cede leadership, albeit grudgingly, as its economy slows and it grows weary of being the security guarantor of last resort.

The prospect is thus not one of clashing titans, but of no titans at all. Regions long accustomed to relying on American resources and leadership to preserve the peace may well be left to fend for themselves. The challenge for American grand strategy as this new century proceeds is thus weaning Europe and East Asia of their dependence on the United States and putting in place arrangements that will prevent the return of competitive balancing and regional rivalries in the wake of an American retrenchment.

A New Atlantic Bargain

The prospect of a diminishing American role in managing European security is already causing concern in Europe. As the United States seeks to lighten its load in the years ahead, Europe's success in spreading democracy and stability will make it a likely candidate for a diminishing U.S.

role. The central issue is not, as in the past, who will balance against Russia. Nor is there anxiety, at least for now, about strategic competition between the United States and Europe. Instead, the key concern is over the reemergence of balancing and rivalries *within* a Europe no longer under American protection. In his 1986 article in *Foreign Policy*, "Europe's American Pacifier," Josef Joffe wrote that America's presence in Europe is central to preventing the return of national rivalries to Europe. Many contemporary analysts believe that Joffe's analysis still holds and that the viability of European integration continues to depend on America's continental commitment.[38]

If the foregoing analysis is correct, however, Europe cannot rely indefinitely on America's protective umbrella to ensure its security and preempt intra-European competition. As they look to the future, prudence thus necessitates that America and Europe forge a vision of European security that is less Atlantic and more European than in the past. Europe is in fact further along in developing such a self-sustaining regional order than is commonly recognized, especially in the United States. Through a steady process of pooling sovereignty, Europe has nurtured a supranational character and identity that make integration irreversible. American power and purpose unquestionably facilitated European integration. American guarantees enabled West Europeans to be comfortable with German recovery and rearmament. And NATO effectively took the weightiest security issues off the European agenda, allowing the European project to focus almost exclusively on economic and political integration.

But Europe is now to a significant extent running on its own steam, making the prospect of less reliance on its American pacifier far less worrisome. The success of the European project stems from the fact that Europe integrated itself internally at the same time that it was integrated into the Atlantic community of capitalist democracies. Germany dealt with its past and made peace with its neighbors, paving the way for a collective process of integration that has produced dramatic results.

Decades of economic and political integration have succeeded in transforming Europe's geopolitical landscape. The Franco-German coalition has established itself as Europe's benign power center, with smaller states arraying themselves in concentric circles around this core. The centripetal force of effective regional unipolarity has replaced the destructive jockeying that plagued Europe during its long decades of multipolarity.

---

[38] See Josef Joffe, "Europe's American Pacifier," *Foreign Policy* 54 (spring 1984): 64–82; and Robert Art, "Why Western Europe Needs the United States and NATO," *Political Science Quarterly* 111, no. 1 (spring 1996): 1–39.

In addition, through a host of institutions and practices—a European parliament, a common market, a single currency—EU members have gradually pooled their sovereignty, enabling the national state to exist comfortably alongside a supranational union. That most of Europe's new democracies are now waiting impatiently for entry into the EU makes clear the appeal of this construction. And the prospect of entry in turn provides impetus behind reform and the resolution of disputes in Central and Eastern Europe.[39]

Despite the continuing success of the European enterprise, both Americans and Europeans need to ensure that the European construction is fully ready to withstand the potential retrenchment of American power. At the same time that the United States continues to shape the evolution of the Atlantic security order, it must also do what it can to strengthen the EU as an independent and durable center of power. Furthermore, the United States and the EU should work hard to attach Russia to the European project, ensuring that Russian power complements rather than challenges the EU's emerging geopolitical weight. Even if it comes at the expense of U.S. influence in Europe or trade across the Atlantic, a stronger and self-sustaining European polity is in America's long-term interests.

Striking a new Atlantic bargain will necessitate that Europe not just aspire to greater geopolitical.influence, but also acquire the requisite military capabilities. In return, the United States should cease its grumbling about an EU that is becoming more autonomous and enthusiastically and unequivocally support Europe's defense efforts.[40] The United States has essentially been telling the Europeans that it welcomes more European defense capability and a more equitable sharing of burdens, but that it really is not interested in sharing power with the EU; Washington enjoys calling the shots. The United States effectively wants to remain the unipolar power, but not to bear the associated costs and responsibilities. Instead, Washington should make clear to Europe that when its new capability is available, the United States will accord the EU greater voice. Capabilities buy and justify influence. This deal should be at the core of a new Atlantic bargain that seeks to lay the foundation for an equitable and lasting partnership.

[39] For further discussion of the long-term implications of integration for European security and the transformation from multipolarity to unipolarity, see Ole Waever, "Integration as Security," in *Atlantic Security: Contending Visions*, ed. Charles Kupchan (New York: Council on Foreign Relations, 1998); and Kupchan, "After Pax Americana."

[40] For a summary of U.S. concerns and why they are misguided, see Charles Kupchan, "In Defense of European Defense," *Survival* 42, no. 2 (summer 2000): 16–32.

East Asia: Sino-Japanese Rapprochement or Multipolar Balancing?

The implications of diminishing American internationalism are less immediate for East Asia than for Europe. Unlike in Europe, the end of the Cold War has not resolved the region's main geopolitical cleavages. As a result, the United States is likely to continue its role as East Asia's extraregional balancer. From this perspective, the United States will effectively gravitate to an Asia-first posture in the years ahead—not because America's interests in Asia are any greater than those in Europe, but because the threats to U.S. interests are far more pressing in Asia than they are in Europe. As a status quo power motivated more by threat than opportunity, the United States will likely sustain its major strategic commitments in East Asia for the foreseeable future.

Nonetheless, it is still important for East Asian countries to work toward a regional security structure that is less dependent on American power. If the United States does practice a more discriminating internationalism in the coming years, East Asia is likely to feel at least some of the consequences. The burgeoning rapprochement between North Korea and South Korea could also affect the scope and tenor of America's strategic commitment in the region. Although the North Koreans have suggested that they might welcome a U.S. presence even after unification, the absence of a geopolitical divide on the Korean peninsula could induce an American retrenchment. Defending South Korea, at least in terms of public diplomacy, remains one of the main missions justifying America's forward presence in East Asia. If that mission disappears, it may be hard to make the case—in the United States as well as in America's regional allies such as Japan—that America's forward strategic posture should continue in its current form. At a minimum, the United States and East Asia's regional powers should begin a dialogue on how to move toward a more self-sustaining and stable regional order.

Preparing East Asia for less reliance on American power is a far more complicated and dangerous than the parallel task in Europe. The key difference is that states in Europe took advantage of America's protective umbrella to deal with the past and pursue an ambitious agenda of regional cooperation and integration. Europeans have accordingly succeeded in fashioning a regional order that is likely to withstand the retraction of American power. In contrast, states in East Asia have hidden behind America's presence, pursuing neither reconciliation nor regional integration. East Asia's major powers remain estranged.

The United States therefore faces a severe tradeoff in East Asia between the dependence on American power arising from its predominant role in the region and the intraregional balancing that would ensue in the wake of an American retrenchment. America's sizable military presence keeps the peace and checks regional rivalries. But it also alienates China and holds in place a polarized political landscape. As China's economy and military capability grow, its efforts to balance against the United States could grow more pronounced. Were the United States to reduce its role as regional arbiter and protector, relations with China would likely improve, but at the expense of regional stability. Japan and Korea would no doubt increase their own military capabilities, risking a region-wide arms race and spiraling tensions.

If the United States is to escape the horns of this dilemma, it must help repair the region's main line of cleavage and facilitate rapprochement between East Asia's two major powers: Japan and China. Just as reconciliation between France and Germany was the critical ingredient in building a stable zone of peace in Europe, so too is Sino-Japanese rapprochement the sine qua non of a self-sustaining regional order in East Asia.

Primary responsibility for improving Sino-Japanese ties lies with Japan. With an economy and political system much more developed than China's, Japan has far more latitude in pushing their relationship forward. As in Europe, economic ties should serve as the vehicle for promoting closer political ties. Japan can also make a major step forward by finally acknowledging and formally apologizing for its behavior during World War II. The United States can further this process by welcoming and helping to facilitate overtures between Tokyo and Beijing. Washington should also help dislodge the inertia that pervades politics in Tokyo by making clear to the Japanese that they cannot indefinitely rely on American guarantees to ensure their security. Japan therefore needs to take advantage of America's protective umbrella while it lasts, pursuing the policies of reconciliation and integration essential to constructing a regional security order resting on cooperation rather than deterrence.

China has its own work to do if its relationship with Japan is to move beyond cold peace. Beijing should respond with unequivocal enthusiasm should Japan address its past more openly. It would be particularly important for Beijing to take advantage of a resolute accounting and apology to shape public opinion and moderate the resentment toward Japan that still runs deep in Chinese society. According to a public opinion survey carried out in 1997, over 40 percent of Chinese have a "bad" impression of Japan, while 44 percent have an "average" impression, and only 14 percent have a good impression. Over 80 percent of respondents indicated that Japan's invasion of China during World War II remains their main association with Japan.[41] Loosening the domestic constraints stemming from these public attitudes is a necessity if rapprochement is to have any chance of getting off the ground.

China could also improve the chances of rapprochement by being more receptive to regular, high-level contact with Japan's politicians and its defense establishment. The two countries established diplomatic relations in 1972, but it was not until 1998 that a Chinese head of state visited Japan. And President Jiang Zemin's visit ended up doing more harm than good because the Japanese government refused to make mention of an apology for the past in the joint communiqué. Jiang then turned the issue into the centerpiece of his trip. High-level visits have nonetheless continued, but they have done little to build momentum behind a real political opening.

Contact between the Japanese and Chinese militaries, although of late picking up in frequency, has been sparse, contributing to estrangement between Beijing and Tokyo. After years of isolation, China's People's Liberation Army has only very recently agreed to engage in regular exchanges of information and personnel. If decades of mutual suspicion are to be overcome, China will need to demonstrate its readiness to participate in broader and more frequent bilateral activities, including joint military exercises. The two countries should also take advantage of the regular regional forums hosted by the Association of Southeast Asian Nations (ASEAN) to advance their bilateral agenda. Whatever the exact formula, it is time for China and Japan to embark on more ambitious efforts to break down the formidable barriers that still stand between them.

If ties between China and Japan do markedly improve, the United States would be able to play a less prominent role in the region, making possible an improvement in its own relations with China. Washington should avoid rhetoric and policies that might induce China to intensify its efforts to balance against Japan and the United States, instead buying time for Sino-Japanese rapprochement to get off the ground. In the great debate over China's future that is now taking place on America's op-ed pages and in its academic journals, both the optimists and the pessimists are way off the mark.[42] It is simply too early to pronounce China either a strategic partner

[41] *Zhongguo Qingnian Bao* (China Youth Daily), February 15, 1997, cited in Kokubun Ryosei, "Japan-China Relations after the Cold War: Switching from the '1972 Framework,'" *Japan Echo* 28, no. 2 (April 2001): 9.

[42] For optimistic views of China's future, see Robert S. Ross, "Beijing as a Conservative Power," *Foreign Affairs* 76, no. 2 (March/April 1997): 33–44; and Nicholas Berry, "China is Not an Imperialist Power," *Strategic Review* 24, no. 1 (winter 2001): 4–10. For pessimistic views, see Richard Bernstein and Ross Munro, "The Coming Conflict with China," *Foreign Affairs* 76, no. 2 (March/April 1997): 18–32; and Constantine Menges, "China: Myths and Reality," *The Washington Times*, April 12, 2001.

or an implacable adversary. Talk of an impending Chinese military threat is both counterproductive and misguided; neither the Chinese military nor its economy is world-class.[43] The United States can therefore afford to adopt a wait-and-see attitude toward China while avoiding provocative moves, such as supporting a Taiwanese policy of moving toward formal independence. China can do its part to strengthen its relationship with the United States by containing saber-rattling over Taiwan, halting the export of weapons to rogue states, and avoiding actions and rhetoric that could inflame territorial disputes in the region.

The prospect of a meaningful rapprochement between China and Japan is obviously far off; I have laid out a vision for the long term, not for tomorrow. Neither China nor Japan appears ready to embark down the path of reconciliation. Nor is the United States about to take steps to reduce its influence in the region; Washington enjoys being Asia's security hub.

At the same time, no one imagined in 1945 that Germany and France would put their historical animosities aside and become the collective core of an integrated Europe. If China and Japan are to have a chance of heading in the same direction, they need to take the small steps now that will lead to lasting change down the road. As Robert Schuman wrote in 1950 as he envisaged Europe's future, "That fusion of interest which is indispensable to the establishment of a common economic system" is "the leaven from which may grow a wider and deeper community between countries long opposed to one another by sanguinary divisions."[44] It is at least plausible that Schuman's wisdom will prove to be as indispensable for peace in Asia as it has been for peace in Europe.

A Global Concert of Regional Powers

As this new century progresses, unipolarity will give way to a world of multiple centers of power. This transition will take place both because of the rise of Europe and because American internationalism will gradually wane over time. If my analysis is correct, the most dangerous consequence of a return to multipolarity is not balancing among North America, Eu-

---

[43] China's GDP in 1999 was $732 billion, while America's was $9.2 *trillion*—over twelve times larger. China's annual defense budget is roughly 5% of that of the United States. International Institute for Strategic Studies, *The Military Balance 2001–2002* (London: International Institute for Strategic Studies, 2000), 25, 194. See also Bates Gill and Michael O'Hanlon, "China's Hollow Military," *The National Interest* 56 (summer 1999): 55–62.

[44] Robert Schuman, "Declaration of 10 May 1950." Text available at: http://europa.eu.int/comm/dg10/publications/brochures/docu/50ans/decl=_en.html#DECLARATION.

rope, and East Asia, but the reemergence of national rivalries and competitive balancing within Europe and East Asia as American retrenchment proceeds. It is for this reason that American grand strategy should focus on facilitating regional integration in Europe and East Asia as a means of preparing both areas to assume far more responsibility for managing their own affairs.

The ultimate vision that should guide U.S. grand strategy is the construction of a concertlike directorate of the major powers in North America, Europe, and East Asia. These major powers would together manage developments and regulate relations both within and among their respective regions. Such regional centers also have the potential to facilitate the gradual incorporation of developing nations into global flows of trade, information, and values. Strong and vibrant regional centers, for reasons of both proximity and culture, often have the strongest incentives to promote prosperity and stability in their immediate peripheries. North America might therefore focus on Latin America, Europe on Russia, the Middle East, and Africa, and East Asia on South Asia and Southeast Asia.

Mustering the political will and the foresight to pursue this vision will be a formidable task. The United States will need to begin ceding influence and autonomy to regions that have grown all too comfortable with American primacy. Neither American statesmen, long accustomed to calling the shots, nor statesmen in Europe and East Asia, long accustomed to passing the buck, will find the transition an easy one.

But it is far wiser and safer to get ahead of the curve and shape structural change by design than to find unipolarity giving way to a chaotic multipolarity by default. It will take a decade, if not two, for a new international system to evolve. But the decisions taken by the United States early in the twenty-first century will play a critical role in determining whether multipolarity reemerges peacefully or brings with it the competitive jockeying that has so frequently been the precursor to great-power war in the past.

3

U.S. Strategy in a Unipolar World

William C. Wohlforth

This book addresses the central puzzle posed by Ikenberry in the introduction: "Why, despite the widening power gulf between the United States and other major states, has a counterbalancing reaction not yet taken place?" In this chapter, I provide an answer: "Because neither theory nor history suggest that a counterbalance is likely given today's distribution of capabilities." In other words, I argue that the absence of a counterbalance—or even the signs of one—is not a puzzle even for a very spare structural reading of realist theory. Among self-interested states, collective action in pursuit of a single goal—such as counterbalancing a hegemon—is very hard to achieve. In the history of ancient and modern states systems, durable hegemonies are common. The conditions that make for counterhegemonic alliances are rare. They are not only absent from the current unipolar system, but they are unlikely to be present for a very long time.

Before the September 11, 2001, terrorist attacks on the United States, many analysts argued that the U.S. grand strategy of global engagement would precipitate counterbalancing by other major powers. Given that the initial American response to the attack was an intensified engagement policy that entailed even greater involvement in the security affairs of Eurasia and heightened demands on the policies of other states, counterbalancing would appear to be an even greater concern. If the world is, as some contributors to this volume believe, on the cusp of a new balancing order, then the United States must proceed very circumspectly in its campaign against terrorism. Will a proactive antiterror strategy provoke counterbalancing among great powers? Because my explanation for the absence of balancing under unipolarity is rooted in the distribution of capabilities itself rather than more ephemeral factors, I do not expect even an intensified counterterror campaign embedded within a renewed U.S. strategy of engagement to provoke systemic counterbalancing on the part of other states.

I base the analysis on the assumption that a sound grand strategy must be attuned to long-term considerations of relative power. I seek to isolate the causal effect of such power considerations by analyzing current world politics as if nothing has changed since the eighteenth century *except* the distribution of material resources. In other words, by excluding all the factors that might mitigate the effect of classical balance-of-power considerations, I employ assumptions that are *most* favorable to the argument that a U.S. strategy of engagement will spark a counterbalance. I acknowledge that this is an analytical procedure that may not be persuasive to most policymakers and many scholars. Yet the arguments both scholars and practitioners make about world politics and U.S. policy presuppose just such a procedure. Regardless of one's stance regarding realism, the power-centric and structural analysis I perform here is necessary to advance the debate.

My objective is to assess one argument in a large and complex debate over U.S. grand strategy. Scholars have proposed many candidate explanations for the absence of balancing behavior after 1991, such as globalization, democracy, and nuclear deterrence. Moreover, balance-of-power considerations are only one contested part of the overall debate over grand strategy. Even realists who highlight the importance of the distribution of capabilities understand that it is but one of the many factors that must figure in the calculations of policymakers. Truth in advertising compels strict limits on any claims that can be made on behalf of the kind of analysis I present here. The ultimate contribution of this chapter is negative. International relations scholarship on the balance of power does not yield a clear finding that impugns the wisdom of a strategy of engagement for a state in America's unipolar position. In the complex calculation of the costs and benefits of engagement, the risk of sparking a counterbalance should not figure prominently. Given that many "disengagers" write as if their preferred strategy is backed up by a preponderance of scholarship on the balance of power, this negative contribution is quite relevant to the debate.

Why No Balancing?

The absence of balancing among the great powers is a fact. To counter-balance, great powers must either increase military strength (internal balancing) or aggregate their capabilities in an alliance (external balancing).[1] During unipolarity's first decade, neither form of balancing took place. After the Cold War's end and the collapse of the Soviet Union in 1991, most major powers cut defense outlays significantly. As table 3.1 shows, military spending by the major powers from 1995–2000 remained at historically low levels, in most cases declining as a share of economic output. And none of the much-heralded moves by other states to coordinate policy—the "European troika" of France, Germany, and Russia; the "special relationship" between Germany and Russia; the "strategic triangle" of Russia, China and India; and the "strategic partnership" between China and Russia—came anywhere close to aggregating capabilities to match the United States. The balancing rhetoric that accompanied these moves masked far more limited objectives: coordinating policy on regional issues; enhancing leverage in policy bargaining with the United States; and "prestige balancing," the technique of using relatively low-cost gestures to distance oneself politically from Washington. Even as efforts to coordinate policy against Washington, these arrangements fell far short, as member states periodically demonstrated a willingness to cooperate closely with the United States when it suited their interests of the day—as, for example, Russia chose to do in the immediate aftermath of the September 11 attacks. By any reasonable benchmark, the current international system is one in which both external and internal balancing among great powers is at a historical low.

Three propositions that are consistent with realist theory solve the mystery of the missing balance. First, balancing is inefficient even in settings where the incentives to balance are strong: tightly interdependent regional systems with aggressive revisionists that are weak enough to be countered. In other words, balancing is hard even in systems like modern Europe, from whose experience most balance-of-power theory is derived. Second, the concentration of capabilities in the United States passes the threshold at which counterbalancing becomes prohibitively costly, and thus the dominant strategy for other major powers is some form of engagement. Third, in the current globally dispersed system, balancing is much less efficient and the threshold concentration of capabilities necessary to sustain unpolarity is far lower than it was in Europe.

[1] Kenneth N. Waltz, *Theory of International Politics* (Reading, Mass.: Addison-Wesley, 1979), 168.

Table 3.1   Defense Expenditure of Major Powers, 1995–2000 Billions Constant 1998 $US
(as % GDP)

	USA	Britain	France	Germany	Russia	China	Japan
1995	298 (3.8)	39 (3)	42 (3.1)	35 (1.7)	43 (4.1)	14 (1.8)	37 (1)
1996	282 (3.5)	40 (3)	41 (3)	34 (1.6)	40 (3.8)	15 (1.8)	37 (1)
1997	281 (3.3)	37 (2.7)	41 (2.9)	33 (1.6)	42 (4.2)	17 (1.9)	38 (1)
1998	274 (3.1)	37 (2.5)	40 (2.8)	33 (1.5)	31 (3.2)	19 (2)	38 (1)
1999	275 (3)	37 (2.5)	40 (2.7)	34 (1.5)	38 (3)	21 (2.1)	38 (1)
2000	281	36	40	33	44	23	38

Source: Stockholm International Peace Research Institute (SIPRI), database on military expenditures: http://first.sipri.org.
Note: All figures for China and Russia are SIPRI estimates.

The Inefficiency of Balancing

Imagine a debate in London in May 1811 on the question at heart of this book: why no counterbalance? Fifteen years of war would have demonstrated French power and threat. Yet, we would have witnessed the failure of five coalitions against France, each ending in disaster as one or more members chose to bandwagon with or hide from Napoleon. We would know that Foreign Secretary George Canning had offered France an *uti possedetis* ("keep-what-you-have") peace, only to see it rejected by Napoleon. France would be at the peak of its power, ruling Spain, Italy, the Low Countries, and much of Germany directly. Austria, Prussia, Norway, and Denmark would be mere satellites of the Grand Empire. Only Britain, Sweden, Portugal, and Russia would be out of Napoleon's grasp, but of these only Britain would actively be balancing France. The small countries on the continent by now would have no choice but to bandwagon. But surely the greatest puzzle of all would be Russia—the one empire other than the British that could actually choose to balance—which would be busily collaborating with France against Britain. St. Petersburg would, in short, be undermining and alienating the *only* possible ally against French hegemony in Europe.[2]

To be sure, balancing eventually did occur in the sixth, final, and finally successful coalition. But that coalition was only made possible by two events: Napoleon's invasion of Russia, which, not surprisingly, had the effect of strengthening the anti-French party in Czar Alexander's court, and by far the most important, the revealed *weakening* of France. Events in Russia and Spain revealed that France was less powerful than previously imagined. As a result, one by one the other great powers concluded that they would be better off joining a winning coalition against France than continuing to accommodate the preferences of a weakening Paris.

[2] See Paul W. Schroeder, *The Transformation of European Politics, 1763–1848* (Oxford: Clarendon Press, 1994), chaps. 6–9.

The example illustrates three theoretical reasons to expect balancing among rational, self-interested states to be difficult. First, as Glen Snyder notes, "The logic of collective goods undercuts . . . balance-of-power theory."[3] The security associated with an international equilibrium can be enjoyed by all states, whether or not they pay for it by balancing. Hence, the standard logic of collective action predicts balancing capabilities are likely to be systematically undersupplied. The implication is that balancing will be inefficient, as in the Napoleonic example.

Second, politics—even international politics—is most often local. Because power—especially the power to take and hold territory—is difficult to project over long distances, for any state the most salient threats and opportunities tend to be nearby. Consequently, states are usually more concerned with their neighborhoods than with the global equilibrium. In the Napoleonic case, Russia opted for engagement with France in part because it had aims against the Ottoman Empire that Britain opposed. All the other powers had similar hopes and gripes—all of which played into Napoleon's hands. As Kenneth N. Waltz points out, balancing may occur despite states' shortsighted intentions.[4] True, but this may make balancing very inefficient, as the systemic imperative may need to reach extremes in order to overwhelm local considerations.

Third, to quote Snyder again, "Rational alliance formation is a matter of optimizing across security gains and autonomy losses."[5] Alliance commitments affect both security and autonomy. Security against a potential hegemon may be purchased through sacrificing autonomy in an alliance. The stronger the potential hegemon, the more explicit and comprehensive the necessary alliance commitment, and the greater the consequent sacrifice in autonomy. The more salient local as opposed to systemic imperatives, the greater the importance of autonomy losses associated with alliance formation relative to the security gains of attaining a systemic equilibrium.

These three theoretical considerations make balance-of-power theory more realistic by explaining why balancing will be inefficient, as in the Napoleonic case.[6] They all arise from the simple assumption that states re-

---

[3] Glen H. Snyder, *Alliance Politics* (Ithaca, N.Y.: Cornell University Press, 1997), 50.

[4] Kenneth N. Waltz, "Reflection on *Theory of International Politics:* A Response to My Critics," in *Neorealism and Its Critics,* ed. Robert O. Keohane (New York: Columbia University Press, 1986).

[5] Snyder, *Alliance Politics,* 48.

[6] I explore this issue further in William C. Wohlforth, "Measuring Power and the Power of Theories," in *Realism and the Balancing of Power: A New Debate,* ed. John A. Vasquez and Colin Elman (Englewood Cliffs, N.J.: Prentice Hall, 2002).

spond to systemic incentives in a roughly rational manner. The only way to reject them is to argue that states are systematically insensitive to relative costs and benefits—that they can be expected to engage in counterbalancing even when it is not in their interest to do so. Some formulations of balance-of-power theory imply such an argument by treating balancing as a system-determined imperative to which states respond in an automaton-like manner, or as a norm that transcends immediate state interests.[7] But there is no compelling reason to accept such an argument when applying balance-of-power theory to the current unipolar system. And while some formulations of realist theory suggest such an argument, there is nothing about realist theory generally that requires it.

To be sure, the more inefficient balancing is, the fewer the circumstances in which balance-of-power theory makes determinate predictions. Instead of being states' dominant strategy most of the time, balancing becomes a highly contingent choice. Even in an international system like the modern European one where the theory should work well, the conditions necessary to foster a strong systemic balancing imperative are rare. Systemic balancing only occurs when members of the prospective anti-hegemonic coalition conclude they have the capability to balance at less cost in the things they value (security, status, prosperity) than bandwagoning with the strongest power or standing aside from the contest. Had France been somewhat stronger (and, perhaps, less reckless), there is little in the historical record to suggest that its hegemony in Europe would not have lasted many decades. And had that been the case, rather than explaining the inefficiency of the anti-French balancing coalitions, these same three theoretical considerations would explain their complete absence.

The Unipolar Threshold

This discussion brings us to one final proposition that is both consistent with realism (though rarely mentioned in standard treatments of balance-of-power theory) and illuminated by the example of Napoleon's Grand Empire. This proposition concerns not the efficiency but the very possibility of balancing. In any system, there is a threshold concentration of power in the strongest state that makes a counterbalance prohibitively

---

[7] See, for example, Michael Nicholson, *Formal Theories of International Relations* (Cambridge: Cambridge University Press, 1989), 26; and Morton A. Kaplan, *System and Process in International Politics* (New York: John Wiley, 1957), 23. These sources are cited in Richard Rosecrance, "Has Realism Become Cost-Benefit Analysis?" *International Security* 26, no. 2 (fall 2001), 134, who makes this same point.

costly. This is what it means to call a system "unipolar."[8] Once again, we should not expect states to engage in counterbalancing when it is manifestly beyond their capability to do so. Once the system is past this threshold, further concentration of capabilities in the hands of the sole pole reinforces rather than undermines equilibrium. And the level of the unipolar threshold—the percentage of power that must be concentrated in the unipolar state in order to preclude systemic balancing—depends on the relative salience of local as opposed to global imperatives. That is, the unipolar threshold will vary in different international systems depending on the number and location of the states that comprise them.

Bearing these theoretical propositions in mind, consider the following three empirical attributes of the current international system.[9]

1. The United States is far more capable relative to other great powers than Napoleonic France—or any other European great power in the last three centuries. The graphs in figure 1 plot rough measures of economic and military capabilities in the European and global international systems since the eighteenth century. More detailed historical research ratifies the impression those rough measures convey: the states responsible for all the classical bids for hegemony in Europe possessed a much smaller initial share of the total capabilities in the great-power subsystem. From a *much* narrower material base than the United States currently possesses, France actually managed to pass the unipolar threshold for the years of the Grand Empire.

2. The United States possesses a much more complete portfolio of material capabilities than any European system leader. The graphs in figure 1 illustrate the conventional wisdom that the United States' post-1991 dominance in military and economic power is unprecedented in modern history. Not only does the United States have a margin of superiority that greatly exceeds that of the British Empire at its peak, it also has the edge in every important dimension of power. By devoting only 3–4 percent of its economy to the military, it generates 55 percent of all defense spending and 80 percent of military research and development among the world's seven most powerful states. It also accounts for 43 percent of economic production, 40 percent of high-technology production, and 50 percent of total research and development expenditures. No state in history could do this. Leading states tended to be either great commercial and naval powers or great land powers—never both.

---

[8] I analyze this question in greater depth in William C. Wohlforth, "The Stability of a Unipolar World," *International Security* 21, no. 1 (summer 1999): 1–36.

[9] The discussion here elaborates on the treatment of these issues in Wohlforth, "The Stability of a Unipolar World."

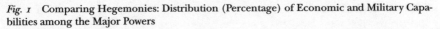

Fig. 1 Comparing Hegemonies: Distribution (Percentage) of Economic and Military Capabilities among the Major Powers

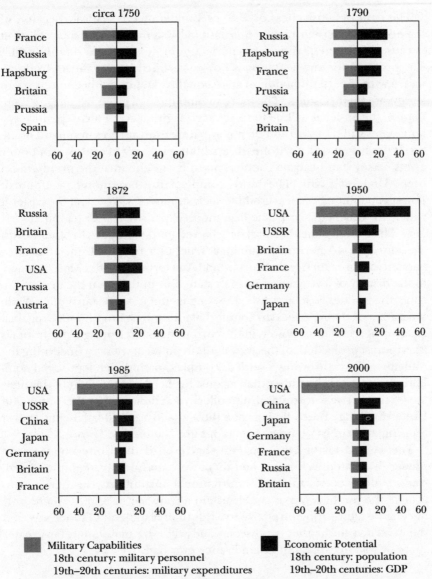

Military Capabilities
18th century: military personnel
19th–20th centuries: military expenditures

Economic Potential
18th century: population
19th–20th centuries: GDP

Sources: Eighteenth-century data: Paul M. Kennedy, *The Rise and Fall of the Great Powers: Economic Change and Military Conflict from 1500 to 2000* (New York: Random House, 1987). GDP, 1870–1985: Angus Maddison, *Monitoring the World Economy, 1820–1992* (Paris: OECD, 1995). GDP, 2000: Central Intelligence Agency, *World Factbook 2001* (http://www.odci.gov/cia/publications/). Military expenditures, 1872–1985: J. David Singer and Melvin Small, "National Material Capabilities Data, 1816–1985," computer file (Ann Arbor, Mich.: Inter-University Consortium for Political and Social Research). Military Expenditures, 2000: Stockholm International Peace Research Institute (SIPRI), database on military expenditures: http://first.sipri.org.

Notes: Germany = Federal Republic of Germany and Russia = USSR in 1950, and 1985. Maddison's estimates are based on states' modern territories. For 1870, I added his estimates for Austria, Hungary, and Czechoslovakia; and Russia and Finland. 2000 GDP figures are calculated using purchasing power parity (PPP) ratios, which, according to the CIA, may overstate the size of China's economy by 25%. China's and Russia's military expenditures for 2000 are SIPRI estimates.

The comprehensiveness of U.S. preponderance is critical. Because of the norm of sovereignty, the international system is de jure anarchic, but because of vast inequalities of material power, it is de facto hierarchical.[10] The problem for any hegemon is how to reconcile the reality of its dominance with the useful fiction of state equality. Hence, all hegemons try to legitimate their position. The more unambiguous a given hegemon's dominance, the easier it will be to foster such legitimacy. In a competitive system, states will try to exploit their comparative advantages in pursuit of status. If the hegemon's portfolio of capabilities is heavy in one class of power assets, lesser states can be counted on to try to enhance the premium on other kinds of assets. The more complete the hegemon's portfolio of power capabilities, the less credible such strategies will be, and the easier it will be for others to accept the hegemon's expansive role as legitimate.

3. The United States has already achieved unipolar status. In other words, the status quo is American dominance. True, after 1991 the United States expanded into areas in Central Europe and Asia formerly under Moscow's sway to the dismay of a weakened Russian state. But in the main theaters of Europe, the Middle East, and Asia, U.S. engagement is the status quo. While most alliance theory concerns counterbalancing by status quo states against an aspiring, revisionist power, in the current system restoring equilibrium is a revisionist project. All of the arguments in political science concerning the difficulty of overthrowing a settled, complex, path-dependent social equilibrium now work for rather than against the hegemon. In light of this literature, the barriers to organizing collective action against the status quo United States are much higher than those that frustrated balancing against aspiring, revisionist would-be hegemons like Napoleonic France.

Theory and history thus suggest that even if the United States were physically located in Eurasia, and there were no nuclear weapons, globalization, democracy, modern international institutions, or new norms against the use of force, it could sustain a unipolar system. It would only need to be a bit stronger relative to rivals than Napoleon's France was, and the evidence shows that it possesses and will long maintain a far greater share of system capabilities than France ever had.

The Geography of U.S. Unipolarity

Of course, the United States is not in Eurasia, while all other great powers and potential great powers are. This simple reality captures two further at-

---

[10] Stephen D. Krasner, *Sovereignty: Organized Hypocrisy* (Princeton, N.J.: Princeton University Press, 1999).

tributes of the current international system that differentiate it from its European predecessors.

4. United States capabilities are "offshore." Geography is a material explanation for reduced threat perceptions. As Stephen M. Walt notes, "States that are nearby pose a greater threat than those that are far away. Other things being equal, states are more likely to make their alliance choices in response to nearby powers than in response to those that are distant."[11] A systemic concentration of power that is separated from all other major players by two oceans is less threatening to others, regardless of U.S. intentions or institutions.

5. The international system is global—and all other great powers are clustered in and around Eurasia. In contiguous international systems such as modern Europe, systemic and local imperatives fuse at a lower threshold than in dispersed systems. A hegemon thus needs more power to stave off a counterbalance, since local concerns are less likely to divert other powers from systemic balancing. It is striking in this context how strong local imperatives were in eighteenth- and nineteenth-century Europe.

The current system is global, rather than regional, and the unipolar state is offshore. These two geographical features dramatically alter the relationship between local and systemic imperatives. Distance reduces the salience of American unipolarity, while proximity maximizes salience of the capabilities of the other great powers vis-à-vis each other. They are much more likely to have aspirations and gripes regarding each other than regarding the distant unipolar power. Local threats and opportunities are thus much more likely to thwart systemic balancing in this than in other systems. Thus, the unipolar threshold is *lower* in the current international system than it was in modern Europe; counterhegemonic balancing is likely to be *less* efficient; and the United States has a far larger and more comprehensive preponderance in the distribution of material capabilities than any leading state in modern history. Simply extending the logic of standard balance-of-power theory to the geographical realities of today's unipolar system suggests:

(a) that other great powers have lower incentives to counterbalance the hegemon than in European systems because balancing brings fewer security gains (owing to the hegemon's offshore location) and greater autonomy losses (owing to location of all other great powers on the Eurasian landmass).

(b) that other great powers face larger collective action problems in fashioning a counterhegemonic alliance than states in analogous posi-

---

[11] Stephen M. Walt, *The Origins of Alliances* (Ithaca, N.Y.: Cornell University Press, 1987), 23.

tions in past international systems. Overcoming the collective action problem requires that one or a few states face particularly salient or concentrated incentives to balance. The greater the extent to which major powers are embedded in regional security systems, the less likely it is that any one will face sufficiently concentrated incentives to pay the up front costs of organizing a counterbalance.

(c) that attempts on the part of individual states to balance via internal efforts are likely to spark local counterbalancing (either through compensatory internal efforts, regional alliances, or alliances with the United States in the classic "checkerboard" pattern) before they substantially constrain the United States.

Standard treatments of balance-of-power theory feature vulnerable, revisionist, centrally located putative hegemons possessing marginal brute power advantages and highly asymmetrical power portfolios in closely integrated international systems. That is, they concern Europe in the eighteenth and nineteenth centuries. And even in that setting, organizing a counterbalance could be precarious and uncertain. By contrast, America's capabilities are relatively greater and more comprehensive than those of past hegemons, are located offshore, they stand behind rather than against the status quo, and the prospective balancing powers are comparatively close regional neighbors embedded in complex regional subsystems containing relatively capable states. The basic propositions set forth above suggest that this is a state of affairs that augurs for stability. Put differently, examining simply the distribution of material capabilities, the system is not in disequilibrium, and the systemic balancing imperative is weak. Simply by considering noncontroversial propositions about the inefficiency of balancing and factoring in geography, the mystery of the missing counterbalance is solved, even if we do not consider nuclear weapons and other clearly important new factors in world politics.

Explaining the Unipolarity Debate

This discussion does leave one puzzle unanswered: why do so many thoughtful people think the current system is "incipiently multipolar"?[12] According to Richard Haass, "As power diffuses around the world, America's position relative to others will inevitably erode."[13] Charles Kupchan sees "a global landscape in which power and influence are more equally

[12] The phrase is Snyder's, *Alliance Politics*, 18.
[13] Richard N. Haass, *The Reluctant Sheriff: The United States after the Cold War* (New York: Council on Foreign Relations, 1997).

distributed" as a "near term" prospect that will bring "the return of competitive balancing" among great powers.[14] Samuel Huntington agrees, arguing that America's unipolar "moment" has already given way to a "uni-multipolar" structure that will soon yield to an unambiguously multipolar one.[15]

One answer is the common tendency of commentators to shift the goal posts. Under bi- or multipolarity, the prolonged absence of a major power war was considered a historical achievement. In those systems, even the temporary abeyance of geopolitical competition among great powers was a striking puzzle that scholars labored long to try to explain. Under unipolarity, scholars appear to take comparatively amicable relations among all the great powers for granted, and suddenly the sine qua non of polar status is the ability to impose solutions to intractable regional conflicts or civil wars within distant states of little or no strategic importance. Thus, in Huntington's view, a truly unipolar state "could effectively resolve all important international issues alone, and no combination of other states would have the power to prevent it from doing so." This is demanding standard, to say the least. When the European great powers failed to get their way in the Balkans in the nineteenth century they did not cease being great powers, just as United States did not lose its superpower status when it failed to prevail in Vietnam. It would never have occurred to any observer of any other interstate system to apply Huntington's definition to any previous hegemon.

A second explanation for inflated expectations of multipolarity's return is the selection of misleading reference points. For example, the only historical referent Huntington identifies for a unipolar system is the Roman Empire at its peak—not a state system at all, nor indeed a system to which anyone before 1991 would have thought to apply the concept of polarity. Compared to a military empire like Rome, any states system seems multipolar.

Perhaps more influential is the memory of the tight bipolar system of the early Cold War. Figure 2 plots a standard measure of the systemic concentration of capabilities for the top six great powers over the last two centuries. What this indicator seeks to capture is the degree to which capabilities are concentrated in the hands of one or a few states within the great-power sub-system. Overall, the story this index tells is that in the post–World War II era capabilities have been much more concentrated than in the nineteenth

[14] Charles A. Kupchan, "Life after Pax Americana," *World Policy Journal* 16 (fall 1999): 20–27.

[15] Samuel P. Huntington, "The Lonely Superpower," *Foreign Affairs* 78, no. 2 (March/April 1999): 35–49.

century. Capabilities were remarkably evenly distributed among great powers in the classical era of the balance of power in Europe. Waltz truly captured the uniqueness of post–World War II international politics with his structural concept of bipolarity. But the highest peacetime levels of overall concentration were in the early bipolar era around 1948–52. It was then that the two superpowers dominated all other great powers to a degree that no state—including the United States—can today. While Soviet decline, Japanese stagnation, and U.S. growth have increased concentration since the mid-1980s, economic and military capabilities are still more dispersed among great powers now than in the early bipolar era. What this means in practice is that the second-tier great powers are relatively more capable vis-à-vis the United States today than they were vis-à-vis the United States and the Soviet Union in the early Cold War. To the extent that expectations concerning the sole superpower at the dawn of unipolarity are influenced by memories the relative dominance of the two superpowers at the dawn of bipolarity, the former is bound to disappoint.

A final explanation for misperceived polarity shifts is the changing composition of the international system—in particular the vast increase in the number of lesser powers compared to great powers. Figure 3 plots the military personnel and general military-industrial capabilities (an index of population, energy use, military personnel, and military spending) of the top five powers as a percentage of the world total. It indicates that the great powers still represent a large proportion of world power capabilities (though, again, not as great as in the early bipolar era). But the dramatic increase in the number of states over the last half century means that there are simply many more states with at least some offensive capability and often substantial defensive capability than in most of the international systems of the past. To the extent that the indicators in figure 3 capture the ability of states to field some kind of military force that can defend territory and local waters, the global balance of defensive power has shifted steadily against the great powers—not surprising given the increased number of lesser states.

The result is again to enhance the salience of local imperatives compared to the systemic balance among great powers. Each great power in each region has to think about more and more capable non-great power neighbors than did the great powers of earlier international systems. At the same time, the ability of great powers to determine the character of relations through the system is less than it was in much simpler and smaller regional systems like nineteenth-century Europe, with fewer and weaker non-great power actors. The effect of a declining ratio of great powers to lesser states was already observable in the latter bipolar era, as commentators continually hailed each instance of regional independence from the superpowers as the return of multipolarity. Waltz showed that they were

Fig. 2   Singer/Small Concentration Index for Top Six Powers

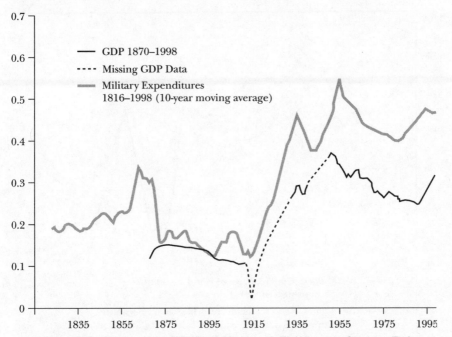

Sources: GDP, 1870–1990: Angus Maddison, *Monitoring the World Economy, 1820–1992* (Paris: Organization for Economic Cooperation and Development, 1995); GDP 1991–1998: Central Intelligence Agency, *World Factbook* (Washington, D.C.: Government Printing Office, various years). Military expenditures, 1872–1985: J. David Singer and Melvin Small, "National Material Capabilities Data, 1816–1985," computer file (Ann Arbor, Mich.: Inter-University Consortium for Political and Social Research). Military expenditures, 1985–1998: International Institute of Strategic Studies, *The Military Balance* (London: IISS, various years).

Notes: Singer and Small's measure of the concentration of power is: standard deviation of the percentage shares of each state divided by the maximum possible standard deviation in a system of size N. The properties of the measure as compared to other measures of concentration in the social sciences are discussed in James Lee Ray and J. David Singer, "Measuring the Concentration of Power in the International System," in *Measuring the Correlates of War*, ed. J. David Singer and Paul F. Diehl (Ann Arbor: University of Michigan Press, 1990).

wrong, in that the system was still bipolar.[16] But they were right that it was less concentrated in the 1970s than in the 1950s. Because expectations today are based on comparisons to the nineteenth century and the early bipolar era, America's inability to impose settlements (at low cost) on dozens of regional states is often taken as evidence that the system is not really unipolar.

The indicators presented in figures 2 and 3 are crude and need to be supplemented by historical research on changing power relationships. But they do convey efficiently what more detailed research appears to rat-

---

[16] Waltz, *Theory of International Politics.*

Fig. 3   Great Power Capabilities as a Percentage of World Total

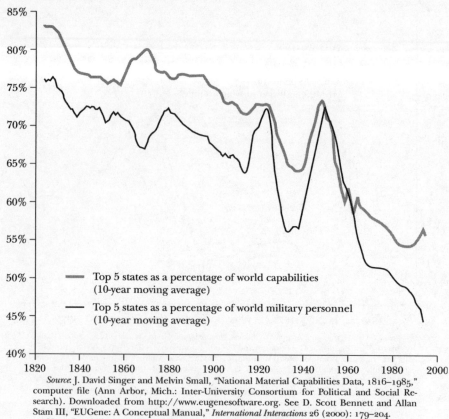

Source: J. David Singer and Melvin Small, "National Material Capabilities Data, 1816–1985," computer file (Ann Arbor, Mich.: Inter-University Consortium for Political and Social Research). Downloaded from http://www.eugenesoftware.org. See D. Scott Bennett and Allan Stam III, "EUGene: A Conceptual Manual," *International Interactions* 26 (2000): 179–204.

Notes: Capabilities represented by Singer and Small's composite index, which combines the following indicators with equal weights: total population, urban population, energy consumption, iron and steel production, military expenditures, and military personnel.

ify: the current system is characterized by an unprecedented hegemony within the great-power subsystem, and a novel proliferation of lesser states outside that subsystem.

Unipolarity, Balancing, and the Case for Disengagement

The structure of the international system has shifted from bipolarity to unipolarity, but American grand strategy has undergone no such transformation. The United States continues to follow a strategy of maintaining a preponderance of power globally and deep engagement in the security affairs of Europe, Asia, and the Middle East. It has adapted rather than abandoned the central institutions and practices it fostered during the bipolar era, expanded NATO to Central Europe, strengthened its military alliance with Japan, and taken on a great many other less heralded new security commitments in areas formally under Moscow's sway. To support this strategy, the United States continues to maintain a military establishment on a scale comparable in absolute terms to the peacetime years of the Cold War.

Such behavioral continuity in the face of structural change has prompted many scholars to argue that it is time to develop a strategy for disengaging the United States from the security affairs of Eurasia. While not all of these scholars are self-described realists, they generally accept the realist premise that a sound grand strategy must be attuned to the systemic distribution of power. They differ on the details but agree on a central proposition: the risks of continuing the strategy of preponderance outweigh the risks of early disengagement.[17] Their argument demands an extremely complex assessment of the costs and benefits of engagement. After September 11, 2001, the main question was naturally whether engagement makes terror attacks against the United States more likely. The analysis in this chapter cannot address that crucial question. What it can do is clarify the relationship between unipolarity, engagement, and balancing behavior.

The current strategy of engagement is consistent with but not necessitated by the system's material structure. Critics of realism are right that a full explanation for America's choice of grand strategy must include path-dependency, inertia, domestic politics, and ideas (though they are wrong that any realist claims structure dictates strategic choice). The strategy is consistent in that the material environment places few restrictions on a strategy of engagement while offering numerous demands for American involvement. Given the increased ratio of lesser states to great powers, and thus the expanding list of intrastate conflicts, as well as the unprecedented concentration of capabilities in the United States, it is not surprising that Washington's involvement is so frequently demanded as well as denounced. But this structure does not require U.S. engagement. Disengagers are right that America *can* "come home." Indeed, because unipolarity dampens traditional great-power threats to the core security of the United States, the current strategy may be difficult to sustain, particularly if Americans perceive a tight link between the engagement strategy and the terrorist threat to their homeland.

---

[17] See Barry R. Posen and Andrew L. Ross, "Competing Visions for U.S. Grand Strategy," *International Security* 21, no. 2 (winter 1996/97): 5–54; Christopher Layne, "From Preponderance to Offshore Balancing: America's Future Grand Strategy," *International Security* 22, no. 1 (summer 1997): 86–124; Eugene Gholtz, Daryl G. Press, and Harvey M. Sapolsky, "Come Home, America: The Strategy of Restraint in the Face of Temptation," *International Security* 221, no. 4 (spring 1997): 5–48; Kupchan, "Life after Pax Americana," 20–27.

In assessing the costs and risks of competing grand strategies, three propositions derived from the foregoing analysis of the distribution of capabilities ought to be considered:

First and most importantly, a continued U.S. grand strategy of engagement will not produce a counterbalance. The debate over balancing dynamics and U.S. grand strategy requires two critical judgments. First, will the systemic balancing imperative soon come to dominate the strategies of the second-tier great powers? That is, in maximizing their preference for security, status, or wealth, will these states find that the systemic imperative to counterbalance U.S. power outweighs more local imperatives when these two levels contradict each other? The second judgment is just as critical but rarely noted: to what extent is balancing behavior contingent on U.S. strategy as opposed to its underlying capabilities? For America cannot choose to become less powerful; it can only decide how and where to wield its latent power. Disengagers must argue that U.S. engagement increases incentives for others to balance substantially over what they would do to counter "disengaged" U.S. potential. As Kenneth Waltz has shown, actors in a competitive system seek to emulate or undercut successful practices.[18] To some degree, America's preponderance will elicit such a competitive response no matter what it does. The question is whether engagement materially affects that response.

I established that the distribution and location of material capabilities suggest that local imperatives will overwhelm the systemic resentment of American power in the concrete strategic choices of other major states. To be sure, American success will elicit strategies of emulation and competition from other states. But my explanation for the missing counterbalance suggests that these responses are not especially sensitive to U.S. strategy.

Second, the strategy may affect levels of cooperation among great powers. Cooperation is hard among states in anarchy. Realists argue that cooperation is contingent on power—either a shared threat or hegemonic dominance. Liberals, institutionalists, and constructivists think cooperation does not require specific power configurations. These different theories have different explanations for post-1991 cooperation that are hard to evaluate on existing data. For realists, cooperation is an outgrowth of U.S. hegemony. The strength of institutions reflects the strength of the state that creates them. If realists are right, then disengagement decreases the leverage available to Washington to effect cooperation, and to build and run the institutions that make its dominance cheaper and more efficient. The United States uses the security dependence of other states to push through cooperative solutions on a variety of issues that favor its in-

---

[18] Waltz, *Theory of International Politics.*

terests.[19] Disengagement reduces security dependence of others and reduces the incentives American policymakers can provide to other actors to forge cooperation.

Many of these levers of influence were on display in the aftermath of the September 11 attacks. While the ultimate outcome of the antiterror campaign will not be known for many years, the initial phase clearly showed the utility of engagement in fostering a coalition against the Taliban and Al Qaeda in Afghanistan. Long-standing relationships with Uzbekistan, for example, coupled with a large supply of carrots and sticks vis-à-vis Russia, helped the United States quickly project power into Central Asia—one of the most remote spots in Eurasia. If the strategy of engagement does not directly generate increased terrorist threats to the U.S. homeland, then, on balance it pays important dividends in responding to unexpected security threats.

Third, the strategy affects the incentives for intra-great-power balancing. I have argued that the absence of a counterbalance against American power is largely a structural result. The absence (or, at least, the muted level) of competitive balancing *among* great powers in Eurasia may be a consequence of U.S. strategy. If America brought its forces home, its latent power would continue to figure in the calculations of other states. Still, the security problem would become more acute. Charles Kupchan argues that "cobinding" through institutions can create stable regional systems in Asia and Europe without direct U.S. engagement.[20] Gholtz, Press, and Sapolsky argue that even without elaborate institutions, these regions can create stable multipolar systems by relying on defense-dominant military postures.[21] These arguments seem more plausible in Europe than Asia, where most regional experts would expect the return of competitive balancing if Washington extracted itself from the area.

The propositions I developed here provide one explanation for low levels of security or prestige competition among great powers since 1990. Constructivist, institutionalist, and liberal theories provide another.[22] We cannot know with confidence which is true (or which is true about which region or issue) because the outcome is overdetermined. On the question of should the United States come home, however, the predictions of

---

[19] For a vivid and well-documented case, see David E. Spiro, *The Hidden Hand of American Hegemony: Petrodollar Recycling and International Markets* (Ithaca, N.Y.: Cornell University Press, 1999).

[20] Charles A. Kupchan, "After Pax Americana: Benign Power, Regional Integration, and the Sources of Stable Multipolarity," *International Security* 23, no. 3 (fall 1998): 40–79.

[21] Gholtz, Press, and Sapolsky, "Come Home, America."

[22] See, for example, G. John Ikenberry, "Institutions, Strategic Restraint, and the Persistence of the American Postwar Order," *International Security* 23, no. 3 (winter 1998/99): 43–78.

different theories diverge. If most realist theories are right, the resultant multipolar regions would become much more competitive strategic environments. Competitive environments could foster more capable actors. Such an environment would affect domestic debates inside critical states—Japan and Germany are prime examples—over whether to create the capabilities and institutions of a great power. Again, the realist and constructivist/liberal explanations of these "anomalous" states would receive a real test if America came home. If American withdrawal sparked an arms race between Japan and China, for example, what sorts of new capabilities and strategies might emerge? In short, it is possible that disengagement could decrease relative U.S. power by creating a more competitive Eurasia that could incubate one or a few fearsome states in the future. Disengagement could thus produce the ironic (or tragic) result that the United States would have to reengage—possibly under even more dangerous circumstances than are imaginable today.

Conclusion

In this chapter I developed an explanation for the absence of competitive balancing among great powers after 1991 that has implications for the debate over U.S. grand strategy. An influential argument holds that a continued strategy of engagement will prompt a counterbalancing reaction on the part of other major powers and therefore that the United States should disengage itself from the security affairs of Eurasia. Given that the initial U.S. response to the terror attacks on New York and Washington was a dramatically enhanced engagement strategy, this argument remains central to long-term strategic planning.

If it can be shown that the international system is not teetering in a precarious disequilibrium and primed for counterbalancing, then the argument for early disengagement loses some force. I accepted as a starting point for analysis the assumption that relative power is important in explaining state behavior and should be considered when framing strategic choices. In order to evaluate the causal effect of such power considerations as rigorously as possible, I sought to isolate them by assuming away all the manifold changes in world politics since the eighteenth century except for changes in the distribution and location of capabilities. That is, the analytical procedure and the assumptions I employed were most favorable to the standard argument that current U.S. grand strategy contradicts the systemic balancing imperative.

My main conclusion is that well-known realist theories of the relations among standard geopolitical variables—the number of states and the distribution, composition, and location of material capabilities—predict that the systemic balancing imperative is very unlikely now to assume the salience it did in seventeenth- to twentieth-century Europe, where balance-of-power theory developed. The balancing imperative—often a weak force in the past—will not soon dominate great-powers' strategic choices in today's novel unipolar system. United States power is too great, too comprehensive, too far offshore, and too deeply enmeshed in (rather than arrayed against) the status quo to provoke a classical counterbalancing reaction. The greater salience of local over systemic imperatives in today's international system means that the United States can be engaged deeply in the security affairs of Eurasia without sparking counterbalancing efforts. Thus, the very feature of the unipolar system that causes many scholars to question its longevity—the ability of regional actors sporadically to defy the preferences of the major powers—actually works to prolong it. For all of these reasons, the United States could in all likelihood decline relative to other great powers for many decades without jeopardizing its ability to continue in its present strategic role in world politics.

The fact that the United States can continue its current strategic course does not mean it should do so. For one thing, if Americans come to perceive a direct link between the engagement strategy and the terrorist threat to their homeland then the strategy's cost will rightly be seen in a new light and the case for "coming home" will be strengthened. And some of the positive attributes of a unipolar system are not contingent on U.S. strategy. Whether or not the United States is engaged, there will be no anti-U.S. counterbalancing coalition and no challenge to U.S. primacy in the policy relevant future.

If, however, there is no direct link between the strategy of engagement and the attractiveness of the U.S. homeland as a target for terror, then the case for engagement is strengthened. By dampening security and status competition among second-tier great powers, the United States keeps Eurasia less competitive and thus less likely to breed tough, militarily powerful states. By keeping other states somewhat dependent on itself for security, Washington obtains leverage on other issues and is in a better position to foster cooperation among self-interested states. Naturally, Washington generally ensures that the resultant cooperative equilibria reflect its interests. The United States obtains large but hard-to-measure gains from the deference it receives in exchange for the forward deployment of its considerable resources. In a pinch, Washington can use its hegemonic position to extract unilateral advantage. Given the fact that engagement is unlikely by itself to drain American resources, an engaged United States in a better position than a disengaged one to respond to a major crisis or unexpected geopolitical challenges. These arguments seemed to be ratified by the initial U.S. response to the unexpected security threat from terrorism.

As daunting as the challenge of terrorism seems in the wake of September 11, the challenge would be even more formidable in a world on the verge of a structural shift to multipolarity. Fortunately, we are not in such a world. Because unipolarity dampens the traditional great-power security threats of power balancing and hegemonic rivalry—the prime security threat for most great powers for most of modern history—the United States and its allies can contemplate innovative and potentially expensive responses—military, economic, and political—to new security threats.

PART II

The Management of Unipolarity

4

Keeping the World "Off-Balance": Self-Restraint and U.S. Foreign Policy

Stephen M. Walt

What a difference a decade makes. The United States spent the 1980s fretting about its imminent decline, only to awake and discover that it was on top of the world. Both Trotsky and Team B turned out to be 180 degrees off, and it was the Soviet Union rather than the capitalist West that ended up on the ash-heap of history. Alarmist fears about an emerging Japanese superpower turned out to be equally misguided, and the "Japan That Could Say No" (to take the title of a best-selling tract by Shintaro Ishihara) became the "Japan That Said 'Uncle' " at century's end. Instead of becoming the "ordinary country" that some anticipated, facing a world "after hegemony," the United States found itself in a position of preponderance unseen since the Roman Empire.[1]

I thank John Ikenberry, Stephen Krasner, and the other contributors to this volume for their comments on earlier drafts of this essay. I have also profited from comments at seminars at Columbia University's Institute for War and Peace Studies and the International Security Program of the Belfer Center for Science and International Affairs at Harvard University. Michelle von Euw and Kate Regnier provided research assistance and logistical support, for which I am also grateful.

[1] Prominent examples of "declinist" thinking include Richard Rosecrance, ed., *America as an Ordinary Country* (Ithaca, N.Y.: Cornell University Press, 1979); and Paul Kennedy, *The Rise and Fall of the Great Powers: Economic Change and Military Conflict from 1500 to 2000* (New York: Random House, 1987). A belief that U.S. power was declining is also implicit in Robert O. Keohane, *After Hegemony: Cooperation and Discord in the World Political Economy* (Princeton, N.J.: Princeton University Press, 1984). Prominent dissenting views include Kenneth Waltz, *Theory of International Politics* (Reading, Mass.: Addison-Wesley, 1979); and Joseph S. Nye, *Bound to Lead: The Changing Nature of American Power* (New York: Basic Books, 1990). Samuel P. Huntington warned of Japanese ascendance in "Why International Primacy Matters," *International*

Just how good is the U.S. position? In 2001, the U.S. economy accounted for roughly one quarter of gross world product and was roughly 40 percent larger than its nearest competitor (Japan). The United States enjoyed robust growth for a decade while Japan has been mired in depression and ran up sizeable budget surpluses for the first time in several decades.[2] The United States now spends as much on defense as the next nine countries combined, and because six of the nine are close U.S. allies, this figure actually understates the U.S. advantage.[3] The United States is the world leader in higher education and advanced technologies, and especially the information technologies and service industries on which future productivity is likely to depend.[4] American society is also unusually open to immigration, new ideas, and new business practices, which makes it more adept at adapting to new conditions. America's situation is not perfect—as the September 2001 terrorist attacks on the World Trade Center and the Pentagon demonstrated all too vividly—but one could hardly ask for much more.[5]

Not surprisingly, most Americans regard this position of primacy as undiluted good news. The bad news, such as it is, however, is that these developments left us intellectually ill-prepared for these new circumstances. It is one thing to exercise leadership when one's principal allies face the same overarching threat and have a strong interest in U.S. protection. It is quite another thing to be the dominant power when the only serious threat is a shadowy transnational terrorist network. Not surprisingly, the past decade has produced a lively debate on U.S. grand strategy, with different authors offering sharply contrasting advice on how the United States should respond to its position as the sole remaining superpower.[6]

Security 17, no 4 (spring 1993): 68–83. Japanese dominance is forecast in Ezra F. Vogel, *Japan as Number One: Lessons for America* (New York: Harper Torchbooks, 1985); and proclaimed in Shintaro Ishihara, *The Japan That Can Say No* (New York: Harper and Row, 1991).

[2] These favorable conditions are now changing: U.S. economic growth slowed dramatically in 2000–2001 and together with the tax cut voted in the spring of 2001, is likely to bring the U.S. federal budget back into deficit in the near future. But neither development threatens the U.S. position as the dominant world power.

[3] Based on data from *The Military Balance, 2001–2002* (London: International Institute for Strategic Studies/Oxford University Press, 2001).

[4] See Joseph S. Nye and William A. Owens, "America's Information Edge," *Foreign Affairs* 75, no. 2 (March/April 1996): 20; and U.S. Department of Commerce, Office of Technology Policy, *The New Innovators: Global Patenting Trends in Five Sectors* (Washington, D.C.: Office of Technology Policy, 1998).

[5] A good summary of the material bases of U.S. preponderance is found in William F. Wohlforth, "The Stability of a Unipolar World," *International Security* 24, no. 1 (summer 1999): 5–41. On the adaptability of American society, see Thomas L. Friedman, *The Lexus and the Olive Tree: Understanding Globalization* (New York: Farrar, Straus and Giroux, 1998), chap. 15.

[6] A good survey of recent writings on U.S. grand strategy is Barry R. Posen and Andrew L. Ross, "Competing Visions for U.S. Grand Strategy," *International Security* 21, no. 3 (winter 1996–97): 5–53. Prominent examples in this genre include William Kristol and Robert Kagan, "A Neo-Reaganite Foreign Policy," *Foreign Affairs* 75, no. 4 (July/August 1996): 18;

This chapter examines an important part of this puzzle, focusing on whether U.S. preponderance is likely to trigger a defensive backlash by other states. For most of its history, U.S. leaders did not have to worry very much about the possibility that other strong states might combine against them. Until the 1890s, the United States was too weak and geographically isolated to provoke widespread opposition, and U.S. leaders were free to concentrate on consolidating the U.S. position in the Western hemisphere. Even after it joined the ranks of the great powers, the United States generally avoided military commitments abroad unless there was an imminent threat to the global balance of power. Instead, the United States let other states bear the costs of keeping each other in check and got directly involed—as in 1917 and 1941—only when one state seemed about to establish a hegemonic position in Europe or Asia.[7] When it became clear that the European powers and Japan were too weak to uphold the balance of power after World War II, however, the United States did establish an extensive array of alliance commitments and began to maintain a large military presence overseas. Although there were occasional tensions with the U.S. alliance system, the major powers of Europe and Asia generally welcomed the commitment of U.S. power and were willing to defer to U.S. leadership.

According to some prominent theories of international politics, the situation now should be quite different. The United States is far and away the most powerful state on the planet, and no other state presently threatens to dominate either Europe or Asia. Because unbalanced power is an asset to its possessor but a potential danger to others, Americans now face the novel prospect that other major powers might concentrate on balancing *them*. At the very least, other states may be more inclined to resist U.S. leadership and look for ways to circumscribe Washington's freedom of action, simply to make sure that the United States does not impose its own preferences too enthusiastically. For the time being, therefore, the ability to formulate an effective foreign policy is likely to depend on whether other states show a strong tendency to balance the United States, and on whether U.S. leaders can devise ways to minimize these tendencies if and when they emerge.

Richard N. Haass, "Foreign Policy in the Age of Primacy," *Brookings Review* 18, no. 4 (fall 2000): 2–7; Robert J. Art, *Selective Engagement: America's Grand Strategy and World Politics* (Ithaca, N.Y.: Cornell University Press, 2003); Nye, *Bound to Lead;* Christopher Layne, "From Preponderance to Offshore Balancing: America's Future Grand Strategy," *International Security* 22, no. 1 (summer 1997): 86–124; and Eugene Gholz, Daryl G. Press, and Harvey M. Sapolsky, "Come Home, America: A Strategy of Restraint in the Face of Temptation," *International Security* 21, no. 4 (spring 1997): 5–48.

[7] See John J. Mearsheimer, "The Future of America's Continental Commitment," in *No End to Alliance: The United States and Western Europe: Past, Present and Future*, ed. Geir Lundestad (New York: St. Martin's, 1998); and idem, *Tragedy of Great Power Politics*, chap. 6.

The remainder of this chapter is organized as follows. Part I examines why states tend to balance against other states and argues that structural theory cannot explain why efforts to balance U.S. power have been remarkably weak since the end of the Cold War. Part II consider several alternative explanations for the absence of any serious attempt to balance U.S. power and argues that balance-of-threat theory provides the best explanation for the surprising dearth of balancing behavior. Part III lays out a set of prescriptions based on these theoretical insights, emphasizing in particular the need for a policy of self-restraint, and identifies several areas where the United States may be departing from these precepts. The conclusion offers several caveats to these recommendations and identifies issues that merit further investigation.

Why Do States Balance?

When considering why other states might join forces against the United States, an obvious place to begin is structural (i.e., "neorealist") balance-of-power theory.[8] According to structural theory, the condition of international anarchy gives states a powerful aversion to unbalanced power. Because weaker states cannot be sure that stronger states will not use their superior capabilities in ways that the weak will find unpleasant, they look for ways to limit the freedom of action of the strong. When the dangers that strong states pose seem especially clear and imminent, weaker states are likely to increase their own military capabilities, form defensive alliances, develop common military plans with their partners, or even initiate war in an attempt to shift the balance of power in their favor.[9]

Balance-of-power theory focuses on the distribution of material capabilities, such as population, economic wealth, natural resources, military forces, etc. It predicts that states will balance against the *strongest* state, defined as the state with the largest accumulation of material sources. The theory therefore implies that existing U.S. alliances will become more delicate, less cohesive, and harder to lead now that the Soviet Union is gone and the United States is overwhelmingly stronger than any other country.

[marginal handwritten note: *nature of int'l system (anarchy)*]

[8] The *locus classicus* here is Kenneth N. Waltz, *Theory of International Politics* (Reading, Mass.: Addison-Wesley, 1979). See also Mearsheimer, *Tragedy of Great Power Politics* (New York: Norton, 2001), and Dale C. Copeland, *The Origins of Major War* (Ithaca, N.Y.: Cornell University Press, 2000).

[9] As Kenneth Waltz recently put it, "As nature abhors a vacuum, so international politics abhors unbalanced power. Faced with unbalanced power, some states try to increase their own strength or they ally with others to bring the international distribution of power into balance." See his "Structural Realism after the Cold War," *International Security* 25, no. 1 (summer 2000): 5–41.

The theory also predicts that other major powers will be looking for ways to limit the unilateral exercise of U.S. power. At a minimum, they will be more reluctant to help the United States pursue its foreign policy objectives; at a maximum, they will join forces to constrain Washington's freedom of action.

Is there any evidence of these tendencies? Yes. Both European and American officials have warned that NATO can no longer be taken for granted and signs of tension within the alliance are increasingly apparent.[10] French foreign minister Hubert Védrine has repeatedly complained about America's position as a "hyperpower" and once declared that "the entire foreign policy of France . . . is aimed at making the world of tomorrow composed of several poles, not just one." German Chancellor Gerhard Schroeder has offered a similar warning, declaring that the danger of "unilateralism" by the United States is "undeniable."[11] The recurring disputes of the past ten years and growing doubts about the U.S. commitment have led NATO's European members to commit themselves to building an independent European defense force for the first time since World War II, despite predictable misgivings on this side of the Atlantic. This initiative has been accompanied by European calls for an EU seat on the United Nations Security Council, a proposal endorsed by Javier Solana, former Secretary-General of NATO and the new European high representative for foreign affairs. Taken together, these developments herald a weakening of transatlantic ties and the emergence of a more forceful European voice in foreign policy.[12]

At the same time, China and Russia have responded to U.S. preponder-

[handwritten marginal note: European balancing efforts]

[10] See Stephen M. Walt, "The Ties That Fray: Why Europe and America Are Drifting Apart," *The National Interest* 54 (spring 1998–99) 3–11; Peter W. Rodman, *Drifting Apart? Trends in U.S.–European Relations* (Washington, D.C.: The Nixon Center, 1999); and Jeffrey Gedmin, "Continental Drift: A Europe United in Spirit against the United States," *The New Republic,* June 28, 1999, 23–24.

[11] Quoted in Craig R. Whitney, "NATO at 50: With Nations at Odds, Is It a Misalliance?" *New York Times,* February 15, 1999, A7. Or as a French academic recently put it: "[The United States] does what it wants. Through NATO it directs European affairs. Before we could say we were on America's side. Not now. There is no counterbalance." Michel Winock, quoted in "More Vehemently Than Ever: Europeans Are Scorning the United States," *New York Times,* April 9, 2000, A1, A8. For a fuller appreciation of Védrine's views, see Hubert Védrine with Dominique Moisi, *France in an Age of Globalization,* trans. Philip Gordon (Washington, D.C.: Brookings Institution, 2001).

[12] See Anne Swardson, "EU to Form European Military Force," *Washington Post,* December 12, 1999, A41; Peter Norman, "EU Edges Closer to Defense Policy," *Financial Times,* February 12, 2000, 5; Stephen Castle, "European Union Seeks Seat on Security Council," *The Independent,* November 18, 1999, 17. For background and analysis, see Francois Heisbourg, "Europe's Strategic Ambitions: The Limits of Ambiguity," Charles C. Kupchan, "In Defence of European Defence: An American Perspective," Jolyon Haworth, "Britain, France and the European Defence Initiative," and Guillaume Parmentier, "Redressing NATO's Imbalances," *Survival* 42, no. 2 (summer 2000): 5–55, 95–112.

ance by seeking to resolve existing points of friction and increasing other forms of security cooperation, an effort that culminated in the signing of a formal treaty of friendship and cooperation in July 2001. Although the treaty was not directed at any specific country, it was explicitly intended to foster a "new international order" and Russian commentators described it as an "act of friendship against America."[13] Russian president Vladimir Putin has also called for increased cooperation between Russia and India and declared that India's emergence as a "mighty, developed, independent state" would be in Russia's interests because it would "help create a balance in the world." Even lesser states are looking for ways to put a leash on the United States: as Venezuelan president Hugo Chavez recently put it, "The twenty-first century should be multipolar, and we all ought to push for the development of such a world. So long live a united Asia, a united Africa, a united Europe."[14]

If one is looking for signs of balancing tendencies, in short, they are not difficult to find.[15] Yet it is striking how half-hearted and ineffective these efforts have been. Disagreements and policy disputes are hardly a new development in U.S. relations with its principal allies, yet there have been no significant defections in the ten years since the Soviet Union imploded. Russia, China, North Korea, and a few others have occasionally collaborated in order to signal their irritation with the United States, but their efforts fall well short of formal defense arrangements and Russia seems equally interested in building close ties with the West. Responses to U.S. preponderance pale in comparison to the powerful coalitions that formed to contain Wilhelmine Germany or the Soviet Union. United States allies may resent their dependence on the United States and complain about erratic U.S. leadership, but the old cry of "Yankee, Go Home" is strikingly absent in Europe and Asia. Instead, the United States is still formally allied with NATO (which has grown by three nations and is likely to add more in the next few years) and has renewed and deepened its military relationship with Japan. Its security ties with South Korea, Taiwan, and several other ASEAN countries remain firm, and its relations with Vietnam are improving. United States relations with India are probably better than they were during much of the Cold War. No one is making a serious effort to forge a meaningful anti-American alliance, despite the enormous dis-

---

[13] See "Russia and China Sign 'Friendship' Pact," *New York Times,* July 17, 2001, A1, A8.

[14] See "India a Great Power: Putin," *Times of India,* October 2, 2000, and Larry Rohter, "A Man with Big Ideas, a Small Country . . . and Oil," *New York Times,* September 24, 2000, section 4, 3.

[15] See Fareed Zakaria, "America's New Balancing Act," *Newsweek,* international edition, August 6, 2001.

parity of power in U.S. hands, and the September 2001 attacks may even have strengthened the U.S. diplomatic position in the short term.[16]

Meanwhile, who are America's principal adversaries? Not the major powers of Europe and Asia, or even the rising power of China. Rather, America's recent enemies have been the isolated and impoverished regimes in Cuba, Iraq, Afghanistan, Libya, and North Korea, a set of regimes that possess little power and even less international support.[17] With enemies like these, who needs friends?

From the perspective of structural balance-of-power theory, this situation is surely an anomaly. Power in the international system is about as *unbalanced* as it has ever been, yet balancing tendencies—while they do exist—are remarkably mild. It is possible to find them, but one has to squint pretty hard to do it. The propensity to balance is weak even though the United States has not been shy about using its power in recent years. How might we account for this apparent violation of realist logic?

Why Other States Are Not Balancing the United States

The lack of a strong anti-American coalition has not gone unnoticed, and several scholars have recently offered several distinct explanations for its absence. Each identifies part of the reason why the world remains "off-balance," but none of these explanations is wholly convincing.

Unipolarity

In a pathbreaking article on the nature of unipolar systems, William C. Wohlforth argues that structural realism can provide a compelling explanation for the current dearth of genuine balancing behavior. His key insight is to recognize that the behavior of the major powers in today's unipolar world is likely to be quite different from their behavior in the bipolar and multipolar worlds of the past. In particular, Wohlforth argues

---

[16] See Josef Joffe, "Who's Afraid of Mr. Big?" *The National Interest*, 64 (summer 2001): 43–52.

[17] In 1999, these states possessed a combined GDP of $194.4 billion. This figure is roughly 2% of U.S. GDP and less than two-thirds the size of the U.S. defense budget. Similarly, their combined defense spending in 1999 was roughly $10.6 billion, compared to roughly $292.1 billion for the United States. See *The Military Balance, 2000–2001* (London: International Institute for Strategic Studies, 2000).

that the unipolar structure of contemporary international politics dis-
courages potential rivals from making a concerted effort to check America's preponderant position. So long as the United States maintains a
healthy economic advantage and a global military presence that is second
to none, other states will not dare to balance against it. Potential rivals will
be unwilling to invite the "focused enmity" of the United States, and key
U.S. allies like Japan and Germany will prefer to free-ride on U.S. protection rather than trying to create stronger military forces of their own.
Hegemonic wars are by definition precluded, and great power competition will be correspondingly mild. Thus, Wohlforth concludes that unipolarity is likely to both long-lived and comparatively peaceful.

As discussed at greater length below, this argument contains a number
of important insights. Because the United States is so far ahead, it is more
dangerous for other states to oppose it openly and tempting for some
states to continue to rely on U.S. protection. Yet there are at least two
problems with Wohlforth's confident claim that no state (or group of
states) would dare to challenge U.S. preponderance.

First, Wohlforth's analysis does not discuss the possibility that secondary
states might try to constrain the United States without engaging in overt
efforts to build a balancing coalition. Secondary states may be reluctant
to openly combine against the United States (for fear of losing its protection or attracting its "focused enmity") but there are a host of lesser actions they can still undertake in order to complicate U.S. calculations and
constrain its freedom of action. For example, Russia may be too weak to
pose much of a danger to the United States, yet its reluctance to cooperate in the wake of NATO's decision to expand eastwards made it more difficult for the Clinton administration to handle its recurring confrontations with Iraq and Serbia. Indeed, had Moscow been less eager to show
Washington that ignoring Russian interests was not cost-free, it might
have joined the West in pressuring Baghdad and Belgrade and helped the
United States avoid the collapse of UNSCOM in 1998 and the Kosovo War
in the spring of 1999. Different Western policies might also make Moscow
more amenable to U.S. requests that it limit the sale of nuclear technology to countries like Iran and put a damper on the emerging Sino-Russian rapprochement.

Similarly, even if China is unlikely to emerge as a true "peer competitor" for several decades, a combination of geography, technological ac-
quisitions, and strategic innovation could enable a revisionist China to
threaten U.S. interests in Asia. Its ability to do this will be affected, in part,
by how much support it receives from other countries (e.g., Russia) and by
whether the United States can count on rapid and efficient help from its

own allies in the region.[18] Unipolarity may discourage active balancing against the United States for the reasons Wohlforth describes, but other states can still engage in low-level efforts to impede U.S. initiatives.[19] And we now know that unipolarity did not deter the Al Qaeda terrorist network from attacking the United States, in order to demonstrate its opposition to the U.S. role in the Middle East and Persian Gulf and to bring the costs of these policies back home to America.

Second, and following from the first point, Wohlforth's structural explanation does not consider whether the propensity to balance against the United States could be affected by the specific military forces that the United States acquires or the ways that the United States chooses to use them. The omission is significant, because today's unipolar structure imposes very few external constraints on what the United States might decide to do. The Cold War imposed a certain discipline on the conduct of U.S. foreign policy, but the absence of any serious rivals makes it easier for foreign and defense policy to be influenced by domestic interest groups, foreign lobbies, or ideological whims. Wohlforth is primarily worried that the United States might reduce its overseas role (which could encourage other states to catch up), and he downplays the possibility that the United States will overreach. Apart from exhorting U.S. leaders to preserve the U.S. lead and maintain existing U.S. overseas commitments (in order to keep the unipolar structure intact), Wohlforth's otherwise impressive analysis does not offer much practical policy guidance.

[margin annotation: unipolarity rationale ignores role of spec. mil. forces]

Institutions and the Western Order

An alternative explanation for the absence of anti-American balancing highlights the unique institutional arrangements binding the United States and its allies together.[20] According to John Ikenberry, the Western order has long rested on the willingness of the United States to commit itself to a set of multilateral institutions that limit its ability to either threaten or abandon its major allies. The permeable nature of the U.S po-

[18] See Thomas J. Christensen, "Posing Problems without Catching Up: China's Rise and Challenges for U.S. Security Policy," *International Security* 25, no. 4 (spring 2001): 5–40.

[19] As the October 2000 bombing of the USS *Cole* illustrates, even very weak actors (in this case, a terrorist group) can impose costs on the United States and force it to adjust its deployment practices.

[20] See G. John Ikenberry, "Institutions, Strategic Restraint, and the Persistence of American Postwar Order," *International Security* 23, no. 3 (winter 1998–99): 45–78; idem, *After Victory: Institutions, Strategic Restraint, and the Rebuilding of Order after Major Wars* (Princeton, N.J.: Princeton University Press, 2001).

litical system also gave potential balancers a variety of ways to monitor and shape U.S. policy, thereby reducing fears that the United States might use its power in ways that would threaten their own interests. These institutions, networks, and norms have broadened and deepened over the past four decades, and Ikenberry now sees them as akin to a formal constitution of the Western order. Accordingly, he regards the Western order as extremely robust (even in the absence of an external threat) and suggests that "stability will be an inevitable feature" of this system for many years to come.[21] But where Wohlforth traces stability to the unipolar material structure of the current system, Ikenberry sees it as the historically contingent, path-dependent product of institutionalized arrangements made over the course of the past five decades.

Ikenberry's account underscores the unusual durability of the U.S.–led alliance system, and the features he identifies account for some of its resilience since the Soviet Union collapsed.[22] Yet the real question is whether the unique qualities of the Western alliance will persist now that the global distribution of power has been transformed by the disappearance of the Soviet Union. Institutions reflect the capabilities and interests of the states that create them, and these interests are likely to shift now that the structure of the system has been transformed.[23] During the Cold War, the United States and its allies had common interests in many areas, and especially on the core issues of national security. Although disagreements arose over out-of-area issues (e.g., Vietnam, Suez) or the fine details of NATO's military strategy (e.g., the debate on "flexible response" in the 1960s), there was little disagreement about what the alliance was for or what its central mission(s) were. Thus, the distribution of capabilities (and thus the definition of interests) and the nature of Western institutions pointed towards a similar set of policies and commitments.

Today, however, the distribution of power gives the United States less reason to commit itself to Europe, gives Europe less reason to be confident about U.S. support, and creates a greater chance for serious conflicts of interest between the United States and its long-time partners. NATO

---

[21] Ikenberry also suggests that "short of large-scale war or a global economic crisis, the American hegemonic order appears to be immune to would-be hegemonic challengers." See Ikenberry, "Institutions, Strategic Restraint, and American Postwar Order," 78.

[22] See also Robert McCalla, "NATO's Persistence after the Cold War," *International Organization* 50, no. 3 (summer 1996): 445–75; Waltz, "Structural Realism after the Cold War."

[23] Waltz makes this point in "Structural Realism after the Cold War," 24–26. Indeed, NATO's principal mission has already changed in important ways, and it is somewhat misleading to think of it as the same institution. See also Lawrence Freedman, "The Transformation of NATO," *Financial Times*, August 6, 2001, 17; Celeste Wallander, "Institutional Assets and Adaptability: NATO after the Cold War," *International Organization* 54, no. 4 (autumn 2000): 705–35.

has persisted because Europeans still want the U.S. "pacifier" to remain in place, and because U.S. leaders have been willing to maintain that role even though there is no serious external threat to any of the European powers. But it is anyone's guess how long this commitment will last, and the Bush administration has made no secret of its desire to reduce the U.S. presence in Europe in order to devote more resources to other priorities.[24] The global war on terrorism is likely to provide the pretext for a further reduction in U.S. forces in Europe, thereby hastening NATO's evolution from a serious military alliance into a looser political confederation.[25]

In the end, Ikenberry's optimism rests on the belief that the existing institutional "glue" is sufficiently sticky to keep the United States and its allies together even if their interests begin to diverge. He may be right, but signs of strain are increasingly evident in the wake of NATO's haphazard interventions in Bosnia and Kosovo, and the Bush administration's nonnegotiable commitment to missile defense, abandonment of the ABM treaty, and continued disregard for its allies' opinions. The United States and Europe need not become enemies, but close friendship (let alone a meaningful alliance) can no longer be taken for granted.[26] European governments have been dismayed by the U.S. rejection of the Comprehensive Test Ban Treaty and the Bush administration's opposition to the Kyoto Protocol on global warming, the global campaign to ban landmines, the treaty to establish an international criminal court, and the verification protocol to the Biological Weapons Convention. The September 2001 attacks may have triggered a renewed sense of unity in the short-term, but earlier differences have not been resolved and are likely to reemerge over time.[27]

These trends are not simply a consequence of the particular objectives of individual leaders or political parties; they also reflect the new structure

[24] According to an unnamed U.S. defense official, "The assumption is that cuts [in U.S. personnel] would primarily come out of Europe." See "Rumsfeld Aides Seek Deep Personnel Cuts in Armed Forces to Pay for New Weaponry," *Wall Street Journal*, August 8, 2001, A3.

[25] That process will be furthered if NATO expansion is linked to closer ties between NATO and Russia, and if NATO turns out to be largely superfluous in the war on terrorism. See James Kurth, "The Next NATO: Building an American Commonwealth of Nations," *The National Interest* 65 (fall 2001): 5–16.

[26] Some of the institutional elements that Ikenberry identifies are probably irrelevant to the question of security commitments. Thus, he argues that transnational business and governmental connections help solidify relations within the American system, but it is not clear why such states require or reinforce the U.S. commitment to fight and die for Europe or Asia.

[27] European leaders emphasized that the U.S. response should be "proportional," and public opinion polls suggest that there are serious misgivings about the U.S. handling of the war in Afghanistan. See Steven Erlanger, "So Far, Europe Breathes Easier over Free Hand Given the United States," *New York Times*, September 29, 2001, B1, B6; and "German Opinion Swings against War," ISN Security Watch, October 25, 2001.

of world politics. The United States was committed to multilateralism during the Cold War because it needed allied support and wanted to keep the Soviet Union isolated. Now that the Cold War is over and the United States sits perched on the pinnacle of power, however, it is loath to let its allies restrict its freedom of action and less interested in multilateral approaches. As one U.S. official explained the decision not to use NATO to wage war in Afghanistan: "The fewer people you have to rely on, the fewer permissions you have to get."[28]

US need/ interest in multilateralism

Viewed as a whole, these trends cast doubt on whether existing Western institutions can hold the United States and its allies together, because institutions can do little if the members are no longer committed to them. Conflicts of interest between the United States and Europe are likely to grow with time, especially if states such as China eventually present a serious challenge to U.S. interests. The Soviet Union threatened U.S. and European interests alike, but a rising China would pose little direct threat to Europe. In the future, European states might even regard China as an attractive strategic partner. The point is not to warn of a dangerous Sino-European alliance, it is merely to underscore that institutions formed in one strategic context are less likely to endure once that context has changed.

Fear of U.S. Retrenchment

Other scholars discount the danger of an anti-American coalition because they believe that America's overseas presence is likely to diminish now that the Soviet threat is gone. Instead of worrying about U.S. dominance, in short, this view suggests that other states are more concerned that the United States might withdraw. Instead of banding together to keep the United States in check, therefore, most of the other major powers are happy to defer to U.S. leadership in the hopes of keeping U.S. forces committed in their regions.[29]

do they really like or military presence?

There is some truth in this interpretation as well, although the United States has yet to liquidate any of its major overseas commitments and is likely to expand some of them as part of the campaign against global terrorism. The United States has also been extremely active on the world stage and has been willing to exercise its power unilaterally on more than one occasion. Other states may worry about a U.S. withdrawal, but there is little sign that it is doing so yet. Thus, this perspective does a good job of

[28] Quoted in Elaine Sciolino and Steven Lee Myers, "Bush Says 'Time is Running Out'; U.S. Plans to Act Largely Alone," *New York Times*, October 7, 2001, 1A.

[29] See Mearsheimer, *Tragedy of Great Power Politics*, chap. 10.

explaining why balancing might be less likely at some point in the future, but it has trouble explaining why balancing tendencies have been so subdued for the past ten years. And if key U.S. allies really believe that a retrenchment is likely, one would expect to see more energetic efforts to develop their own defense capabilities, as opposed to the modest efforts seen to date.

To summarize: each of these explanations offers useful insights into why other states are not balancing against the United States, despite its historically unprecedented concentration of economic and military power. But each tells only part of the story and none offers detailed advice for how the United States can remain an activist, preponderant power without eventually generating a countervailing coalition. Let us therefore return to the more general question of why alliances form and consider the U.S. position from a slightly different perspective.

Balance-of-Threat Theory

The anomaly of states failing to balance U.S. power largely vanishes if we focus not on power but on *threats*.[30] As I have argued at length elsewhere, balance-of-threat theory helps explain why most of the other major powers did not ally against the United States after World War II, when the United States controlled nearly half of the world economy, had sole possession of atomic weapons, and possessed large conventional forces as well. It also goes a long way to explaining why balancing has not occurred to any significant degree today.

Balance-of-threat theory argues that states form alliances to balance against *threats*. Threats, in turn, are a function of power, proximity, offensive capabilities, and aggressive intentions. Other things being equal, an increase in any of these factors make it more likely that other states (and especially other major powers) will regard the possessors of these traits as threatening and begin to look for some form of protecting themselves.

Gauging the balance of threats is not always easy, however. No one has yet devised a valid way to aggregate the different components of threat, and measuring each of these factors can be difficult in itself. As a result, it is sometimes hard to determine which of several possible threats is the most serious. Before World War II, for example, states in Central and East-

---

[30] See Stephen M. Walt, *The Origins of Alliances* (Ithaca, N.Y.: Cornell University Press, 1987); and idem, "Testing Theories of Alliance Formation: The Case of Southwest Asia," *International Organization* 42, no. 2 (spring 1988): 275–316.

ern Europe did not balance vigorously against Nazi Germany because they also faced threats from each other and from the Soviet Union.[31] When threats are diffuse or indeterminate, states are more likely to remain neutral or hedge their bets in other ways.

When a particular state does appear especially dangerous, however, the optimal response is to get some other state to bear the costs of containing it.[32] Thus "buck passing" is the preferred response to most threats. When there is no one to pass the buck to, however, major powers prefer to balance against the most threatening state(s) rather than choosing to "bandwagon" with it. Bandwagoning is risky because allying with a threatening state requires trust in its continued benevolence. Because intentions can change, strong states usually choose to form defensive coalitions to contain the most threatening power, rather than trying to deflect the threat by joining forces with it.

Taken together, the four components of threat go a long way toward explaining why other states have not done very much to balance against the United States. Moreover, balance-of-threat theory also subsumes the partial explanations offered by Wohlforth, Ikenberry, and others.

Power   In general, states with great power are threatening to others, because other states can never be sure how they will use these capabilities. As a state's power increases, moreover, other states will worry that it might be able to use its capabilities with impunity, and they will be likely to take action to prevent this. Up to a point, therefore, increases in a state's relative power will increase the tendency for others to balance against it. Thus, balance-of-power theory is not wrong; it is merely incomplete. Power is one of the factors that affects the propensity to balance, although it is not the only one nor always the most important.

Of course, a state's willingness to balance depends in part on whether doing so is likely to be effective.[33] This consideration explains why weak states are more likely to bandwagon than medium and major powers are: because they can do little to affect the outcome, they must seek the winning side at all costs.[34] By the same logic, a state could grow so powerful

---

[31] See Stephen M. Walt, "Alliances, Threats, and U.S. Grand Strategy," *Security Studies* 1, no. 3 (spring 1992): 457.

[32] Emphasizing the prevalence of "buck passing" is Mearsheimer, *Tragedy of Great Power Politics*, chap. 6.

[33] As Waltz noted, states that balance are safer "provided . . . that the coalition they join achieves enough defense or deterrent strength to dissuade adversaries from attacking." See *Theory of International Politics*, 127. For a recent formal analysis of these issues, see Robert Powell, *In the Shadow of Power: States and Strategies in International Politics* (Princeton, N.J.: Princeton University Press, 1999). I discuss Powell's arguments in more detail below.

[34] In the words of Annette Baker Fox, "Instead of moving to the side of the less powerful and thereby helping to restore the balance, [small states] tended to comply with the de-

that other states might be reluctant to try to balance against it. The leading state's level of preponderance might fall short of true hegemony if it lacked the capacity to physically dominate the globe, yet other states might still decline to balance so as not to provoke the leading power to focus its superior capabilities on them. Moreover, the strongest power can also do more to reward states that choose to bandwagon, especially if it can persuade others that they will be rewarded (but not devoured) if they flock to its banner.

As noted above, the same logic underpins Wohlforth's claim that unipolarity will be durable and peaceful and thus provides some of the justification for a strategy of primacy. If the United States is big enough, the argument runs, other states will be dissuaded from challenging its position and may not even try to check its freedom of action. Thus, the relationship between power and balancing is curvilinear: states balance against power but *only up to a point.* If a state's power continues to grow beyond that point, others states will regard balancing as increasingly futile and will be less and less inclined to try it.

Although this argument appears to challenge the neorealist claim that states tend to balance, it is not really a violation of the theory. As Waltz has noted repeatedly, states in anarchy must adopt policies of self-help (or expect to suffer the consequences). So long as power is not too heavily skewed, buck passing and balancing are the most promising "self-help" strategies. If one state does become preponderant, however, bandwagoning may be the rational response. Thus, the United States has long enjoyed a hegemonic position in the Western Hemisphere, both because its immediate neighbors have been too weak to challenge it directly and because other great powers have been preoccupied by events in their own regions.[35] This argument implies that other states might be more likely to balance against the United States were its power to decline, which in turn suggests that the United States has ample incentive to preserve its material superiority.

mands of the more powerful and thus to accentuate any shift in the balance of forces. . . . Viewed in this way, the small state's characteristic behavior may be described as 'anti-balance of power' while that of a great power is characteristically 'pro-balance of power.' " See her *The Power of Small States: Diplomacy in World War II* (Chicago: University of Chicago Press, 1959), 185.

[35] Indeed, Wohlforth suggests that "second-tier states" (by which he means all the major powers save the United States) "face structural incentives similar to lesser states in a region dominated by one power, such as North America." This view implies that the global structure of power now resembles the hegemony that the United States has long enjoyed in the Western hemisphere. See Wohlforth, "Stability of a Unipolar World," 25. It is also worth noting that the two countries that did challenge the United States—Castro's Cuba and the Sandinista regime in Nicaragua—had to rely on Soviet support in order to do so, paid an enormous price, and in the case of the Sandinistas, ultimately failed.

Yet several caveats should be acknowledged as well. First, this prescription makes sense only if one is fairly confident that the United States is well past the critical threshold beyond which other states are unlikely to balance. If the United States has not yet reached the point of inflection (i.e., where the propensity to balance begins to decline) then increases in power will tend to provoke anti-American coalitions.

Second, power is only one of the elements that states consider when deciding whether or not to balance. As discussed below, the tendency for other states to join forces against the United States will increase if the United States acquires especially threatening capabilities or if it uses its power capriciously, rather than using it in ways that other states regard as beneficial to their own interests.[36] It makes sense not to balance a preponderant power if aligning with it brings tangible benefits, but if one is going to face its "focused enmity" anyway, one might as well try to organize the combined capabilities that can keep the dominant power at bay. Thus, it is not simply a matter of what the United States *has*; how other states respond will also depend on what they think the United States will *do*.

Third, as already discussed, there is a range of possible responses that other states may make, ranging from all-out bandwagoning to free-riding, to passive noncooperation, to tacit opposition, and on to active balancing. States may not want to attract the "focused enmity" of the United States, but they may be eager to limit its freedom of action, complicate its diplomacy, sap its strength and resolve, maximize their own autonomy and reaffirm their own rights, and generally make the United States work harder to achieve its objectives. Such actions would fall well short of forming an explicit alliance directed against the United States, but U.S. policymakers would still find them troubling.[37]

By itself, therefore, the effects of power are probably indeterminate. America's current preponderance does worry other states and provides a modest incentive for them to balance, but it may also inhibit their willingness to take direct action to bring the United States to heel. By itself, therefore, power does not determine what other states are likely to do.

Proximity   Because the ability to project power declines with distance, states that are nearby pose a greater threat than those that are far away.

---

[36] See Francois Heisbourg, "American Hegemony? Perceptions of the U.S. Abroad," *Survival* 41, no. 4 (winter 1999–2000): 5–19.

[37] Similarly, peasants and other individuals with little material power or social status often devise elaborate strategies to subvert or limit the predations of more powerful actors. See James C. Scott, *Weapons of the Weak: Everyday Forms of Peasant Resistance* (New Haven, Conn.: Yale University Press, 1985); and idem, *Domination and the Arts of Resistance: Hidden Transcripts* (New Haven, Conn.: Yale University Press, 1990).

The geographic position of the United States is thus a tremendous asset, and it goes a long way toward explaining why other states are less worried by the concentration of power in U.S. hands. Because it is extremely difficult to project power across water and onto a foreign shore, U.S. power is less threatening to others and they are less inclined to balance against it.[38] America's geographic isolation also reduces the likelihood of territorial disputes with other major powers and allows the United States to take a more detached view of many international developments.

Moreover, because the other major powers lie in close proximity to one another, they tend to worry more about each other than they do about the United States. This feature explains why the United States is such a desirable ally for many Eurasian states: its power ensures that its voice will be heard and its actions will be felt, but it lies a comfortable distance away and does not threaten to dominate its allies physically. As a European diplomat puts it, "A European power broker would be a hegemon. We can agree on U.S. leadership, but not on one of our own."[39] Similarly, Asian allies like Japan, Korea, and Taiwan favor a strong U.S. commitment because they see other states (and each other) as potentially dangerous and because they regard the physical presence of U.S. troops as a nonthreatening guarantor of regional stability.[40] Geography also explains why it would be difficult to conjure up an anti-American coalition combining Russia, China, and India, unless the United States acted in a remarkably myopic and aggressive fashion.

Offensive Power   Other things being equal, states are more threatening when they acquire specific military capabilities (such as highly mobile, long-range military forces) or political capacities (such as a potentially contagious ideology) that pose a direct danger to the territorial integrity or political stability of other powers.[41] Accordingly, other states are more

---

[38] The "stopping power of water," is emphasized by John Mearsheimer in *Tragedy of Great Power Politics*, chap. 4. Although Mearsheimer explicitly rejects the idea of an "offense-defense" balance, he acknowledges that geographic features (such as large bodies of water) can make conquest more difficult.

[39] Quoted in Robert J. Art, "Why Western Europe Needs the United States and NATO," *Political Science Quarterly* 111, no. 1 (spring 1996): 36. See also Christoph Bertram, *Europe in the Balance: Securing the Peace Won in the Cold War* (Washington, D.C.: Carnegie Endowment for International Peace, 1996).

[40] See Nye, "Case for Deep Engagement," *Foreign Affairs* 74, no. 4 (July 1995): 90–102; Thomas C. Christensen, "China, the U.S.–Japan Alliance, and the Security Dilemma in East Asia," *International Security* 23, no. 4 (spring 1999): 49–80; and Richard K. Betts, "Wealth, Power and Instability: East Asia and the United States after the Cold War," *International Security* 18, no. 3 (winter 1993–94): 34–77.

[41] This is a central tenet of so-called offense-defense theory. For the most thorough statement of this argument, see Stephen Van Evera, *Causes of War*, vol. 1, *The Structure of Power and the Risks of War* (Ithaca, N.Y.: Cornell University Press, 1999). For critiques, see Richard K. Betts, "Must War Find a Way? A Review Essay," *International Security* 24, no. 2 (fall 1999):

likely to balance when states with large material resources acquire these particular specialized offensive capabilities. By contrast, when a state can defend its own territory but cannot attack others with high confidence, their incentive to balance against it will decline.

As noted above, the physical isolation created by the Atlantic and Pacific oceans reduces the direct military threat that the United States poses to other states, thereby reducing their propensity to balance. But this effect should not be overstated, given that other states are clearly worried about America's unparalleled power-projection capabilities. Thus Chinese military officials see the world as comprised of "one pole, but many powers," identify "U.S. hegemonism and power politics" as the central security problem in the world, and are acutely attentive to the global reach of U.S. military capabilities. Chinese, Russian, and European leaders have also been sharply critical of U.S. plans to develop national missile defenses, correctly seeing them as a potential threat to their own deterrent capabilities.[42]

In a general sense, the physical presence of U.S. ground forces in Europe or Asia is less threatening than its capacity to strike hostile targets virtually anywhere in the globe. Similarly, we should expect other states to be especially worried by the current campaign to create a national missile defense system (which would threaten other states' deterrent capabilities) or the potent air capabilities demonstrated by the United States in the 1991 Gulf War, the 1999 intervention in Kosovo, and the recent war in Afghanistan. According to balance-of-threat theory, increasing U.S. *offensive* capabilities will increase the tendency for other states to balance against the United States. By contrast, developing and deploying U.S. power in defensive modes (as in South Korea or Western Europe) is likely to reassure allies without provoking potential foes.

Offensive Intentions   States are more likely to balance when they believe others have especially aggressive intentions.[43] The logic here is straight-

---

166–98; and Keir Lieber, "Grasping the Technological Peace: The Offense-Defense Balance and International Security," *International Security* 25, no. 1 (summer 2000): 77–104.

[42] See David Shambaugh, "China's Military Views the World: Ambivalent Security," *International Security* 24, no. 3 (winter 1999/2000): 52–79; Erik Eckholm, "Missile Wars: What America Calls a Defense China Calls an Offense," *New York Times*, July 2, 2000, section 4, 3; and Igor Ivanov, "The Missile Defense Mistake: Undermining Strategic Stability and the ABM Treaty," *Foreign Affairs* 79, no. 5 (September-October 2000): 15–20; and Thom Shanker, "Russians Resist Rumsfeld Effort to Set Aside ABM Treaty," *New York Times*, August 14, 2001, A9. See also the colloquium on "A Consensus on Missile Defense?" in *Survival* 43, no. 3 (autumn 1994): 61–94.

[43] Robert Powell has developed a formal model portraying alignment decisions in a world of three states. In its simplest form, the model suggests that states will usually prefer to wait or bandwagon rather than balance, depending in part on the available "technology of coercion" and on whether forming an alliance yields increasing or decreasing returns to scale. In

forward: because known aggressors are by definition harder to appease, the only choice is to assemble a countervailing coalition that is strong enough to stop them.

Here again, the United States gains by being perceived as *comparatively benign*. This does not mean that the United States always acts benevolently or that it is incapable of aggressive behavior. Rather, it means that most of the world's major powers do not see U.S. intentions as especially hostile or aggressive. This judgment probably reflects the relaxed nature of U.S. imperialism as well as the legacy of Cold War cooperation; as great powers go, the United States has been rather mild-mannered. Although some states are understandably concerned that U.S. power may be used to undermine their interests, none of the major powers seem to be worried that the United States will try to conquer them. The United States may be self-righteous, overweening, and occasionally trigger-happy, but it is not trying to acquire additional territory. As a result, other states are somewhat less inclined to balance against its otherwise daunting capabilities.[44]

Taken together, the principle sources of threat explain why balancing behavior has been muted thus far. The United States is by far the world's most *powerful* state, but it does not pose a significant *threat* to the vital interests of most of the other major powers.[45] Other states are wary of U.S. capabilities, but they are nowhere near as alarmed as the European powers were by Wilhelmine Germany in the first decade of the twentieth century, or by Nazi Germany in the 1930s. Similarly, the American threat to the medium powers of Europe and Asia is much less worrisome than the threat formerly posed by the Soviet Union, which combined power, proximity, offensive capabilities, and aggressive intentions in an especially alarming package.[46]

---

the model, this result occurs because the incentive to be on the winning side of a war outweighs the desire to reap a larger share of the postwar benefits. Powell's model is limited to the analysis of alignment decisions in wartime (the first move in the model is a decision by one state to attack one or both of the other two) and Powell admits that balancing may be more likely in prewar situations. Powell also notes that "the terms of the tradeoff between balancing and bandwagoning change if the attacker is more willing to use force than the other two states. . . . This lowers the payoff to bandwagoning and makes balancing more likely." In other words, the incentive to balance or bandwagon is affected by the judgment that states make about the intentions of others. Although Powell claims that his results challenge balance-of-threat theory, his conclusions are in fact not all that different. See *In the Shadow of Power*, chap. 5, especially 190.

[44] As noted earlier, this is a central theme in Ikenberry's analysis of the Western order.

[45] China may be a partial exception to this generalization, with Russia as a potential second candidate.

[46] See Walt, *Origins of Alliances*, chap. 8; and idem, "Alliance Formation and the Balance of World Power," *International Security* 9, no. 4 (spring 1985): 3–43.

Impediments to Balancing

Balancing behavior is not automatic, and the main impediments to effective alliance formation help reinforce the U.S. position.[47] First, potential balancers may try to pass the buck to one another, hoping that their allies bear the brunt of the effort to deter, contain, or defeat an aggressor. If they buckpass or free-ride too much, however, the balancing coalition will not acquire enough strength to succeed or may simply dissolve amid mutual mistrust and recrimination.[48] Second, potential balancers must recognize their shared interests and communicate them to one another, and have to be able to trust each other enough to make workable defensive arrangements. Finally, to be truly effective, allies must coordinate strategy and avoid the temptation to seek unilateral advantages when opportunities to do so arise.

Given these potential pitfalls, a clever great power can try to thwart efforts to form a balancing coalition.[49] Aggressive states can try to mask the full extent of their ambitions, potential allies can be co-opted with bribes, and defensive coalitions can be split by offering concessions to one opponent but not to others. And if they are especially skillful, even powerful and aggressive states may defuse opposition long enough to accomplish their aims.[50]

Summary

Balance-of-threat theory provides a compelling explanation for the absence of anti-American balancing both during and after the Cold War. Balance-of-threat theory largely subsumes the alternative explanations for the lack of a strong desire to balance U.S. power, and the impediments just described explain why states that might wish to form an anti-American coalition will face significant practical obstacles.

[47] Thus, Napoleon once remarked: "How many allies do you have? Five, ten, twenty? The more you have, the better it is for me." Quoted in Karl E. Roider, *Baron Thugut and Austria's Response to the French Revolution* (Princeton, N.J.: Princeton University Press, 1987), 327.

[48] On these tendencies, see Mancur Olson and Richard Zeckhauser, "An Economic Theory of Alliances," *Review of Economics and Statistics* 48, no. 3 (August 1966): 266–79; Barry Posen, *The Sources of Military Doctrine* (Ithaca, N.Y.: Cornell University Press, 1984), especially 63–64; and Mearsheimer, *Tragedy of Great Power Politics*, chap. 8.

[49] On Adolf Hitler's efforts to impede the balancing process, see Walt, "Alliances, Threats, and U.S. Grand Strategy."

[50] Bismarck's conduct of the Wars of German Unification (1864, 1866, 1870) is a classic example of this sort of statecraft. Under his leadership, Prussia fought three wars, unified Germany, and fundamentally altered the balance of power in Europe, yet without provoking a countervailing coalition.

These arguments raise the obvious question: is the danger of an anti-American coalition so remote as to be of little practical concern? The answer is no, for two reasons. First although it would require several acts of folly to bring such a coalition about, the United States is more likely to commit such acts if it assumes that the geopolitical costs will be negligible. Second, keeping the world "off-balance" is very much in the U.S. interest even if other states are disinclined to form an anti-U.S. alliance. The ability of the United States to achieve its foreign policy objectives at relatively low cost will depend in large part on whether other powers are inclined to support or oppose U.S. policies, and whether others find it easy or difficult to coordinate joint opposition to U.S. initiatives. The more other states worry about U.S. preponderance, the more likely they are to take steps—however modest and covert—designed to undermine or obstruct U.S. efforts. The United States is likely to be both more secure and better able to achieve its chosen ends if other states do not see its preponderant position as especially worrisome. Thus, even if an anti-American alliance is presently unlikely, U.S. policymakers should try to reduce other states' incentives to interfere or resist in limited but still problematic ways. Let us now consider how the United States can achieve that general objective.

A Strategy of Self-Restraint

The United States cannot alter its geographic position (save by giving up territory or by conquering more), and it cannot change the distribution of capabilities either rapidly or unilaterally (save by rapidly disarming or by wrecking its own economy deliberately). Accordingly, the recommendations set forth here assume that the United States will continue to hold its current position of primacy, and they focus on ways that it can diminish the *offensive* elements of U.S. power or attempt to convey benign intentions whenever possible.

Maintain U.S. Capabilities

As discussed earlier, the enormous disparity between the United States and the other major powers helps keep the world "off-balance." Because the U.S. possesses such large advantages, it can provide benefits for states whose interests are compatible with its own. If U.S. power were to decline significantly, other states would have less to gain from cooperating with the United States and less to lose by challenging it. United States strength can be a source of attraction and may even deter some adversaries from acting to thwart U.S. aims. Thus, maintaining its material superiority is the first step towards discouraging the formation of a countervailing coalition.

Unfortunately, with great power comes great ambition, and usually, more than a little arrogance. The more powerful a state is, the more it can hope to accomplish and the less it will display a "decent respect for the opinions of mankind." In the near term, therefore, the main danger is that the United States will either squander its power in ill-chosen adventures or use its power in ways that reinforce the concerns of other states. Accordingly, the policy recommendations set forth below focus on ways that the United States can make its preponderance less worrisome to the rest of the international community.

"Mailed Fist, Velvet Glove"

As just noted, U.S. preponderance makes other states more sensitive to the ways that U.S. power is used. As a result, the United States should take care to use its power judiciously, and especially where military force is concerned. Americans should worry when generally pro-U.S. publications such as the *Economist* describe the United States as "too easily excited; too easily distracted; too fond of throwing its weight around," or when knowledgeable foreign experts describe the United States as a "rogue superpower" or a "trigger-happy sheriff."[51]

Three specific recommendations follow. First, the United States should use force with forbearance, asking questions first and shooting later. Although it will occasionally be necessary to use force preemptively so as to minimize casualties or convey resolve, U.S. preponderance gives it the luxury of taking a more relaxed and deliberate view of many international developments. States whose existence might be endangered if they failed to act quickly may have to preempt threats and respond vigorously to highly ambiguous warnings. Because the United States is objectively so secure, however, it can usually rely on policies of deterrence and retaliation rather than preemption, and reserve the latter tactic for those rare circumstances when it faces a potentially lethal danger.[52] In general, the

---

[51] See *The Economist*, September 21, 1996; Heisbourg, "American Hegemony?" 10–15; and also Martin Walker, "What Europeans Think of America," *World Policy Journal* (summer 2000): 26–38.

[52] For example, although U.S. officials did have genuine grounds for launching cruise missile strikes on Afghanistan and Sudan in 1998, the decision to strike on the basis of ambiguous information ignored the larger geopolitical effects of appearing overly eager to use force. For a harsh assessment of these actions, see David Hoile, *Farce Majeure: The Clinton Ad-*

United States should follow the prescription once expressed by President Woodrow Wilson, who declared that the United States "can afford to exercise the self-restraint of a truly great nation, which realizes its own strength and scorns to misuse it."[53]

Second, the United States can reduce the threat posed by its overawing power by giving other states some say over the circumstances in which it will use force. As Ikenberry has emphasized, confining the use of force to multilateral contexts is an effective way to assuage potential fears about the unilateral exercise of U.S. power. This point has been lost on conservative opponents of the United Nations and other international institutions, who fail to recognize that multilateral institutions help the United States exercise its power in a way that is less threatening (and therefore more acceptable) to others. Although exceptions will arise from time to time, the United States should for the most part rely on a "buddy system" to regulate the large-scale use of its military power. Specifically, if it cannot persuade one or more other major powers to join it, then the United States should refrain from using force.[54] This policy might also increase other states' incentives to maintain good relations with Washington, because close ties with the United States will give them a greater influence over how Washington chooses to use its power.[55]

Third, given that the United States now wants broad support for its war against terrorism, it would be wise to reciprocate the foreign support it has recently sought by making some concessions of its own. Committing itself to a serious effort to negotiate a replacement for the Kyoto Protocol on global warming would be an ideal first step, and would go a long way to defuse lingering fears of U.S. unilateralism. Similarly, the United States could accelerate preparations for a new global trade round and declare that it was especially interested in lowering its own barriers against exports from the developing world, even if this hurts some special interests

---

ministration's Sudan Policy, 1993–2000 (London: European-Sudanese Public Affairs Council, 2000).

[53] Quoted in P. Edward Haley, Revolution and Intervention: The Diplomacy of Taft and Wilson with Mexico, 1910–1917 (Cambridge, Mass.: MIT Press, 1970), 100.

[54] This sort of "buddy system" serves two purposes. First, it legitimates U.S. dominance by making it part of a larger group. Second, it safeguards the U.S. against gross misjudgments: if we cannot persuade anyone else that the use of forced is called for, U.S. leaders should probably reconsider the wisdom of this policy. Needless to say, support from Great Britain alone will normally not suffice to legitimate the use of force by the United States.

[55] Daniel Deudney and John Ikenberry argue that the norm of multilateral consultation regarding the use of force was a central element of the Western system that emerged during the Cold War. See Daniel Deudney and G. John Ikenberry, "Realism, Structural Liberalism, and the Western Order," in Unipolar Politics: Realism and State Strategies after the Cold War, ed. Ethan B. Kapstein and Michael Mastanduno (New York: Columbia University Press, 1999); and Ikenberry, After Victory.

here at home. It is also an ideal time to improve relations with Russia, by making sure that issues like NATO expansion and missile defense are handled in a manner that is acceptable to Moscow.[56] The common element in these various initiatives is to show that the United States is willing to compromise with other countries, and willing to use its power in ways that advance others' interests as well as its own.

A final element of the "velvet glove" approach is that the United States should go easy on promoting democracy. Encouraging democracy is a worthy goal on normative grounds and U.S. policy can sometimes exert positive effects on occasion. Promoting democracy can also be extremely destabilizing (especially in multiethnic societies lacking well-established democratic traditions) and is likely to appear intrusive and self-congratulatory to foreign elites.[57] At the very least, the United States should not make exporting democracy the centerpiece of its foreign policy.

Practice "Random Acts of Self-Abnegation"

U.S. preponderance allows it to impose its preference on other states in many circumstances, or to ignore the preferences of others and merely go its own way irrespective of what other states want.[58] This capacity is a great asset, of course, but it can easily tempt the United States into precisely the sort of unilateralist behavior that concerns even longstanding U.S. allies. The more that the United States insists on its own way, the more others are likely to resent U.S. power and search for ways to restrict it. Thus, unilateralist actions like the Helms-Burton Act (which sought to impose penalties on foreign firms conducting business in Cuba) or the recent decisions to reject a series of prominent international conventions carry symbolic costs that may ultimately outweigh the alleged benefits of rejection.[59]

---

[56] Russia is more likely to accept NATO expansion if the door to its own entry is opened wider, and it is clearly willing to accept missile defenses in the context of mutually agreed revision to the 1972 Anti-Ballistic Missile treaty.

[57] See Thomas Carothers, *Aid to Democracy: The Learning Curve* (Washington, D.C.: Carnegie Endowment for International Peace, 2000); and Jack L. Snyder, *From Voting to Violence: Democratization and Nationalist Conflicts* (New York: W.W. Norton, 2000). On the difficulty of creating truly liberal societies when the proper political culture is absent, see Markus Fischer, "Thoughts on the Liberal Peace," Discussion Paper 00–1, International Security Program, Belfer Center for Science and International Affairs, Harvard University (March 2000).

[58] See Lloyd Gruber, *Ruling the World: Power Politics and the Rise of Supranational Organizations* (Princeton, N.J.: Princeton University Press, 2000).

[59] As Canadian foreign minister Lloyd Axworthy commented in response to the Helms-Burton Act: "This is bullying. But in America, you call it 'global leadership.' " Quoted in "Talk Multilaterally, Hit Allies with a Stick," *New York Times,* July 21, 1993, E3. The United States stood apart when 178 other countries voted to implement the Kyoto Protocol in July

By the same logic, the United States would do well to offer genuine concessions when it can, simply to minimize others' concerns that it is indifferent to their interests and amour propre. In other words, recognizing that verbal statements of benign intent are little more than "cheap talk," the United States can best communicate its benevolence by making more credible signals to this effect. And to be credible, these gestures must entail some cost to the United States. Thus, the Clinton administration wisely abandoned its initial opposition to a German candidate for the position of managing director of the International Monetary Fund, thereby allaying concerns about U.S. dominance and avoiding a potentially costly dispute with its closest allies.[60] This approach also implies a willingness to accept less-than-perfect agreements that are still a net benefit to U.S. interests.[61]

A related tactic would be to "denationalize" international policy discussions by framing them in terms of a search for "best practices." Instead of viewing international collaboration as a bargaining process in which different national positions are openly negotiated, the United States should orient collaborative efforts around the exchange of technical expertise and professional advice. This approach has gained favor in a number important areas, including environmental cooperation, commercial regulation, international law enforcement, and international antiterrorist efforts.[62] By conducting collaboration primarily via day-to-day consultations between the relevant bureaucrats, professional elites, and technical experts, this approach would diminish the sense that the United States was "imposing" its own preferences on its weaker partners. It also increases the likelihood that the United States might alter its own practices

---

2001, single-handedly scuttled the verification protocol to the Biological Weapons Convention (which was supported by fifty-four other nations, including our NATO allies and Japan), and is aligned with strange bedfellows like China, Iraq, and Libya in opposing creation of an International Criminal Court.

[60] See James Blitz et al., "The Camdessus Succession," *Financial Times*, March 17, 2000, 14.

[61] For example, the Bush administration rejected the verification protocol to the Biological Weapons convention on the grounds that it was not perfectly verifiable and that its inspection provisions might expose U.S. pharmaceutical companies to industrial espionage. Yet the agreement would have had at most marginal effects on the level of U.S. transparency (which is already very high), and would have forced less open societies to provide far greater openness than they do at present. Although the protocol was not *perfectly* verifiable, it would have made it much riskier for states to try to evade their treaty commitments by developing biological weapons in secret.

[62] See Peter C. Haas, ed., *Knowledge, Power, and International Policy Coordination,* special issue, *International Organization* 46, no. 1 (winter 1992); Anne-Marie Slaughter, "The Real New World Order," *Foreign Affairs* 76, no. 5 (September/October 1997): 183–97, and idem, "Governing the Global Economy through Government Networks," in *The Role of Law in International Politics: Essays in International Relations and International Law,* ed. Michael Byers (New York: Oxford University Press, 2000).

in light of the experience of other actors. Ideally, the outcome could be the best of both worlds: the United States (and others) develop workable solutions on some area of common concern (such as terrorism or transnational crime), while the United States shows it is willing to engage in genuine give-and-take.

These prescriptions do not require the United States to abandon important interests and does not mean that the United States should not insist on its own way on occasion. Rather, it suggests that the United States should look for issues where letting weaker states win costs us something but not much. By visibly refraining from using the full extent of its power, and by not seeking every advantage that primacy might confer, the United States can reduce other states' concerns about its capabilities and reduce their incentive to join forces against us. The United States likes to think of itself as a "benevolent hegemon," but it needs to make sure its benevolence is apparent to others.

Keep Clients under Control

The ability of the United States to keep the world "off-balance" rests in part on avoiding unnecessary quarrels with foreign powers. In addition to minimizing the direct threat that U.S. power poses to others, the United States must also ensure that its allies and clients do not act in ways that encourage third parties to see it as overly dangerous. If the United States allows its allies to behave in a bellicose or provocative fashion, they may drag it into conflicts that might otherwise have been avoided.

This problem will be especially acute when dealing with client states who enjoy high levels of domestic support in the United States, and it may actually be worse now that the Cold War is over. Because most U.S. citizens have been indifferent to foreign affairs, the *relative* impact of groups with strong and focused agendas has probably increased.[63] Domestic lobbies may exert even greater influence than they did before, simply because most Americans are indifferent. If U.S. politicians allow these domestic considerations to influence their policies, and especially if the desire to placate domestic lobbies dominates their strategic calculations, then the United States is in effect allowing its foreign policy to be made in Taipei, Miami, Jerusalem, or Warsaw rather than in Washington. Although America's present preponderance might lead some to conclude that there is little risk in backing these traditional clients, letting them determine

[63] See James M. Lindsay, "The New Apathy," *Foreign Affairs*, 79, no. 5 (September/October 2000): 2–8.

U.S. policy may lead to conflicts that might otherwise have been avoided. Thus, if client states want to rely on U.S. protection, the United States must insist that they not take actions that could exacerbate its relations with others.

Do Not Treat Potential Adversaries as a Monolith

During the Cold War, the United States sometimes lumped leftist or Marxist regimes together and viewed them as part of an undifferentiated communist "monolith." Although some U.S. officials held more subtle views (and developed strategies that reflected this awareness), the general tendency to regard any leftist or socialist regime as a potential tool of the Kremlin often led to self-fulfilling spirals of hostility with these regimes.[64]

Because the United States has an important interest in discouraging other states from joining forces against us, it should guard against this tendency to lump states together and view them as part of some larger anti-American movement. To take the most obvious example, depicting North Korea, Iraq, Iran, and Libya as a set of anti-American "rogue states"—let alone an "axis of evil"—ignores the important differences between these states, blinds us to the possibility of improving relations with some of them, and encourages them to cooperate with one another even more.[65] Similarly, Samuel P. Huntington's forecast of a looming "clash of civilizations" could become a dangerous self-fulfilling prophecy if it becomes the guiding framework for the conduct of U.S. foreign policy.[66] If we assume that cultural differences make non-Western states inherently hostile to the United States, we are likely to behave in ways that will reinforce these differences and we will overlook opportunities to keep potentially hostile blocs divided. Even if there are significant obstacles to the formation of a strong anti-American coalition, does the United States really want to give other states a greater incentive to overcome them?

This lesson is especially pertinent in the aftermath of the September 11

[64] See Robert Pastor, *Condemned to Repetition: The United States and Nicaragua* (Princeton, N.J.: Princeton University Press, 1987); Walter Lafeber, *Inevitable Revolutions: The United States in Central America* (New York: W. W. Norton, 1984); and W. Anthony Lake, "Wrestling with Third World Radical Regimes: Theory and Practice," in *U.S. Foreign Policy: Agenda 1985–86*, ed. John W. Sewell, Richard E. Feinberg and Valeriana Kallab (New Brunswick, N.J.: Transaction Books, 1985).

[65] See Robert S. Litwak, *Rogue States and U.S. Foreign Policy: Containment after the Cold War* (Washington, D.C.: Woodrow Wilson Center Press, 2000).

[66] See Samuel P. Huntington, *The Clash of Civilizations and the Remaking of World Order* (New York: Basic Books, 1997), and see also Stephen M. Walt, "Building Up New Bogeymen," *Foreign Policy* 106 (spring 1997): 176–89.

why we shouldn't have gone to Iraq

attacks. Although some U.S. officials favored a broad campaign against all terrorist groups (or suspected sponsors, such as Iraq), cooler heads have prevailed and the United States has thus far eschewed such a risky course. Broadening the war to countries like Iraq would jeopardize international support, divert U.S. assets away from the groups that actually struck the United States, and encourage various anti-American groups to support each other even more vigorously. Unless the United States has clear evidence that foreign powers are helping terrorists wage war against us, the proper strategy is "divide-and-conquer," keeping the terrorists isolated and giving their potential allies good reasons to cut them loose. Labeling regimes we do not like an "axis of evil," as President Bush did in his February 2002 State of the Union address, merely alarms potential allies, casts doubt on U.S. judgment, and limits our own flexibility in dealing with these very different countries.

Emphasize Defense; Eschew Offense

best for a power

Balance-of-threat theory implies that states will be more likely to balance against the United States if its military capabilities appear to be heavily oriented toward offense. By contrast, military forces that are designed to protect the U.S. or its allies will be less dangerous to others and less likely to provoke a balancing response.[67]

As critics of offense-defense theory have noted, distinguishing between offensive and defensive weapons and force postures can be extremely difficult, particularly at the level of individual weapons systems.[68] In general, however, force postures that protect territory without threatening others, and that lack the capacity to attack foreign territory, are likely to be less threatening than force postures that emphasize offensive conquest.[69]

From this perspective, the ideal U.S. posture would be the forward deployment of *defensively* oriented military forces. United States ground

---

[67] Theoretical support for this proposal may be found in Charles L. Glaser, "Realists as Optimists: Cooperation as Self-Help," *International Security* 19, no. 3 (winter 1994–95): 50–90; and Andrew Kydd, "Sheep in Sheep's Clothing: Why Security Seekers Do Not Fight Each Other," *Security Studies* 7, no. 1 (winter 1997): 114–55.

[68] See Jack Levy, "The Offensive-Defensive Balance in Military Technology: A Theoretical and Historical Analysis," *International Studies Quarterly* 28, no. 2 (1984): 219–38; John J. Mearsheimer, *Liddell Hart and the Weight of History* (Ithaca, N.Y.: Cornell University Press, 1988), 36, n. 61; and Jonathan Shimshoni, "Technology, Military Advantage, and World War I: A Case for Military Entrepreneurship," *International Security* 15, no. 3 (winter 1990–91): 187–215.

[69] Thus the military forces (and doctrines) of the former Soviet Union were explicitly oriented towards offensive action and helped provoke the countervailing coalition that subsequently encircled them.

troops and tactical aircraft could be deployed overseas to defend key allies, as they currently do in Japan, Germany, and South Korea. By eschewing large offensive capabilities (such as long-range bombers), the United
States would appear less threatening to others and would be less likely to
provoke defensive reactions.[70]

Unfortunately, such a sharp distinction would be difficult to maintain
in practice. It would be impossible to remove all the offensive potential
from current U.S. forces without significantly weakening overall U.S. capabilities and depriving the United States of options it would like to retain. And if the much-ballyhooed "revolution in military affairs" has real
substance to it, it is likely to enhance the ability of the United States to
project destructive military force throughout the globe. The war in
Afghanistan suggests that U.S. power projection capabilities continue to
improve, and other states are unlikely to find this a comforting trend.

How would such a development affect the geopolitical position of the
United States and the attitudes of other countries? On the one hand, re-
verting to an "offshore balancing" strategy and relying on increased
strategic mobility and power projection might eliminate the tensions
caused by the presence of large U.S. forces in places like Okinawa. On the
other hand, a force posture of large, highly offensive forces based in the
continental United States would also provide less credible protection to
other states (thereby removing the pacifying effects of the current U.S.
presence), but it *would* still be seen as threatening by some other countries. It is entirely possible, therefore, that a radical restructuring of the
U.S. military posture could increase the degree to which other states saw
us as threatening and make it harder for the United States to attract allied
support.[71]

Foreign reactions to U.S. plans to develop missile defenses suggest that
this is not merely a theoretical possibility. Nuclear weapons are still the
"trump cards" of international politics, and a combination of missile defenses and large, highly accurate offensive forces would look a lot like a
first-strike capability to most other countries, especially those with small
and relatively primitive arsenals. Thus, if missile defense can be made to
work, it could give the United States the capacity to threaten other states
with impunity. At the very least, it would make it more difficult for poten-

---

[70] See Shambaugh, "China's Military Views the World," 57–62.

[71] For analyses advocating greater reliance on air-based or sea-based power projection capabilities, see Karl Mueller, "Flexible Power Projection for a Dynamic World: Exploiting the
Potential of Air Power," and Owen R. Coté Jr., "Buying . . . from the Sea": A Defense Budget
for a Maritime Strategy," both in *Holding the Line: U.S. Defense Alternatives for the Early 21st Century,* ed. Cindy Williams (Cambridge, Mass.: The MIT Press, 2001). Interestingly, neither
Mueller nor Cote discuss how other states are likely to react to their proposed alternatives.

tial adversaries to deter the use of U.S. conventional forces by threatening nuclear escalation. Thus, it is hardly surprising that Russia, China, and several U.S. allies view this initiative with misgivings.[72] And it does little good to declare that the system is intended only as a defense against limited attacks by so-called rogue states, because other states cannot be sure that the United States will not try to expand the system at some point in the future.[73]

For all of these reasons, other states are likely to be alarmed by U.S. efforts to build even a "limited" version of NMD. Although such a policy is unlikely to trigger an anti-U.S. alliance all by itself, it would certainly make such a development more likely.

Defend the Legitimacy of U.S. Preponderance

Balancing behavior will be less likely if foreign elites hold positive images of the United States, share similar outlooks on most global problems, and in general regard U.S. preponderance as benevolent, beneficial, and legitimate. Not surprisingly, other states seek to portray the U.S. position as unfair and illegitimate, both to raise doubts about U.S. motives and to convince each other that a more balanced world would be preferable. Thus, Chinese officials habitually warn about the dangers of U.S. "hegemonism," French elites complain about America's cultural impact, and

---

[72] As one Russian commentator puts it, "In the past ten years, the United States has enjoyed the position of being the only remaining world power. During this time, the idea of an overseas invasion in order to protect human rights and defend U.S. interests has gradually become an acceptable and even commonplace understanding among the American political and security elite. . . . [But] until recently, no member of the nuclear club has had to fear an external invasion. . . . Successful future deployment of a national missile defense could change this reality. . . . This is exactly the situation both Russia and China fear: an invasion to defend the independence of Georgia, or Taiwan, or to stop a 'genocide,' or whatever else the American president might take as evidence of a lack of 'peaceful intentions.' This is why the Russians fear missile defense." See Alexander Altounian, "Why Russians Fear Missile Defense," *Washington Post*, August 15, 2001, A19.

[73] Chinese and Russian officials have warned that U.S. development of NMD would force them to build additional weapons or develop countermeasures. The director-general for arms control at the Chinese Ministry of Foreign Affairs, Sha Zukang, summarized China's position by admitting that "to defeat your defenses we'll have to spend a lot of money . . . but otherwise the United States will feel it can attack anyone at any time, and that isn't tolerable." U.S. assurances that the system was limited to attacks by rogue states have been unpersuasive; in Sha's words, "How can we base our own national security on your assurances of good will?" See Eric Eckholm, "China Says U.S. Missile Shield Could Force a Nuclear Buildup," *The New York Times*, May 11, 2000, A1, A6. Chinese President Jiang Zemin recently reaffirmed this position, telling U.S. reporters that U.S. deployment of defenses would lead China "to increase our defense capability in keeping with the development of the international situation." See "In Jiang's Words: 'I Hope the Western World Can Understand China Better,'" *New York Times*, August 10, 2001, A8.

the Iraqi government seeks to portray the United States as a heartless great power that is indifferent to the human sufferings that its far-flung foreign policy imposes on weaker states.

In addition to the normal sorts of geopolitical competition, therefore, the United States must also defend the legitimacy of its own position. And this means being aware of how U.S. policy appears to other countries. The Bush administration may have been correct to reject the Kyoto protocol, for example, but it was a diplomatic gaffe for the world's wealthiest country (and the largest producer of greenhouse gases) to declare that it was renouncing the treaty because it "was not in [our] economic best interests."[74] Similarly, other states will rarely be persuaded when the United States justifies unpopular policies by declaring that U.S. national security is at stake, given that the United States is easily the most secure great power in modern history.[75]

In particular, the United States needs to improve its capacity to communicate effectively in the Arab and Islamic world. The hatred that provoked the September 11 attacks is partly a reaction to U.S. policy in the region—and especially its reflexive support for Israel—but it is also fueled by a combination of myths and accusations promoted by anti-U.S. groups and governments.[76] To overcome these misperceptions, the United States should launch a broad-based public information campaign in the region, using every instrument and channel at its disposal. In addition to preparing diplomats to engage with local media outlets like Al Jazeera (the Qatar-based news network that reaches some 35 million Arabs), the United States should also increase its own Arabic-language broadcasts and develop Arabic-language websites to reach the growing Internet-savvy populations in these countries.

Fortunately, the United States possesses formidable assets in this sort of ideational competition. Not only is English increasingly the lingua franca of science and international business, but the American university system is now a potent means of co-opting and socializing foreign elites.[77] Stu-

[74] Quoted in "EU: Disgust over Bush's Kyoto Decision," *Agence France Presse*, March 29, 2001.

[75] Thus, U.S. allies in Europe are skeptical of U.S. missile defense plans in part because they do not see the threat as particularly serious. See Philip H. Gordon, "Bush, Missile Defense, and the Atlantic Alliance," *Survival* 43, no. 1 (spring 2001): 23–25.

[76] For example, many Arabs believe (incorrectly) that U.S. sanctions are responsible for the deaths of thousands of Iraqi children, when the real cause is Saddam Hussein's refusal to use the UN "oil for food" program.

[77] There were nearly half a million foreign students at U.S. universities in 1997–98, while only 113,956 U.S. students were studying abroad. The disparity is even more striking when England is excluded; for example, there were 46,958 Chinese students and 47,073 Japanese students at U.S. universities in 1997–98, but only 2,116 and 2,285 American students in China and Japan respectively. See *Open Doors 1997–98* (New York: Institute for International Education, 1999).

dents studying in the United States become familiar with U.S. mores, while absorbing the prevailing U.S. attitudes about politics and economics.[78] Not all of them have positive experiences or end up adopting favorable attitudes toward the United States, but many of them do.

The effects of America's dominant role in global education are reinforced by the pervasiveness of U.S. mass media.[79] Although the shadow cast by American culture generates a hostile backlash on occasion, this element of America's "soft power" is probably a potent but relatively non-threatening weapon in the ideational struggle for the hearts and minds of foreign elites.[80]

Much of America's "soft power" rests on instruments and capabilities that are not (and should not be) subject to political control. "Cultural diplomacy" will be more effective when it is not part of an explicit propaganda campaign, and the socializing effects of being educated in the United States might vanish if the U.S. government tried to organize it for explicit purpose of co-optation. Nonetheless, the United States should probably consider ways to wage this war of legitimacy more effectively. One obvious strategy would be to adopt a more generous approach to foreign aid and other forms of financial assistance, although it would require a sea-change in public and congressional attitudes to implement such a policy.[81] And because we still know relatively little about how social and political values are transmitted from one country to another, the impact of (and proper role for) U.S. "soft power" is also a worthy topic for more sustained scholarly research.[82]

---

[78] This tendency will be especially pronounced in U.S. business schools and public policy programs, because each tends to emphasize the U.S. commitment to free markets and liberal institutions.

[79] The top twenty-five highest grossing films of all time are all American productions, even if one omits U.S. ticket sales and looks solely at foreign revenues. Based on figures downloaded from http://www.worldwideboxoffice.com on May 9, 2000.

[80] On "soft power," see Nye, *Bound to Lead*, and G. John Ikenberry and Charles A. Kupchan, "Socialization and Hegemonic Power," *International Organization* 44, no. 3 (summer 1990): 283–315.

[81] The United States spent approximately 1% of GDP on its nonmilitary international affairs budget in 1962, but spends only 0.2% of GDP today. These are not the budgetary allocations of a country that is really serious about how it conducts diplomacy. See Robert J. Lieber, "Three Propositions About America's World Role," in *Eagle Rules? Foreign Policy and American Primacy in the Twenty-First Century*, ed. Lieber (Upper Saddle River, N.J.: Prentice-Hall, 2001), 10.

[82] See Frank Ninkovich, *U.S. Information Policy and Cultural Diplomacy* (New York: Foreign Policy Association, 1994); Juliet Antunes Sablosky, "Reinvention, Reorganization, Retreat: American Cultural Diplomacy at Century's End, 1978–1998," *Journal of Arts Management, Law, and Society* 29, no. 1 (spring 1999): 30–46; and Neil M. Rosendorf, "Socio-cultural Globalization: Concepts, History, and America's Role," in *Governance in a Globalizing World*, ed. Joseph S. Nye and John Donahue (Washington, D.C.: Brookings Institution, 2000).

Conclusion

The formation of a cohesive anti-American coalition is not inevitable, and may not even be likely.[83] But the likelihood that some states will try to balance against us (even if only a rather tentative and tacit fashion) will increase if the United States acts in ways that threaten their interests. When such actions would reduce U.S. security or jeopardize its ability to pursue particular interests, it behooves Americans to search for policies that could override or dampen these tendencies. In the preceding pages, I have tried to sketch what some of these policies could be.

In general, I have argued that a policy of self-restraint is most likely to keep the rest of the world "off-balance" and minimize the opposition that the United States will face in the future. The central theme of the recommendations set forth above is the need to make reassurance a constant concern of U.S. foreign policy. Throughout the Cold War, the United States repeatedly sought to remind its allies that its commitment to them was credible. To do this, the United States deployed military forces on foreign territory, conducted joint military exercises, sent top officials on innumerable visits, and made verbal commitments in hundreds of public speeches. Now that the Cold War is over and the United States is essentially unchecked, U.S. leaders have to make a similar effort to convince other states of their good will, good judgment, and sense of restraint. And U.S. leaders cannot just say it once and then act as they please: reassuring gestures have to be repeated and reassuring statements have to be reiterated. Needless to say, the more consistent its words and deeds, the more effective U.S. pledges are likely to be.

Unfortunately, it is hard to be optimistic about America's ability to implement such a strategy. Great power may or may not corrupt, but it certainly tempts; and self-restraint is not a cardinal U.S. virtue. Moreover, by requiring the United States to become even more actively engaged around the world, and especially in the Middle East and Central Asia, the current campaign against terrorism is likely to reinforce the fears and resentments that gave rise to Al Qaeda in the first place. The longer this effort takes, and more it requires the United States to interfere in other countries' business, the greater the chance of a hostile backlash later on. Thus, even if the current distribution of power calls for a policy of self-restraint, one suspects that the United States will end up meddling more than it should, building more than it should, and probably building the

[83] Here I differ from Christopher Layne, "The Unipolar Illusion: Why New Great Powers Will Rise," *International Security* 17, no. 4 (spring 1993): 5–51.

wrong sorts of weapons. The Bush administration's first year in office does not afford much grounds for optimism, given their repeated insensitivity to the opinions of others and their willingness to chart a solo course on a range of different issues.[84] The administration appeared to be doing better in the immediate aftermath of the September 11 attacks, but it has reverted to its earlier unilateralism now that the initial challenge has been met.[85]

Even so, we should keep this warning in perspective. The United States *is* the most secure great power in history, and most states would be delighted to exchange their position for ours. Geography, history, and good fortune have conspired to give the United States a remarkable array of advantages and retaining those advantages does not require the genius of a Bismarck (or even a Kissinger). At a minimum, Americans can be grateful for that. But the United States still has an interest in retaining the good wishes of most other countries, if only because its ability to accomplish positive ends will decline if other states are resentful or fearful, and if they are looking for opportunities to throw dust in Uncle Sam's eyes. And if the United States ends up hastening the demise of its existing alliances and creating new ones that are opposed to it, we will have only ourselves to blame.

---

[84] According to Theo Sommer, former editor of *Die Zeit,* "[Bush] offers everyone consultations, partners and rivals alike; he promises to keep in touch; that is why he assures everyone, you cannot talk about an American go-it-alone attitude. Yet the conversations are aimed at conversion, not compromise." Quoted in Thom Shanker, "White House Says the U.S. Is Not a Loner, Just Choosy," *New York Times,* July 31, 2001, A1, A10.

[85] For a skeptical forecast on this point, see Steven E. Miller, "The End of Unilateralism? Or Unilateralism Redux?" *Washington Quarterly* 25, no. 1 (winter 2001–2): 15–29. Or as Republican foreign policy advisor Richard Perle told an international conference of defense officials in February 2002, "Never has the United States been more unified, never has it been more purposeful, never has it been more willing, if necessary, to act alone." Quoted in Colleen Barry, "U.S. Allies Express Reservations in Face of Washington's Resolve to Broaden War on Terrorism," *AP Online,* February 3, 2002.

5

Defying History and Theory: The United States as the "Last Remaining Superpower"

Josef Joffe

A hegemonial power may be defined in two parts. First, it should be able to defy all challengers, whether they come singly or in combination. Rome was such a power, Britain was not because it had to fight its major wars with the help of others. But in a nuclear setting, superior deterrent/defensive capabilities are not enough. For any nation with a second-strike force can deter each and all. Though Russia and China, Britain and France possess that distinction, they are not hegemonial powers.

So there is a second condition. A hegemon must also enjoy a surplus of usable, not just deterrent, power. Its interests and its influence must extend throughout the entire system; its sway over critical outcomes—strategic, diplomatic, economic—must exceed the capabilities of its rivals by a comfortable margin. A hegemon must wield large positive, not just negative, power.

By that measure, only the United States is a hegemonic power, and uniquely so. Of all former greats, only Rome fits the description although, for precision's sake, it should be classified as an empire. For at the height of its power, after it had subjugated the lands between the British Isles, Carthage, and the Levant, Rome was virtually coterminous with the then-international system itself. Its successors—the Papacy or the Holy Roman Empire, Habsburg Spain or the France of Louis XIV, nineteenth-century Britain or twentieth-century Germany—were only would-be hegemons. True, the sun never set on Charles V's empire, Britain ruled the waves in the nineteenth century, and Nazi Germany went all the way to the gates of Moscow and Cairo. But they were vulnerable to combinations of other powers that prevailed over them in the end. Nor was Britain a real exception. To uphold its exalted position, it depended on allies—all the way to World War II when it was almost done in by a single foe, Nazi Germany.

America is unique in time and space. Others might be able to defy the United States, but they can neither compel nor vanquish it—except in the meaningless sense of nuclear devastation that will be mutual. The sweep of its interests, the weight of its resources, and the margin of its usable power are unprecedented. None other than Hubert Védrine, the French foreign minister, has made the point in all its glory—though grudgingly, one must assume. "The United States of America," he proclaimed, "today predominates on the economic, monetary [and] technological level, and in the cultural area. . . . In terms of power and influence, it is not comparable to anything known in modern history." In short, the United States is a *hyper-puissance*, a "hyper-power."

History and theory suggest that this cannot last. Power will always beget power, and inordinate power will provoke inordinate internal effort among the lesser players and/or combinations among them. Why hasn't it done so already, given that America became the "last remaining superpower" at the turn of the 1990s? Several answers are possible.

One argument against the classical-realist prediction—that balancing shall prevail—comes in a number of guises, such as liberal institutionalism, "complex interdependence," or constructivism. These are modern-day versions of older creeds: Kantian liberalism in the eighteenth, Angellian trade optimism in the late nineteenth, and international legalism in the early twentieth century, as embodied in the League of Nations. All of them would explain the "dog that did not bark in the night" by way of transcendence.

In explaining why balancing has not "kicked in" against the United States, antirealist theory would claim that the system is *not* destiny; structure qua distribution of power cannot explain behavior, at least not in our day and age. Other forces are said to drive the actions of state. Rules and norms, democratic culture and economic interaction have dethroned "structure" as the ultimate arbiter of international politics. Hence the puzzle of this book—"why has counterbalancing not yet set in?"—is said to be no puzzle at all. It is simply the wrong question.

Arguments from transcendence have not worked very well in the previous three centuries. Indeed, since dawning of the Democratic Age (1776 in America, 1789 in France), "power politics," as the older realist moniker had it, was alive and well while balancing has ranged from coalition building to global war. But that does not dispense with the inductionist fallacy: there is no immutability in regularity. So neoliberal theory certainly has a prima facie point: balancing against the United States has *not* set in; nor is the serious kind—alliances, let alone war—visible on the horizon of political reality. Why not?

History, the first cousin of international relations, provides a second possible answer to the puzzle: balancing takes time to ripen. Sometimes it happens very quickly; by 1792, much of Europe had taken up arms against the three-year-old French Revolution, and by 1815, Europe's would-be ruler Napoleon was vanquished. In the case of Stalin's Russia, the *renversement des alliances* crystallized within a year of Nazi Germany's defeat in 1945. These were instances of a very rapid response. But other "reaction-formations" took much longer.

In the case of the Third Reich, concerted, system-wide balancing kicked in only nine years after Hitler's accession and rapid rush to rearmament; the defining moment was America's entry into World War II in December 1941 (and then only because it was attacked by Japan first, with Hitler declaring war a few days later). Bismarck's Germany enjoyed a much longer break. After its unification in 1871, Germany was undoubtedly the premier power on the continent. But only at the beginning of the twentieth century did it begin to face formalized, multistate opposition, when France, Russia, and Britain coalesced in the Entente of 1907.[1] Antihegemonial war, that is, World War I, did not break out until 1914, forty-three years after the Second Reich's rise to regional preeminence.

What about Britain, the nation that comes closest to hegemony *à l'américaine?* Arguably, Britain *never* inspired the massive balancing that undid Europe's hegemonic pretenders from Habsburg to Soviet Russia. True, Britain faced a succession of challengers plus their cohorts: Spain, Holland, France, Russia (in Central Asia), Wilhelmine and Hitlerian Germany. But a determined coalition of major powers that would lay low Britannia? In fact, the pattern went the other way. Britain was always the balancer, not the "balancee," to coin a phrase.

History and Hegemony: Models for the United States

History suggests that the United States may not be such an extraordinary exception to the realist rule. The curious cases of Britain and Bismarck

[1] More informal balancing, especially by Russia, can be traced back to 1890 when post-Bismarck Germany refused to renew the vaunted "Reinsurance Treaty" by which Berlin pledged to remain neutral in case of unprovoked Austrian aggression against St. Petersburg.

Germany, both of which detained at least partial primacy—maritime or continental—shift the inquiry from structure and second-image analysis to the third answer: state behavior. Does the career of these two powers—which enjoyed a long, or in the German case, longish run against fate—deliver some insights pertaining to twenty-first-century America? Or does the "last remaining superpower" defy historical comparison?

Not quite. To be sure, America's hegemonial dimensions dwarf those of Britain and post-1871 Germany. But there is a basic structural similarity. Like them, the United States possesses primacy, but not supremacy, a condition that would allow it to impose its will everywhere and every time. The difference between primacy/hegemony and supremacy is the presence or absence of worthy competitors. Britain and Germany faced plenty of them: France, Austria, Russia, Japan, and eventually America. So does the United States today. There is the EU—with two nuclear powers and an economy cum population larger than America's. Minus its Soviet empire, Russia still stretches across ten time zones while retaining an overkill nuclear arsenal. Japan has the world's second-largest economy, and nuclear-armed China boasts the world's largest population. India, second in population, looms as could-be competitor down the road.

Yet they are not ganging up on the United States. If behavior might be a key to the puzzle, we must ask: what distinguishes America's—as well as Britain's and Bismarck's—grand strategy from the course of those who *were* brought down by countervailing coalitions? To begin, one should define the "positional logic" of a hegemon. An actor like the United States, who exceeds all the others in terms of invulnerability and influence, should want to secure a structure of power that perpetuates its exalted position. The "last remaining superpower" should strive to remain precisely that.

How? This hegemon has only three choices. Choices one and two are merely theoretical; only three appears practicable. The first might be supremacy. Yet that ambition would stultify even a Behemoth like twenty-first-century America. Even a more modest variant of the supremacy gambit—keeping rivals from rising to the top—would defy contemporary realities. For "keeping the others down" ultimately implies preventive war, a very costly, if not suicidal approach in an age of second-strike capabilities.

The second choice would be the opposite of the first. A near-autarkic power, the United States could retreat into nuclear-armed isolation. This is equally unpromising because the United States would have to let go of those vital interests that transcend physical safety, renouncing its stake in order beyond borders. But once the United States had emerged from its nineteenth-century cocoon, it has reflexively stressed "milieu goals" over "possession goals," defining its well-being in terms of a compatible international environment—from the "Open Door" via the Fourteen Points and the Atlantic Charter to making Europe "whole and free again."

That leaves only the third choice: keeping players two, three, four . . . from ganging up against number one—from undermining its interests and vitiating its preferences. The "categorical imperative" is this: "Act in such a way as to keep others from joining forces to balance or best you." Conceptually, the quest is for position rather than possession. Operationally, it breaks down into two variants, which could be labeled "Britain" (3a) and "Bismarck" (3b).

Turning from abstract structural logic to the hurly-burly of history, how do these nineteenth-century models relate to twenty-first-century America? Briefly, Britain's strategy was to capitalize on the great advantage of insularity—to stay aloof from the quarrels of Europe, when possible, and to intervene, usually with others, against the would-be hegemonist of the day, when necessary. The game was to reduce the reasons for ganging up by pursuing extracontinental interests or to break up the gang when it formed nonetheless.

Bismarck's grand strategy was at the opposite extreme: not intermittent intervention, but permanent entanglement. To banish the "nightmare of coalitions" (Bismarck's term for "ganging up"), the "Iron Chancellor" sought to cement better relations with all contenders than they might establish among themselves. As long as all these relationships converged in Berlin like spokes in a hub, Germany would be the manager, not the victim of European diplomacy. Consciously or not, the United States has adopted a grand strategy that is a bit of "Britain" and a good deal more of "Bismarck."[2]

Balancing à la Britain

Henry VIII was the first to render his country's grand strategy explicit with the maxim *Cui adhaero praeest*—"prevail will those whom I support." By 1577, Elizabeth I was the "Umpire betwixt the Spaniards, the French, and the Estates," wrote an admiring chronicler. "France and Spain are . . . the Scales in the Balance of Europe, and England the Tongue or the Holder of the Balance."[3]

In Winston Churchill's words: "For four hundred years the foreign policy of England has been to oppose the strongest, most aggressive, most

---

[2] For an elaboration of the following, see my " 'Bismarck' or 'Britain'? Toward an American Grand Strategy after Bipolarity," *International Security* 19, no. 4 (spring 1995): 94–117.

[3] William Camden, *The History of the Most Renowned and Victorious Princess Elizabeth*, 4th ed. (London: M. Flesher, 1688), 233.

182

dominating Power on the Continent. . . . Faced by Philip II of Spain, against Louis XIV under William III and Marlborough, against Napoleon, against William II of Germany, it would have been easy . . . to join with the strongest and share the fruits of his conquest. However, we always took the harder course, joined with the less strong Powers, made a combination among them, and thus defeated and frustrated the Continental military tyrant."[4]

This is the traditional, if also idealized, rendition of British grand strategy. In the great European struggles for hegemony, Britain engineered those continental coalitions that stopped the Habsburgs and the Hitlers. It would fight with and against France, the Netherlands, Austria and Prussia-Germany. The basic principle was "antihegemonism without entanglement." In the words of Castlereagh: "When the Territorial Balance of Europe is disturbed," Britain "can interfere with effect. . . . We shall be found in our Place when actual danger menaces the System of Europe; but this Country cannot, and will not, act upon . . . Principles of Precaution."[5] And: "Our true policy has always been not to interfere except in great emergencies and then with a commanding force."[6]

Extraordinarily successful, this strategy secured Britain's status as the only global power for about three centuries. Until World War I, when Britain lost an entire generation in the trenches of Flanders, the strategy was also enormously economical. As Spain, France, Austria, and the Netherlands exhausted themselves in endless continental war, Britain played out the essential advantages of an island-based sea power.

Analogous to the United States, British geographic insularity granted it immunity from direct attack as long as the Royal Navy controlled its maritime moat. Mastery of the seas multiplied options and reduced costs. Compared to the expense of keeping and moving large armies, the dispatch of the fleet (in the U.S. case, add the carrier and air force) was not just cheaper. It allowed for speed, hence strategic surprise at points chosen by the attacker. Like America's at Midway, Britain's decisive battles were won at sea—against the Armada and at Trafalgar—and at far smaller cost than Napoleon's victory at Borodino.

[4] In a speech to the Conservative members of the Foreign Affairs Committee in March 1936. As reproduced in Winston S. Churchill, *The Gathering Storm*, vol. 1, *The Second World War* (Boston: Houghton Mifflin, 1948), 207–208.

[5] "Lord Castlereagh's Confidential State Paper of May 5, 1820," appendix A in A. W. Ward and G. P. Gooch, eds., *The Cambridge History of British Foreign Policy, 1783–1919* (New York: Macmillan, 1923), vol. 2 (1815–1866), 632. (For this quote, I am indebted to Henry A. Kissinger, *Diplomacy* [New York: Simon and Schuster, 1994], 88.)

[6] "Lord Bathurst to Lord Castlereagh, October 20, 1820," in *Correspondence, Despatches, and Other Papers of Viscount Castlereagh*, ed. Charles William Vane, marquess of Londonderry, vol. 12 (London: John Murray, 1853), 56.

The name of the game was balance, not conquest—at least in Europe. North America, India, and East Asia were other stories. Tipping the scales (exploiting "synergy") is cheaper than having to field the full range of countervailing power.

Even more economical than breaking up hostile coalitions ex post facto is to provide no incentives for "ganging up" ex ante. By withdrawing from the European system after victory, Britain routinely removed itself as a target. The no-conquest rule also reduced *future* costs by leaving no permanent enmities on the books. Unlike those "arch enemies" France and Germany, Britain could thus maximize alliance options for the next round. And so, Britain could always mastermind those superior coalitions that brought down the hegemonist *du jour.* This presaged American grand strategy in the two World Wars: wait out the trend, then intervene decisively on the side of the status quo.

Bismarck's "League of Peace"

The opposite paradigm, and one more apropos for present-day America, was designed by Bismarck after Germany's unification in 1871. This new player was now the mightiest actor on the continental stage—akin to the U.S. globally. "What had become clear to Europe was that primacy had passed from France to Germany," notes the British historian John A. Grenville, and he quotes Disraeli to make the point: "You have a new world. . . . The balance of power has been entirely destroyed."[7] But precisely for that reason, the Second Reich was also the most vulnerable player in the great-power game.

Isolation à la Britain was impossible for Germany, encircled as it was by four great powers, one of which, France, permanently plotted *revanche.* Bismarck's enduring problem was Frederick the Great's "cauchemar des coalitions" on a grander scale. Germany could best any challenger, but not fend off all at once. The solution to this existential problem was limned in Bismarck's fabled Kissinger Diktat. It was the creation of a "universal political situation in which all the powers except France need us and, by dint of their mutual relations, are kept as much as possible from forming coalitions against us."[8] Bismarck's metaphor for the Second Reich was the "Bleigewicht am Stehaufmännchen Europa," the dead weight in

---

[7] *Europe Reshaped, 1848–1878* (Hassocks: Harvester Press, 1976), 358.
[8] The Diktat ("dictation") was formulated in Bismarck's summer retreat Bad Kissingen on June 15, 1877. In Johannes Lepsius et al., eds., *Die Grosse Politik der Europaischen Kabinette,* vol. 2, *Der Berliner Kongress, seine Voraussetzungen und Nachwirkungen, 1871–1877* (Berlin: Deutsche Verlagsgesellschaft fur Politik und Geschichte, 1924), 154.

the tumbler doll that was Europe. The simile implied that Germany had to manage Europe's fragile equilibrium from the center. Berlin had to neutralize the forces that drove Russia and Austria toward collision in the Balkans, that threatened to embroil Britain and Russia in the arc of crisis running from Turkey to Afghanistan, and that might tempt either of the three to look for French help.

How to generate the "dead weight?" For a few years, Bismarck tried going it alone *à l'anglaise*. But when he realized that Germany lacked both gravity and invulnerability, Bismarck contracted a lasting case of pactomania. The centerpiece was the Dual Alliance with Austria (1879) against Russia. Two years later, that axis was embedded in a revived Three Emperors' League with Russia, where each pledged benevolent neutrality to the others in a war with a fourth power, that is, France. Thus, Bismarck added the "Saburov Rule" to the "Kissinger Diktat." "All politics," he told the Russian ambassador in Berlin, "can be reduced to this formula: Try to be in a threesome as long as the world is governed by the precarious equilibrium of five great powers. That is the true protection against coalitions."[9]

By 1883, Bismarck's alliances covered half of Europe, including Serbia, Rumania, and Italy. Finally, after the Three Emperors League had collapsed under the weight of Austro-Russian rivalries in the Balkans, Bismarck struck a secret deal with the tsar: the legendary Reinsurance Treaty of 1887. In it, each pledged benevolent neutrality in case the other was attacked by its main foe—Germany by France, Russia by Austria.

What was the purpose of these contradictory, indeed, mendacious commitments? Bismarck did not construct his system in order to aggregate power, but to *devalue* it—balancing and stalemating *à la* Britain, but in totally un-British ways. He dreaded the marriage of Germany's flanking powers. And so this intricate web would preserve Germany's position by making hostile coalitions—indeed, war itself—impossible. If all but France were bound to Berlin, if none could move without being tripped by that net, each would stay in place—and with this arrangement came stability for the European status quo so profoundly destabilized by the enormous, but not supreme power of the Second Reich.

The Grand Strategy of Hubs and Spokes

Recalling these two historical models helps to limn an answer to why the United States remains in the cozy position of an unchallenged number

---

[9] Quoted in William Langer, *European Alliances and Alignments, 1871–1890* (New York: Alfred E. Knopf, 1956), 199.

one. America is bit like Britain and a lot like Bismarck's Germany—but on a global scale and with far more clout than either. To Britain's insularity and superior navy, the United States has added an unmatched air force and the greatest deterrent of them all: nuclear weapons. Though virtually neutralized as a weapon of the offense, this revolutionary technology has unhinged one mechanism of the balance of power. Nuclear weapons cannot be aggregated like the armies of yore.

Even if Russia, China et al. coalesced, the United States could still deter them as long as it can inflict unacceptable damage on each and all. In the conventional arena, numbers mattered; on the nuclear chessboard, it is the speed, reach, and invulnerability of retaliatory weapons and C³I systems. Ganging up in the nuclear age does not threaten America's core security. Indeed, because they can deter all comers, nuclear weapons are an isolationist's dream.[10] Nuclear weapons explain in realist-structuralist terms why the classical balance-of-power has not kicked in against the United States: it does not and cannot work, at least not in an existential way.

But unlike yesterday's Britain, the United States no longer has the isolationist option. Britain was not really part of the European great-power system; by pursuing overseas expansion, Britain rarely offered a target for countervailing alliances on the continent.[11] Contemporary America is more like Bismarck's Germany writ large. Its interests and its presence span the globe; the United States is always in harm's way. Nor can the United States rely on the other great powers to stalemate each other (how would the EU balance China?). Hence there is little opportunity for synergistic intervention at the margin.

The United States plays the British game only regionally—when it masterminds a coalition against Saddam Hussein in 1990 or the Afghan Taliban regime in 2001. Or when it tips the scales in favor of NATO's intervention against the Serbs in the War of the Yugoslav Succession—first in Bosnia in 1995 and then in the Kosovo in 1999. Like Britain, the United

[10] See the seminal contribution by Kenneth N. Waltz, *The Spread of Nuclear Weapons: More May Be Better*, Adelphi Papers No. 171 (London: International Institute for Strategic Studies, 1981). Robert W. Tucker has written that nuclear weapons "give substance to the long-discredited isolationist dream. So long as it is clear that they will be employed only in the direct defense of the homeland, they confer a physical security that is virtually complete, and that the loss of allies cannot alter." "Containment and the Search for Alternatives: A Critique," in *Beyond Containment*, ed. Aaron Wildavsky (San Francisco: Institute for Contemporary Studies Press, 1983), 81.

[11] One significant exception is the Seven Years War (1756–1763), which began as the "French and Indian Wars" in North America. Once it had broken out, both Britain and France began to cast about for allies in Europe. Thus, a war on the periphery deteriorated into an all-European melee at the center.

States tries to minimize itself as a target by staying offshore as an over-the-horizon presence in the Western Pacific and the Mediterranean. Where the United States does commit ground forces, their presence is accepted as legitimate—as in Japan, South Korea, and Western Europe. A critical exception to this rule was a contingent of six thousand U.S. troops in Saudi Arabia since the Gulf War. Interestingly, this was one of the ostensible reasons for the attack of the bin Laden terror network against New York and Washington in 2001. But the global game is essentially a Bismarckian one, and that may be one explanation for the "dog that did not bark in the night." Recall the Kissinger Diktat. The task was to create a system "in which all the powers except France need us and . . . are kept as much as possible from forming coalitions against us." The fitting metaphor is that of hub and spokes. The hub is Washington, and the spokes are Western Europe plus the NATO newcomers in Eastern Europe, Japan, China, Russia, and the Middle East. In the aftermath of the war in Afghanistan, India has become a candidate-member of the system. For all their antagonisms against the United States, the "spokes' " relationships with the "hub" are as yet more important to them than their ties to one another. Let us examine each spoke separately.

The Far East

In the Pacific, the United States has fought wars against Japan, North Korea/China, and North Vietnam (supported by the Soviet Union). Yet today, the United States has better relations with Russia, China, Japan, and South Korea (and of course Taiwan) than these states have with one another. Lesser states like Thailand would rather huddle under the American umbrella than be exposed to the larger Pacific powers. That might also become true for America's former nemesis, Vietnam, which moved a bit closer toward the American orbit when Bill Clinton became the first American president to visit the country in November 2000.

Though China and Russia are always touting their "strategic partnership," as first announced in 1997, both covertly look to the United States as an implicit ally against each other. At any rate, their "strategic partnership" fails to translate into anything tangible, let alone into an alliance. All of Asia counts on the U.S. security guarantee to keep Japan from converting its economic riches into military prowess. And though each has played its own game with North Korea, China and Russia have been quite content to let the United States carry the burden of constraining Pyongyang's nuclear ambitions.

All of this may change if the two Koreas unify. At that point, the ostensible reason for the American military presence in the South (protection against the North) will fall away. Reunified Korea might ask the United States to leave. On the other hand, this has not happened in reunited Germany, even though the strategic threat from the East faded a decade ago. Germany likes to keep a diminished U.S. force on its soil (about 75,000) for at least two reasons. One, the United States keeps underwriting NATO as an *Atlantic* alliance—a useful beast to have around in case of Russia's resurgence or another war in the Balkans. Second, this presence still helps to shorten the shadow of German power, thus reassuring everybody else in Europe. As foreign minister Fischer put it, the withdrawal of the U.S. force might open a "security gap," Europe might then be forced into a role that it would neither be able nor willing to assume.[12] Korea might be animated by analogous calculations.

The Middle East

In the most labile region of the World, the United States inserted its spoke forty years ago by ending the imperial careers of Britain and France during the Suez War of 1956. Now everybody but Iraq and Iran looks to Washington to help sort out their ancient quarrels. While the United States dispenses side-payments in the form of economic and military aid to its various clients, it tacitly guarantees everybody's security against everybody else. As its revolutionary fervor wanes, Iran might rediscover the traditional geopolitical interests that underwrote the shah's alliance with the United States. Indeed, situated between a Russian colossus in the north and a revisionist Iraq to the south, Iran's natural extraregional partner is America.

When the PLO and Jordan made peace with Israel in the mid-1990s, the signing took place in the Rose Garden of the White House. In its quest for statehood, the PLO has sidled up to the United States in order to gain leverage against Israel. When a crisis threatens to get out of hand, as did Intifada II beginning in 2000, both Israelis and Palestinians take their complaints to Washington, hoping to have Mr. Big exact concessions that neither could extract on its own. When local culprits like Iraq needs chastening, the United States takes the lead, as it did in 1990, or again in 2002. Bismarck could not even have dreamt of such a successful hub-and-spokes operation in nineteenth-century Europe.

The point is again a realist one. It is structure qua power that allows the

[12] Address to NATO's Parliamentary Assembly in Berlin, November 18, 2000, as reported in "U.S. Troops Are Indispensable," *Welt am Sonntag*, November 19, 2000, 2.

United States to play this game so successfully. It isn't just America's good offices that draw key regional players to the Washington "hub." If it were, the EU would be so much more successful at gaining a foothold in the region. But it is only number one that can back up its mediation, as Bismarck could not at the Congress of Berlin in 1878, with tangible military guarantees and side-payments. Brokers must be not only "honest," but also muscular.

Europe

Western Europe has been linked to the Washington hub since 1945—if also for reasons that have lost their force since the end of the Cold War. Since De Gaulle, who came to power in 1958, France has pursued a half-hearted balancing strategy against the United States, trying to turn the EU into a competitive orbit. The game always falls short of real rivalry. Britain, Germany, Italy, even France need the United States as security lender of last resort—as balancer against a resurgent Russia as well as against each other. It is quite useful to have an extracontinental player in the game who is bigger than each and all, but also more of an elephant than a *Tyrannosaurus rex*. Also, Europe is a very long way from an *e pluribus unum* and thus not very good at producing "public goods" like security.

After three years of Europe's humiliation by the Serbs, it was American cruise missiles that sobered up Messrs. Karadzic and Milosevic. Ditto in the Kosovo engagement of 1999 when the European NATO members only took to the air after the United States had come around to leading the posse (and to offering most of the air power). Ditto during the antiterror war in the wake of the attack on September 11 when only the United States could have mustered the clout to harness a worldwide coalition against the culprits.

Stung by its impotence in the Balkan wars, Europe has decided on an intervention force of sixty thousand soldiers by 2003 that might operate independently of the United States in peace-keeping or police operations. Given the exigencies of training, rotation, and readiness, this force would actually have to grow by a factor of at least three. For effective autonomy, Europe would also have to acquire an additional triple capability: long-range (satellite-based) intelligence and assessment, long-range projection forces, long-range precision-munitions.

This task contends with declining post–Cold War defense budgets. But assume Europe puts its money where its mouth is. This leaves the EU with the biggest question of them all: would it *want* to intervene alone, that is, without a reinsurance policy underwritten by the U.S. cavalry, so to speak? In a setting that actually entailed peace *enforcement*, that is, real war fighting, sensible policymakers would want to have a Plan B with an American component. But if the United States is to be in on the crash, it would naturally want to be in on the takeoff. And so the tie must hold.

Post-Soviet Russia and Eastern Europe

After the self-dissolution of the Soviet Union in 1991, Washington managed to recruit Boris Yeltsin's Russia into its orbit, proffering the same option to his successor Vladimir Putin. It was George Bush who eased Moscow's fall from empire, while running interference for Helmut Kohl as he fumbled his way to reunification. It was Bill Clinton who defined the terms of Russia's association with the Western alliance, who controlled Russia's access to IMF funds (as Bismarck did when he closed the Berlin bourse to Russian bond sales in 1887). The United States also manned the gate through which Poland, Czechia, and Hungary could march into NATO.

Evidently, Russia will not want to play second-fiddle to the United States forever. But as Russia regains its former power, Europeans—especially the Poles, the easternmost members of NATO—will once more fully appreciate the value of the Atlantic security tie. For the first time ever, Warsaw now sees its future in an embrace of Germany, which can make or break its entry into the EU. But in terms of physical security, nothing can replace the United States in the minds of the Poles and other East Europeans. Whence it follows that the United States, to borrow from Secretary of State Madeleine Albright, remains the "indispensable" power in the European subsystem as long as the EU does not harness its enormous resources under a single will.

At any rate, the "hub" tends to have more options than the "spokes." This was illustrated by changing Russian grand strategy after the Twin Tower attack in 2001 when Moscow swiftly gravitated to the American side. Indeed, Putin's Russia then offered itself as the main strategic partner of the United States, delivering bases in Uzbekistan and Tadjikistan as well as precious intelligence to the U.S. while supplying the foes of the Taliban with arms and ammunition. Assuming that it endures, this shift from the outside to the inside of the great power club highlights the essential implication of the hub-and-spokes model: secondary powers would rather bandwagon with today's number one than balance against it.

The United States and the World: Different Beast, Different Jungle

America is an XXL Bismarck Reich—the indispensable impresario of all critical endeavors, and precisely for that reason not (yet) the object of encirclement. Nonetheless, let us pursue the analogy to the end and ask: why did Bismarck's "hub-and-spokes" system fail so miserably by century's end?

One classical answer is the stupidity of his successors and the hoary ambitions of Wilhelm II. A few months after Bismarck's dismissal, the Foreign Office's Paul Kayser remarked: "After a quarter of a century of genius, it is a real blessing to be able to be as homely and matter of fact as other governments."[13] Bismarck's heirs certainly lived up to that sigh of relief. The first blow against complexity was struck when the new regime refused to renew the Reinsurance Treaty with Russia because that secret compact conflicted with Germany's pledges to Austria. The new chancellor Leo von Caprivi was heard to confess that he simply could not keep several balls up in the air at once, as Bismarck had done.

A more profound answer was offered in Sir Eyre Crowe's famous Memorandum of 1907. There were two possible interpretations of German strategy. Either the Kaiser was reaching for hegemony—or "all her excursions and alarms, all her underhand intrigues do not contribute to . . . a well-conceived . . . system of policy." So what was it—hegemonial or haphazard? Intentions did not matter, Crowe concluded. The critical point was the relentless growth of German material power that would feed Germany's ambition, turning it into a "formidable menace to the rest of the world" even without "malice aforethought."[14] In other words, the system was destiny, and so Germany's growing power called for balance and containment—for "ganging up."

A third problem with Bismarck's hub and spokes was Germany's precarious position as "semihegemonial power": strong enough to hold off each, but not all. To keep all spokes centered on Berlin required a strong and invulnerable hub—real hegemony. Without that strength, Germany could not keep these rods in place forever. Russia was encroaching on Austria in the Balkans. France, hungering to undo the defeat of 1871, was determined to break the entire wheel. Thus an alliance between Russia and France, the two revisionists, was an ever-present threat. And materialize it did—not the least because the manager became Europe's main problem when it began to grope for mastery after 1890.

What lesson does this analogy hold for the United States, the XXL version of the Bismarckian model? How does this number one remain in its present position? The answer requires a digression on some crucial differ-

---

[13] The head of the Colonial Section, as quoted by Walther Frank, "Der Geheime Rat Paul Kayser," *Historische Zeitschrift* 168 (1943): 320. Citation from Gordon A. Craig, *From Bismarck to Adenauer* (New York: Harper and Row, 1965), 21.

[14] For a lengthy exposition of the memorandum see Sybil Crowe and Edward Corp, *Our Ablest Public Servant: Sir Eyre Crowe, 1864–1925* (Braunton: Merlin Books, 1993), 110–19.

ences between the Reich and the United States. The United States is a
different beast, and so is the realm through which it roams.

America irks and domineers, but it does not conquer. It tries to call the
shots and bend the rules, but it does not go to war for land and glory. Indeed, the last time the United States actually did so was in the Philippines
and Cuba a hundred years ago. This is a critical departure from traditional great-power behavior. For the balance-of-power machinery to
crank up, it makes a difference whether the others face a usually placid
elephant or an aggressive T. rex. Rapacious powers are more likely to
trigger hostile coalitions than nations that contain themselves, so to
speak.

In the old days, counteralliances formed so rapidly because expansion
and war was the full-time job of the world's potentates. The contrast with
today is not a matter of superior American virtue, as a long string of interventions from Latin America to the Middle East amply confirms. The
stakes have changed.

Why doesn't the United States follow in the footsteps of Charles, Louis,
et al.? Setting aside war for strategic resources like oil and water in the
Middle East, or population wars as in Africa, what is the point of conquering land and people? Land in the developed world spells not riches, but
more agricultural surpluses and hence higher support payments and
taxes. Machiavelli thought it easier to acquire gold with good soldiers
than vice versa.[15] But as Saddam's soldiers found out in Kuwait City, the
money was gone—whisked away at the speed of a modem.

Population as such has also been devalued in the postagrarian, post-
"cannon-fodder" age. In the twenty-first-century economy, as in modern
war, sheer numbers count for less and less, and technological sophistication for more and more. But highly motivated specialists need not be subjugated; almost as mobile as capital, they go where the return on their skill
is highest, as tens of thousands of Indian, Chinese, Israeli, and European
computer scientists in Silicon Valley demonstrate. Information-driven
"modes of production" have separated profit from (territorial) possession. Invasion is not as lucrative as in eras past, and those who do not conquer do not provoke war.

Nor does a counteraggregation of power deal very well with the postmodern nature of power. Let's make no mistake about it. "Hard" power—
men and missiles, guns and ships—still counts. It remains the ultimate, existential currency of power. But on the day-to-day transaction level, "soft

---

[15] "For gold alone will not produce good soldiers, but good soldiers will always produce
gold." *The Prince and The Discourses* (New York: Modern Library, 1950), 310.

power" is the more interesting coinage.[16] It is "less coercive and less tangible." It grows out of "the attraction of one's ideas, with "agenda setting," with "ideology" and "institutions," and with holding out big prizes for cooperation, such as the vastness and sophistication of one's market.[17]

"Soft power" is cultural-economic power and very different from its military kin. The United States has the most sophisticated, though not the largest, forces in the world and this sophistication keeps growing by leaps and bounds, as the Afghan war demonstrated. But it is in a class of its own in the soft-power game. On that table, none of the others can match America's pile of chips—from McDonald's to Microsoft, from Hollywood to Harvard. This type of power—a culture that radiates outward and a market that draws inward—rests on pull, not on push; on acceptance, not on imposition. Nor do the many outweigh the one. In this arena, Europe, Japan, China, and Russia cannot meaningfully gang up on the United States like in an alliance of yore. All of their movie studios together could not break Hollywood's hold because if size mattered, India, with the largest movie output in the world, would rule the roost. Nor could all their universities together dethrone Harvard and Stanford. For sheer numbers do not lure the best and the brightest from abroad who keep adding to the competitive advantage of America's top universities.

Against soft power, aggregation does not work. How does one contain power that flows not from coercion but seduction? Might it work in the economic sphere? There is always the option of trading blocs cum protectionism. But would Europe (or China or Japan) forego the American market for the Russian one? Or would Europe seek solace in its vast internal market alone? If so, it would forgo the competitive pressures and the diffusion of technology that global markets provide. The future is mapped out by Daimler Chrysler, not by a latter-day "European Co-Prosperity Sphere."

This is where the game has changed most profoundly. The old game of nations was, in the end, zero sum: My gains are your losses. But the new game is different. Not only do all win and lose together; that was true in 1914, too, when the great powers did march off into the trenches, though on many counts, they were even more interdependent or integrated than today. (Direct investments were higher as fraction of GDP.) Today, advanced nations worry less about another's disproportionate relative gains because the connection between strategy and economics has loosened.

In theory, the United States should worry greatly about China's

---

[16] The term was introduced by Joseph S. Nye in his *Bound to Lead: The Changing Nature of American Power* (New York: Basic Books, 1990).

[17] Ibid., 188, 31–32.

growth—as did Britain about Germany's at the turn of the nineteenth century. Yet instead of plotting preventive war, the United States accepts a $50 billion trade deficit with China, viewing it as a carrot that will recruit China to the status quo and allow welfare to trump warfare. Britain and Napoleonic France blockaded each other's trade because the strategic imperative dwarfed the economic one in their battle for sheer survival. Today, Europe and America inflict only mild tit-for-tat retaliation on each other because they are deadly afraid of destroying the global trading system. America's rivals would rather deal with the former's "soft power" by competition and imitation because the costs of economic warfare are too high—provided, of course, that strategic threats do not reemerge.

How does such an explanation relate to international relations theory? Is it a third-image/realist or a second-image/ neoliberal model? It is both, but structure qua distribution of power still matters most. The United States, though endowed with a surfeit of "soft power," could not play out its unique role unless ensconced at the apex of the hierarchy—with a vast margin of usable resources that help it to act as "hub" and enforcer of the rules. As in the domestic arena, rules and norms ultimately depend on order, hence on the pacifying impact of power.

And so, United States "soft power" cannot be divorced from its "hard power." Otherwise, the EU, blessed with a rich civilization and a U.S.–size economy, would be an equal in terms of global influence. Yet it is not because it must do without the ultima ratio. The spread of America's "soft power" across the globe cannot be explained apart from the country's victory in the Second World War and the Cold War. Second, this pacific currency of power trumps its more violent variants only where strategic threats are muted, if not moot. International terrorism, it should be noted, is not a *strategic* threat.

The same goes for other variables of second-image analysis. The new "modes of production"—the devaluation of territory, population, and mass manufacturing—certainly play a role in softening the classical balance-of-power game. And so does the expansion of the democratic and postnational realm. But these benign features depend on the stability that rests on a hierarchy of power and the absence of existential threats. Only where these threats have waned—as in the "Berlin-Berkeley Belt"—do postmodern and neoliberal values thrive. Yet where these threats persist, as in the Belgrade-Baghdad-Beijing Belt, regular spasms of violence have racked the Balkans, the Middle East, and Africa. In this segment, both democratic development and the logic of mutual gain remain victims of the Hobbesian calculus. At worst, the outcome is strife, at best, as in East Asia, it is a neoclassical balancing system where rising and status-quo powers vie for a new distribution of power, with war always lurking in the background.

The "no-conquest" rule informing American grand strategy is a second-image variable, too. As argued earlier, balances form more rapidly against a T. rex than against an elephant. In explaining the elephantine nature of U.S. behavior, neoliberal theory might fall back on the Kantian vision; it would postulate that liberal-democratic polities, of which the United States is the foremost exemplar, are inherently peaceful. But such an answer is at best only a partial one. From the "shores of Tripoli" in 1801 to the war against Al Qaeda in 2001, the United States has not exactly been a model of Kantian virtue—though it stopped conquering a hundred years ago. Why? Again, "hard power"—the stuff of realism—furnishes the rest of the answer. A nation stronger than each and all can dispense with force and wield other cudgels, be they economic or diplomatic. In general, those who have power need not inflict force; power is when it need not be used. So goodness flows from great power, too.

Balance and Power after Bipolarity

"Pourvu que ça dure," was the wary counsel of Napoleon's mother Laetitia. Bismarck's hub-and-spokes operation is hardly a reassuring precedent. He managed to keep Europe's number one out of encirclement for twenty years; then, the inexorable slide toward World War I began. Sooner or later, rivals *will* balance against number one. Why should America fare better than history and theory suggest?

Actually, balancing has already begun—though with an interesting new twist. Given the argument so far—why balancing against the U.S. has *not* materialized—this verdict seems to open up a vexing paradox. To crack it, it helps to distinguish between three different types of balancing: psycho-cultural, politico-diplomatic, and military-strategic—a distinction to which classical balance-of-power theory has paid no attention. Roughly, the first is high, the second is medium, the third is low to nil.[18] Why is this so, and what are the implications for U.S. grand strategy?

Psycho-Cultural Balancing

In Europe, but also elsewhere, this type comes in the guise of three indictments. First, America is morally retrograde. It executes its own people, and it likes to bomb others. It is the land of intolerant, fundamentalist re-

---

[18] For an elaboration, see Josef Joffe, "Who Is Afraid of Mr. Big?" *The National Interest* (summer 2001): 43–53.

ligion. The United States will not submit to the dictates of global goodness; it will not respect climate conventions, nor ratify the International Criminal Court or the Land Mine Ban. Internationally, it is "Dirty Harry" and "Globocop" rolled into one—an irresponsible and arrogant citizen of the global community.

Second, America is socially retrograde. It is the land of "predatory capitalism" (thus former German chancellor Helmut Schmidt) that denies critical social services, like health insurance, to those who need it most. Instead of bettering the lot of the poor and unskilled, mainly dark-skinned minorities, it shunts them off into prison. America accepts, nay admires, gross income inequalities whereas the rest of the civilized world cherishes the social justice that comes with redistribution. The United States lets its state school system rot, not to speak of the public infrastructure.

Third, America is culturally retrograde. It gorges itself on fatty fast food, wallows in tawdry mass entertainment, starves the arts and prays only to one God, which is Mammon. Instead of subsidizing the good and the high-minded, the United States ruthlessly sacrifices the best of culture to pap and pop. Its great universities (for the rich and well-connected only) conceal vast illiteracy and ignorance of the world. In matters sexual, America is both prurient and prudish.

America, in short, gets it both coming and going. It is puritanical and self-indulgent, Philistine and elitist, sanctimonious and crassly materialist. It is a society where solidarity and community, taste and manners are ground down by rampant individualism. Whatever the caricature's fidelity, there is deeper problem with such an indictment. Europe, indeed, most of the world, also wants what America is. Nobody has ever used a gun to drive Frenchmen into one of their 780 McDonald's. No force need be applied to make the rest of the world buy clothes or watch films "Made in U.S.A." The problem, in short, is America's gargantuan "soft power."

Hence, other governments must deploy the force of law to *stop* their citizens from imbibing all things American. This is where "cultural balancing" turns operative. In 1993, the French coaxed the EU into adding to its commercial treaties a "cultural exception" clause exempting cultural products, high or low, from normal free-trade rules. Other European nations impose informal quotas. The purpose is a balance-of-power policy of sorts. It is to contain American cultural clout—to build trade walls instead of real turrets and battlements. The enemy is not America the Conqueror, but America the Beguiling.

And seduction is subversion. America is not just number one in terms of strategic and soft power. It is also modernity's global engine. Like any revolution, this one, too, threatens old power, status, and entitlement structures. Unwritten social contracts that have upheld traditional notions of distributive justice are under attack from abroad, and "abroad" is "America"; hence the conflation of "globalization" with "Americanization." To catch up, Europe et al. have to become at least partly what America already is; no wonder that they dislike the idea as well as its purveyor. The natural "reaction-formation," as Professor Freud would pontificate, is to assert one's own moral-cultural superiority, holding it up against the depraved ways of America. Or to project one's angst about modernity's cruel progress on that vast canvas that is the United States.

Hence the psycho-cultural balancing against an America that is what Europe and Westernizing societies fear to become, but cannot totally avoid. The "enemy," against whom resistance is due, was described by a French foreign minister thus: an "ultraliberal market economy, rejection of the state, nonrepublican individualism, unthinking strengthening of the universal and 'indispensable' role of the USA, common law, *anglophonie*, Protestant rather than Catholic concepts."[19]

Political-Diplomatic Balancing

Save for such devices as the French-inspired "cultural exception" clause, there is no hard-and-fast counteraction against the Beguiler. The struggle against Temptress America is high on vocality, but low on penalties. In the political arena, the duel has more palpable repercussions. The problem is an obvious one. First, how to constrain an economy that seems to defy the usual strictures of the international market—why else would the dollar rise in tandem with exploding trade deficits? Second, how to contain an America that dominates the diplomatic field from Pyongyang to Jerusalem, from the WTO to the IMF, from the heavens above (where it is working on missile defense) to the grounds below (where it refuses adherence to the land mine ban)?

In the political realm, the demise of bipolarity did have consequences. With Cold War discipline gone, the Europeans can afford to balance against Mr. Big in ways that help their own farmers while hurting those of the United States (which is also no stranger to the "consumer protection" game). On weightier matters than GM foods and hormone beef, Europe's common currency makes a better case in point. Nary a politician or pundit has failed to stress the *political* rewards of monetary union, with the euro touted as bulwark and counterweight against the Almighty Dollar. Indeed, the language is straight out of the balance-of-power vocabulary.

[19] Hubert Védrine, as quoted in Tony Judt, "The French Difference," *New York Review of Books*, April 12, 2001, 19.

Turning into a coequal reserve currency and unit-of-account, the argument goes, the euro will impose discipline on America's profligate ways by curbing its power to issue debt in its own currency. And so, the euro will bring about a bipolar or, along with the yen, tripolar system in the financial arena.

Politico-diplomatic balancing has kicked in against the United States long ago. Since the Gulf War, the EU has fitfully tried to insert itself into the Israeli-Palestinian peace process in order to break the U.S. monopoly on mediation. As the United States tries to hang on to the "dual containment" of Iran and Iraq, the EU has insisted on a "cultural dialogue" with Tehran while ridiculing George W. Bush's "axis of evil" terminology and warning him stridently not to go to war against Iraq. To curtail U.S. influence in the region, the French have opened separate diplomatic channels to Baghdad and Tehran, escalating the competition against the United States in 2001 when they openly condemned the Anglo-American bombing of Iraq.

With his counterpart Vladimir Putin at his side, French president Jacques Chirac has castigated American missile defense plans while in Moscow. Diplomatic balancing can also involve doing nothing at critical moments. When the Bush administration was caught in a terse standoff with China over its crippled spy plane held on Hainan Island in April 2001, its European allies reacted with deafening silence. Such parries belong into the category of "subcritical balancing" for they fall far short of formal counteraggregations of power. So do the routine invocations of "strategic partnership" between Moscow and Beijing, which entail neither partnership nor strategic consequences.

More interesting (and novel) is the indirect, nay, unconscious "ganging up" against number one. Their common denominator is the attempt to constrain American power within universal or at least regional control regimes. One example is the European, Russian, and Chinese opposition to missile defense. The message to the United States is: "You must adhere to time-honored arms control regimes as embodied in the ABM Treaty." Yet the purpose, perfectly logical from a balancing perspective, is to suppress a quantum leap in what is seen as excessive American power. Assume that missile defense really works. In that case, it will not only devalue the strategic arsenals of the lesser players. It will also add to America's "proactive" power by enhancing its escalation dominance. If the United States could really shield itself, it could inhibit Chinese sallies against Taiwan or intervene against any "rogue state" with little risk to itself. That would grant a nice margin of usable power to the United States, a prospect that does not assure the rest of the world.

Other examples are the Land Mine and the Comprehensive Test Ban treaties to which the United States refuses to adhere. Again, the lesser players correctly see America's waywardness in balance-of-power terms. Antipersonnel mines deliver a nice shield for power projection abroad while continued nuclear testing helps to build more sophisticated, say, subkiloton, warheads that might just be more usable. That, too, worries those who worry about unbridled American power.

Or take America's refusal to submit to climate conventions. Though the issue is framed in terms of global good citizenship, the underlying point is again untrammeled American power. The fear is that the United States will strengthen its economic position relative to the rest if it continues to take liberally from the global commons by refusing to limit its CO[cf15]2 output. Picking up on the bitter recriminations against the United States during the negotiations about the Kyoto climate protocol in The Hague in November 2000, the *Economist* noted: "Some European ministers made it clear that they wanted Americans to feel some economic pain more than they wanted a workable agreement."[20]

America's refusal to submit to the International Criminal Court also involves an unarticulated balancing game. For both sides, the issue is American power. Clearly, the United States does not want international bodies to pass judgment on its interventions by way of prosecuting malfeasants in its military ex post facto. Clearly, the Europeans see the ICC as yet another regime that might deter the use of force not sanctioned by international bodies such as the UN.

The general point is this: hegemonic powers are loath to submit to international regimes they do not dominate. Lesser powers like them precisely because they strengthen the many against the one. In a world that does not (yet) gang up formally against the "last remaining superpower," international regimes have become the functional equivalent of classical balance-of-power politics. Number one knows it, and so do numbers two, three, and four. Because this game is played by allies as well as nondeclared adversaries, it is high on implicit intent and low on explicit affirmation.

Strategic Balancing

Because America's existential sting is well-concealed or well-contained, "real" balancing against this hegemon falls short of the classic pattern; it is internal, illicit, or implicit. Internal balancing is what the Russians and Chinese do when they try to preserve (Moscow) or expand (Beijing) their military panoplies. Illicit balancing goes by the name of international ter-

---

[20] "Oh No, Kyoto," *The Economist*, April 7, 2001, 81.

ror. It is deployed against the United States more or less privately, as by
Saudi freelance bombardier bin Laden, or more or less officially, by those
Islamic countries suspected as sources of "state-sponsored terrorism." Im-
plicit balancing is what the EU does when it fields a rapid-reaction force
(RRF) under the umbrella of its European Defense and Security Policy
(ESDP).

The label "implicit" is deliberately chosen. For its purpose is not to
countervail the United States in the ways of a classic alliance. The size of
the RRF is as modest as its objective. The latter was laid down in the "Pe-
tersberg Tasks": policing rather than war-fighting, peace maintenance
rather than peace enforcement. These tasks dovetail realistically with the
RRF's compact size of sixty thousand (akin to the international total deployed in the Kosovo after the bombing in 1999).

Nonetheless, the European rhetoric on the RRF is shrouded in equivo-
cation. Atlanticist stalwarts like Britain and, to some extent, Germany talk
about a force-within-NATO. Usual suspects like France depict the RRF as
first step toward a full-fledged EU army. One French official, speaking
anonymously, has put it with Gallic acerbity: "The train [of an independent European defense policy] is already moving. NATO is not on board.
It is not the engine. It is not even in the tender or even in the passenger
compartment."[21] This is how Washington views the RRF. Hence, the three
D's issued as early as 1998: The ESDP must not *diminish* or *duplicate*
NATO, nor *discriminate* against non-EU NATO members.

Whatever the European rhetoric, the ESDP is a balancing mechanism *in
nuce.* The thrust is implicit rather than explicit. Its purpose is not to oppose the United States outright, but to enhance Europe's relative power
vis-à-vis the United States with an asset that might increase European autonomy and/or diminish U.S. preponderance. As such the RRF is a perfect example for "neo-ganging up." It unfolds *within*, not between alliances. It is not a duel here and now, but a down payment on the future.

Implications for U.S. Grand Strategy

Why, then, is there no "real" balancing against the American hegemon?
The short answer is twofold: America's surfeit of "soft," especially eco-

---

[21] For Richard, see Robert Locke, "France Fires Fresh Salvo at Britain over Euro Army,"
Sunday Times (London), December 10, 2000. For the anonymous French official, see Anton
LaGuardia, "America Tries to Stop EU Going It Alone on Defense," *Telegraph* (London), December 16, 2000. As quoted in Christopher Layne, "Death Knell for NATO? The Bush Administration Confronts the European Security and Defense Policy," *Policy Analysis* 394 (April
4, 2001): 3.

nomic, power can be contained only at enormous welfare costs to the containers, that is, by self-isolation. It can only be devalued—by superior competitive performance. America's hard power, on the other hand, need not be balanced in the traditional way because this peculiar hegemon behaves like an pachyderm rather than a T. rex. This beast inspires discomfort, not existential angst, pace Messrs. Saddam, Milosevic, and bin Laden.

This assessment may not be reassuring to others. After all, great power creates balancing incentives willy-nilly. An elephant, no matter how benign, is no pussycat. For America's rivals and friends, the critical issue is not the history or virtue of this beast, but its behavior. Setting aside those "rogue states" which have been the routine targets of American hard power, why should numbers two, three, four . . . want to remain willing participants in America's hub-and-spokes scheme?

Bismarck's prescription was: maintain a constellation "in which all the powers except France need us." But his creation failed in the end because it was so precarious. Battered by unyielding conflicts among the other great powers Bismarck could not control, it ultimately fell under the weight of Germany's soaring ambitions. Bismarck could only hope for a stalemate, and he had little else to invest in the game than manipulation, maneuver, and mendacity. His main assets were negative payoffs: stick to the status quo so as to avoid worse—great-power war. He was, in modern parlance, no institution builder; he did not engineer international structures that would give all the other players *positive* incentives to stay in the game.

This is where a critical difference between the United States and the Bismarckian Reich emerges, and with a crucial normative lesson to boot. In the second half of the twentieth century, America *was* an institution builder, as illustrated by a whole alphabet soup of acronyms: UN, IMF, GATT, OEEC/OECD, NATO, World Bank, WTO, PfP, plus a host of subsidiary Cold War alliances like ANZUS, SEATO, and CENTO. The United States bestrode the world as provider of public goods that cemented America while serving the needs of others. Previous hegemons were in business for themselves.

Whence it follows that numbers two, three, four . . . will prefer cooperation with number one to anti-American coalitions as long as the United States remains the foremost provider of global/regional public goods. The essence of public goods is that anybody can profit from them once they exist. That gives the lesser players a powerful incentive to maintain the existing order and to accord at least grudging acceptance to the purveyor of those benefits. Conversely, it diminishes their incentives to gang up on him. The current system does not abound with alternative powers that would uphold international security or financial stability.

While the others surely resent America's clout, they have also found it useful to have a player like the United States in the game. Europe and Japan regularly suffer from America's commercial hauteur, but they also suspect that the United States is the ultimate guarantor of the global free-trade system. Britain and France were only too happy to let American cruise missiles bludgeon the Serbs to the negotiating table. Ditto four years later in the Kosovo war. The Arabs hardly love the United States, but they did cooperate when George Bush mobilized an international posse against Saddam Hussein in 1990 because they could not contain him on their own. And so again in 2001 when Bush the Younger harnessed a worldwide coalition against terrorism.

When lesser powers cannot deter China in the Straits of Taiwan, or persuade North Korea to denuclearize, it is nice to have one special actor in the system who has the will and the wherewithal to do what others wish, but cannot achieve on their own. Indeed, he is indispensable. In the language of public-goods theory: there must always be somebody who will recruit individual producers, organize the startup, and generally assume a disproportionate burden in the enterprise. That is as true in international affairs as it is in grassroots politics.

Charles, Philip, et al. sought to conquer; the United States has built institutions, which is another word for "public goods"—that is the difference. Even brilliant statesmen like Bismarck or Disraeli never thought much beyond Germany or Britain; Bismarck's purpose was not to do good for Europe, but for Germany. Nor did he devise systems that would transcend the narrow purpose of stalemating power for the benefit of the country in the middle. But the genius of American diplomacy in the second half of the twentieth century was building institutions—structures that would advance American interests by serving those of others.

Why pay the bill? By providing security for others—in Europe, the Middle East, and the Pacific—the United States has also bought security for itself. Stability is its own reward because it prevents worse: arms races, nuclear proliferation, conflicts that spread. Enlarging NATO, though costly to the American taxpayer, brings profits to both Poland and the United States because anything that secures the realm of liberal democracy benefits its leading representative. Shoring up the World Trade Organization (WTO), even when it pronounces against Washington, is still good for America because, as the world's largest exporter, it has the greatest interest in freer trade.

Are the costs of "public goods" production intolerable? The problem is that the bulk of the world's great institutions was built during the Cold War—when it was clearly in the interest of number one to shoulder the burden and sign the checks. Since then, it is no longer so clear that the

United States puts more resources into international institutions than it seeks to draw from them. America's old penchant for free trade is now diluted by preferences for "managed trade," which is a euphemism for regulated trade.

If it cannot achieve consensus, the United States will act unilaterally, as with the Helms-Burton sanctions bill (directed against non-American investments in Cuba or Iran), or bilaterally, as with Britain in the low-level bombing war against Iraq. If Congress does not like certain UN policies, it will withhold membership dues. If the United States sees a promise in "Star Wars, Mark II," it will withdraw unilaterally from existing arms control treaties. In 1990, Bush the elder diligently harnessed a coalition against Iraq; in 2002, Bush the younger went into the same arena with the message: follow or not, the United States will act. The risk is evident: as the United States diminishes its investment in global public goods, others will feel the sting of American power more strongly. And the incentive to discipline Mr. Big will grow, as it has in the course of the Bush II administration.

For the United States to prevail where Bismarck failed, the choices are all to clear. Primacy does not come cheap, and the price is measured not just in dollars and cents, but above all in the currency of obligation. Conductors manage to mold eighty solo players into a symphony orchestra because they have fine sense for everybody else's quirks and qualities—because they act in the interest of all. Their labor is the source of their authority. And so a truly great power must do more than merely deny others the reason and opportunity for "ganging up." It must also provide essential services. Those who do for others engage in systemic supply-side economics: they create a demand for their services, and that translates into political profits also known as "leadership."

Power exacts responsibility, and responsibility requires the transcendence of narrow self-interest. To succeed longer than did Bismarck, the task is "Bismarck-plus." As long as the United States continues to provide such public goods, envy and resentment will not escalate into fear and loathing that spawn hostile coalitions. "Do good for others in order to do well for yourself," is the proper maxim for an unchallenged number one. To endure in the twenty-first century, this hegemon must serve his own interests by serving those of others. And he must abide by the lessons of the second half of the twentieth century—the era of institution-building that was the finest moment of American diplomacy.

6

Incomplete Hegemony and Security Order in the Asia-Pacific

Michael Mastanduno

Is U.S. unipolarity better understood as an ephemeral "moment," soon to be overtaken and forgotten, or as an international "system" with its own logic and dynamics and with the potential to endure for several decades beyond the 1990s? The analysis contained in this chapter leans closer to the latter position than to the former. My presumption is that the persistence of unipolarity depends not only on the maintenance of asymmetrical power relations, but, just as critically, on the ability of the United States to institutionalize and maintain legitimacy for an American-centered international order. Hegemony, more so than unipolarity, is the key concept.

The ability of the United States to translate its preponderant power into a durable hegemonic order will be sorely tested in the Asia-Pacific region. Economic dynamism, political diversity, and fluid relations among major powers whose future prospects are uncertain characterize the contemporary Asia-Pacific. China is a rising power simultaneously asserting its global status, testing its regional influence, and transforming its domestic politics. Japan remains a leading commercial and technological power that has experienced a decade of economic and political uncertainty.

This essay was initially prepared for the East-West Center–sponsored project, "Security Order in the Asia-Pacific." A version will appear in *Managing Security in Asia: Toward a Normative Contractual Order?* ed. Muthiah Alagappa (Stanford University Press, forthcoming).

India strikes many as a wakening giant determined to assert itself as a legitimate great power.

Suspicions and resentments deeply embedded in the history of the region continue to linger some fifty years after the end of the Second World War.[1] The experience of Japanese imperialism prior to and during the war continues to shape political sentiment in China, Korea, and parts of Southeast Asia.[2] Both the growth of Chinese power and the unpredictability of North Korea concern Japan. Numerous flashpoints that could lead to bilateral or regional military conflict include the troubled relationship between China and Taiwan, instability and ethnic conflict in Indonesia, the continued division of the Korean Peninsula, and the Kashmir dispute between India and Pakistan.[3] One does not need to be unduly pessimistic to recognize the potential for instability and conflict in this critical area of world politics.

How is order to be maintained in this region? No universally accepted definition of security "order" exists among political scientists. The most commonly cited definition is probably that offered by Hedley Bull, who defined international order broadly as the "pattern of international activity that sustains those goals of the society of states that are elementary, primary, or universal."[4] Definitions of order are contentious because any particular international order benefits some actors and privileges some values at the expense of others. Nevertheless, most political scientists would probably accept that a successful regional order involves the absence of a major war among the states in the region. It also involves the management, and ideally the successful resolution, of regional disputes short of major war. Finally, order necessitates the peaceful accommodation of international change, or, as T. V. Paul and John Hall put it recently, "The success of an international order is predicated on the extent to which it can accommodate change without violence."[5]

---

[1] One recent example is the controversy sparked by a conference intended to play down Japan's record of atrocities during its prewar occupation of China. The conference was sharply criticized by the Chinese government and by some historians and others in Japan. See Howard French, "Japanese Call '37 Massacre a War Myth, Stirring Storm," *New York Times*, January 23, 2000.

[2] Ralph Cossa noted in a recent analysis of Korean-Japanese relations that "unfortunately, one of the few things that the people of the South and North have in common is a mutual distrust of Japan." Ralph Cossa, ed., *U.S.–Korea–Japan Relations: Building toward a "Virtual Alliance"* (Washington, D.C: CSIS Press, 1999), 195.

[3] Prior to his visit in March 2000, President Clinton referred publicly to the Indian subcontinent as "the most dangerous place in the world today." See Jane Perlez, "U.S. and India, Trying to Reconcile, Hit Bump," *New York Times*, March 22, 2000.

[4] Hedley Bull, *The Anarchical Society: A Study of Order in World Politics* (New York: Columbia University Press, 1977), 16.

[5] T. V. Paul and John Hall, introduction to *International Order and the Future of World Politics* (Cambridge: Cambridge University Press 1999), 2.

The purpose of this chapter is to examine the role of U.S. hegemony in the creation and maintenance of security order in the Asia-Pacific. The hegemonic pathway to order should be distinguished from other pathways. Order might be maintained, for example, by the operation of the balance of power, whether bipolar (involving the United States and China, for example) or multipolar. It might result from the functioning of a diplomatic concert among the major powers in the region, or from the emergence of a pluralistic security community. Order might also result from the broadening and deepening of international institutions—institutions sufficiently legitimate and powerful to constrain the potentially destabilizing behavior of member states.

In contrast to these possible pathways, hegemony refers to the creation and maintenance of security order due to the capabilities and behavior of a dominant state. The hegemonic pathway is directly relevant to the contemporary Asia-Pacific because the United States possesses a preponderance of material capabilities and has been eager to take on the responsibility as a stabilizer of the regional security order.

A set of related arguments are advanced in this chapter. The first is a reminder that hegemony has material and nonmaterial components. A unipolar distribution of power, by itself, is not sufficient to establish hegemony. There must also be some meaningful degree of acquiescence on the part of other major states in the region. In a hegemonic order, the leader must have followers, and the more these followers are willing to recognize the hegemonic order as legitimate and share its values and purposes, the more durable the order will be.

Second, a hegemonic order does exist in the Asia-Pacific. The United States has constructed that order over the course of the postwar era and has continued to advance it after the end of the Cold War. Hegemony has contributed in significant ways to the maintenance of regional security. United States power and presence has helped to keep traditional major power rivals in the region from engaging in significant conflict and has helped to reassure smaller states who traditionally have been vulnerable to larger regional powers. The United States has played a key role in managing and defusing regional crises. And, by promoting economic liberalization in the region, U.S. officials helped to disarm the nationalist economic competition that historically has been associated with political conflict.

There are limits to what hegemony has contributed to regional order. United States officials have helped to defuse regional crisis, but have proved unable to foster any fundamental resolution of those crises or to address their underlying causes. Similarly, the United States has helped to discourage conflict among major regional powers, yet has been unable to promote any significant improvements in relations among those powers. Hegemony has contributed to security order but has been, in effect, a holding operation: it has kept the security environment from deteriorating yet without creating any enduring solutions to regional security problems.

Third, the U.S. hegemonic order is incomplete. One regional power, Japan, has embraced the U.S-centered order and found its security in the maintenance of that order. A second regional power, China, is considerably more ambivalent, despite the fact that the United States has made it a foreign policy priority to integrate China into the existing order. A third major player, India, is similarly ambivalent about U.S. hegemony, and the United States has only recently begun any serious attempt to integrate India.

Fourth, the United States faces a set of significant challenges in its effort to sustain and consolidate a hegemonic order in the region. It has the daunting task of completing hegemony through the successful engagement of China and India. It must also maintain domestic support for its hegemonic role and manage the political resentments that inevitably arise when there are gross asymmetries in the global distribution of power and prestige.[6] The fact that these challenges are interrelated makes their effective resolution all the more difficult.

Finally, and despite its obvious shortcomings, I argue that the pathway of U.S. hegemony has significant advantages over other pathways in the contemporary Asia-Pacific. There are pathways that are more desirable, but not feasible in the near term. There are pathways that are feasible, but less desirable as a means to secure order. The U.S. hegemonic order is by no means ideal. But, in light of the alternatives and the distinctive political context of the contemporary Asia-Pacific, U.S. hegemony is sufficiently attractive and tolerable to persist meaningfully into the future.

Hegemony and Order

It is somewhat ironic that during the time period most political scientists consider the high point of U.S. hegemony—the 1950s and 1960s—the term *hegemony* hardly appeared in the international relations literature. The term came into usage during the 1970s, when many U.S. political scientists addressed the issue of "declining hegemony." Hegemony and hegemonic stability became central themes in international relations scholar-

---

[6] The attacks on the United States of September 11, 2001, obviously constitute the most dramatic expression to date of anti-American resentment.

ship during the 1980s.[7] As is the case for many core concepts, hegemony has multiple meanings and different analysts stress different ones. The most important point for the purposes of this chapter is to recognize both the material and nonmaterial aspects of hegemony.

One common understanding equates hegemony with a particular distribution of material resources—one in which there exists an unambiguously dominant state.[8] Hegemony, in this view, is essentially equivalent to unipolarity. Some scholars focus exclusively on the international economic structure, while others suggest that a state must be dominant in the distribution of military as well as economic power to qualify as hegemonic.[9]

Others contend that hegemony connotes more than the asymmetrical distribution of resources, whether economic or military. Hegemony should be understood in terms of the ability to control effectively important international outcomes; it is associated not just with material power but with social purpose. Charles Kindleberger popularized this idea with his now well-known argument that one leading state needed to undertake a series of tasks to assure one critical outcome—the robust functioning of a liberal economic order.[10] Robert Keohane argued more generally that hegemonic states possessed the capabilities to "maintain the regimes they favor."[11] During the 1980s and 1990s, Bruce Russett, Susan Strange, and Henry Nau each challenged the conventional wisdom of the United States as a hegemonic power in decline by pointing to the continued U.S. ability to produce the international outcomes it preferred, such as liberal trade, democratization, and the nuclear peace.[12] A hegemonic state has the power to shape the rules of the international game in accordance with its

---

[7] Major contributions include Robert G. Gilpin, *The Political Economy of International Relations* (Princeton, N.J.: Princeton University Press, 1987); Robert O. Keohane, *After Hegemony: Cooperation and Discord in the World Political Economy* (Princeton, N.J.: Princeton University Press, 1984); Susan Strange, "The Persistent Myth of Lost Hegemony," *International Organization* 41, no. 4 (autumn 1987): 551–74; A useful review is Peter Katzenstein, Keohane, and Stephen Krasner, "International Organization and the Study of World Politics," *International Organization* 53, no. 4 (autumn 1998): 645–86.

[8] Krasner operationalizes hegemony in this fashion in "State Power and the Structure of International Trade," *World Politics* 28, no. 3 (autumn 1976): 317–47.

[9] A good example of the former is David A. Lake, *Power, Protection, and Free Trade: International Sources of U.S. Commercial Policy, 1887–1939* (Ithaca, N.Y.: Cornell University Press, 1988).

[10] Charles P. Kindleberger, *The World In Depression, 1929–1939* (Berkeley: University of California Press, 1973).

[11] Robert O. Keohane, "The Theory of Hegemonic Stability and Changes in International Economic Regimes, 1967–1977," in *Change in the International System*, ed. Ole Holsti, Randolph M. Siverson, and Alexander L. George (Boulder, Colo.: Westview Press, 1980), 136.

[12] Bruce M. Russett, "The Mysterious Case of Vanishing Hegemony: Or, Is Mark Twain Really Dead?" *International Organization* 39, no. 2 (spring 1985): 207–31; Strange, "The Persistent Myth of Lost Hegemony"; and Henry R. Nau, *The Myth of America's Decline: Leading the World Economy into the 1990s* (Oxford: Oxford University Press, 1990)

own values and interests. An important implication is that a hegemonic distribution of power will not always produce the same international outcomes; outcomes depend on the particular priorities and purposes of whatever state happens to dominate.

A third meaning of hegemony is embedded in the question of whether international outcomes benefit other states as well as the hegemonic state. Does the hegemonic state promote the common good, or does it merely exploit others for its particularistic gain? Scholars distinguish benign from malign hegemony, leaders from dominators, and collective goods producers from predators. Although it makes sense to identify different styles of hegemonic behavior, the key point is that hegemony is unlikely to endure if it is primarily coercive, predatory, or only beneficial to the dominant state. Put differently, leaders must have followers. Hegemony requires some level of consent on the part of other major actors in order to sustain itself. The most durable hegemonic order is one in which there exists a meaningful consensus on the right of the hegemonic state to lead, and on the social purposes it projects. Gramsci's depiction of hegemony as a power relationship that is internalized, or reproduced and sustained through ideological acceptance, is relevant here.[13] One might say that hegemony works best when it is least noticed, or when others as a routine state of affairs accept it.[14] Or as Bruce Cumings put it recently, "Hegemony is most effective when it is indirect, inclusive, plural, heterogeneous, and consensual—less a form of domination than of form of legitimate global leadership."[15]

Hegemony, then, requires a preponderance of material resources, a sense of social purpose, the ability to control international outcomes of importance to the dominant state, and some degree of consent and acceptance from other states in the system. Two qualifications are in order. First, the ability to control outcomes should not be taken to imply that the hegemonic state controls *all* international outcomes, or that it wins all the

[13] Useful discussions of Gramsci and hegemony are found in Robert Cox, "Gramsci, Hegemony, and International Relations: An Essay in Method," *Millennium* 12, no. 2 (summer 1983): 162–75; and Keohane, *After Hegemony*.

[14] A recent *Foreign Affairs* essay by Richard N. Haass is instructive in this regard. Haass argues that the United States should not strive for hegemony, but for a concert of great powers. But his idea of a concert is a system in which other major powers are persuaded to accept conceptions of order that reflect the particular interests and values of the United States. As "common" values he points to economic openness; humanitarian intervention because people, not just states, enjoy rights; the control and reduction of nuclear weapons; and limits on the use of force. See Richard Haass, "What to Do with American Primacy," *Foreign Affairs* 78, no. 5 (September/October 1999): 37–49.

[15] Bruce Cumings, "The United States: Hegemonic Still?" in *The Interregnum: Controversies in World Politics, 1989–1999*, ed. Michael Cox, Ken Booth, and Tim Dunne (Cambridge: Cambridge University Press 1999), 484.

time.[16] No state enjoys that luxury, and to establish that as the threshold for hegemony is simply to create a straw man.[17] But in a hegemonic system we should be able to identify, as Russett does, a set of key international outcomes that are consistent with the preferences and purposes of the dominant state. The hegemonic state should be pivotal in setting the rules of the game, even if it does not prevail in every particular conflict.

Second, some degree of consent from other relevant states does not imply that we should expect to see unbridled enthusiasm or public displays of affection for the hegemonic order. In a system of sovereign states in which prestige matters domestically and internationally, it is natural to expect government officials to express reservations or protests about the accumulation of power in the hands of a single state. But for French or Chinese officials to complain in a public setting that the United States is a "hyperpower," or to assert that a unipolar world is a dangerous one, is not the same as forming a balancing coalition against U.S. preponderance.[18] Although public criticism may be a precursor to serious opposition, the more important issues to consider are whether other states are actively resisting the hegemonic order, and to what extent they accept the purposes of the hegemonic state as legitimate and even internalize them as their own.

The Gradual Emergence of the U.S. Hegemonic Order

The United States emerged as a great power during the late nineteenth and early twentieth centuries.[19] It came out of World War I as the world's leading source of manufactured output, financial credit, and foreign direct investment.[20] The dramatic growth in U.S. economic power, juxta-

[16] Even early in the postwar era when the United States was so dominant and others countries so devastated, the United States did not win every battle. See G. John Ikenberry, "Rethinking the Origins of American Hegemony," *Political Science Quarterly* 104 (fall 1989): 375–400; and Michael Mastanduno, *Economic Containment: CoCom and the Politics of East-West Trade* (Ithaca, N.Y.: Cornell University Press, 1992).

[17] Journalists are sometimes tempted to do this. Arnold Beichman asks how the United States can be a superpower if it is "paying tribute" to North Korea or is Saddam Hussein is still a "functioning dictator." See Beichman, "What U.S. Superpower?" *Washington Times*, January 4, 2000.

[18] Those who anticipate the early demise of U.S. hegemony and the unipolar structure often cite expressions of resentment or anxiety as evidence of mobilization against the hegemonic order. See, for example, Christopher Layne, "The Unipolar Illusion: Why New Great Powers Will Rise," *International Security* 17, no. 4 (spring, 1993): 5–51.

[19] Fareed Zakaria, *From Wealth to Power: The Unusual Origins of America's World Role* (Princeton, N.J.: Princeton University Press, 1999).

[20] Jeffry Frieden, "Sectoral Conflict and U.S. Foreign Economic Policy, 1914–1940," *International Organization* 42, no. 1 (winter 1988): 59–90; and Paul Kennedy, *The Rise and Fall of*

posed to the relatively modest role the United States played in interwar economic diplomacy, prompted Kindleberger's often cited phrase that the United States was "able" but not "willing" to lead the world economy during the depression years. The relative economic power of the United States increased further during World War II, and of course following that conflict the United States did assume a more prominent global role both militarily and economically.

United States officials consistently envisioned international order and their global role in ideological as well as material terms. World War II was fought not simply to adjust the balance of power among leading states; it was also importantly a struggle against fascism, an ideological competitor to democracy and liberalism as organizing principles for political life. The commitment of U.S. officials to a fundamental transformation of the domestic political economies of the defeated powers reflected the deep conviction that fascism was evil and had to be eliminated as an alternative path to political order.

A similar sentiment, of course, informed the U.S. crusade against communism. United States hegemony during the Cold War was never complete in that the Soviet Union posed a geopolitical challenge and represented a viable ideological alternative. It is tempting, in light of the contemporary political context, to underestimate the appeal that communist ideology held, particularly in the so-called Third World, during the 1950s and 1960s. Until the 1980s, U.S. officials felt the best they could do was to "contain" communism so that it did not penetrate and undermine the capitalist and (sometimes) democratic order under construction in various parts of the world. The end of the Cold War in 1989 represented not just the demise of the Soviet Union as a superpower challenger to the United States, but also the demise of the ideological alternative it presented for domestic and international political order.

Another, albeit softer, challenge to U.S. hegemony emerged as the Cold War ended. Japan and the United States, close military allies during the Cold War, by the 1980s also became significant economic competitors in possession of the world's two largest economies. Japan's economic challenge was comprehensive and multifaceted. The ability of Japanese firms to outcompete their U.S. counterparts in merchandise trade was only the most visible manifestation. Japan also challenged the United States for control at the frontier of advanced technologies with military as well as commercial applications. And, during the 1980s, the two countries

---

the Great Powers: Economic Change and Military Conflict from 1500 to 2000 (New York: Random House, 1988).

"traded places" with Japan becoming the world's largest creditor and the United States the world's largest debtor.[21]

The Japanese challenge was, in a particular sense, ideological as well. The widespread view in academic and policy circles was that Japan's economic success was based on "developmental capitalism"—an alternative, Asian way to organize a capitalist political economy.[22] In contrast to the more laissez-faire model offered by the United States, the Japanese model emphasized tight alliances and long-term relationships among manufacturing firms, close collaboration between industry and government, a commitment to state-led industrial policy and export promotion, the selective protection of home markets, and reliance on banks rather than equity markets for corporate funding. This model seemed to be working during the 1980s—so well, in fact, that a debate emerged within U.S. policy circles over whether the United States should emulate Japan by adopting an industrial policy of its own and perhaps creating an executive agency with the seeming foresight of Japan's Ministry of International Trade and Industry. As Japan's success mounted, its usually reticent foreign policy officials become more assertive at touting the advantages of their economic model. They urged the World Bank, for example, to stress the key role of government intervention in its 1993 study of the origins and lessons of the Asian economic miracle.[23]

The challenge of developmental capitalism was accentuated by the economic accomplishments of the broader Asia-Pacific region. The countries of East and Southeast Asia grew at an average annual rate of roughly 6 percent for almost two decades, well above the global annual average of about 2 percent.[24] Sustained, high rates of growth enabled the region to take on greater significance in the world economy. Asia was no longer on the periphery; in fact, prominent political economists such as Robert Gilpin foresaw a fundamental shift in the center of global economic activity, and by implication, geopolitical influence, from Europe to Asia.[25] The Asia Pacific began to assume more of a regional identity, symbolized by the emergence of APEC and the initiation in 1993 of annual meetings of

[21] Clyde V. Prestowitz Jr., *Trading Places: How We Are Giving Our Future to Japan and How to Reclaim It*, 2d ed. (New York: Basic Books, 1990).

[22] Chalmers Johnson, *MITI and the Japanese Miracle: The Growth of Japanese Industrial Policy, 1920–1975* (Stanford, Calif.: Stanford University Press, 1982); and Prestowitz, *Trading Places*.

[23] World Bank, *The East Asian Miracle: Economic Growth and Public Policy* (New York: Oxford University Press, 1993).

[24] Michel Oksenberg, "The Asian Strategic Context," in *America and the East Asian Crisis: Memos to a President*, ed. Robert Zoellick and Philip D. Zelikow (New York: Norton, 2000), 8–9.

[25] Gilpin, *Political Economy of International Relations*.

the region's leaders. This dawning of the "Pacific Century" and the distinctiveness of Asia's approach to political economy went hand in hand. A common metaphor depicted Asia's thriving economies as geese flying in formation behind the leadership of Japan.

The picture that emerges at the end of the 1990s is strikingly different. Throughout the past decade Japan experienced economic stagnation. Japan's "bubble economy" burst in the early 1990s, and the subsequent efforts at recovery have been hampered by some of the very features of the Japanese model that accounted for Japan's postwar success.[26] Lifetime employment commitments and long-term relationships among firms made the Japanese economy far less flexible than that of the United States in responding to economic downturns. The same close links between banks, firms, and government that helped to allocate capital effectively during the high growth years have proved to be a constraint at a time when many banks are insolvent and carrying bad loans. Industrial policy was an effective instrument for the mobilization of an economy to catch up in the production of commodities such as automobiles and memory chips. As Japanese officials recognize, industrial policy has turned out to be far less effective as an instrument for innovation at the frontier of technology.[27] The tendency of Japanese politicians to defer to the professional expertise of the bureaucracy, viewed as a great asset in the consistent implementation of the postwar growth strategy, has proven a liability in an era in which Japan lacks an overall strategy and requires political leadership and vision to change direction.

The Asian financial crisis of 1997–98 further accentuated the weakness of developmental capitalism. The pressure of volatile international capital movements exposed a host of domestic economic vulnerabilities in some of the most promising "young tigers" of East and Southeast Asia. These problems included the overextension of credit to inefficient enterprises and real estate developers, inadequate supervision of domestic financial systems, a lack of transparency in current and capital account activity, excessive short-term borrowing to cover current account deficits, and the use of reserves to defend overly rigid exchange rates.[28] In the course of

---

[26] For elaboration, see Michael Mastanduno, "Models, Markets, and Power: Political Economy and the Asia-Pacific, 1989–1999," *Review of International Studies* 26 (fall 2000): 493–507; and Rosemary Foot and Andrew Walter, "Whatever Happened to the Pacific Century?" in *The Interregnum: Controversies in World Politics, 1989–1999*, ed. Michael Cox, Ken Booth, and Tim Dunne (Cambridge: Cambridge University Press, 1999).

[27] Scott Callon, *Divided Sun: MITI and the Breakdown of Japanese High Technology Industrial Policy, 1975–1993* (Stanford: Stanford University Press, 1995).

[28] Morris Goldstein, *The Asian Financial Crisis: Causes, Cures, and Systemic Implications* (Washington, D.C.: Institute for International Economics, 1998); and Richard Cooper, "Asian Financial Crisis: Future Outlook and Next Steps," in *America and the East Asian Crisis: Memos to a President*, ed. Robert Zoellick and Philip D. Zelikow (New York: Norton, 2000).

only several years, the common characterization of the region by academics and policy analysts has swung from "Asian miracle" to "crony capitalism." The latter depiction likely overplays Asian weaknesses, just as the former probably overplayed Asian strengths.

In the years ahead, the Asian model of political economy is more likely to be modified than abandoned outright. Japan's stagnation and the financial crisis should not be taken to imply either Asia's economic collapse or the triumph of the American form of capitalism. These seminal events of the 1990s do suggest, however, that the Asian model no longer carries the ideological appeal it enjoyed previously as a superior form of capitalist development.

The geopolitical position of the United States is also strikingly different at century's end. At the end of the Cold War, the U.S. position in global terms appeared to be one of military dominance and relative economic decline. Ten years later, the military superiority of the United States has probably increased. Even though the Cold War has ended, U.S. defense spending has remained at the average levels of the Cold War and continues to dwarf that of any other state, allied or not. The U.S.–led interventions in the Persian Gulf at the beginning of the 1990s and especially in Kosovo at the end served as uncomfortable reminders, even to America's closest allies, of the sizable disparity between the United States and other countries in intelligence gathering capacity, defense technologies, and power projection capabilities.

The United States simultaneously has recovered a position of relative economic superiority. Its economy thrived through the 1990s as those of its major competitors struggled. United States–based firms and the economy as a whole have taken greater advantage of the revolution in information technology than have the economies of other states. What appeared at the end of the 1980s to be a struggle for technological supremacy between Japan and the United States appears, a decade later, to have been resolved in favor of the latter. The Asian crisis accentuated the U.S. relative advantage; the U.S. economy proved less vulnerable than many had expected to the contagion effect of the Asian downturn. And, U.S. markets are recognized as crucial by countries seeking to export their way out of decline, while Japan has taken criticism from within the region and beyond for its reluctance to stimulate regional recovery by opening its markets and maintaining the strength of its currency.

Some fifty years after the end of the Second World War, the United States finds itself atop a unipolar distribution of material capabilities. As William Wohlforth recently emphasized, U.S. preeminence is unprecedented: "Never in modern international history has the leading state been so dominant economically and militarily."[29] Among today's major powers, only the United States retains the full array of great power attributes—military, economic, and what Joseph Nye and others have termed the "soft" power attributes of ideological or cultural power.[30]

The idea of an international structure dominated by the United States may be reassuring to some and is obviously distasteful or threatening to others.[31] But the preponderance of the United States in material capabilities should not be taken to imply U.S. control over all or even most international outcomes. Even a cursory glance at international events during the 1990s suggests the limits to U.S. power over outcomes—Saddam Hussein remained in place in Iraq, other Western nations undermined U.S. economic sanctions, and adversaries in the Middle East and in the Balkans continued to defy U.S.–crafted initiatives to resolve their differences. The attacks of September 11, 2001, also dramatically suggested limits on the ability of the United States to secure its own territory in the face of a weaker yet determined adversary. Yet, it is also the case that crucial outcomes in world politics, for better or worse, are increasingly consistent with U.S. core values.[32] As a status quo power the United States prefers, and currently enjoys, peace defined as the absence of serious conflict among major global powers. The general trend in favor of liberalized trade and financial markets reflects U.S. preferences. The extreme statism of command economies, along with the moderate statism associated with developmental capitalism and import substitution industrialization has fallen out of favor. The attributes of political governance favored by the United States (e.g., democracy, liberalism) are not universally practiced but have a far greater appeal than they have had in the past.

During the 1990s, U.S. officials adopted a geopolitical strategy designed to preserve and extend preponderance. That strategy included efforts to discourage the rise of great power challengers, the selective use of international institutions (e.g., the WTO, the IMF) to reflect and spread U.S. core values, and engagement in key regions where economic power and

[29] William C. Wohlforth, "The Stability of a Unipolar World," *International Security* 24, no. 1 (summer 1999): 13.

[30] Joseph S. Nye, *Bound to Lead: The Changing Nature of U.S. Power* (New York: Basic Books, 1990); and Nau, *The Myth of America's Decline*.

[31] For contrasting views see Robert Kagan, "The Benevolent Empire," *Foreign Policy* 111 (summer 1998): 24–35; and Charles William Maynes, "The Perils of (and for) an Imperial America," *Foreign Policy* 111 (summer 1998): 36–49.

[32] See the arguments made by Russett, "The Mysterious Case of Vanishing Hegemony," Strange, "The Persistent Myth of Lost Hegemony," and Cumings, "The United States: Hegemonic Still?"

potential geopolitical influence are concentrated.[33] The two most important regions are Europe and Asia. In Europe, U.S. strategy has centered on the maintenance and expansion of NATO to promote regional stability and discourage great power challengers. United States officials supported German unification on the condition that Germany remain in NATO and have encouraged European defense initiatives only to the extent that they remain subordinate to NATO. The U.S. hegemonic strategy for Asia takes a different institutional form but reflects similar grand strategic objectives.

Incomplete Hegemony in the Asia-Pacific

The U.S. Hegemonic Strategy for Asia

The end of the Cold War presented the U.S. officials with several options for pursuing order in the Asia-Pacific. The United States could have adopted the role of "offshore balancer" by withdrawing its forward presence from the region and encouraging a multipolar balance of power to emerge.[34] Alternatively, U.S. officials could have focused on building and strengthening regional security and economic institutions as the principal pathway to order. A third possibility might have been to organize a coalition of states to contain whatever state appeared prepared to mount a challenge to regional order. In light of its size and ambition, China would be the most likely prospect for that role.[35] United States officials have given priority to none of the foregoing options. Instead, they have pursued a hegemonic strategy—one that reserves a special role for the United States as the principal guarantor of regional order.

The most important institutional feature of the U.S. hegemonic strategy is the cultivation of a set of special relationships with key states in the region. Bilateralism, rather than multilateralism, is the key to the U.S. approach. The most important bilateral relationship is with Japan, reflecting the continuity between America's Cold War and post–Cold War regional strategy. United States officials similarly have maintained their bilateral alliance structure and commitment to South Korea. Instead of using these

[33] Mastanduno, "Preserving the Unipolar Moment: Realist Theories and U.S. Grand Strategy after the Cold War," *International Security* 21, no. 4 (spring 1997): 49–88.

[34] Layne "The Unipolar Illusion."

[35] Robert Ross believes the region is already bipolar. See Robert S. Ross, "The Geography of the Peace: East Asia in the Twenty-First Century," *International Security* 23, no. 4 (spring 1999): 81–117.

alliances to balance China, however, the core U.S. strategy has been to develop a special relationship with China as well. Clinton administration officials termed their approach to China "comprehensive engagement"; they envisioned a partnership that is less than an alliance but considerably more cooperative than competitive. The overall U.S. approach to the region might be thought of in terms of a "hub and spokes" arrangement: U.S. officials have sought to craft a series of special relationships designed to assure key regional players that their relationship with Washington is both crucial and indispensable.[36]

The manner in which the United States has treated multilateral security institutions in Asia clarifies further its hegemonic strategy. United States officials tended to view multilateral initiatives skeptically during the Cold War, particularly after the failures of SEATO and CENTO. During the 1990s, they have been more supportive and encouraging of multilateralism as a complement to core bilateral security relationships. For example, in a 1993 speech in South Korea, President Clinton focused attention on the crucial role of bilateral alliances, and also called for the promotion of new multilateral dialogues in the region on the full range of common security challenges.[37]

For U.S. officials, multilateral initiatives afford a useful way to engage the participation of various Asian states in regional security affairs, while not undermining the core hegemonic strategy. Asian security institutions can play a positive role in fostering communication and confidence building measures, but are not sufficiently developed to take on a central role in the management and resolution of regional security problems. Thus it is not surprising that U.S. officials have supported the Asian Regional Forum (ARF) as a vehicle for ASEAN members to voice their security concerns and explore the potential for preventive diplomacy and maritime cooperation. United States officials similarly have supported the Northeast Asia Cooperation Dialogue (NEACD) among China, Japan, Russia, the United States, and the two Koreas. NEACD offers the United States a "safe" way to involve Japan and Russia in regional security dialogue, as well as an opportunity to defend and explain U.S. bilateral alliances with Japan and South Korea to suspicious Chinese and Russian officials.[38]

United States officials clearly view multilateral initiatives as supplements to, not substitutes for, core bilateral security relationships. In times

---

[36] Josef Joffe analyzes hub-and-spoke strategies for hegemonic powers in Josef Joffe, "'Bismarck' or 'Britain'? Toward an American Grand Strategy after Bipolarity," *International Security* 19, no. 4 (spring 1995): 94–117.

[37] Ralph Cossa, "U.S. Approaches to Multilateral Security and Economic Institutions in Asia," *Pacific Forum CSIS* (unpublished, 2000).

[38] Ibid.

of crisis they turn not to these regional institutions but prefer instead to rely on U.S.–led diplomatic efforts and institutional structures that the United States can more comfortably control. In the North Korean nuclear crisis of 1994 the United States relied on ad hoc diplomacy and established a new entity, KEDO (Korean Peninsula Energy Development Organization) to implement its agreement. During the Asian financial crisis, U.S. officials rebuffed Japan's proposal for a regional financing facility and instead concentrated the management of the crisis on the more comfortable terrain of the IMF.

The U.S. intention to serve as the principal source of regional order is symbolized and reinforced by its forward military presence. Early in the 1990s, the United States scaled back its troop commitments in East Asia and about the same time relinquished its naval facilities in the Philippines at the request of that government. These moves were read in the region and elsewhere as the beginnings of U.S. withdrawal. By 1995, U.S. officials made clear that this was not the case, and in fact that their intention was the opposite. The United States planned, in the words of the Pentagon's East Asia strategy document, to maintain a forward political and military commitment to East Asia of "indefinite duration." This included the stabilization of the U.S. troop presence in the region at about 100,000.[39] The United States also intended to maintain its dominant position in maritime East Asia. United States alliances with Japan and South Korea provided secure access in Northeast Asia. In Southeast Asia, the U.S. Navy would rely on "places, not bases." By the end of the 1990s U.S. officials had concluded access agreements for naval facilities in Indonesia, Malaysia, Singapore, and Brunei, along with a status-of-forces agreement with the Philippines.[40]

A final component of the U.S. hegemonic strategy might be called a commitment to a forward economic presence in Asia. United States officials have consistently and aggressively promoted the spread of liberal international economic policies in Asian states inclined to be more comfortable with the practices of developmental capitalism. Economic openness plays into U.S. economic interests, particularly given U.S. competitiveness in the export of services, agriculture, and advanced technology. It plays into U.S. security interests since U.S. officials have consistently held that liberalism and economic interdependence promote more

[39] U.S. Department of Defense, *United States Security Strategy for the East Asia-Pacific Region*, Report of Office of International Security Affairs (Washington, D.C.: Government Printing Office, 1995); Nye, "The Case for Deep Engagement," *Foreign Affairs* 74 (July/August 1995): 90–102; and Nye, "The 'Nye Report' Six Years Later," *International Relations of the Asia-Pacific* 1, no. 1 (2001): 95–104.

[40] Ross, "The Geography of the Peace," 85–86.

peaceful and cooperative political relations. It is not surprising that U.S. officials have reacted negatively and decisively to initiatives that seemed to suggest closed regionalism or managed trade. In the early 1990s the United States opposed, and worked hard to assure that Japan would oppose, Malaysia's proposal for an East Asian Economic Group that would exclude the United States. United States officials expressed concern at the highest levels and hinted that exclusionary economic arrangements in East Asia might force the United States to reevaluate security commitments.[41] The role of the United States in APEC has been to push member states more decisively and quickly in the direction of liberalization. United States officials have promoted trade liberalization bilaterally in negotiations especially with Japan, China, and South Korea, and multilaterally through the WTO. They have pushed financial liberalization in Asia under the auspices of the "Washington Consensus" developed and implemented by the IMF and World Bank.[42]

Hegemony and Regional Order: Contributions and Limits

The United States has crafted a hegemonic strategy for the Asia Pacific to serve its own geopolitical and economic interests. Yet, in the process, U.S. hegemony is also making important contributions to regional order. Hegemony has promoted order, but it is also important to recognize the limitations of U.S. hegemony as the principal mechanism for regional order.

One important contribution of the U.S. position in Asia has been to keep potential power rivals at bay. Japan and China are major powers, each with the capacity to be great military powers. They share geographic proximity and an unfortunate history of conflict and mutual recrimination. Events such as the recent conference in Japan reconsidering the 1937 massacre at Nanking, or recent remarks by Tokyo governor Shintaro Ishihara to the effect that Japan must be prepared to put down Korean or Chinese "uprisings," serve to reopen old wounds and keep hostilities alive.[43]

---

[41] Joseph M. Grieco, "Realism and Regionalism: American Power and German and Japanese Institutional Strategies during and after the Cold War," in *Unipolar Politics: Realism and State Strategies after the Cold War*, ed. Ethan Kapstein and Mastanduno (New York: Columbia University Press, 1999), 328–39.

[42] Robert Wade, "The Coming Fight over Capital Flows," *Foreign Policy* 113 (winter 1998–99): 41–54.

[43] On the first incident, see footnote 1. On the second, see "Mr. No Blames the Victim," *Asian Wall Street Journal*, April 12, 2000. Ishihara used a racial slur in referring to potential Korean or Chinese rioters.

The Japanese-Chinese relationship has the makings of a classic security dilemma, and one reinforced by hard memories and ethnic conflict. As Tom Christensen noted recently, "Although Chinese analysts presently fear U.S. power much more than Japanese power, in terms of national intentions, Chinese analysts view Japan with much less trust and, in many cases, with a loathing rarely found in their attitudes about the United States."[44] Chinese attitudes and suspicions obviously factor into Japan's own anxieties about the rising power and intentions of its large neighbor. In this circumstance, U.S. hegemony plays a critical role in keeping the negative aspects of the relationship from spiraling in a dangerous direction. Through its alliance and commitment to defend Japan, the United States make it possible for Japan to avoid having to confront China directly.

A direct Japanese approach to China would only confirm Chinese fears of a revanchist Japan. Although Chinese officials are reluctant to admit it, they recognize that the U.S.–Japan alliance constrains as well as protects Japan. That alliance, combined with the U.S. partnership with China, helps to reassure China that it does not need to confront Japan directly. The balancing game U.S. officials must play is a delicate one: too strong an alliance with Japan arouses Chinese fears of containment, while too strong a partnership with China to the neglect of Japan arouses Japanese fears of abandonment. The difficulty of the diplomatic task only serves to reinforce the fact that in the absence of a U.S. hegemonic role, the chances of Japanese-Chinese geopolitical competition would increase substantially.

Second, U.S. hegemony helps to assure the security of smaller states in the region. In many circumstances, hegemonic power can reasonably be feared by smaller states as a threat to their security and territorial integrity. In the Asia-Pacific context, the opposite is more likely to be the case. The U.S. presence is more a source of reassurance than of threat.

One reason is that the smaller powers of Northeast and Southeast Asia live in potentially dangerous neighborhoods. They coexist with larger powers that have varying geopolitical ambitions and conflicts among themselves.[45] And, there is an array of unresolved territorial disputes that can serve as possible flashpoints for larger conflicts. The United States, in this setting, can play the role of "honest broker" more credibly than any other large power. It has geopolitical interests of its own, but does not

[44] Thomas J. Christensen, "China, the U.S.–Japan Alliance, and the Security Dilemma in East Asia," *International Security* 23, no. 4 (spring 1999): 52.

[45] Although China claims the entire South China Sea as its territorial waters, India recently announced it would hold unilateral and bilateral naval exercises there. See "India Challenges China in South China Sea," *STRATFOR.COM Global Intelligence Update*, April 26, 2000.

have territorial ambitions. It also possesses power projection capabilities that other major powers in the region lack, granting it credibility as the potential enforcer of regional order. In Northeast Asia, the U.S. presence in both Japan and South Korea helps to reassure the latter in the presence of its more powerful neighbors. The U.S. maritime presence in Southeast Asia similarly helps the smaller ASEAN states to deal more comfortably with China.

Although most Southeast Asian states (Singapore is an exception) are reluctant to grant the United States access to their bases to preposition military equipment, most also acknowledge and welcome the role that U.S. forward deployed forces play in maintaining regional stability.[46]

A third contribution of U.S. hegemony to order involves the management of security crises that have the potential to escalate to local war and the possibility of broader regional conflict. The United States has assumed for itself a major role in responding to and defusing regional crises. The 1999 conflict between India and Pakistan over Kashmir is an apt example. That conflict came closer to a general war than was publicly acknowledged at the time. Pakistan established positions in Indian-controlled Kashmir during the spring of 1999. India responded with a general military mobilization, which eventually led Pakistan to preparations of its own. Although neither side expected a full-scale war, the potential for these two nuclear powers to stumble into one was not insignificant. This concern led to a frenzied response at the highest levels of the U.S. government. President Clinton intervened personally and stayed in regular phone contact with the leaders of both sides, urging each to show restraint and respect the sanctity of the line of control. Most analysts credit Clinton with a significant (albeit short-term) success in persuading Pakistan prime minister Sharif to withdraw his forces.[47]

United States officials similarly have taken the lead role in seeking to discourage North Korea's nuclear ambitions. They fear that a nuclear North Korea would damage nonproliferation norms generally and within the Asia-Pacific region. An important concern is that a nuclear North Korea, in the context of Russia and China's existing possession of nuclear weapons, would create incentives for Japan eventually to reconsider its nonnuclear status. United States officials crafted the arrangement in 1994 in which North Korea agreed to a nuclear moratorium in exchange for economic assistance provided by the United States, South Korea, and

[46] Oksenberg, "The Asian Strategic Context," 10. He notes that even China quietly acknowledges the constructive role of U.S. forces, though not publicly out of concern those forces might be used to defend Taiwan.

[47] John Lancaster, "War Was Narrowly Averted; Kashmir Conflict Flared Dangerously," *Washington Post*, July 26, 1999.

Japan through KEDO. Asian states did not respond in a decisive manner to North Korea until the United States engaged and took the lead. In 1999, the United States again promised economic concessions, this time to induce North Korea not to conduct tests of its long-range missiles. The North Korean test program was especially alarming to Japan; in August 1998 North Korea sent a missile directly over Japanese airspace. United States officials recognize that the North Korean threat is immediate for its Asian allies, and more remote with regard to the U.S. homeland.[48] It took the initiative nonetheless to develop a concerted response among Washington, Seoul, and Tokyo, and urged Moscow and Beijing to use whatever influence they could to restrain North Korea.[49]

The United States has also intervened in the increasingly tense standoff between China and Taiwan. The goal of the Clinton administration was to deter China from seeking a military solution (the Taiwan Relations Act of 1974 calls for the United States to come to Taiwan's aid if it is attacked) and to dissuade Taiwan from provocative acts of independence. China fired missiles close to Taiwan in March 1996, in anticipation of Taiwanese elections. These actions were meant to intimidate Taiwan and had the temporary effect of stalling shipping in the Taiwanese straits. The United States responded by dispatching two aircraft carriers and about fourteen other warships to the area. The United States intended through its strategy of "calculated ambiguity" to deter possible Chinese aggression and simultaneously to signal its willingness to maintain a close partnership with China. It prepared to take similar steps early in 2000, as China once again escalated its rhetoric (this time, without launching missiles) in anticipation of another Taiwanese election.[50]

Fourth, U.S. hegemony has contributed to regional order by helping to stave off in the Asia-Pacific the kind of nationalist economic competition (and attendant political friction) that plagued the world economy during the 1930s. The potential for beggar-thy-neighbor policies certainly existed during the late 1990s. The Asian financial crisis was a profound shock that plausibly could have led to closed markets, competitive devaluations, and a downward spiral of trade and growth. The management of this crisis was

[48] Assistant Secretary of State J. Stapleton Roy testified in early 2000 that North Korea's missiles "are unlikely to be used against U.S. territory, but they are a growing threat to U.S. allies and U.S. forces around the world." John Donnelly, "Intelligence Officials: Missile Attack on U.S. Unlikely," *Defense Week*, February 14, 2000.

[49] Morton I. Abramowitz and James T. Laney, *U.S. Policy toward North Korea: Next Steps*, Council on Foreign Relations Task Force Report (1999), 10–11; and Philip Shenon, "North Korea Agrees to End Missile Testing in Exchange for Economic Aid," *New York Times*, September 13, 1999.

[50] Robert G. Kaiser and Steven Mufson, "Analysts Differ on Whether China Crisis Looms," *Washington Post*, March 16, 2000.

found in Washington rather than Tokyo. During the crisis, the U.S. Federal Reserve eased interest rates to assure global liquidity and maintain high growth in the United States. As the crisis eased, the United States fueled recovery by taking in the huge flood of exports from emerging economies as well as from China and Japan.[51] The U.S. response to the crisis reflected its broader regional economic strategy of seeking to liberalize the developmental capitalist markets of Japan and Southeast Asia, and at the same time opening and integrating China into the liberal world economy.

It is important to recognize the limitations of hegemony as a means to promote regional order. In its essence, the U.S. hegemonic project in the Asia-Pacific is more a "holding action" than a progressive strategy for improving security relations. It is an effort to stabilize a status quo that reflects U.S. dominance. Although U.S. officials have worked hard to keep relations among major powers in the region from deteriorating, it is not clear that they have envisioned a plan for resolving the long-standing tensions in those relationships. In fact, since the United States does not want to encourage a balancing coalition against its dominant position, it is not clear that it has a strategic interest in the full resolution of differences between, say, Japan and China or Russia and China. Some level of tension among these states reinforces their individual need for a special relationship with the United States.

United States officials have managed and defused regional crises in Asia without any fundamental resolutions of the underlying disputes. The series of U.S.–initiated economic concessions to North Korea, for example, are more an effort to buy time than a plan to transform the politics of the Korean Peninsula. United States diplomacy toward the China-Taiwan dispute also proceeds in this spirit. And, U.S. attempts to proceed more aggressively to solve regional disputes are not always welcome. A Clinton administration offer to build on the success of crisis management and mediate the ongoing dispute over Kashmir was rebuffed by India, which felt that U.S. diplomacy in the past had sided too closely with the position of Pakistan.[52]

There are also limits to what hegemony can accomplish in regional economic relations. The United States played a vital role as market of last resort during the Asian crisis—a role that no other state within or outside the region was prepared to play. But, by itself the United States simply

---

[51] The United States, in the words of the *Financial Times*, was "an anchor of stability" during the crisis. See the editorial, *Financial Times*, April 15, 2000.

[52] "India and Pakistan: The Elephant and the Pekinese," *The Economist*, March 18, 2000, 25–27. Indian concerns were only magnified as the United States moved closer to Pakistan in its efforts to craft a response to the attacks of September 2001.

can't engineer enduring prosperity in the region. First and foremost, the United States needs the active cooperation of Japan.[53] The inability or unwillingness of Japan to pull out of its stagnation or to open further its economy will be a continuing source of pressure on the regional economy regardless of whatever initiatives the United States takes. The economic collapse of Japan, or of China, within the context of the Asian crisis would have posed a stabilization challenge beyond the capacity of any single state, even with the support of international institutions, to manage effectively.

United States Hegemony Is Incomplete

The limits of U.S. hegemony as a pathway to order must be recognized in a different sense as well. A complete hegemonic order, I argued earlier, requires not just preponderant capabilities but also some meaningful degree of acquiescence on the part of other states, especially major ones, in the maintenance of that order. At the end of the first post–Cold War decade, the United States finds that it has forestalled any serious challenges, individual or collective, to its hegemonic position. It also has earned the strong support of one major power in the region, but has some distance to cover to obtain the acquiescence of two others.

The strong alliance between Japan and the United States developed during the Cold War has persisted after the Cold War. This was not a foregone conclusion. Many analysts, neorealists in particular, anticipated at the end of the Cold War that Japan would distance itself from the United States and adopt a more independent and perhaps assertive foreign policy. Kenneth Waltz argued in 1993 that Japan was on the verge of transformation; all that remained was for it to "reach for the great power mantle."[54] But Japan has not done this, at least not in the sense anticipated by Waltz. Its willingness to continue to define its national security priorities in terms of its special relationship with the United States in part reflects changes in Japan's national identity that have evolved over the postwar era, and in part the effectiveness of a U.S. strategy designed to assure Japan that its interests would be best served by remaining, in effect, as a junior partner in a U.S.–centered regional and global order. This is not to suggest that Japan's continued acquiescence can be taken for granted. On

[53] This argument is elaborated by Michael H. Armacost, "Japan: Policy Paralysis and Economic Stagnation," in *America and the East Asian Crisis.*

[54] Kenneth N. Waltz, "The Emerging Structure of International Politics," *International Security* 18, no 2 (fall 1993): 55.

the contrary, the uncertainty and fear of abandonment inherent in any alliance relationship is pronounced in the post–Cold War strategic context, since there is no longer any central strategic threat to provide a core rationale for the alliance. United States officials appreciated the need, by the middle of the 1990s, to play down bilateral economic conflicts and focus attention instead on repairing and expanding their bilateral security relationship with Japan. That relationship will demand sustained attention in the uncertain security environment of the Asia-Pacific.[55]

The U.S. relationship with China poses a different problem. On one hand, it is by no means certain that China is committed to mount a revisionist challenge to U.S. hegemony. China's interest in economic modernization, and in particular its inclination to integrate more fully into the institutions of the capitalist world economy such as the WTO, suggest otherwise. On the other hand, it is equally clear that China remains uncomfortable playing a subordinate role in a U.S.–centered order. Chinese rhetoric, in particular its stated commitment to foster a transformation from U.S. hegemony to a multipolar world, is designed to reinforce this point. A key problem for U.S. officials is that China defines its geopolitical interests partly in material terms and partly in terms of status. During the Clinton era the United States committed to comprehensive engagement and a partnership with China in an effort to convince Beijing that it would be secure and prosperous in a U.S.–centered order. The Bush administration has been less willing to embrace China as a "partner," yet still eager to enlist Chinese cooperation in U.S. economic and geopolitical initiatives. United States officials, in overall terms, have achieved limited success. Their strategy has not yet managed both to satisfy China's economic interests and accommodate its desire for respect and recognition as a legitimate great power.

If, in the case of China, the United States has reached out with mixed results, in the case of India, the problem is similar but the U.S. effort during the first post–Cold War decade proved fairly minimal. India, like China, perceives itself as a rising power with legitimate security concerns and a claim to major power, and eventually great power, status. International prestige is as important to India as it is to China, and from India's perspective, the United States treats it more as a less developed country than as an emerging great power. United States officials lecture India on its nuclear proliferation and reluctance to sign the Comprehensive Test Ban Treaty, even as the U.S. Senate rejects that same treaty. India also per-

---

[55] U.S. officials were reminded of this in 1998: after North Korea test-fired its missile over Japan, Japanese officials announced plans to develop their own intelligence gathering satellites.

ceives that the United States favors China excessively and unfairly in terms of economic and diplomatic attention. This is especially irritating because India, like the United States, is a large multicultural democracy. India and the United States also share an emerging economic interest in that both are at the forefront of the development of internet and other information technology. The United States, despite its overall commitment to regional stability and the evolution of its hub-and-spoke security strategy in the Asia-Pacific, has been slow to seize the initiative and improve bilateral relations with this key regional power. The Clinton visit to India in March 2000—remarkably, the first by a U.S. President since 1978—was an important initial step in the right direction, though considerably more work remains to be done.[56]

Can U.S. Hegemony Endure?

United States officials speak on an engagement with the Asia-Pacific region of indefinite duration and imply that hegemony is sustainable over the long term. Many scholars are skeptical and point to growing discomfort and discontent about U.S. dominance in a unipolar setting expressed by actors in the region.[57] United States hegemony clearly cannot last forever. But it did endure through the first post–Cold War decade. Can it be sustained for another decade, perhaps two? No one can say with certainty, but it is possible to point to a set of related challenges that U.S. officials must address effectively if the hegemonic pathway to order in the Asia-Pacific is to be sustained and strengthened. Even those most confident in the durability of unipolarity suggest that the United States must "play its cards right" in order to sustain it.[58]

A first challenge is that of completing hegemony. This is no easy task. It involves integrating China and India while simultaneously maintaining the support of Japan. The United States does enjoy some advantages. It can count on the fact that all three powers have an interest in a regional stability that allows prosperity to grow. None would welcome a nuclear arms race or war on the Korean Peninsula or Indian subcontinent. None have a strategic interest in Japanese economic collapse, or political chaos and fragmentation in China with its attendant refugee flows and environ-

---

[56] See Jane Perlez, "U.S. and India, Trying to Reconcile, Hit Bump," *New York Times*, March 22, 2000.

[57] For example, Tyler Marshall and Jim Mann, "Goodwill toward U.S. Is Dwindling Globally," *Los Angeles Times*, March 26, 2000, and Christopher Layne, "What's Built Up Must Come Down," *Washington Post*, November 14, 1999.

[58] Wohlforth, "The Stability of a Unipolar World," 8.

mental problems.[59] United States officials also hold strong cards in the effort to integrate China and India economically. The fact that China's economy has been increasingly dependent on the world economy in general and U.S. markets, investment, and technology in particular is an important source of leverage for the United States.[60] In India's case, there is considerable room to overcome constraints on bilateral trade and investment in both labor-intensive sectors (e.g., textiles) and in high technology, and to integrate India effectively into international economic institutions such as the WTO and APEC. One difficulty, of course, is that increased wealth and prosperity are necessary but probably not sufficient means to integrate these two powers. Their status demands are equally important and even harder to accommodate. Symbolic political gestures (similar to the initiative of including Russia in the "G-8" of industrial democracies) are useful to pursue. But U.S. officials will quickly be forced to address the need to share decision-making authority substantively as well as symbolically.

A second challenge is to maintain domestic support for the political and economic strategies to sustain hegemony. United States officials succeeded during the 1990s, but one could argue that they had it relatively easy. They managed to defuse security crises without being drawn into a major military role. Sustained economic prosperity in the United States helped to mitigate any lingering concerns over burden sharing and unfair trade practices—concerns that decisively shaped domestic political debate over Asia policy at the beginning of the decade. Opinion polls suggest that the U.S. public is supportive of U.S. engagement in Asia, but also is not deeply informed and is sensitive to the costs of engagement.[61] In this domestic political context, U.S. officials proved effective at pursuing hegemony quietly and cheaply during the 1990s.

The next decade may prove less accommodating. A major military crisis in the Taiwan Straits or Korean Peninsula would strain and possibly undermine domestic support for the hegemonic strategy in Asia. The domestic test would prove most severe if the United States found itself intervening and taking casualties while its closest ally in the region, Japan, begged off a direct role for political or constitutional reasons. United

[59] Nye, "Implications for U.S. Policy of Power Shifts between China and Japan," in *America and the East Asian Crisis*, 162.

[60] Good recent discussions include Paul Papayounou and Scott Kastner, "Sleeping with the Potential Enemy: Assessing the U.S. Policy of Engagement with China," *Security Studies* 9 no. 1 (fall 1999): 164–95; and William J. Long, "Trade and Technology Incentives and Bilateral Cooperation," *International Studies Quarterly* 40, no. 1 (March 1996): 77–106.

[61] For the supporting data see John E. Rielly, ed., *American Public Opinion and U.S. Foreign Policy 1999* (Chicago: Chicago Council on Foreign Relations, 1999).

States officials have worked with their Japanese counterparts to head off this "nightmare scenario" by strengthening and clarifying Japan's responsibilities under the U.S.–Japan Security Treaty. Whether and how the new arrangements would work in an actual crisis remains to be seen.[62]

A sustained economic downturn in the United States would similarly complicate U.S. strategy. The incentives for Asian trading states to embrace a U.S.–centered security order are increased to the extent that U.S. officials are willing to tolerate sizable trade deficits.[63] Slower growth in the United States, however, could rekindle both protectionist pressures and the resentment directed at Asian trading partners perceived to benefit unfairly from the asymmetrical openness of the U.S. market. In relations with Japan and South Korea, the politically charged issue of whether the United States should be defending states with prosperous economies, and perfectly capable of defending themselves, would be raised anew. A strategic partnership with China—a potential adversary perceived to be taking advantage of the United States economically—would similarly come under serious strain.

United States officials face more generally the domestic challenge of maintaining support for comprehensive engagement of China, which is necessarily a long-term strategy. An alternative approach to China policy began to crystallize by the end of the 1990s. Members of the so-called Blue Team—a loose collection of academics, members of Congress and their staffers, and some intelligence and military officials—promote the view that China is a rising and already hostile power destined to threaten vital U.S. interests.[64] Blue Team advocates call for the United States to take a harder line on China's human rights and unfair trade practices, restrict technology transfers, and provide more vigorous support for Taiwan. They have the potential in U.S. politics to mobilize human rights activists, the Taiwan lobby, opponents of religious persecution, and foreign policy conservatives. The powerful U.S. business community is arrayed against this coalition, but its ability to prevail is not a foregone conclusion—especially because it cannot control China's behavior, which is a key factor in the domestic debate. United States officials must win this domestic struggle, while deflecting the charge of appeasement, in order to pursue a consistent engagement strategy toward China.

---

[62] Japanese willingness to deploy naval forces to assist U.S. forces operating against Afghanistan—under consideration as of October 2001—would be an important step in advancing bilateral security cooperation.

[63] The U.S. merchandise trade deficit in 1999 was a record $271 billion, much of it with Japan and China. In 1989, at the height of U.S. economic conflict with Japan, the overall deficit was only $92 billion. John Burgess, "It's a Record: A $271 Billion Deficit," *Washington Post National Weekly Edition,* February 28, 2000.

[64] Robert G. Kaiser and Steven Mufson, "Blue Team Draws a Hard Line on Beijing," *Washington Post,* February 22, 2000.

A third challenge is for U.S. officials to manage the temptations of arrogance, triumphalism, and unilateralism. These are perennial temptations for any dominant state in whatever international order. The United States, perhaps because its preponderant power is coupled with a domestic political tradition that strongly imbues foreign policy with the values of society, seems especially inclined to preach its virtues, impose its values, and dictate rather than consult. But this type of behavior inevitably creates political resentment and backlash. It has the potential to provoke the very kind of balancing behavior that the U.S. hegemonic strategy has been designed to forestall.

By the end of the 1990s, U.S. officials found themselves confronting these reactions quite directly. Several U.S. initiatives—NATO expansion, the bombing of Kosovo, and the announced intention to modify the ABM Treaty—combined to stress the U.S.–Russia relationship and prompt Russia to explore "antihegemonic" options. Chinese officials similarly reacted negatively to what they viewed as U.S. arrogance in the May 1999 bombing of the Chinese embassy in Belgrade, scandals over Chinese nuclear espionage, and renewed public criticism from the United States over China's human rights practices. India resented U.S. demands for nuclear restraint as the United States defied the international community by rejecting ratification of the Comprehensive Test Ban Treaty. States in Southeast Asia chafed at the triumphalism that seemed to accompany the U.S. response to the Asian financial crisis. Even America's closest ally, Japan, voiced serious complaints over U.S. unilateralism in the handling of North Korea.[65]

How much and what type of damage these events will ultimately assess to the U.S. hegemonic position remains to be seen. But at the very least U.S. behavior will prompt major states in the region to explore their alternatives. In 1999, the Russian prime minister suggested that India, China, and Russia form a partnership to counter the global power of the United States. The presidents of China and France spent time during a recent summit to ponder common responses to U.S. "hyper-power." United States officials have found, among the permanent five of the U.N. Security Council, that they face a potential standoff between Russia and China on one side, the United States and Britain on the other, and France holding a swing vote. Former national security advisor Brent Scowcroft offered recently that the United States does not consult effectively and does not think much about the effects of its actions on others: "We behave to much of the world like a latter-day colonial power." State Department officials

---

[65] Japanese officials were reportedly furious that U.S. officials unilaterally declared in 1998 that funding for North Korean nuclear reactors—most of which is coming from Japan—could go ahead despite North Korea's missile firing over Japan. See Marshall and Mann, "Goodwill toward U.S. is Dwindling Globally."

recognize all of this as the essence of what they have come to call their "hegemony problem," but they have yet to figure out how to solve it.[66]

Conclusion: U.S. Hegemony and Other Pathways to Regional Order

United States hegemony is by no means an ideal solution to the security problems of the contemporary Asia-Pacific. It is incomplete, there are limits to what it can achieve, it makes other states uncomfortable, and at least at some levels it makes the United States uncomfortable as well. Nevertheless, in the near term it remains the best available pathway to regional order. It is easy to find fault with hegemony. But in the particular circumstances of the Asia-Pacific, it is difficult to find an alternative pathway that combines desirability and feasibility in a more adequate way.

Although there are plausible candidates, it is difficult in the near term to imagine another actor playing a regional hegemonic role more effectively. A Japanese hegemony would require a more open economy and society than Japan has been prepared to contemplate even in the face of severe economic crisis. Beyond the economic sphere, it would confront the constraints imposed on a more prominent Japanese regional presence by the legacy of Japanese colonialism.[67] There is also the intriguing question, raised recently by Masaru Tamamoto, of whether hegemony in any form is fundamentally unthinkable for Japan in political and cultural terms due to the postwar transformation of Japanese political identity.[68]

Few would contend that Chinese hegemony is unthinkable in that same sense. On the contrary, a recent essay by David Kang points to the long tradition of Chinese hegemony in the Asian past.[69] Whether or not contemporary China holds hegemonic ambitions, Chinese hegemony today is constrained by capabilities. One must rely on a series of highly optimistic projections to anticipate a smooth Chinese transformation for developing economy to regional hegemon. The need for continued economic reform, the fragility of the banking system, technological backwardness, the uncertainty of political transition, and the challenge of

[66] Scowcroft is quoted in Marshall and Mann, "Goodwill toward U.S. is Dwindling Globally." See also STRATFOR.COM, "Asian Alliance on the Horizon," Global Intelligence Update, October 14, 1999; James Hackett, "A New Anti-American Axis?" *Washington Times*, February 24, 2000; and Tyler Marshall, "Anti-NATO Axis Could Pose Threat," *Los Angeles Times*, September 27, 1999.

[67] Parts of the discussion of this section borrow from Ikenberry and Mastanduno, eds., *International Relations Theory and the Asia-Pacific* (Columbia University Press, forthcoming).

[68] Masaru Tamamoto, "Ambiguous Japan: Japanese National Identity at Century's End," in *International Relations Theory and the Asia-Pacific*.

[69] David Kang, "Culture and Hierarchy: The Chinese System and Stability in Asia," in *International Relations Theory and the Asia-Pacific*.

maintaining political and social stability as economic growth proceeds all point to the difficulty of a Chinese path to regional hegemony. There is additionally the more fundamental issue of how others in the region—Japan, Korea, other ASEAN states—would react to a serious Chinese bid to replace the United States.

Hegemony is obviously not the only pathway to order. Some analysts anticipate in the Asia-Pacific the return to a more traditional multipolar balance of power.[70] Multipolarity is plausible if one assumes the relative decline of the United States and the emergence of Japan, China, India, and perhaps Russia and Indonesia as roughly equivalent great powers. As a mechanism for order, a multipolar balance in contemporary Asia would face significant challenges. These include the uneven spread of military and especially nuclear capabilities among the major contenders; the existence of numerous flashpoints that increase the potential that conflicts would begin and escalate; and the potential inflexibility of alliance commitments due to long-standing friendships (e.g., United States and Japan) and rivalries (e.g., Japan and China). It would be a mistake to assume that a new multipolarity in Asia would operate similarly and provide the kind of relative stability enjoyed by European powers during the nineteenth century, and it is thus not surprising that analysts who foresee multipolarity generally expect the Asia-Pacific to be "ripe for rivalry."

A bipolar balance of power could plausibly emerge as a result of an action and reaction process on the part of China and the United States. A precondition would be the sustained development of Chinese economic, technological, and military capabilities. One could imagine, to the detriment of the regional and global economy, a political division with states in the region lining up behind one or the other power. The order created in this scenario would depend on the staying power of the two—and only the two—rivals. If China can develop sufficient capacity to challenge U.S. hegemony, then Japan, with a more powerful and sophisticated economy, is certainly capable of challenging China. Russia and India, major land powers with sizable populations, share many, if not all, of the potential great-power attributes of China. A future bipolarity could end with one pole standing or with several more emerging. The two major powers also would need to manage the risks that made the Cold War so predictably dangerous. Bipolarity encourages intense ideological conflict and the tests of resolve associated with brinkmanship. The United States and So-

---

[70] Aaron L. Friedberg, "Ripe for Rivalry: Prospects for Peace in a Multipolar Asia," *International Security* 18, no. 3 (winter 1993/94): 5–33; and Richard K. Betts, "Wealth, Power, and Instability: East Asia and the United States after the Cold War," *International Security* 18, no. 3 (winter 1993/94): 34–77.

viet Union managed those tests well—or were they simply lucky? China and the United States would face additional challenges as long as their nuclear capabilities remained asymmetrical, and as long as the United States claimed as an ally a political entity that China considers part of its own territory.

Finally, a pluralistic security community would be a more desirable pathway to order than hegemony, bipolarity, or multipolarity. In a security community a group of states share interests and values with sufficient commonality that the use of force to settle conflicts among them becomes essentially unthinkable.[71] This regional future would entail, in effect, the "Europeanization" of the Asia-Pacific—a coherent and self-conscious political community organized around shared values, interconnected societies, and effective regional institutions. Political community would become the core organizing principle of regional order, offering to states within it the value of joint membership and a sense of identity beyond their borders. The community would possess institutions and mechanisms to foster integration and resolve political conflict.

The circumstances required for the emergence of pluralistic security communities are difficult to attain, and as a result, this regional order may be the least likely.[72] The existence of a shared and deeply felt sense of political community among peoples across the borders of sovereign states is an elusive condition that cannot easily be engineered by state leaders. History and geography make this a special challenge in the Asia-Pacific. Would shared political identity be trans-Pacific or East Asian? What are its core values, and on what common cultural, religious, or other type of foundation does it rest? The absence of political community is a feature of the Asia-Pacific region unlikely to erode any time soon. Pluralistic security communities also rely on the robust presence of democratic government; the Asia-Pacific is marked instead by a significant diversity of regime types, and many of those that are democracies are still in the early phases of political development.

United States hegemony, then, may be the least problematic of an inherently problematic set of pathways to regional order. The fact that political community remains elusive, that historical resentments run deep, and that mutual suspicion characterizes much of the politics of the region create space for U.S. hegemony. No one loves a global hegemon. But U.S. hegemony is sufficiently benign to be at least tolerable—even to states

---

[71] See Emmanuel Adler and Michael Barnett, eds., *Security Communities* (Cambridge: Cambridge University Press, 1998).

[72] For a discussion of community-based security orders and their prerequisites, see Bruce Cronin, *Community under Anarchy: Transnational Identity and the Evolution of International Cooperation* (New York: Columbia University Press, 1999).

with great-power aspirations of their own. In these circumstances, the on-going challenge for U.S. officials interested in the preservation of hege-monic order will be to build on the progress already made while main-taining domestic support for this post–Cold War grand strategy.

PART III

The Institutions and
Ideology of Unipolarity

7

Democracy, Institutions, and American Restraint

G. John Ikenberry

O ne of the most puzzling aspects of world order after the Cold War is the persistence of stable and cooperative relations among the advanced industrial democracies and, more generally, the absence of balancing among the great powers. Despite the collapse of bipolarity and dramatic shifts in the global distribution of power, America's relations with Europe and Japan have remained what they have been for decades: stable, cooperative, and interdependent. Most observers have expected dramatic shifts in world politics after the Cold War, such as the return of multipolar great-power rivalry, the rise of competing regional blocs, and the decay of economic multilateralism. Yet even without the Soviet threat and Cold War bipolarity, and despite the extreme—indeed, unprecedented—character of the power disparities between the United States and the other major states, the United States along with Japan and Western Europe have reaffirmed their alliance partnerships, contained political conflicts, expanded trade and investment between them, and avoided a return to strategic rivalry and great-power balance. The United States started the 1990s as the world's only superpower and grew even

This chapter draws on G. John Ikenberry, "Institutions, Strategic Restraint, and the Durability of Western Order," *International Security* 23, no. 3 (winter 1998/99): 43–78; and *After Victory: Institutions, Strategic Restraint, and the Rebuilding of Order after Major War* (Princeton, N.J.: Princeton University Press, 2001).

more powerful through the decade, but its longstanding partnerships in Asia, Europe, and elsewhere around the world remain stable.

As the introduction to this book indicates, the persistence of the post-war American-led order is particularly a puzzle for dominant strands of realist theory. Realist theories are inadequate to explain both the durability of Western order and its important features, such as its extensive institutionalization and the consensual and reciprocal character of relations within it. To be sure, decades of balancing against Soviet power reinforced cooperation among these countries, but the basic organization of Western order predated the Cold War and survives today without it. Hegemonic theory is more promising as an explanation, but it too misses the remarkably liberal character of American hegemony and the importance of international institutions in facilitating cooperation and overcoming fears of domination or abandonment. For all these reasons, it is necessary to look beyond realism for an understanding of order among the advanced industrial societies.

To explain the absence of post–Cold War balancing between the major states—and the more general durability of relations among the industrial democracies—we need to turn realist theories of order on their head. It is actually the ability of the Western democracies to overcome or dampen the underlying manifestations of anarchy (order based on balance) and domination (order based on hegemony) that explains the character and persistence of Western order. Realist theories miss the institutional foundations of Western political order—a logic of order in which the binding and constraining effects of institutions and democratic polities reduce the incentives of Western states to engage in strategic rivalry or balance against American hegemony. The Western states are not held together exclusively because of external threats or the simple concentration of power. Rather, Western order has a structure of institutions and open polities that bind major states together, thereby mitigating the implications of power asymmetries and reducing the opportunities of the United States to abandon or dominate other states. The institutional character of the postwar order—made possible and credible by democratic regimes—is critical to an adequate explanation for the absence of power balancing after the Cold War.

This institutional explanation of Western order is developed in four steps. First, I argue that the basic logic of order among the Western states was set in place during and immediately after World War II, and it was a logic that addressed the basic problems emerging from both inside and outside the Western world. Two postwar settlements emerged after 1945: one responding to the problem of Soviet power and the spread of communism and the other responding to the problems of power disparities and regional rivalries within the West. Political and institutional bargains infused these two settlements—and they continue to influence American relations with Europe and Asia in the aftermath of the Cold War.

Second, Western order reflects the efforts of the United States and other nations to grapple with a basic constitutional problem: how to build a durable and mutually acceptable order among a group of states with huge power asymmetries. In order to gain the cooperation and compliance of secondary states, the United States had to both restrain and commit its power so as to reassure weaker states that it would not dominate or abandon them. Cooperative order is built around a basic bargain: the hegemonic state gets commitments by secondary states to participate within the postwar order, and in return the hegemon places limits on the exercise of its power. The weaker states do not fear domination or abandonment—reducing the incentives to balance—and the leading state does not need to use its power assets to enforce order and compliance. In effect, institutions create constraints on state action that serve to *reduce the returns to power*, that is, they reduce the long-term implications of asymmetries of power. This is precisely what constitutions and the rule of law do in domestic political orders. Limits are set on what actors can do with momentary power advantage. Losers realize that their losses are limited and temporary—to accept those losses is not to risk everything nor will it give the winners a permanent advantage. It is because the Western postwar order has found institutional ways to reduce the returns to power that it is so stable and mutually acceptable.

Third, the Western postwar order has also been rendered acceptable to Europe and Japan because American hegemony is built around decidedly liberal features. The penetrated character of American hegemony, creating transparency and allowing access by secondary states, along with the constraining effects of economic and security institutions, has provided mechanisms to increase confidence that the participating states would remain within the order and operate according to its rules and institutions. American hegemony has been rendered more benign and acceptable because of its open and accessible internal institutions.

Fourth, the Western order has actually become more stable over time because the rules and institutions have become more firmly embedded in the wider structures of politics and society. This is an argument about the *increasing returns to institutions*, in this case Western security and economic institutions. Over the decades, the core institutions of Western order have sunk their roots ever more deeply into the political and economic structures of the states that participate within the order. The result is that it is becoming increasingly difficult for "alternative institutions" or "alternative leadership" to seriously emerge. Western order has become institutionalized and path dependent—that is, more and more people will have to disrupt their lives if the order is to radically change. This makes wholesale change less likely.

Overall, the durability of Western order is built on two core logics. First, the institutions and practices of the order serve to reduce the returns to power, which lowers the risks of participation by strong and weak states alike. This, in turn, makes a resort to balancing and relative gains competition less necessary. Second, the institutions also exhibit an "increasing returns" character, which makes it more and more difficult for would-be orders and would-be hegemonic leaders to compete against and replace the existing order and leader. Although the Cold War reinforced this order, it was not triggered by it or ultimately dependent on the Cold War for its functioning and stability.

The implication of this analysis is that the West is a relatively stable and expansive political order. This is not only because the United States is an unmatched economic and military power today, but also because it is uniquely capable of engaging in strategic restraint, reassuring partners and facilitating cooperation. Because of its distinctively penetrated domestic political system, and because of the array of power dampening institutions it has created to manage political conflict, the United States has been able to remain at the center of a large and expanding hegemonic order. Its capacity to win in specific struggles with others within the system may rise and fall, but the larger Western order remains in place with little prospect of decline.

Postwar Bargains and Settlements

Forecasts of post–Cold War breakdown and disarray missed an important fact: in the shadow of the Cold War a distinctive and durable political order was being assembled among the major industrial countries. It is a multifaceted American-centered order organized around a layer cake of security alliances, open markets, multilateral institutions, and forums for consultation and governance. It is an order built on common interests and values among the advanced industrial countries and anchored in capitalism and democracy. But it is also an engineered political order built on American power, institutional relationships, and political bargains, particularly with Europe and Japan.

The core of today's international order is built on two grand bargains that the United States has made with other countries around the world. One is a realist bargain that grew out of the Cold War. The United States provides its European and Asian partners with security protection and access to American markets, technology, and supplies within an open world economy. In return, these countries agree to be stable partners who provide diplomatic, economic, and logistical support for the United States as it leads the wider international order. The other is a liberal bargain that addresses the uncertainties of American power. Asian and European states agree to accept American leadership and operate within an agreed upon political-economic system. In return, the United States opens itself up and binds itself to its partners. In effect, the United States builds an institutionalized coalition of partners and reinforces the stability of these long-term mutually beneficial relations by making itself more "user friendly"—that is, by playing by the rules and creating ongoing political processes with these other states that facilitate consultation and joint decision making. The United States makes its power safe for the world and in return the world agrees to live within the American system. These bargains date from the 1940s but continue to undergird the post–Cold War order.

These bargains—and the overall American-centered system—are a product of two order-building exercises after World War II. One is familiar and commonly seen as the defining feature of the postwar era. This was the containment order, organized around superpower rivalry, deterrence, containment, and ideological struggle between communism and the free world. Truman, Acheson, Kennan, and other American foreign policy officials were responding to the specter of Soviet power, organizing a global anticommunist alliance and fashioning an American grand strategy under the banner of containment. America's strategy was to "prevent the Soviet Union from using the power and position it won . . . to reshape the postwar international order."[1] This is the grand strategy and international order that was swept away in 1991.

But there was another order created after World War II. Here American officials were working with Britain and other countries to build a new set of relationships among the Western industrial democracies. The political settlement among these countries was aimed at solving the problems of the 1930s. This was a political order whose vision was articulated in such statements as the Atlantic Charter of 1941, the Bretton Woods agreements of 1944, and the Marshall Plan speech in 1947. Unlike containment, there was not a singular statement of strategy and purpose. It was an assemblage of ideas about open markets, social stability, political integration, international institutional cooperation, and collective security. Even the Atlantic Pact agreement of 1949 was as much aimed at reconstruction and inte-

---

[1] John Lewis Gaddis, *Strategies of Engagement: A Critical Appraisal of Postwar American National Security Policy* (New York: Oxford University Press, 1982), 4.

grating Europe and binding the democratic world together as it was an alliance created to balance Soviet power.[2]

The American system is based on a vision of open economic relations, intergovernmental cooperation, and liberal democratic society. But the most consequential aspect of the order is its security structure. Although the United States remained deeply ambivalent about extending security guarantees or forward deploying troops in Europe and Asia, it ultimately bound itself to the other advanced democracies through alliance partnership.[3] This strategy of security binding has provided a structure of commitments, restraints, and mechanisms of reassurance between the democratic alliance partners.

The American-centered alliances have always been doing more "work" than is usually appreciated.[4] The traditional understanding of alliances is that they are created to balance against external power and threats. But America's postwar alliances with Europe and Japan were created to do a lot more. The alliances have been as active in stabilizing and managing relations between alliance partners as in countering hostile states. This was true even during the Cold War but it is fundamentally the case today. The alliances serve to bind Japan, the United States, and Western Europe together and thereby reduce conflict and the potential for strategic rivalry between these traditional great powers. The alliances help these states establish credible commitment to a cooperative structure of relations. The alliances provide institutional mechanisms that allow each state to gain access to the policy-making processes in the others. Europe and Japan have institutionalized mechanisms for influencing the exercise of American military power. Moreover, by binding Germany to Western Europe and Japan to the United States, the alliances helps mute security-dilemma-driven conflict and strategic rivalry that might otherwise breakout in Europe and East Asia. The alliances allow the United States to both project power around the world and to limit and channel how that power is exercised. These functions of the alliances fit together—and they constitute a long-term institutional bargain between the United States and its European and Asian partners.

[2] See Mary N. Hampton, "NATO at the Creation: U.S. Foreign Policy, West Germany, and the Wilsonian Impulse," *Security Studies* 4, no. 3 (spring 1995): 610–56; and Hampton, *The Wilsonian Impulse: U.S. Foreign Policy, the Alliance, and German Unification* (Westport, Conn.: Praeger, 1996).

[3] On the complex, ambivalent, and evolving American thinking on its postwar security commitment to Europe, see Marc Trachtenberg, *A Constructed Peace: The Making of the European Settlement, 1945–1963* (Princeton, N.J.: Princeton University Press, 1999); and Melvin Leffler, *A Preponderance of Power: National Security, The Truman Administration, and the Cold War* (Stanford, Calif.: Stanford University Press, 1992).

[4] This argument is developed in Ikenberry, *After Victory*.

This system of alliances and multilateral institutions are the core of today's world order. American power both undergirds this system and is transformed by it. By enmeshing itself in a postwar web of alliances and multilateral commitments, the United States was able to project its influence outward and create a relatively secure environment in which to pursue its interests. But that order also shapes and restrains American power and makes the United States a more genial partner for other states. Likewise, the array of institutions and cooperative security ties that link Europe, the United States, Japan, and others creates a complex and stable order that in shear size overwhelms any alternative global order. Russia, China, or any other combination of states or movements are structurally too small to mount a fundamental challenge to this system. It is an order built on multifaceted cooperative arrangements, wealthy and advanced economies, and a preponderance of military power.

The Institutional Logic of Western Order

The institutional logic of Western order that today mitigates incentives for power balancing can best be isolated by looking at its first appearance after 1945. The most fundamental strategic reality after World War II was the huge disparity of power between the great powers who had fought the war—and, in particular, the commanding hegemonic position of the United States. George Kennan, in a major State Department review of American foreign policy in 1948, pointed to this new reality: "We have about 50% of the world's wealth but only 6.3% of its population. . . . Our real task in the coming period is to devise a pattern of relationships which will permit us to maintain this position of disparity without positive detriment to our national security."[5] It is the examination of the choices and options that the United States and the major European and Asian states faced after the war that allows us to see the underlying institutional logic of postwar order.

In a commanding postwar position, the United States had a tremendous range of options. It could dominate—use its power to prevail in the endless distributive struggles with other states. It could abandon—wash its hands of Europe and Asia and return home. Or it could seek to convert its favorable postwar power position into a durable order that commanded the allegiance of the other states within it. A legitimate political order is

[5] Kennan, Memorandum by the Director of the Policy Planning Staff (Kennan) to the Secretary of State and the Under Secretary of State (Lovett), February 24, 1948, *Foreign Relations of the United States*, 1948, vol. 1 (Washington, D.C.: Government Printing Office, 1975), 524.

one where its members willingly participate and agree with the overall orientation of the system.[6] To achieve a legitimate order means to secure agreement among the relevant states on the basic rules and principles of political order. States abide by the order's rules and principles because they accept them as their own.

To gain the willing participation of other states, the United States had to overcome their fears that America might pursue its other options: domination or abandonment. In this situation, the critical element to order formation was the ability of the United States to engage in "strategic restraint"—to convey to its potential partners credible assurances of its commitments to restrain its power and operate within the agreed upon rules and principles of postwar order. In the absence of these assurances, the weaker states of Europe and Japan would have serious incentives to resist American hegemony and engage in strategic rivalry and perhaps counterbalancing alliances.

It was precisely because the United States had the ability to engage in strategic restraint that a durable and legitimate postwar order was possible. This logic of restraint—institutionalized during the Cold War—persists today and radically reduces the incentives for power balancing. In effect, the United States agreed to move toward an institutionalized and agreed upon political process and to limit its power—made credible by binding institutions and open polities—in exchange for the acquiesce and compliant participation of secondary states. At the heart of the Western postwar order is an ongoing trade-off: the United States agrees to operate within an institutionalized political process and, in return, its partners agree to be willing participants.

More specifically, the United States had an incentive to move toward a settlement after the war with "constitutional" characteristics—that is, an order in which basic institutions and operating principles establish expectations and limit on what the leading state can do with its power.[7] In effect, this array of institutional agreements reduce the implications of "winning" in international relations, or to put it more directly, they serve to reduce the returns to power. This is fundamentally what constitutional institutions do within domestic orders. They set limits on what a state that gains disproportionately within the order can do with those gains, thereby reducing the stakes of uneven gains.[8] This means that they reduce the possibilities that a state can turn short-term gains into a long-term power ad-

---

[6] See David Beetham, *The Legitimation of Power* (London: Macmillan, 1991).

[7] See Alec Stone, "What Is a Supranational Constitution? An Essay in International Relations Theory," *The Review of Politics* 56, no. 3 (summer 1994): 441–74.

[8] See discussion in Jon Elster and Rune Slagstad, eds., *Constitutionalism and Democracy* (New York: Cambridge University Press, 1988).

vantage.[9] Taken together, constitutional agreements set limits on what actors can do with momentary advantages. Losers realize that their losses are limited and temporary—to accept those losses is not to risk everything nor will it give the winner a permanent advantage.

The role of institutional limits on power can be seen within domestic constitutional polities. When a party or leader wins an election and takes control of the government, there are fundamental and strictly defined limits on the scope of the power that can be exercised. A newly elected leader cannot use the military to oppress or punish his rivals, or use the taxing and law enforcement powers of government to harm or destroy the opposition party. The constitution sets limits on the use of power—and this serves to reduce the implications of winning and losing within the political system. To lose is not to lose all and winning is at best a temporary advantage. As a result, both parties can agree to stay within the system and play by the rules.

Limits on power are never as clear cut, absolute, or guaranteed in relations between states. The underlying conditions, even in highly complex and integrated orders, is still anarchic. But where institutions can be established that provide some measure of mutually binding constraints on states, and where the polities of the participating states are liberal democratic in character, the conditions exist for a settlement with constitutional characteristics.

But why would a hegemonic state want to restrict itself by agreeing to limits on the use of hegemonic power? The answer is that a constitutional settlement conserves hegemonic power, and this is for two reasons. First, if the hegemonic state calculates that its overwhelming power advantages are only momentary, an institutionalized order might "lock in" favorable arrangements that continue beyond the zenith of its power. In effect, the creation of basic ordering institutions are a form of hegemonic investment in the future. The hegemonic state gives up some freedom on the use of its power in exchange for a durable and predictable order that safeguards its interests in the future.

This investment motive rests on several assumptions. The hegemonic state must be convinced that its power position will ultimately decline. If it does, it should want to use its momentary position to get things that it wants accomplished. On the other hand, if the new hegemon calculates that its power position will remain preponderant into the foreseeable future, the incentive to conserve its power will disappear. Also, the hegemon must be convinced that the institutions it creates will persist beyond its

[9] See Adam Przeworski, *Democracy and the Market* (New York: Cambridge University Press, 1991), 36.

own power capabilities—that is, it must calculate that these institutions have some independent ordering capacity.[10] If institutions simply are reflections of the distribution of power, the appeal of an institutional settlement will obviously decline. But if institutions are potentially "sticky," powerful states that are farsighted enough to anticipate their relative decline can attempt to institutionalize favorable patterns of cooperation with other states that persist even as power balances shift.

The second reason why a hegemon might want to reach agreement on basic institutions, even if it means giving up some autonomy and short-term advantage, is that is can reduce the "enforcement costs" for maintaining order. The constant use of power capabilities to punish and reward secondary states and resolve conflicts is costly. It is far more effective over the long term to shape the interests and orientations of other states rather than directly shape their actions through coercion and inducements.[11] A constitutional settlement reduces the necessity of the costly expenditure of resources by the leading state on bargaining, monitoring, and enforcement.

But it remains a question why weaker states might not just resist any institutional settlement at all after the war and wait until they are stronger and can negotiate a more favorable settlement. There are several factors that might make this a less attractive option. First, without an institutional agreement, the weaker states will lose more than they would under a settlement, where the hegemonic state agrees to forego some immediate gains in exchange for willing participation of secondary states. Without an institutional settlement, bargaining will be based simply on power capacities, and the hegemonic state will have the clear advantage. The option of losing more now in order to gain more later is not an attractive option for a weak state that is struggling to rebuild after war. Its choices will be bi-

---

[10] The argument that international regimes and institutions, once created, can have an independent ordering impact on states comes in several versions. The weak version of this claim is the modified structural realist position that sees lags in the shifts of regimes as power and interests change. See Stephen D. Krasner, "Structural Causes and Regime Consequences: Regimes as Intervening Variables," in *International Regimes*, ed. Krasner (Ithaca, N.Y.: Cornell University Press, 1983), 1–12. The stronger version entails assumptions about path dependency and increasing returns. For a survey, see Walter W. Powell and Paul J. DiMaggio, eds., *The New Institutionalism in Organizational Analysis* (Chicago: University of Chicago Press, 1991), introduction, 1–38.

[11] This point is made by Lisa Martin, "The Rational State Choice of Multilateralism," in *Multilateralism Matters*, ed. John G. Ruggie (New York: Columbia University Press, 1993), 110. See also Margaret Levi, *Of Rule and Revenue* (Berkeley: University of California Press, 1988), 32. The argument that hegemons will want to promote normative consensus among states so as to reduce the necessity of coercive management of the order is presented in G. John Ikenberry and Charles A. Kupchan, "Socialization and Hegemonic Order," *International Organization* 44, no. 3 (summer 1990): 283–315.

ased in favor of gains today rather than gains tomorrow. The hegemon, on the other hand, will be more willing to trade off gains today for gains tomorrow. The difference in the two time horizons is crucial to understanding why a constitutional settlement is possible.

A second reason that weaker states might opt for the institutional agreement is that—if the hegemon is able to credibly demonstrate strategic restraint—it does buy the weaker state some protection against the threat of domination or abandonment. As realist theory would note, a central concern of weak or secondary state is whether they will be dominated by the more powerful state. In an order that has credible restraints on power, the possibility of indiscriminate and ruthless domination is mitigated. Just as importantly, the possibility of abandonment is also lessened. If the hegemonic state is rendered more predictable, this means that the secondary states do not need to spend as many resources on "risk premiums," which would otherwise be needed to prepare for either domination or abandonment. In such a situation, the asymmetries in power are rendered more tolerable by secondary states.

Taken together, the Western postwar order involves an institutional bargain: the leading state gets a predictable and durable order based on agreed upon rules and institutions—it gets the acquiescence in this order by weaker states, which in turn allows it to conserve its power. In return, the leading state agrees to limits on its own actions—to operate according to the same rules and institutions as lesser states—and to open itself up to a political process in which the weaker states can actively press their interests upon the more powerful state. The hegemonic or leading state agrees to forego some gains in the early postwar period in exchange for rules and institutions that allow it to have stable returns later, while weaker states are given favorable returns up front and limits on the exercise of power.

Varieties of Postwar Power Restraints

Even if there are reasons why the leading and secondary states might favor a constitutional order, it is not obvious that they will accept the risks seemingly inherent in such an order. For self-regarding states to agree to pursue their interests within cobinding institutions, they must convey to each other a credible sense of commitment—an assurance that they will not abandon their mutual restraint and exploit momentary advantages.[12] The United States and its partners were able to overcome the risks of a highly

[12] For a discussion of the general problem of credible commitment and its importance to institutional development and the rule of law, see Barry Weingast and Douglass C. North,

asymmetrical order because of three features: its "reluctant" orientation toward hegemonic domination; the open and penetrated character of the American polity; and the constraining effects of postwar economic and security institutions. In each of these ways, the postwar order was established in a way that served to limit the returns to power.

The first way in which the United States provided reassurances to its partners was in its basic orientation toward postwar order—that it was a "reluctant hegemon" in many respects, and that it fundamentally sought agreement among the Western states on a mutually acceptable order, even if this meant extensive compromise. It is revealing that the initial and most forcefully presented American view on postwar order was the State Department's proposal for a postwar system of free trade. This proposal did not only reflect an American conviction about the virtues of open markets, but it also was a vision of order that would require very little direct American involvement or management. The system would be largely self-regulating, leaving the United States to operate within but without the burdens of direct and ongoing supervision.

This view on postwar trade reflected a more general American orientation as the war came to an end. It wanted a world order that would advance American interests, but it was not eager to actively organize and run that order. It is in this sense that the United States was a reluctant superpower.[13] This general characteristic was not lost on Europeans, and it mattered as America's potential partners contemplated whether and how to cooperate with the United States. To the extent the United States could convey the sense that they did not seek to dominate the Europeans, it gave greater credibility to America's proposals for a constitutional settlement. It provided some reassurance that the United States would operate from within limits and not use its overwhelming power position simply to dominate.

More generally, the overall pattern of American postwar policies reflected a self-conscious effort by administration officials to infuse the postwar system with a sense of legitimacy and reciprocal consent. When American officials began to organize Marshall Plan aid for Europe, for example, there was a strong desire to have the Europeans embrace American aid and plans as their own—thus enhancing the legitimacy of the overall postwar settlement. At a May 1947 meeting, George Kennan argued that it was important to have "European acknowledgement of re-

---

"Constitutions and Commitment: The Evolution of Institutions Governing Public Choice in Seventeenth-Century England," *Journal of Economic History* 44 (1989): 803–32.

[13] See Richard Holt, *The Reluctant Superpower: A History of America's Global Economic Reach* (New York: Kodansha International, 1995). See also Geir Lundestad, "Empire by Invitation? The United States and Western Europe, 1945–1952," *The Journal of Peace Research* 23 (September 1986): 263–77.

sponsibility and parentage in the plan to prevent the certain attempts of powerful elements to place the entire burden on the United States and to discredit it and us by blaming the United State for all failures." Similarly, State Department official Charles Bohlen argued that United States policy should not be seen as an attempt "to force 'the American way' on Europe."[14] The United States wanted to create an order that conformed to its liberal democratic principles, but this could only be done if other governments embraced such a system as their own.

This orientation was also reflected in the compromises that the United States made in accommodating European views about the postwar world economy. The British and the continental Europeans, worried about postwar depression and the protection of their fragile economies, were not eager to embrace America's stark proposals for an open world trading system, favoring a more regulated and compensatory system.[15] The United States did attempt to use its material resources to pressure and induce Britain and the other European countries to abandon bilateral and regional preferential agreements and accept the principles of a postwar economy organized around a nondiscriminatory system of trade and payments.[16] The United States knew it held a commanding position and sought to use its power to give the postwar order a distinctive shape. But it also prized agreement over deadlock, and it ultimately moved a great distance away from its original proposals in setting up the various postwar economic institutions.[17]

A second way that the United States projected reassurance was structural—its own liberal democratic polity. The open and decentralized character of the American political system provided opportunities for other states to exercise their "voice" in the operation of the American hegemonic order, thereby reassuring these states that their interests could be actively advanced and processes of conflict resolution would exist. In

[14] "Summary of Discussion on Problems of Relief, Rehabilitation and Reconstruction of Europe," May 29, 1947, *Foreign Relations of the United States*, 1947, vol. 3 (Washington, D.C.: Government Printing Office, 1972), 235.

[15] The strongest claims about American and European differences over postwar political economy are made by Fred Block, *The Origins of International Economic Disorder* (Berkeley: University of California Press, 1977), 70–122.

[16] The 1946 British Loan deal was perhaps the most overt effort by the Truman administration to tie American postwar aid to specific policy concessions by allied governments. This was the failed Anglo-American Financial Agreement, which obliged the British to make sterling convertible in exchange for American assistance. See Richard Gardner, *Sterling-Dollar Diplomacy: The Origins and the Prospects of Our International Economic Order* (New York: McGraw Hill, 1969); and Alfred E. Eckes Jr., *A Search for Solvency: Bretton Woods and the International Monetary System, 1944–71* (Austin: University of Texas Press, 1971).

[17] See John Gerard Ruggie, *Winning the Peace: America and World Order in the New Era* (New York: Columbia University Press, 1996), chap. 5.

this sense, the American postwar order was a "liberal hegemony," an extended system that blurred domestic and international politics as it created an elaborate transnational and transgovernmental political system with the United States at its center.[18]

There are actually several ways in which America's penetrated hegemony has served to reinforce the credibility of the United State's commitment to operating within an institutionalized political order. The first is simply the transparency of the system, which reduces surprises and allays worries by partners that the United States might make abrupt changes in policy. This transparency comes from the fact that policy making in a large, decentralized democracy involves many players and an extended and relatively visible political process. But it is not only that it is an open and decentralized system, but it is also one with competing political parties and an independent press—features that serve to expose the underlying integrity and viability of major policy commitments.[19] The open and competitive process may produce mixed and ambiguous policies at times, but the transparency of the process at least allows other states to make more accurate calculations about the likely direction of American foreign policy, which lowers levels of uncertainty and provides a measure of reassurance—which, everything else being equal—provides greater opportunities to cooperate.

Another way in which the penetrated hegemonic order provides reassurances to partners is that the American system invites (or at least provides opportunities for) the participation of outsiders. The fragmented and penetrated American system allows and invites the proliferation of a vast network of transnational and transgovernmental relations with Europe, Japan, and other parts of the industrial world. Diffuse and dense networks of governmental, corporate, and private associations tie the system together. The United States is the primary site for the pulling and hauling of transatlantic and trans-Pacific politics. Europeans and Japanese do not have elected officials in Washington—but they do have representatives.[20] Although this access to the American political process is not fully recipro-

---

[18] This section and the next draw on Daniel Deudney and G. John Ikenberry, "The Sources and Character of Liberal International Order," *Review of International Studies* 25, no. 2 (April 1999): 179–96.

[19] This point is made in James Fearon, "Domestic Political Audiences and the Escalation of International Disputes," *American Political Science Review* 88 (September 1994): 577–92.

[20] For the transnational political process channeled through the Atlantic security institutions, see Thomas Risse-Kappen, *Cooperation among Democracies: The European Influence on U.S. Foreign Policy* (Princeton, N.J.: Princeton University Press, 1995). On the U.S.–Japanese side, see Peter J. Katzenstein and Yutaka Tsujinaka, " 'Bullying,' 'Buying,' and 'Binding': U.S.–Japanese Transnational Relations and Domestic Structures," in *Bringing Transnational Relations Back In*, ed. Risse-Kappen (New York: Cambridge University Press, 1995), 79–111.

cated abroad, the openness and extensive decentralization of the American liberal system assures other states that they have routine access to the decision-making processes of the United States.

The implication of penetrated hegemony is that the United States is not as able to use its commanding power position to gain disproportionately in relations with Japan and Europe—or at least it diminishes the leverage that would otherwise exist. For example, there is little evidence that the United States has been able to bring more pressure to bear on Japanese import policy, even as its relative power capacities have seemingly increased in the 1990s with the end of the Cold War and the slump in the Japanese economy. Beginning in July 1993 with the signing of a "framework" agreement, the Clinton administration launched a series of efforts to pin Japan to numerical import targets, including threatened sanctions to boost American automobile imports. But despite repeated American efforts in February 1994 and the spring of 1995, Prime Minister Hosakawa, helped by protests from the European Union, was able to largely resist American pressure.[21] The advent of the World Trade Organization also has provided additional ways for Japan to narrow trade dispute to specific issues, bring international procedures of review into play, and diminish the capacity of the United States to use its hegemonic power for economic advantage.[22] The open and penetrated character of the United States serves to fragment and narrow policy disputes, creates a more level playing field for European and Japanese interests, and reduces the implications of hegemonic power asymmetries.

A final way in which reassurance was mutually conveyed was in the institutions themselves, which provided "lock in" and "binding" constraints on the United States and its partners, thereby mitigating fears of domination or abandonment. The Western countries made systematic efforts to anchor their joint commitments in principled and binding institutional mechanisms. Governments might ordinarily seek to preserve their op-

[21] See Andrew Pollack, "U.S. Appears to Retreat from Setting Targets to Increase Japan's Imports," *New York Times,* July 10, 1993; David Sanger, "Hosakawa's Move Foils U.S. Strategy," *International Herald Tribune,* April 11, 1994; Nancy Dunne and Michito Nakamato, "Wiser U.S. to Meet Chastened Japan," *Financial Times,* May 18, 1994; and Reginald Dale, "Japan Gains the Edge in Trade War," *International Herald Tribune,* September 13, 1994.

[22] As Clyde V. Prestowitz Jr. writes: "In the past, the United States would have attempted to negotiate a bilateral settlement with the potential imposition of sanctions lurking in the background as an incentive to reach an agreement. Under the new WTO rules, however, all disputes are supposed to be submitted to the WTO for compulsory arbitration and unilateral imposition of trade sanctions is illegal. . . . But if America then attempts to solve the problem unilaterally by imposing sanctions, Japan could have the U.S. sanctions declared illegal by the WTO. Knowing this, Japanese officials have refused even to meet with U.S. negotiators . . . and have effectively told the United States to buzz off." Prestowitz, "The New Asian Equation," *The Washington Post,* April 14, 1996, C1.

tions, to cooperate with other states but to leave open the option of disengaging. What the United States and the other Western states did after the war was exactly the opposite: they built long-term economic, political, and security commitments that were difficult to retract. They "locked in" their commitments and relationships, to the extent that this can be done by sovereign states.[23]

The logic of institutional binding is best seen in security alliances. Alliances have often been formed not simply or even primarily to aggregate power so as to balance against external threats, but rather to allow alliance partners to restrain each other and manage joint relations. Alliances have traditionally been seen as temporary expedients that bring states together in pledges of mutual assistance in the face of a common threat, a commitment specified in the *casus foederis* article of the treaty. But as Paul Schroeder and others have noted, alliances have also been created as *pacta de contrahendo*—pacts of restraint.[24] They have served as mechanisms for states to manage and restrain their partners within the alliance. "Frequently the desire to exercise such control over an ally's policy," Schroeder argues, "was the main reason that one power, or both, entered into the alliance."[25] Alliances create binding treaties that allow states to keep a hand in the security policy of their partners. When alliance treaties are *pacta de contrahendo*, potential rivals tie themselves to each other—alleviating suspicions, reducing uncertainties, and creating institutional mechanisms for each to influence the policies of the other.

The practice of mutual constraint only makes sense if international institutions or regimes can have an independent ordering impact on the actions of states. The assumption is that institutions are sticky—that they can take on a life and logic of their own, shaping and constraining even the states that create them. When states employ institutional binding as a strategy, they are essentially agreeing to mutually constrain themselves. In effect, institutions specify what it is that states are expected to do and

[23] For an important argument about why democratic states are particularly inclined to engage in "binding," see Daniel Deudney, "Binding Sovereigns: The Practices, Structures, and Geopolitics of Philadelphian Systems," in *Constructing Sovereignty*, ed. Thomas Biersteker and Cynthia Weber (New York: Cambridge University Press, 1996), 190–239.

[24] See Paul W. Schroeder, "Alliances, 1815–1945: Weapons of Power and Tools of Management," in *Historical Dimensions of National Security Problems*, ed. Klaus Knorr (Lawrence: University Press of Kansas, 1975), 227–62. As Schroeder notes, the internal constraint function of alliances was earlier observed by George Liska. See Liska, *Nations in Alliance: The Limits of Interdependence* (Baltimore: Johns Hopkins Press, 1962), 116; *Imperial America: The International Politics of Primacy* (Baltimore: Johns Hopkins Press, 1967), 9–11 and 20–21; and *Alliances and the Third World* (Baltimore: Johns Hopkins Press, 1968), 24–35.

[25] Schroeder, "Alliances, 1815–1945," 230.

make it difficult and costly for states to do otherwise.[26] Binding mechanisms include treaties, interlocking organizations, joint management responsibilities, agreed upon standards and principles of relations, and so forth. These mechanisms raise the "costs of exit" and creates "voice opportunities," thereby providing mechanisms to mitigate or resolve the conflict.[27]

The Bretton Woods economic and monetary accords exhibit the logic of institutional lock-in. These were the first accords to establish a permanent international institutional and legal framework to ensure economic cooperation between states. They were constructed as elaborate systems of rules and obligations with quasi-judicial procedures for adjudicating disputes.[28] In effect, the Western governments created an array of functionally organized transnational political systems. Moreover, the democratic character of the United States and the other Western countries facilitated the construction of these dense interstate connections. The permeability of domestic institutions provided congenial grounds for reciprocal and pluralistic "pulling and hauling" across the advanced industrial world.

It was here that the Cold War's security alliances provided additional institutional binding opportunities. The old saying that NATO was created to "keep the Russians out, the Germans down, and the Americans in" is a statement about the importance of the alliance structures for locking in long-term commitments and expectations. The American-Japanese security alliance also had a similar "dual containment" character. These institutions not only served as alliances in the ordinary sense as organized efforts to balance against external threats, they also provided mechanisms and venues to build political relations, conduct business, and regulate conflict.

Binding institutions have been particularly important for Germany and Japan. Both countries were reintegrated into the advanced industrial world as "semi-sovereign" powers; that is, they accepted unprecedented

[26] This view accords with our general view of what institutions are and do. As Lorenzo Ornaghi argues: "The role of institutions in politics is to give the rules of the game, in that, by reducing the uncertain and unforeseeable character of interpersonal relations, insurance is mutually provided." Ornaghi, "Economic Structure and Political Institutions: A Theoretical Framework," in *The Economic Theory of Structure and Change,* ed. Mauro Baranzini and Roberto Scazzieri (Cambridge: Cambridge University Press, 1990), 27.

[27] For an attempt to use this logic of binding to explain European union, see Joseph Grieco, "The Maastricht Treaty, Economic and Monetary Union and the Neo-Realist Research Programme," *Review of International Studies* 21 (1995): 21–40.

[28] See Harold James, *International Monetary Cooperation since Bretton Woods* (New York: Oxford University Press, 1995).

constitutional limits on their military capacity and independence.[29] As such, they became unusually dependent on the array of Western regional and multilateral economic and security institutions. The Western political order in which they were embedded was integral to their stability and functioning. The Christian Democrat Walther Leisler Kiep argued in 1972 that "the German-American alliance . . . is not merely one aspect of modern German history, but a decisive element as a result of its preeminent place in our politics. In effect, it provides a second constitution for our country."[30] This logic of Germany's involvement in NATO and the EU was reaffirmed recently by the German political leader Karsten D. Voigt: "We wanted to bind Germany into a structure that practically obliges Germany to take the interests of its neighbors into consideration. We wanted to give our neighbors assurances that we won't do what we don't intend to do."[31] Western economic and security institutions provide Germany and Japan with a political bulwark of stability that far transcends their more immediate and practical purposes.

The recent revision of the U.S.–Japan security treaty in May 1996 is another indication that both countries see virtues in maintaining a tight security relationship regardless of the end of the Cold War or the rise and fall of specific security threats in the region.[32] Even though the threats in the region have become less tangible or immediate, the alliance has been reaffirmed and cooperation and joint planning have expanded. Part of the reason is that the alliance is still seen by many Japanese and American officials as a way to render the bilateral relationship more stable by binding each to the other.[33] The cobinding aspects of NATO have also partially

[29] On the notion of semisovereignty, see Peter J. Katzenstein, *Policy and Politics in West Germany: The Growth of a Semi-sovereign State* (Philadelphia: Temple University Press, 1987). For a discussion of Japanese semisovereignty and the postwar peace constitution, see Masaru Tamamoto, "Reflections on Japan's Postwar State," *Daedalus* 125, no. 2 (spring 1995): 1–22.

[30] Quoted in Thomas A. Schwartz, "The United States and Germany after 1945: Alliances, Transnational Relations, and the Legacy of the Cold War," *Diplomatic History* 19, no. 4 (fall 1995): 555.

[31] Quoted in Jan Perlez, "Larger NATO Seen as Lid on Germany," *International Herald Tribune*, December 8, 1997.

[32] President Clinton and Prime Minister Hashimoto signed a Joint Declaration on Security on April 17, 1996, which was a revision of the 1978 Guidelines for U.S.–Japan Defense Cooperation. The agreement declared that the U.S.–Japanese security treaty of 1960 "remains the cornerstone" of their policies, that their forces in Japan would engage in policy coordination for dealing with regional crises, and on a reciprocal basis provide equipment and supplies. Overall, the Japanese made a commitment to actually move toward closer security relations with the United States.

[33] Peter J. Katzenstein and Yutaka Tsujinaka argue that "the security relationship between the United States and Japan is best described by 'binding,' with the United States doing most of the 'advising' and Japan most of the 'accepting.' By and large since the mid-1970s defense cooperation has increased smoothly and apparently to the satisfaction of both militaries. Since that cooperation involved primarily governments and subunits of governments imple-

driven its expansion. This view of NATO as "architecture" that would stabilize relations within Europe and across the Atlantic rather than primarily an alliance to counter external threats was first signaled in Secretary of
State Baker's famous speech in the aftermath of the fall of the Berlin
Wall.[34] Some supporters of NATO expansion see it as an insurance policy
against the possibility of future resurgent and revisionist Russia.[35] But others, particularly in the Clinton administration, see the virtues of expansion more in terms of the stabilizing, integrating, and binding effects that
come from NATO as an institution.[36]

All these characteristics have helped to facilitate a rather stable and
durable political order. American strategic restraint after the war left the
European more worried about abandonment than domination, and they
actively sought American institutionalized commitments to Europe. The
American polity's transparency and permeability fostered an "extended"
political order—reaching outward to the other industrial democracies—
with most of its roads leading to Washington. Transnational and transgovernmental relations provide the channels. Multiple layers of economic,
political, and security institutions bind these countries together in ways
that reinforce the credibility of their mutual commitments. The United
States remains the center of the system, but other states are highly integrated into it, and its legitimacy diminishes the need for the exercise of coercive power by the United States or for balancing responses from secondary states.

Increasing Returns to Postwar Institutions

The bargains struck and institutions created at the early moments of postwar order building have not simply persisted for fifty years, but they have
actually become more deeply rooted in the wider structures of politics
and society of the countries that participate within the order. That is,
more people and more of their activities are hooked into the institutions
and operations of the American liberal hegemonic order. A wider array of

---

menting policy, 'binding' results primarily from transgovernmental relations." Katzenstein
and Tsujinaka, " 'Bullying,' 'Buying,' and 'Binding,' " 80. See also Richard Finn, "Japan's
Search for a Global Role," in *Japan's Quest: The Search for International Role, Recognition, and Respect,* ed. Warren S. Hunsberger (New York: M. E. Sharpe, 1977), 113–30.

   [34] See Michael Smith and Stephen Woolcock, *The United States and the European Community
in a Transformed World* (London: Pinter/Royal Institute of International Affairs, 1993), 1.

   [35] See Zbigniew Brzezinski, "NATO—Expand or Die?" *New York Times,* December 28, 1994.

   [36] See Michael Cox, *U.S. Foreign Policy after the Cold War: Superpower without a Mission?*
(London: Royal Institute of International Affairs, 1995), 79–83.

individuals and groups, in more countries and more realms of activity, have a stake—or a vested interest—in the continuation of the system. The costs of disruption or change in this system have steadily grown over the decades. Together, this means that "competing orders" or "alternative institutions" are at a disadvantage. The system is increasingly hard to replace.

The reason institutions have a "lock in" effect is primarily because of the phenomenon of increasing returns.[37] There are several aspects to increasing returns to institutions. First, there are large start-up costs to creating new institutions. Even when alternative institutions might be more efficient or accord more closely with the interests of powerful states, the gains from the new institutions must be overwhelmingly greater before they overcome the sunk costs of the existing institutions.[38] Moreover, there tend to be learning effects that are achieved in the operation of the existing institution that give it advantages over a start-up institution. Finally, institutions tend to create relations and commitments with other actors and institutions that serve to embed the institution and raise the costs of change. Taken together, as Douglass North concludes, "the interdependent web of an institutional matrix produces massive increasing returns."[39]

American postwar hegemonic order has exhibited this phenomenon of increasing returns to its institutions. At the early moments after 1945, when the imperial, bilateral, and regional alternatives to America's postwar agenda were most imminent, the United States was able to use its unusual and momentary advantages to tilt the system in the direction it desired. The pathway to the present liberal hegemonic order began at a very narrow passage where really only Britain and the United States—and a few top officials—could shape decisively the basic orientation of the world political economy. But once the institutions, such as Bretton Woods and GATT, were established, it became increasingly hard for competing visions of postwar order to have any viability. America's great burst of insti-

[37] Both rational choice and sociological theories of institutions offer theories of institutional path dependency—both emphasizing the phenomenon of increasing returns. See Paul Pierson, "Path Dependence and the Study of Politics" (unpublished paper, 1996).

[38] On sunk costs, see Arthur L. Stinchcombe, *Constructing Social Theories* (New York: Harcourt, Brace, 1968), 108–18.

[39] North, *Institutions, Institutional Change, and Economic Performance* (New York: Cambridge University Press, 1990), 95. For discussions of path dependency arguments and their implications, see Stephen Krasner, "Approaches to the State: Conceptions and Historical Dynamics," *Comparative Politics* 16 (January 1984): 223–46; and Paul Pierson, "When Effect Becomes Cause: Policy Feedback and Political Change," *World Politics* 45, no, 4 (July 1993): 595–628. For a survey of the literature of path dependency, see Stephen K. Sanderson, *Social Evolutionism: A Critical History* (London: Basil Blackwell, 1990).

tution building after World War II fits a general pattern of international continuity and change: crisis or war opens up a moment of flux and opportunity, choices get made, and interstate relations get fixed or settled for a while.[40]

The notion of increasing returns to institutions means that once a moment of institutional selection comes and goes, the cost of large-sale institutional change rises dramatically—even if potential institutions, when compared with existing ones, are more efficient and desirable.[41] In terms of American hegemony, this means that, short of a major war or a global economic collapse, it is very difficult to envisage the type of historical breakpoint needed to replace the existing order. This is true even if a new would-be hegemon or coalition of states had an interest in and agenda for an alternative set of global institutions—which they do not.[42]

While the increasing returns to institutions can serve to perpetuate institutions of many sorts, American hegemonic institutions have characteristics that particularly lend themselves to increasing returns. First, the set of principles that infuse these institutions—particularly principles of multilateralism, openness, and reciprocity—are ones that command agreement because of their perceived fairness and legitimacy. Organized around principles that are easy for states, regardless of their specific international power position, to accept, the institutional pattern is more robust and easy to expand. Moreover, the principled basis of hegemonic order also makes it more durable. This is John Ruggie's argument about the multilateral organization of postwar international institutions: "All other things being equal, an arrangement based on generalized organizing principles should be more elastic than one based on particularistic interests and situational exigencies."[43] Potential alternative institutional orders are at an added disadvantage because the principles of the current institutional order are adaptable, expandable, and easily accepted as legitimate.

Second, the open and permeable character of American hegemonic in-

---

[40] See Peter Katzenstein, "International Relations Theory and the Analysis of Change," in *Global Changes and Theoretical Challenges: Approaches to World Politics for the 1990s,* ed. Ernst-Otto Czempiel and James N. Rosenau (Lexington, Mass.: Lexington Books, 1989), 291–304.

[41] This notion of breakpoint or critical juncture is not developed in the increasing returns literature, but it is implicit in the argument, and it is very important for understanding the path dependency of American hegemony.

[42] Major or great-power war is a uniquely powerful agent of change in world politics because it tends to destroy and discredit old institutions and force the emergence of a new leading or hegemonic state. Robert Gilpin discusses the possibility that with the rise of nuclear weapons, this sort of pattern of global change may end, thereby leaving in place the existing hegemonic order. See Gilpin, *War and Change in World Politics* (New York: Cambridge University Press, 1981), epilogue, 231–44.

[43] John G. Ruggie, "Multilateralism: The Anatomy of an Institution," in *Multilateralism Matters,* 32–33.

stitutions also serves to facilitate increasing returns. One of the most important aspects of increasing returns is that once a particular institution is established, other institutions and relations tend to grow up around it and become interconnected and mutually dependent. A good analogy is computer software, where a software provider like Microsoft, after gaining an initial market advantage, encourages the proliferation of software applications and programs based on Microsoft's operating language. This, in turn, leads to a huge complex of providers and users who are heavily dependent on the Microsoft format. The result is an expanding market community of individuals and firms with an increasingly dense set of commitments to Microsoft—commitments that are not based on loyalty but on the growing reality that changing to another format would be more costly, even if it were more efficient.

The penetrated character of American hegemony encourages this sort of proliferation of connecting groups and institutions. A dense set of transnational and transgovernmental channels are woven into the trilateral regions of the advanced industrial world. A sort of layer cake of intergovernmental institutions span outward from the United States across the Atlantic and Pacific.[44] Global multilateral economic institutions, such as the IMF and WTO, are connected to more circumscribed governance institutions, such as the G-7 and G-10. Private groups, such as the Trilateral Commission and hundreds of business trade associations, are also connected in one way or another to individual governments and their joint management institutions. The steady rise of trade and investment across the advanced industrial world has made these countries more interdependent, which in turn has expanded the constituency within these countries for a perpetuation of an open, multilateral system.

What this means is that great shifts in the basic organization of the American hegemonic order are increasingly costly to a widening array of individuals and groups who make up the order. More and more people have a stake in the system, even if they have no particularly loyalty or affinity for the United States and even if they might really prefer a different order. As the postwar era has worn on, the operating institutions of the American hegemonic order have expanded and deepened. More and more people would have their lives disrupted if the system were to be radically changed—which is another way of saying that the constituency for preserving the postwar political order among the major industrial coun-

[44] See Cheryl Shanks, Harold K. Jacobson, and Jeffrey H. Kaplan, "Inertia and Change in the Constellation of International Governmental Organizations, 1981–1992," *International Organization* 50, no. 4 (autumn 1996): 593–628.

tries is greater than ever before. It is in this sense that the American post-war order is stable and growing.

The dominance of the United States has sparked complaints and resistance in various quarters of Europe and Asia—but it has not triggered the type of counterhegemonic balancing or competitive conflict that might otherwise be expected. Some argue that complaints about America's abuse of its commanding power position have grown in recent years. Unwillingness to pay United Nations dues; the Helms-Burton Act, which inhibits trade with Cuba; and resistance to commitments to cut greenhouse gases—these and other failures are the grist of European and Asian complaints about American predominance. But complaints about the American "arrogance of power" has been a constant minor theme of postwar Western order. Episodes include the "invasion" of U.S. companies into Europe in the 1950s, the dispute over Suez in 1953, the "Nixon shocks" in 1971 over the surprise closure of the gold window, failure of America to decontrol oil prices during the 1970s energy crisis, and the Euro-missiles controversy of the early 1980s. Seen in postwar perspective, it is difficult to argue that the level of conflict has risen.

The Bush administration has raised the visibility of America's ambivalence toward making multilateral commitments. In the early months of 2001, it rejected a series of international treaties and agreements and unsettled relationships worldwide.[45] But it has also shown some sensitivity to the rising chorus of complaints about what Europeans and others see as a new unilateralist tendency in American foreign policy. Its championing of national missile defense has continued but the proposals have evolved in an effort to make them more acceptable to its allies and Russia. The terrorist acts of September 11 have also led to a reorientation of American policy toward a more coalition-based approach. There is at least a hint that the administration understands that by tying itself to a wider grouping of states it is more effective. To effectively fight terrorism, the United States needs partners—it needs military and logistical support of allies, intelligence sharing, and the practical cooperation of front-line states. The simple logic of problem solving moves the United States into the realm of multilateral, rule-based foreign policy.

The institutional and reciprocal character of the Western system encourages this collaborative approach to terrorism. European and other world leaders trooped into Washington in the weeks following the September 11 attacks. Each offered its support but also weighed in on how

[45] See Gerard Baker, "Bush Heralds Era of U.S. Self-Interest," *International Herald Tribune*, April 24, 2001.

best to wage the coming campaign. Prime Minister Tony Blair is the best example of this strategy of engaging America. The British leader tied himself to the American antiterrorist plan but in doing so he made it a Anglo-American—and even alliance-based—campaign. By binding itself to the superpower, Britain gains a stake in the struggle but also a voice in the policy. At least in the initial months after September 11, allied diplomacy showed the dynamic character of the Western system: the United States has ready friends and America's allies have ready access to American decision making. The American-centered system provides a spider web of relations that helps reinforce the bargains and cooperative structures. Allied interactions tend to moderate policy, soften the sharp edges of allied disagreements, and move the countries toward a more concerted strategy.

Today, as in the past, the differences tend to be negotiated and resolved within intergovernmental channels—even while the Europeans, Americans, and Japanese agree to expand their cooperation in new areas, such as international law enforcement, the environment, and nonproliferation. More importantly, despite complaints about the American abuse of its hegemonic position, there are no serious political movements in Europe or Japan that call for a radical break with the existing Western order organized around American power and institutions. It is the stability of the order, in spite of policy struggles and complaints, that is more remarkable than any changes in the character of the struggles or complaints.

Conclusion

The character of American power is as interesting and remarkable as the fact of its existence. American domination or hegemony is very unusual, and the larger Western political order that surrounds it is unique as well. Fundamentally, American hegemony is reluctant, penetrated, and highly institutionalized—or in a word, liberal. This is what makes it unusual, and it is also what makes it so stable and expansive. The postwar order is the product of both power and institutions. The order would not have taken shape if not for the material power capabilities of the United States. But the specific character of that power was also a reflection of the ideas and practices of the American polity.

Even with the end of the Cold War and the shifting global distribution of power, the relations between the United States and the other industrial countries of Europe and Asia remain remarkably stable and cooperative. The incentives for a return to a balance-of-power order among the major states are rooted in this durable and legitimate arrangement. This chapter offers two major reasons why American hegemony has endured and facilitated cooperation and integration among the major industrial countries rather than triggered balancing and estrangement. Both reasons underscore the importance of the liberal features of American hegemony and the institutional foundations of Western political order.

First, the United States moved very quickly after the war to ensure that relations among the liberal democracies would take place within an institutionalized political process. In effect, the United States offered the other countries a bargain: if the United States agrees to operate within mutually acceptable institutions, thereby muting the implications of power asymmetries, the other countries would agree to be willing participants. The United States got the acquiescence of the other Western states, and they in turn got the reassurance that the United States would neither dominate nor abandon them.

The stability of this bargain comes from its underlying logic: the postwar hegemonic order is infused with institutions and practices that reduce the returns to power. This means that the implications of winning and losing are minimized and contained. A state could "lose" in intra-Western relations and yet not worry that the winner will be able to use those winnings to permanently dominate. This is a central characteristic of domestic liberal constitutional orders. Parties that win elections must operate within well-defined limits. They cannot use their powers of incumbency to undermine or destroy the opposition party. They can press the advantage of office to the limits of the law, but there are limits and laws. This reassures the losing party; it can accept its loss and prepare for the next election. The features of the postwar order—and, importantly, the open and penetrated character of the American polity itself—has mechanisms to provide the same sort of assurances to America's European and Asian partners.

Second, the institutions of American hegemony also have a durability that comes from the phenomenon of increasing returns. The overall system—organized around principles of openness, reciprocity, and multilateralism—has become increasingly connected to the wider and deeper institutions of politics and society within the advanced industrial world. As the embeddedness of these institutions has grown, it has become increasingly difficult for potential rival states to introduce a competing set of principles and institutions. American hegemony has become highly institutionalized and path dependent. Short of large-scale war or a global economic crisis, the American hegemonic order appears to be very immune from would-be hegemonic challengers. Even if a large coalition of states had interests that favored an alternative type of order, the benefits of change would have to radically higher than those that flow from the present system to justify change. But there is no potential hegemonic state (or coalition of states) and no set of rival principles and organizations even on the horizon. The world of the 1940s contained far more rival systems, ideologies, and interests than the world of the 1990s.

The American hegemonic order fits this basic logic. Its open and penetrated character invites participation and creates assurances of steady commitment. Its institutionalized character also provides mechanisms for the resolution of conflicts and creates assurances to continuity. Moreover, the interconnections and institutions of the partnership have spread and deepened. Within this liberal and institutionalized order, the fortune of particular states will continue to rise and fall. The United States itself, while remaining at the center of the order, also continues to experience gains and losses. But the mix of winning and losing across the system is distributed widely enough to mitigate the interest that particular states might have in replacing it. In an order where the returns to power are low and the returns to institutions are high, stability will be its essential feature.

8

Transnational Liberalism and American Primacy; or, Benignity Is in the Eye of the Beholder

John M. Owen IV

The persistence of America's military primacy presents at least two puzzles. First, why is unipolarity lasting so long? How is it that, in defiance of so many predictions since the early 1990s, the U.S. lead over the next most powerful state remains so massive? Second, why does the imbalance of international power persist? How is it that no coalition of states has emerged capable of counterbalancing U.S. power? These puzzles are analytically distinct inasmuch as, according to neorealist theory, only a state can be a pole.[1]

Alliances affect the balance of power among states, but have no bearing on the number of poles. Thus in principle a unipolar system need not be imbalanced; the United States could be the only state with enough power

The author thanks the Sesquicentennial Fellowship and the Miller Center for Public Affairs at the University of Virginia and the Center of International Studies at Princeton University for generous support, and the Rothermere American Institute and Nuffield College at the University of Oxford for the use of their facilities. He is indebted to Mark Haas, John Ikenberry, Charles Kupchan, Sean Lynn-Jones, Henry Nau, William Wohlforth, and an anonymous referee for comments on previous drafts. He also thanks Rachel Vanderhill for research assistance.

[1] Cf. Kenneth N. Waltz, *Theory of International Politics* (Reading, Mass.: Addison-Wesley, 1979); Randall L. Schweller, *Deadly Imbalances: Tripolarity and Hitler's Strategy of World Conquest* (New York: Columbia University Press, 1998); and William C. Wohlforth, "The Stability of a Unipolar World," *International Security* 24, no. 1 (summer 1999): 5–41.

to rate polar status, yet be counterbalanced by an alliance of nonpolar states.

William Wohlforth adequately answers the unipolarity puzzle. In a chapter of this book that he authored, Wohlforth argues that the U.S. lead over other states is so huge that, barring an unlikely Soviet-style collapse, America will have a preponderance of world military power for many years to come. Wohlforth and other contributors to this book are less convincing as to why America continues to enjoy being on the heavy end of an imbalance of power. The United States does produce 23 percent of gross world product, but the European Union (EU) produces 20 percent, China 12 percent, and Japan 7 percent.[2] In principle, then, a balance could emerge were some combination of these states and nuclear-armed Russia sufficiently motivated to increase capabilities and form an alliance. Most contributors to this book begin their answers to this question by adopting the assumption, standard to much international relations theory, that states are unitary rational actors that respond predictably to environmental stimuli. That the United States is physically far away from all potential challenger states; that those challengers are too busy counterbalancing one another to bother with America; that Washington displays no offensive intentions toward others; that U.S. predominance is so highly institutionalized and its behavior thus so predictable; that America is indispensable to stability in too many regions: these explanations all contain truth, but all imply that any reasonable state would see U.S. primacy as not worth trying to overthrow, as perhaps even beneficial.

The trouble is that not all actors see America in such benign terms. And thus some countries are indeed trying to counterbalance the United States. If counterbalancing is the taking of internal or external measures to increase one's military capabilities relative to a particular state or alliance, then China has slowly but surely been counterbalancing U.S. power since the early 1990s.[3] Russia increasingly took counterbalancing steps as the past decade wore on, although it never threw itself wholeheartedly into the effort. (In my conclusion I discuss how the terrorist attacks on America of September 11, 2001, caused Russia and evidently China to abandon counterbalancing, at least temporarily.)

In this chapter I argue that ideological distance from the United States is crucial to whether a given potential counterbalancer becomes an actual

[2] The figures are for 1999. Central Intelligence Agency, *World Fact Book*, http://www.cia.gov/cia/publications/factbook/geos/xx.html#Econ.

[3] I do not consider India a potential challenger to U.S. predominance at present. It may have the potential to balance against America in the medium to long term. See Baldev Raj Nayar, "India as a Limited Challenger?" in *International Order and the Future of World Politics*, ed. T. V. Paul and John A. Hall (New York: Cambridge University Press, 1999), 213–33.

one. Those major powers that are acquiescing to U.S. primacy—Japan and the major powers of the European Union—are doing so because they are dominated by liberal elites who strongly wish for their societies to uphold individual autonomy by limiting the power of the state and minimizing its links with religion. By no means do all liberals around the world approve of all internal or external U.S. policies; indeed, some Bush administration policies on missile defense, the environment, and other policies have alienated many of them. Yet liberals understand that the United States seeks to uphold the same domestic order they believe fundamental to their nations' interests. They perceive U.S. hegemony as benign, U.S. values as universal. Understanding this fundamental concurrence of values and hence interests among liberals, the United States promotes liberalism in most regions of the world and treats liberal countries with trust, thereby reinforcing their acquiescence to U.S. power.

China, by contrast, has counterbalanced U.S. power because it is dominated by antiliberal elites. Russian policy has oscillated between these extremes because its elite is divided between liberals and various types of antiliberals. Antiliberals, including communists, ultranationalists, and (in the Muslim world) theocrats, vehemently reject certain or all facets of liberalism and hence many of the purposes to which America puts its power. They correctly believe that, if the United States had its way, every country in the world would be a liberal democracy; that is, America seeks to override their own visions for their countries as well as to destroy their prospects for holding power. Fearing America's ends, they seek to defend themselves against any imposition of America's will. Meanwhile, for the same ideological reasons, U.S. treatment of these countries has been less benign than of Western Europe and Japan, thereby confirming the antiliberals' perceptions of American purposes.

Thus the absence of a balance of international power is a function of the degree to which liberalism has penetrated ruling elites in those countries capable of helping bring about such a balance. Enough potential challengers countries are dominated or at least influenced by liberal elites so as to preserve American primacy.

My argument has much in common with that of Thomas Risse. Unlike Risse, however, I see the ascendancy of liberal norms and institutions less as constitutive of a security community and more as constitutive (and derivative) of American hegemony. The United States has actively promoted liberal institutions as a way to extend and preserve its influence in Europe and Asia. As a liberal myself, I do agree that U.S. hegemony is peculiarly benign. Not only does it allow smaller countries relatively more influence over the hegemon, but it also promotes human flourishing—freedom and prosperity—better than any alternative yet tried. Thus my emphasis on hegemony is not meant as a radical critique, but rather as a recognition of the interaction of power and ideas in international relations.[4]

The Argument

Ultimately, states balance against power that is being, or that they fear may be, used against them. Not all concentrations of power intimidate all states. Carl von Clausewitz implies an explanation for this discrimination in his definition of war: "an act of violence intended to compel our enemy to fulfill our will."[5] What, then, if B already fulfills state A's will? Insofar as B does so, A will have less reason to use force against B, and B will have less reason to counterbalance A. B could fulfill A's will, at least concerning issues of importance to A, under a number of conditions. A may have already conquered B. Or A and B may share a dangerous enemy. The most familiar type of enemy is a third state C. But A and B may also share an enemy that seeks to overturn their common norms of political order, that is, an ideological enemy. The more important are those shared norms to A, the less reason A has to impose its will upon B, and the less reason B has to counterbalance A's power.

Thus the norms held by states—more precisely, by the elites who govern them—can affect whether they choose to counterbalance a given state, and hence whether power in the international system is ultimately balanced. A state's strategic preferences derive not solely from its relative material power, but rather from an interaction between relative power and relative ideology, that is, the ideological distance between its governing elites and those of other states.[6] An ideology shapes strategic preferences because it gives its holders not only a program for domestic politics but also a transnational group affiliation. This affiliation provides a basis for identifying with certain foreign states and against others. If elites of one ideology have influence over foreign policy, the state will follow one set of

[4] Thus I agree with such writers as Tony Smith, "National Security Liberalism and American Foreign Policy," in *American Democracy Promotion: Impulses, Strategies, and Impacts*, ed. Michael Cox, G. John Ikenberry, and Takashi Inoguchi (New York: Oxford University Press, 2000), 85–102; and Samuel Huntington, "Why International Primacy Matters," *International Security* 17, no. 4 (spring 1993): 69–70.

[5] Carl von Clausewitz, *On War*, ed. Anatol Rapaport (New York: Penguin, 1982), book 1, chap. 2, 101.

[6] For more on ideological distance and the balance of power, see Mark L. Haas, "Systemic Ideology and National Threat: Ideological Affinity and Threat Perception in International Relations" (Ph.D. diss., University of Virginia, 2000), chap. 1. On the influence of domestic properties on state preferences, see Andrew Moravcsik, "Taking Preferences Seriously: A Liberal Theory of International Politics," *International Organization* 51, no. 4 (autumn 1997): 513–53.

strategic preferences; if elites of a competing ideology have influence, the state will follow a different set of preferences.

Political Groups and Identities

Identity is a vague notion, nowhere more than in recent international relations literature. By identity I mean the particular set of social groups to which an actor belongs, or what Georg Simmel calls the "intersection of social circles." An individual's identity is the particular overlap among his group memberships. A given person will belong to any number of groups: for instance, males, husbands, accountants, graduates of Moscow State University, residents of St. Petersburg, Russians. No two persons belong to precisely the same set of groups, and thus each person has his own identity. It is important to note at the outset that any group implies an "out-group," a set of individuals that do not belong to the group. The group "males" has no meaning without the group "females," and vice versa. Social differentiation is necessary to identity formation.[7]

The type of group relevant to international relations is a *political group*, in other words, a group constituted by a plan for ordering social life. Political groups are much more important to their members than are most other types of social groups. Power, material goods, and deeply held values are at stake in the political order. Thus a person will typically derive greater utility from the gains of his political group than from the gains of his nonpolitical groups. Suppose I am a plumber and a monarchist. If plumbers as a group gain total resources—say, if an epidemic of leaky pipes breaks out—I shall personally gain probably little more than the utility derived from whatever my share of the gains are, plus some minimal psychic gain from having my pride in being a plumber bolstered. Should the set of monarchists gain resources, however—say, if we gain a large number of converts—my utility gains should be much greater: society becomes more likely to embody my deeply held values; I may also use the new influence of monarchists to gain power and wealth for myself. Put negatively, the probability that I shall have to submit to republicanism, a domestic order to which I deeply object, will have decreased. That political groups compete for higher stakes is evident in the use of force by many such groups under certain conditions.

[7] Georg Simmel, "The Web of Group Affiliations" ("Die Kreuzung sozialer Kreise," *Soziologie* [Munich: Duncker & Humblot, 1922], 305–44), trans. Reinhard Bendix, in Simmel, *Conflict and the Web of Group-Affiliations* (Glencoe, Ill.: Free Press, 1955).

The tactics of political groups are familiar. Significant for our purposes are the temporary alliances one political group typically forms with another group with which it shares an enemy and thus an interest. Having alliances with groups that have different goals for social life is not necessarily a sign that a political group lacks principles. It may well be rather a sign that the group is currently in a more urgent struggle with a third political group.

In the modern world virtually all persons belong to at least one political group, namely, a state. The social context for a state is global. The plan for ordering social life that constitutes a given state is that world politics should never work to its detriment. Thus Fredonians' interests can never completely harmonize with those of non-Fredonians, who see Fredonia's advantage not as good per se but at best as instrumental to their own state's advantage. With many sets of non-Fredonians much of the time, interactions are positive-sum, and thus Fredonia can cooperate in pareto-improving transactions with other states. But deliberate self-abnegation is exceedingly rare among states.[8]

Within any given state are elites involved in domestic politics. These elites thereby belong to ideological political groups, each constituted by a distinct vision for ordering common life within the state.[9] Such visions only emerge as negations of opposing visions; an ideology always opposes and is opposed by some alternative. Monarchists and republicans, communists and fascists, secular liberals and Islamic theocrats, all are mutually constitutive and mutually negating. Because similar ideas and social conditions often exist in more than one state at once, likeminded ideologues in two or more states typically see themselves as part of a *transnational ideological group* that is in competition with one or more opposing transnational groups. A given group is not necessarily centralized or regulated, nor do its members even necessarily interact with one another. It need not be as tight as the Comintern was. Its members need only be conscious of their shared political cause. As such, their members will derive positive utility from the gains of the group anywhere, and negative utility from the gains of opposing groups.[10]

[8] Thus, in my argument, the norm of "other-help" cannot take hold in international politics. Only when two nation-states unite will their members enter such a norm vis-à-vis one another. Cf. Alexander Wendt, *Social Theory of International Politics* (New York: Cambridge University Press, 1999).

[9] Cf. Carl Schmitt, *The Concept of the Political*, trans. George Schwab (New Brunswick, N.J.: Rutgers University Press, 1976).

[10] David Skidmore, "Introduction: Bringing Social Orders Back In," in *Contested Social Orders and International Politics*, ed. Skidmore (Nashville: Vanderbilt University Press, 1997), 5–6. Skidmore refers to competing domestic social orders whose members form cross-na-

States versus Ideological Groups

States, of course, are particularly potent political groups inasmuch as, when functioning properly, they have a monopoly on the legitimate use of force in a given territory. They may thus coerce obedience much more efficiently than nonstate political groups. Yet transnational ideological groups command allegiance as well, because they implicate the very question of domestic order. A member of such a group will have an integrated conception of her state's interests. The national interest for her will include not only protection from foreign conquest, but also the particular way of life prescribed by her ideology, which in turn implies certain domestic political institutions. Sovereignty is a necessary condition for the particular way of life she favors, but that priority does not lead her to set aside domestic ideology when thinking about foreign policy. Instead, as argued below, domestic ideology colors her perceptions of which states threaten her state's physical security and which mean her state well.

Fredonian monarchists, then—a group comprising at least a subset of Fredonian elites—belong to two distinct but overlapping political groups. Even if all Fredonians are monarchists, millions of monarchists are not Fredonians. Yet, Fredonian monarchists will strive to reconcile the interests of the two groups, inasmuch as they will believe that Fredonia's interests demand not only safety from foreign states but also a head of state determined by heredity rather than election.

The extent to which an elite will identify with his ideological group over and against his country will vary with which component—sovereignty or domestic order—of his conception of the national interest is more threatened. If the greater threat is a domestic ideological enemy, he will defend his ideology more vigorously and identify more strongly with fellow ideologues in other countries. The limiting case is a civil war, in which he may invite foreigners to help him kill his fellow citizens who are ideological enemies.[11] If the greater threat is foreign conquest, he will defend his country's security more vigorously and identify more with fellow nationals of whatever ideology. The limiting case is an international war, in which he joins ideological enemies who are fellow citizens in killing foreigners regardless of ideology. When the ratio of internal to external threats approaches one-to-one, as when his government faces no serious threats to

---

tional coalitions, rather than to transnational ideological groups, but the concept is virtually the same.

[11] Cf. Karl Deutsch, "External Involvement in Internal War," in *Internal War: Problems and Approaches,* ed. Harry Eckstein (New York: Free Press, 1964), 103.

sovereignty *or* his favored domestic order, he will feel moderate solidarity with both his ideological group and his nation-state, and will tend to see no conflict between the two groups.[12]

Identities and Strategic Preferences

To the extent that a state promotes its governing ideology domestically or internationally, friends and foes will generally regard it as an instrument of that ideology. Revolutionary states are notorious for such promotions, but "normal" states engage in them as well.[13] Elites in other states will thus far project their ideological allegiances and hatreds onto an ideology-promoting state. Those elites who adhere to the ideology will derive positive utility from that state's gains; those who oppose the ideology, negative utility. As outlined above, the intensity of these utility gains and losses will vary directly with the degree to which these adherents face ideological threats in their own countries. In normal times, members of an ideological group will simply be complacent about the gains of states that exemplify their ideology.

Thus most Czechoslovaks feared Germany in 1938 not simply because Germany was rearming, but because they inferred from Nazi ideology that Hitler intended to destroy their country. (Most Sudeten Germans did not fear German power.) Thus, too, noncommunist Czechoslovaks ten years later feared the Soviet Union not simply for its power, but for the domestic order it intended to impose on their country. Communist Czechoslovaks, far from fearing Soviet power, participated in its expansion by carrying out the Prague coup d'état of February 1948. And thus today, most elites in the Czech Republic do not fear America's vast power precisely because they share America's liberal vision for societal order; indeed, they have abetted an expansion of U.S. power by bringing their country into NATO. Or consider the wide divergence in threat perception by Italian elites after the fall of Mussolini in 1943. Communists and socialists in Italy

---

[12] The process is similar to what Steven David has called "omnibalancing," or the balancing of domestic and foreign threats in which leaders of many Third World countries engaged during the Cold War. David, however, explicitly downplays any role for ideology in the production of threats. Steven R. David, *Choosing Sides: Alignment and Realignment in the Third World* (Baltimore, Md.: Johns Hopkins University Press, 1991).

[13] On revolutionary states and ideological promotion, see Stephen M. Walt, *Revolution and War* (Ithaca, N.Y.: Cornell University Press, 1996); on promotion by normal states, see John M. Owen IV, "The International Promotion of Domestic Institutions," *International Organization* 56, no. 2 (spring 2002): 375–409.

feared the United States and wanted no part of Marshall aid or the North Atlantic alliance. Instead, they desired an alignment with the Soviet Union and welcomed increases in Soviet power. By contrast, liberals and Christian Democrats perceived American and Soviet power in terms precisely the opposite of those of their leftist counterparts.[14] Few Italian elites seem to have feared power per se, but only power used for a purpose that would thwart their vision for Italy.

A skeptic might concede that in many states elites disagree over alignment strategy, and even that ideology might cause some such disagreements. But does an elite's ideological group affiliation survive her coming to power? In separating internal from external politics, mainstream systemic international relations theory implies that once an elite begins to govern a state, her preferences will respond to external rather than internal dynamics, and those external dynamics will have little or nothing to do with the regime type of her state or others.

I argue, by contrast, that taking power does not eliminate an elite's concern for her country's internal institutions. She will tend to retain her prior strategic preference ordering to the extent that the ratio of physical to ideological threats to her conception of the national interest remains constant. Indeed, she will seek to create conditions that will solidify her preferred alliances in the future. She will try to create economic actors in her society that are materially interested in following her preferences. She will use her power to encourage economic interdependence with states with which she wants to align. She will seek membership for her country in international organizations whose members are states with which she wants to align. She will discourage trade and investment with states against which she wants to align.

James Monroe was a lifelong antimonarchist, and his convictions changed not at all when he became America's president in 1821. Those convictions were partly responsible for his proclamation of what became known as the Monroe Doctrine in December 1823, which purported to exclude the influence of the Old World from the New. Monroe cited not only the power of the European states, but their monarchism, which implied to Monroe and other American elites that they would put their power to a purpose inimical to U.S. interests. "The *political system* of the allied powers is *essentially different* in this respect from that of America," Monroe declared. "We owe it, therefore, to candor and to the amicable re-

---

[14] Donald Sassoon, "Italian Images of Russia, 1945–56," in *Italy in the Cold War: Politics, Culture, and Society, 1948–58*, ed. Christopher Duggan and Christopher Wagstaff (Oxford: Berg, 1995), 189–202.

lations existing between the United States and those powers to declare that we should consider any attempt on their part to *extend their system* to any portion of this hemisphere as dangerous to our peace and safety [italics added]." It is significant that Monroe issued his doctrine weeks after France had used 100,000 troops to restore absolute monarchy in Spain; indeed, Monroe cited this intervention as evidence of the Europeans' designs on the New World.[15] Monarchism was a carrier of European influence; republicanism, of U.S. influence.

Changes in Strategic Preferences

Still, an elite's strategic preferences will tend to change, whether he is in or out of power, along with the ratio of physical-to-domestic-order threats described above. When he needs help achieving his preferred domestic order less than help securing the nation's survival, an elite's solidarity with ideological confreres abroad will reduce accordingly. At an extreme, should he find his country attacked by a foreign enemy, he will seek allies where they may be found. An obvious case is the Anglo-Soviet-American Grand Alliance of the Second World War. A less severe case that produced tension between elites of similar ideologies in different states is Indo-American relations during much of the Cold War. In the early 1960s, the primary threat to India's national interest was not domestic antiliberalism but China. Indian elites thus aligned their country with the Soviet Union, by then itself well on its way to enmity with China; thus did India alienate the United States. Indo-American relations were further degraded in the early 1970s when the Nixon administration, seeking to contain Soviet influence, tilted toward Pakistan. Only since the collapse of the Soviet Union have relations between India and the United States moved toward their more natural cooperative state.[16] Thus, international events feed back onto domestic elite preferences.

Events within a state may also alter strategic preferences. First, certain types of ideologies ascribe a higher value to orthodoxy than to choice; Marxism-Leninism is more doctrinaire than liberalism. The former type

---

[15] The text of Monroe's address is available at http://www.yale.edu/lawweb/avalon/monroe.htm.

[16] See, for example, Stephen M. Walt, "Testing Theories of Alliance Formation: The Case of Southwest Asia," *International Organization* 42, no. 2 (spring 1988), esp. 299–302. On the tilt toward Pakistan, see Henry A. Kissinger, *White House Years* (Boston: Little, Brown, 1979), chap. 21. On recent improvements in Indo–U.S. relations, see Stephen P. Cohen, "India Rising," *Wilson Quarterly* 24, no. 3 (summer 2000): 32–39, 42–43, 46–53.

of ideology makes for comparatively fragile alignments.[17] Thus the Sino-Soviet split began in the late 1950s, as the Chinese communists believed that Nikita Khrushchev and other Soviet leaders, in repudiating Stalinism, had fallen into heresy. The seriousness with which Mao Zedong and his subordinates took this heresy is seen in the long theoretical and historical disputations between Soviet and Chinese officials in the late 1950s and early 1960s.[18]

Second, should threats to an elite's vision for domestic order fade away, she will have less need of foreign allies with whom she shares that vision. This situation also began to afflict Sino-Soviet relations in the late 1950s. In 1949–50, when the Sino-Soviet alliance was first negotiated, Mao needed the alliance in part to help solidify the position of the newly victorious Communist party within China itself. Much of the "right-wing national bourgeoisie" remained in China, and Mao openly desired Soviet moral and material help in suppressing it.[19] A decade later, communist rule was more secure, and Mao's need for friendship with the Soviet communist exemplar was correspondingly reduced. Of course, elites may still have nonideological reasons for wanting to maintain an alliance, for example, enduring economic ties that were originally built for ideological reasons.

Finally, elites may simply abandon the ideology that produced the strategic preferences in question. Their country may lose a war to a victor who coerces them to abandon the old ideology. Or, an ideology may simply fail to live up to its promises. Thus did countless communists in the Soviet bloc become disillusioned with Marxism-Leninism as permanent economic stagnation arrived in the 1970s.

Ideological alignments, then, are conditional. But as argued below, the conditions under which they hold seem to obtain today, at least as regards alignments with and against the United States.

[17] Stephen M. Walt, *The Origins of Alliances* (Ithaca, N.Y.: Cornell University Press, 1987), 35–37; John M. Owen IV, *Liberal Peace, Liberal War: American Politics and International Security* (Ithaca, N.Y.: Cornell University Press, 1997), 35–36; and Haas, "Systemic Ideology and National Threat," chap. 1.

[18] See on the web site of the Woodrow Wilson Center's Cold War International History Project, http://cwihp.si.edu. See, for example, Zhang Shu Guang and Chen Jian, eds. and trans., "The Emerging Disputes between Beijing and Moscow: Ten Newly Available Chinese Documents, 1956–58"; and, specifically on Soviet worries about Chinese communist ideology, see V. M. Zubok, ed. and trans., "A New 'Cult of Personality': Suslov's Secret Reports on Mao, Khrushchev, and Sino-Soviet Tensions, December 1959."

[19] Mao Zedong, telegram to CCP Central Committee, January 2, 1950, http://cwihp.si.edu/cwihplib.nsf/16c6b2fc83775317852564a400054b28/33fcb42f9ceb78e3852564b900657767?OpenDocument; Chen Jian and Yang Kuisong, "Chinese Politics and the Collapse of the Sino-Soviet Alliance," in *Brothers in Arms: The Rise and Fall of the Sino-Soviet Alliance, 1945–1963*, ed. Odd Arne Westad (Washington: Woodrow Wilson Center Press, 1998), 250.

Why No Balance of Power Today?

Western Europe and Japan

Neither Western Europe nor Japan has devoted significant resources to counterbalancing U.S. power. In the 1990s, real military spending in the major European Union (EU) countries and Japan was either flat or declined (see Table 8.1). Far from opposing the expansion of U.S. power, the European allies helped expand it by participating in the Kosovo air war of 1999, a war, it must be noted, that was fought for liberal purposes. The only countervailing evidence is the French plan to make the new sixty-thousand-person EU Rapid Reaction Force independent of NATO; but the British and Germans oppose this French intention. As for Japan, it has embarked on a theater missile defense program, but as a reaction to North Korean provocation and with the cooperation of the United States.[20] Far from attempting to form any anti-U.S. alliance, Tokyo in 1997 renewed the U.S.–Japanese security treaty. It is not the case that these U.S. allies approve of all American policies; indeed, most loudly opposed the unilateral policy changes of the Bush administration in 2001 such as abandonment of the Anti-Ballistic Missile Treaty or the Kyoto Protocol on the environment. But even prior to September 11, they were reacting through diplomacy rather than by counterbalancing U.S. military might.

Why this acquiescence to U.S. primacy? Along with North America, the countries of Japan and Western Europe are the most thoroughly penetrated by liberal elites and their values. In the cases of Germany and Japan, Ikenberry and Kupchan have argued that Washington took great pains after the Second World War to encourage the development of a liberal elite. United States leaders understood that manipulating the material incentives facing these states was not sufficient to guaranteeing their contentment with American hegemony. United States leaders sought also to change the substantive beliefs of elites. These states were now no longer to seek empires; rather, they were to submit to American protection and a U.S.–sponsored liberal economic order, and to see this new international system as not only necessary under the circumstances but *good*.[21]

---

[20] Richard Tanter, "Japan and the Coming East Asian Explosion," *Arena Magazine* 42 (August 1999): 44.

[21] Ikenberry and Kupchan, "Socialization." If as Geir Lundestad argues the American "empire" was "by invitation," it is significant that the invitation was extended by liberal elites; European Marxists wanted no part of it. See Lundestad, "Empire by Invitation? The United States and Western Europe, 1945–52," *Journal of Peace Research* 23 (September 1986): 263–77; and John Lewis Gaddis, *We Now Know: Rethinking Cold War History* (New York: Oxford University Press, 1997), chap. 2.

Table 8.1. Military Spending, 1995–99, in Billions of 1995 $U.S.

	1995	1996	1997	1998	1999	Rank (1999)
United States	278.9	263.7	262.2	256.1	259.9	1
Japan	50.1	51.1	51.3	51.3	51.2	2
France	47.8	46.6	46.8	45.5	46.8	3
Germany	41.2	40.3	38.9	39	39.5	4
United Kingdom	33.8	34.4	32.3	32.0	31.8	5
Russia	25.7	23.4	24.9	18.1	22.4	7
China	12.5	13.7	14.9	16.9	18.4	8

Source: Stockholm International Peace Research Institute, http://projects.sipri.se/milex/ mex_major_spenders.html.

Crucial to this shift in values was what Ikenberry and Kupchan call *internal reconstruction*, namely, the imposition of liberal-democratic domestic institutions on West Germany, Italy, and Japan. The links between the democratization of the defeated powers and American hegemony have been insufficiently analyzed, but it is clear that such links existed in the minds of U.S. leaders. Thus a 1945 State Department memorandum on Italy, approved by President Truman:

> Our objective is to strengthen Italy economically and politically so that truly democratic elements of the country can withstand the forces that threaten to sweep them into a new totalitarianism. Italian sympathies naturally and traditionally lie with the western democracies, and, with proper support from us, Italy would tend to become a factor for stability in Europe. The time is now ripe when we should initiate action to raise Italian morale, make a stable representative government possible, and permit Italy to become a responsible participant in international affairs.[22]

Note that, in order to embrace a U.S.–dominated international order, Italian elites had to accept American norms concerning the proper ordering of *domestic* society. The same reasoning was applied to the Germans and Japanese.[23]

The U.S. strategy worked spectacularly well. Although Japan and Ger-

[22] G. Warner, "Italy and the Powers, 1943–49," in *The Rebirth of Italy 1943–50*, ed. S. J. Woolf (London: Longman, 1972), 47–48.

[23] On American democracy promotion more generally, see Tony Smith, *America's Mission: The United States and the Worldwide Struggle for Democracy in the Twentieth Century* (Princeton, N.J.: Princeton University Press, 1994); Thomas Carothers, *Aiding Democracy Abroad: The Learning Curve* (Washington, D.C.: Carnegie Endowment for International Peace, 1999); Larry Diamond, *Developing Democracy: Toward Consolidation* (Baltimore: Johns Hopkins University Press, 1999); and Gideon Rose, "Democracy Promotion and American Foreign Policy: A Review Essay," *International Security* 25, no. 3 (winter 2000/01): 186–203.

many regained their old economic power, there is no serious possibility that either will use that power to challenge American predominance. The two societies are heavily dependent on the U.S. economy, but in neither state do political elites find that dependence intolerable. Germany and Japan are not challenging the United States because Germans and Japanese fundamentally agree with Americans on the good life and the good society: blood and iron have given way to Coca-Cola and plastic. On the things that matter most, America's will is their will. Because they are liberal, Germany and Japan have no good reason to devote dear resources to balancing against the United States. In turn, the United States treats its fellow liberal states relatively kindly, knowing that the chances are close to nil that those allies will use their gains to threaten it.

Russia

Russia's American policy is more difficult to characterize. Real Russian military spending declined in the 1990s (see Table 8.1); the country's steep economic deterioration is the simplest explanation, but were the Kremlin sufficiently motivated, it could nonetheless have maintained constant military spending. It is further significant that despite its continuing massive nuclear arsenal, Russia made no attempt to blackmail the United States. Analysts agree that in the early 1990s, Russian policy was pro-American, to the point of applauding the eastward expansion of NATO. As the decade wore on, however, Russia began confronting the United States more.[24] It opposed U.S.–NATO actions in the former Yugoslavia, particularly the Kosovo intervention of 1999.[25] It courted an alignment with China, culminating in the "treaty of friendship and peace" of July 2001 that was obviously intended as a first step toward counterbalancing America.[26]

The forces driving Russian foreign policy in the decade after 1991 were unusually complex, not least because Russian domestic politics was bewilderingly complicated and prone to unexpected jarring shifts thanks in part to the methods of President Boris Yeltsin. But both the ambivalence and the general downward trend in Russian policy toward the United

---

[24] Michael McFaul, "Russia's Many Foreign Policies," *Demokratizatsiya* 7, no. 3 (summer 1999): 393–412; Sergei Medvedev, "Power, Space, and Russian Foreign Policy," in *Understandings of Russian Foreign Policy*, ed. Ted Hopf (University Park: Pennsylvania State University Press, 1999), 15–55; Paul Marantz, "Neither Adversaries nor Partners: Russia and the West Search for a New Relationship," in *The Foreign Policy of the Russian Federation*, ed. Roger Kanet and Alexander Kozhemiakin (New York: Macmillan, 1997), 89–96.

[25] McFaul, "Russia's Many Foreign Policies," 404–408.

[26] Patrick E. Tyler, "Russia and China Sign 'Friendship' Pact," *New York Times,* July 17, 2001, A1.

States until late 2001 correlate to the limited and declining influence of political liberals in Russia itself.

Unlike their counterparts in Western Europe and Japan, many influential Russian elites are antiliberal. The United States won the Cold War, but not by militarily defeating the Soviet Union; hence it could not impose liberalism on the vanquished in 1991 as it had done in 1945. The manner in which America triumphed, however—by economically outlasting its Soviet rival—did inspire many Russians to embrace political as well as economic liberalism. Thus a powerful cohort of political liberals continues to exercise influence in Russia. But their influence is diluted by communists, ultranationalists, and pragmatic nationalists. From the start, Russia's political liberals have strongly tended to favor aligning with rather than against the United States. The communists and ultranationalists have pushed for counterbalancing, while moderates have pushed for a middle way of neither supporting nor opposing America.[27] With such ideological heterogeneity, we should expect incoherent foreign policy.

Furthermore, the macrotrend of the 1990s toward anti-Americanism correlates to the macrotrend away from domestic Russian liberalism. In the early 1990s, Boris Yeltsin was firmly in the liberal camp and his liberal advisers—men such as Yegor Gaidar and Andrei Kozyrev—were at the height of their power. As economic reform failed, the crisis in Chechnya worsened, and communists gained power in the Duma, Yeltsin empowered nonliberals such as Aleksandr Korzhakev, Yevgeny Primakov, and finally Vladimir Putin (although Yeltsin never completely cut off the liberals).[28] It is surely no accident that efforts to strengthen relations with China accelerated following Putin's accession to power.[29]

[27] Alex Pravda, "The Politics of Foreign Policy," in *Developments in Russian Politics*, 4th ed., ed. Steven White et al. (London: Macmillan Press, 1997), 208–26; Neil Malcolm, Alex Pravda, Roy Allison, and Margot Light, *Internal Factors in Russian Foreign Policy* (Oxford: Clarendon Press, 1996), esp. the table on p. 24. On the 1992–95 period, Pravda and Malcolm write that Russian "preferences and stances on external issues broadly correspond to those on internal affairs." Pravda and Malcolm, "Conclusion," ibid., 291; see also 287. See also McFaul, "Russia's Many Foreign Policies"; and Elizabeth Wishnick, "Prospects for the Sino-Russian Partnership: Views from Moscow and the Russian Far East," *Journal of East Asian Affairs* 12, no. 2 (summer/fall 1998): 421.

[28] What Alex Pravda and Neil Malcolm write of the 1991–95 period is more generally true of the 1990s: "The phases through which Russian external policy passed broadly corresponded to stages in internal political development." Pravda and Malcolm, "Conclusion," in *Internal Factors in Russian Foreign Policy*, 301. It is important to recognize, too, that many actors pushed for acquiescence to U.S. power out of material interest, e.g., in International Monetary Fund aid. Many of those actors, however, were deliberately created by liberals hoping to tie Russia to the West. See Michael McFaul, "A Precarious Peace: Domestic Politics in the Making of Russian Foreign Policy," *International Security* 22, no. 3 (winter 1997/98): 5–35.

[29] "Partners of Inconvenience: The Russo-Chinese Partnership," *Economist*, January 20, 2001, 4.

At the same time, Washington has arguably treated Russia in a less friendly manner than it has Japan or Western Europe. The United States intervened militarily in the Balkans knowing of Russia's strong objections. Before September 11, the United States never took seriously the proposal to offer NATO membership to Russia. The most obvious reason why is that, like other former communist countries such as Slovakia, Romania, and Bulgaria, Russia has not proven itself to be a stable liberal democracy. The wisdom of these American policies is not at issue here; they were, on balance, probably correct.[30] The issue is rather that the United States must treat semiliberal countries with less trust and deference than its liberal friends; and in so doing, it reinforces the mistrust Russian antiliberals feel toward America.

China

China evidently has been counterbalancing U.S. power slowly but steadily since 1991. In sharp contrast to other second-tier powers, China consistently raised real military spending during the latter half of the 1990s (see table 8.1). It is modernizing its navy and air force, partly through purchases of hardware from Russia.[31] It is improving the range and accuracy of its missiles; it recently launched a navigation positioning satellite to upgrade missile accuracy.[32] Doubtless Japan, India, the ASEAN states, Russia, and of course Taiwan are among the objects of China's military buildup. But the timing of the improvements suggests that the primary object is the United States: U.S. air power in the Gulf War of 1991[33] and the Kosovo air war of 1999[34] both spurred Chinese military initiatives. Furthermore, official statements by the People's Liberation Army and, increasingly, the Communist party itself make clear that America is thought to be China's main enemy.[35] During the Kosovo war, the *People's Daily* "accused the

[30] For an argument (prior to 9/11) that Russia should be admitted to NATO, see Bruce Russett and John Oneal, *Triangulating Peace: Democracy, Interdependence, and International Organizations* (New York: W. W. Norton, 2001), 288–97.

[31] John Pomfret, "U.S. Now a 'Threat' in China's Eyes," *Washington Post*, November 15, 2000, A1.

[32] Pomfret, "U.S. Now a 'Threat' "; International Institute for Strategic Studies, *The Military Balance 1999–2000* (London: IISS, 1999), 171.

[33] Avery Goldstein, "Great Expectations: Interpreting China's Arrival," *International Security* 22, no. 3 (winter 1997): 43.

[34] David Shambaugh, "China's Military Views the World: Ambivalent Security," *International Security* 24, no. 3 (winter 1999): 57–61.

[35] Ibid., 52–79; Alastair Iain Johnston, "China's New 'Old Thinking': The Concept of Limited Deterrence," *International Security* 20, no. 3 (winter 1995): 5–42; Pomfret, "U.S. Now a 'Threat' in China's Eyes."

United States of seeking to become 'Lord of the Earth' and compared contemporary U.S. hegemony to the aggression of Nazi Germany."[36] Avery Goldstein writes,

> Early in the post-Cold War era, it would certainly appear that China and the United States rather quickly have come to focus on each other as the two key players in the game and to view each other's actions as potentially threatening. Each worries about allegedly shifting balances of military power and mutual perceptions of resolve. The early signs suggest that a bipolar East Asia would be dominated by recurrent Sino-American conflict.[37]

As already mentioned, China moved steadily toward an alignment with Russia; it has also courted a similar relationship with India, albeit with less success.[38]

China's determination to counterbalance U.S. power follows from the apparent absence of political liberals among its ruling elites. If any liberals exist among China's elites they are keeping their preferences well hidden. Observers agree that the ideological spectrum among Chinese elites is much narrower than it was in the 1980s. Having witnessed the collapse of the Soviet Union under Gorbachev's reforms, officials in the Chinese Communist party (CCP) seem determined to retain the party's monopoly on political power, and so entertain no thoughts of meaningful political liberalization.[39] Elites do disagree over the pace of economic reform and integration into the world economy. The economic reformers, led by Premier Zhu Rongji, labored long to gain Chinese entry into the World Trade Organization. Economic reactionaries have been much less willing to offer concessions to the United States in order to gain WTO membership and evidently have challenged Zhu's power at times over the issue.[40] But it is not at all clear that economic reformers would oppose military balancing against the United States, or that, if they did, they would have any influence.

Even if Zhu's cohort comprises closet political liberals, China's Leninist

---

[36] Shambaugh, "China's Military Views the World."

[37] Goldstein, "Great Expectations," 64. Goldstein adds that if Asia became multipolar rather than bipolar, China's suspicions of the United States would be diluted.

[38] On India, see Martin Sieff, "Commentary: India Slides into Sino-Russian Orbit," United Press International, January 15, 2001, provided by Comtex, http://www.comtexnews.com.

[39] Michael D. Swaine, *China: Domestic Change and Foreign Policy* (Santa Monica, Calif.: RAND, 1995), 4–14.

[40] David E. Sanger, "At the Last Hour, Down to the Last Trick, and It Worked," *New York Times,* November 17, 1999, A14.

regime prohibits them from implementing their preferences. For all practical purposes, Chinese elites hold a view of society fundamentally opposed to that propounded by the West. Thus Chinese elites do have much to fear from U.S. power: were America to impose its will on China, China would have a new, more liberal regime, just as Japan and Germany have and just as the Soviet Union was acquiring as it collapsed. That regime would not only uphold human rights and thereby halt Chinese state-building, it would also allow political competition, and thus end the CCP's fifty-three-year monopoly on political power. Given separatist sentiments in Tibet, Xinjiang, and Inner Mongolia, it could even lead to the breakup of the world's last great formal empire; that in turn would render the Taiwan question moot. Every U.S. criticism of China's human rights record, every pronouncement by American entertainers in favor of Tibet, every American eulogy for the brave Tiananmen Square protesters of 1989, every use of force by Washington to promote democracy, reminds Beijing of America's vision for China's domestic order. And hence, every increase in U.S. relative power alarms China's rulers.

At the same time, the United States has treated China even less obligingly than it has Russia. It sends spy aircraft to Chinese coastal waters to monitor naval developments. It continues to signal to Beijing its determination to prevent, with force if necessary, any coerced reunification with Taiwan. When President Bush announced his missile defense program on May 1, 2001, he portrayed Russia as a partner and potential democracy, but mentioned China only in passing.[41] Were China now a liberal democracy, one can easily imagine reductions in tensions over these various issues. All in all, it is clear that profound ideological differences are at least partly responsible for the difficult Sino-American relationship, and hence for Chinese attempts to counterbalance the United States.

If Chinese counterbalancing has been slow, it is likely because of current Chinese weakness and dependence on the West. China is simply too far behind America in terms of wealth and technology.[42] Economic reformers, starting with the late Deng Xiaoping, have created conditions under which the Chinese economy depends on continuing relations with the United States. United States influence over the WTO has given Washington special leverage over Beijing, but in the eyes of the CCP elites, that leverage is temporary. Should China continue to gain power at its recent

---

[41] Said Bush: "Today's Russia is not yesterday's Soviet Union. Its government is no longer Communist. Its president is elected. Today's Russia is not our enemy, but a country in transition with an opportunity to emerge as a great nation, democratic, at peace with itself and its neighbors." The implicit comparison with China was as obvious as it was devastating. See the full text at http://www.whitehouse.gov/news/releases/2001/05/20010501-10.html.

[42] Wohlforth, "Stability of a Unipolar World."

rate, we may be saying twenty-five years hence that Beijing began balancing against the United States after the Tiananmen Square massacre in June 1989, when political liberalism was effectively crushed.

Conclusion

The United States may occupy a unique position in the history of the modern states system. It has a preponderance of military power (as well as economic leverage and cultural influence), yet is not generating counterbalancing. Part of the answer must be that, unlike the Spain of Charles V or the France of Louis XIV or Napoleon Bonaparte, America is not using its power to conquer more territory. It is surely enriching itself, but other states are growing rich along with it while maintaining their sovereignty. Yet, American restraint and the increasing returns paid to states that acquiesce to its power cannot be sufficient to explain the persisting imbalance of world power. As the world was forcefully reminded on September 11, 2001, many actors want no part of these increasing returns and perceive anything but benignity and restraint when they observe America.

These actors tend to be the same actors who reject political liberalism. They want their states to counterbalance U.S. power because they fear, with reason, that that power could be used against them, indeed is already being so used. Elites fear not power per se, but power likely to be put to a purpose inimical to what they see as their nation's interests. Antiliberals who hear American lectures on human rights, and suffer real or threatened American economic sanctions, conclude that Washington's will for their countries is sharply at odds with their own. To defend their ability to build and preserve an antiliberal order—be it Leninist, theocratic-Islamic, or some other—they must build their countries' militaries and, where possible, form alliances with likeminded states.

By contrast, liberal elites of the world tend to perceive in American power no threat to their fundamental visions of societal order. They may vehemently disagree with various American external and internal policies, but on the issues that matter most their will is similar to that of the United States. It makes no sense for them to advocate devoting precious resources to bring about a balance of world power. Thus Japan and Western Europe, thoroughly dominated by liberal elites, have acquiesced to U.S. primacy; China, thoroughly dominated by antiliberals, has counterbalanced; and Russia, with a lingering liberal elite of waning but persistent influence, has lurched toward and away from counterbalancing. The absence of an international balance of power, then, is due in large part to there being too few antiliberals in countries able to help effect such a balance.

Paradoxically, the terrorist attacks that so devastated the United States on September 11, 2001, augmented America's international power by placing the country at the head of an instant international antiterrorist coalition. On that infamous day, the U.S. government found itself with a new primary ideological enemy and thus a different aspect of domestic order to defend, namely, domestic order itself. Promoting and defending liberalism became secondary to defeating Islamist terrorism. In turn, elites around the world who faced the same ideological enemy—or believed that they did—saw an opportunity to bandwagon with America. Most significantly, Russian elites who had resisted liberalism and hence U.S. power suddenly found themselves in the same ideological group as the United States, a group seeking to preserve the legitimacy of the state itself by restoring its ability to protect its citizens and wealth. The major threat to Russia's interests, at least in the minds of the Putin government, was already the chronic rebellion in Chechnya. Russians blame the Chechen rebels for the wave of terrorism that struck various parts of Russia in 1999.[43]

Of course, the radical Islamists who perpetrated the September 11 attacks, and the governments that supported them, are far from being anarchists. They rather desire an extremely rigid domestic order that wholly excludes non-Islamist influence. But the means they have chosen to secure that end constitute a threat against order within those states that stand in their way. The long-term importance of this newfound Russo-American common purpose is evident in statements suggesting that the Russian government is dropping its objections to NATO expansion and U.S. missile defense. Even China, faced with abandonment by Russia and an Islamist threat within its own Xinjiang province, at least began to abandon its anti-American rhetoric and diplomacy.[44] This alignment pattern, so beneficial to U.S. primacy, will last only so long as defeating Islamist terrorism remains a priority for these governments. At the time of this writing, it is not at all clear how long that will be.

What is clear is that after September 11, as before, American military primacy owes a great deal to the congruence between the purposes to which the United States puts its power and the purposes of elites in so many states that could, if they chose, help to challenge that primacy. So

[43] "Chaos in the Caucasus," *Economist,* October 9, 1999, 23. One need not condone Russia's brutal policies in Chechnya to acknowledge the Russian perception that Russia and the United States face a common enemy.

[44] David E. Sanger, "Russia, China, and the U.S.: In Terror, at Last a Common Enemy for the Big Three," *New York Times,* October 28, 2001, sec. 4, 1.

long as the United States uses its power in ways consistent with the goals of those elites, those states should eschew counterbalancing, and U.S. primacy should endure. America is indeed a benign superpower. But benignity is in the eye of the beholder; and to the benefit of the United States, the balance of world power is in the hands of actors who behold a benign America precisely because America's ideological enemies are theirs as well.

9

U.S. Power in a Liberal Security Community

Thomas Risse

S hortly after the United States faced an unprecedented terrorist attack on September 11, 2001, the North Atlantic Treaty Organization
(NATO) invoked Article 5 of the North Atlantic Treaty, the mutual
assistance clause, for the first time in its history. Originally, this article as
well as NATO in general was meant to protect Western Europe against a
Soviet attack and to insure American assistance of its European allies
rather than the other way round. Moreover and interestingly enough, the
George W. Bush administration, which was not particularly well known
for a multilateralist foreign policy prior to September 11, changed course
and immediately entangled itself in a broad coalition of allies against international terrorism—from the United Nations Security Council to
NATO and the Arab world. This is particularly significant in light of the
fact that the United States does not need its allies' capabilities to conduct
a *military* campaign against international terrorism, as the war in Afghanistan demonstrated. But the Bush administration recognized immediately
that the fight against terrorism requires sustained efforts in multilateral

A first draft of this paper was presented to the conference "American Unipolarity and the
Future of the Balance of Power," Woodrow Wilson Center, Washington, D.C., May 18–19,
2000. I thank the participants, particularly G. John Ikenberry, as well as an anonymous reviewer, for their insightful comments and suggestions.

diplomacy as well as international cooperation in intelligence gathering and law enforcement.

I argue in this chapter that the "central puzzle" of this book—"Why, despite the widening gulf between the United States and the other major states, has a counterbalancing reaction not yet taken place?"—is not a puzzle. Changing our theoretical lens tells us why the absence of counterbalancing is not very surprising. I use liberal and institutionalist theories of international relations informed by constructivist insights to make my points. The social structure of the current international system is indeed unprecedented in modern history, but not because of the (undisputed) preeminence of American power. Rather, with the exception of China, all current great powers in the international system are liberal and capitalist democracies. Russia is a transition state and it is doubtful whether it qualifies as a major power anytime soon. The current world order is dominated by liberal states. Liberal democracies not only rarely fight each other, as the "democratic peace" argument correctly claims, they form security communities that effectively reduce the security dilemma to insignificant levels and exclude the possibility of great-power war among them. Three features of security communities produce this outcome of stable peace: collective identities and shared values; transnational political, economic, and cultural interdependence; and international structures of governance regulating social order.

While much of the current world order is no longer characterized by anarchy, liberal security communities do not entirely eliminate conflict among liberal states. Dependable and enduring expectations of stable peace do not equal a state of harmony among democracies. Moreover, the social structure of security communities represents a "first-order" institution that constitutes actors and their identities in the current international system. It does not explain particular choices and foreign policies of states and national governments. To account for these choices, we have to draw on insights from liberal theory of international relations emphasizing domestic politics and structures as well as from institutionalist theories focusing on the impact of international ("second-order") institutions that regulate interstate behavior. NATO and the EU represent such second-order institutions in the liberal security community and serve to translate the constitutive principles and norms of the community into rules of appropriate behavior mitigating the unavoidable conflicts. Complaints about U.S. unilateralism and arrogance make sense in light of these norms and rules. The response of both European and Asian members of the security community to the perceived misuse of U.S. power has always been to strengthen the institutional ties through increased "binding" rather than weakening them. Once again, binding behavior rather than counterbalancing has been the European response after September 11, 2001, when the Bush administration threatened to revert to unilateral behavior.

Why Has There Not Been a Balancing Response to U.S. Power?

Most answers to the question why there has not been any serious balancing response to U.S. power in the post–Cold War era start with realist assumptions and then take liberal and/or institutionalist propositions on board in various ways.

U.S. Power Is So Overwhelming That Counterbalancing Is Impossible

William Wohlforth argues that the power differential between the United States and any other power or combination thereof at the turn of the century is so enormous as to make a balancing response prohibitive and too costly.[1] But what about counteralliances? Here, things tend to get more complicated. Wohlforth argues that "alliances are not structural" and that it is more difficult for alliances to form enduring coalitions against a hegemon than it is for a single power to balance against another one.[2] Two pages later, Wohlforth goes as far as to argue that "if the EU were a state, the world would be bipolar."[3] Of course, the EU is not a state in the Weberian sense and is unlikely to become one. But it is on its way toward a European federation and has all the institutional ingredients—from the single market to the single currency to the new European Security and Defense Policy (ESDP)—to be able to overcome the hurdles for counteralliance building. In terms of aggregate power capabilities, there is no question that the EU matches U.S. economic power. The EU is, of course, way behind the U.S. in military capabilities—from military expenditures to conventional high-tech weaponry and power projection capacities. But French and British nuclear forces combined with a hypothetical German decision to invest in nuclear capabilities could easily lead to a European nuclear second-strike capability against the United States. Hypothetically speaking, Europe could easily go nuclear to balance the United States if it

[1] See William Wohlforth, "The Stability of a Unipolar World," *International Security* 24, no. 1 (1999): 5–41. See also Wohlforth's contribution to this volume.
[2] Ibid., 29.
[3] Ibid., 31.

wanted to. What is lacking are not the economic capacities and resources, but the willingness to do so. The EU's collective identity is that of a "civilian power"[4] that tries to pursue its goals in world affairs primarily through nonmilitary means and "soft power."[5] This identity is particularly entrenched within the continent's leading power, Germany. It is precisely this civilian identity that largely explains the EU's widely deplored incapacity to act decisively in violent conflicts along its periphery as experienced in former Yugoslavia during the 1990s. Thus we need to explain the *unwillingness* to form a counterhegemonic alliance against the United States, not the lack of potential resources.

There Will Be a Counterbalancing Response Sooner or Later

This argument[6] is hard to disconfirm as long as the time frame is not specified. As argued above, only Europe and the EU have the material capability to mount such a challenge to U.S. power in the contemporary world system. If there are first signs, we would need to find them in recent European behavior. What about European moves to develop a more coherent defense and security policy in the aftermath of the war in Kosovo, particularly the Helsinki decisions of December 1999? There is no question that EU leaders are concerned about their dependency on U.S. military power and that this dependency became apparent during the war. The war in Kosovo served as a catalyst to push forward efforts to put some teeth into the European "common" foreign and security policy. Kosovo did not cause these efforts, but represents a further step toward a European foreign policy from the Maastricht and Amsterdam treaties onward. Does this amount to first steps at counterbalancing with more serious attempts following, say, ten years down the road?

There is simply not much "there" there in terms of building a European defense and power-projection capability that might be able to match U.S. military capabilities in the foreseeable future. The planned European rapid deployment force will be good for robust peacekeeping, but not for much more. The ESDP is not about building a European version of Tirpitz's navy program in the nineteenth-century German Reich, but about

[4] See Hanns W. Maull, "Germany and Japan: The New Civilian Powers," *Foreign Affairs* 69, no. 5 (1990): 91–106.

[5] Joseph Nye, *Bound to Lead: The Changing Nature of American Power* (New York: Basic Books, 1990).

[6] Christopher Layne, "The Unipolar Illusion: Why New Great Powers Will Rise," *International Security* 17, no. 4 (1993): 5–51; Stephen Walt, "The Ties That Fray: Why Europe and America Are Drifting Apart," *The National Interest* 54 (winter 1998/99): 3–11.

developing a common European foreign policy as a further step toward European political integration. Once this is accomplished, the EU might not ask the United States each time it becomes active in world affairs, and a common European foreign policy will remain different from U.S. foreign policy. But it will continue along the path of a civilian power that sees no need to match U.S. military capabilities. Once again, there is a cheap balancing response available to the Europeans, nuclear weapons, but no indication that the EU, let alone Germany, is starting to move along this path.

U.S. Foreign Policy Discourages Potential Rivals from Balancing Behavior

This argument starts from realist assumptions, but then moves from the system level to the unit level of analysis. Distinctive features of American foreign policy have prevented a counterbalancing response so far. Michael Mastanduno, for example, has argued that the Bush and Clinton administrations have in fact pursued a grand strategy of preserving U.S. primacy in the world system.[7] John Ikenberry claims that U.S. hegemony is characterized by reluctance, openness, and a high degree of institutionalization.[8] Benign hegemony results from the openness of the U.S. political system and from the American efforts of basing its hegemony on a dense set of multilateral institutions. Both characteristics of this particular hegemony give lesser powers ample opportunities to voice their concerns and to influence U.S. policies. As a result, the United States has managed to keep potential rivals happy in the post–Cold War era, and there is little reason to assume that this will change in the near future. At the same time, benign hegemony guarantees U.S. dominance in the international system and makes sure that a possible transition to a multipolar world might actually be managed rather smoothly.

This argument ultimately rests on liberal and institutionalist assumptions about international order and leaves realism further behind. In a realist world, benign hegemony depends on the willingness of the hegemonic power to play by its own rules, which begs the question why the lesser powers should trust it. Ikenberry's propositions only make sense if

---

[7] Michael Mastanduno, "Preserving the Unipolar Moment: Realist Theories and U.S. Grand Strategy after the Cold War," *International Security* 21, no. 4 (1997): 49–88.

[8] G. John Ikenberry, "Institutions, Strategic Restraint, and the Persistence of American Postwar Order," *International Security* 23, no. 3 (1998/99): 43–78.

the norms of multilateral institutions exert enough independent causal influence on state behavior to guarantee that smaller states in the system are happy with U.S. power. This is rather close to an emphasis on security communities.

I find this amalgamation of residual realism, liberalism, and institutionalism empirically more convincing than the arguments reviewed so far. We need to "look more closely at *this* particular hegemon" in order to determine "why *this* particular institutional agenda was pursued."[9] We need to look at U.S. identity. But the argument is rather United States-centric. Viewed from abroad, U.S. foreign policy during the past ten years does not look entirely reassuring. Outside the United States, there is a perception of American unilateralism in both trade and security relations—from the Helms-Burton Act to the failure to ratify the Comprehensive Test Ban Treaty, efforts to destroy the Anti-Ballistic Missile (ABM) regime, and the American refusal to join in the global regime against climate change.[10] A thorough review of U.S. foreign policies toward the UN, multilateral arms control efforts, and NATO over the past ten years shows increasing unilateralism.[11] The same holds true for the Bush administration's response to international terrorism—after initial multilateral moves. As Ernst-Otto Czempiel put it, "Hegemony can be disguised as consensus power."[12] If, as Kupchan suggests in this book, current U.S. foreign policy only partly shows benign hegemony, but also includes bullying and unilateralism as well as a decreasing willingness to be the global protector of last resort, why has this not given rise to balancing behavior by the other major powers?

To answer the question, I take Ikenberry's arguments as my point of departure, but add that we also need to look more closely at the *particular characteristics* of the potential U.S. competitors in the contemporary international system to determine why they have not mounted a serious counterchallenge.

[9] John G. Ruggie, "Multilateralism: The Anatomy of an Institution," *International Organization* 46, no. 3 (1992): 592.

[10] For example, see Matthias Dembinski and Kinka Gerke, eds., *Cooperation or Conflict? Transatlantic Relations in Transition* (Frankfurt: Campus Verlag/St. Martin's Press, 1998); Jürgen Wilzewski, "Back to Unilateralism: The Clinton Administration and the Republican-Lead Congress," in *Cooperation or Conflict?* 23–43; Michael Minkenberg and Herbert Dittgen, eds., *The American Impasse: U.S. Domestic and Foreign Policy after the Cold War* (Pittsburgh, Penn.: University of Pittsburgh Press, 1996).

[11] Bernd W. Kubbig, Matthias Dembinski, and Alexander Kelle, "Unilateralismus als alleinige außenpolitische Strategie? Die amerikanische Politik gegenüber UNO, NATO und der Chemiewaffen-Organisation in der Ära Clinton," HSFK-Report, 3/2000, Frankfurt am Main, Hessische Stiftung Friedens-und Konfliktforschung," May 2000.

[12] Ernst-Otto Czempiel, *Amerikanische Außenpolitik* (Stuttgart: Kohlhammer, 1979), 231.

Relations among Major Powers in the Current World Order: A Liberal Security Community

Debates about U.S. foreign policy, unipolarity, and the absence of power-balancing against the world's "only superpower" mostly overlook the fact that the contemporary world system is dominated by liberal and capitalist democracies. Among the great powers, only the People's Republic of China and Russia are the two remaining nondemocracies with Russia still being in a painful transition process. More than 80 percent of the major powers' GDP and of their military expenditures is concentrated among liberal democracies. A quick look at the world's "top ten" list using several indicators yields similar results:[13] Among the world's top ten in terms of GNP, GNP per capita, energy production, and manufacturing, the only nondemocracy making the list in more than one category is China. If we use indicators for information age technologies or for education, non-democracies drop out altogether, while democratizing states such as South Korea and Taiwan enter the world's leaders in these categories. The only category that is still populated by nondemocracies such as China, North Korea, or Pakistan and with transition states such as Russia, concerns military might. However, most analysts agree that the United States is so far ahead of everybody else concerning military power to render "top ten" lists pretty meaningless in this category.

I argue in the following that liberal democracies dominate the current world order, that they form a security community, and that this explains the absence of counterbalancing against the United States. Following Alexander Wendt, we need to distinguish among several possible social structures in the international order. "Anarchy is what states make of it."[14] This statement does not mean that "anything goes" in international life, but that "anarchy" understood as the absence of a world government can lead to several possible social structures of world politics among which a realist world dominated by the security dilemma is only one. States (and increasingly nonstate actors) create the international order through their interactions, and it makes a huge difference whether they consider each other as potential friends or foes.

Enduring liberal democracies rarely fight each other, and therefore, the security dilemma is almost absent in interactions among them. The literature about the "democratic peace" is enormous and the proposition does

[13] Data compiled from *Encyclopaedia Britannica: Deluxe CD 2000* (Oxford, 1999).

[14] Alexander Wendt, "Anarchy Is What States Make of It: The Social Construction of Power Politics," *International Organization* 88, no. 2 (1992): 384–96; and Wendt, *Social Theory of International Politics* (Cambridge: Cambridge University Press, 1999).

not require further elaboration here.[15] The democratic peace finding has survived many barrages of criticism[16] and some studies even go further arguing that stable democracies never have and never will fight each other.[17] More important, recent quantitative studies suggest that economic interdependence measured in trade dependence of GDP and joint membership in international organizations (IOs) also add to peaceful relations among states.[18] Interdependence effects and IO membership are apparently not as robust as the consequences of joint democracy, but they add to the absence of war among states.

Joint democracy, economic interdependence, and highly institutionalized international relations—these are empirical indicators for what Karl W. Deutsch called a "pluralistic security community" in 1957, defined as "a group of people which has become 'integrated.' By INTEGRATION we mean the attainment, within a territory, of a 'sense of community' and of institutions and practices strong enough and widespread enough to assure, for a 'long' time, dependable expectations of 'peaceful change' among its population." The sense of community is defined as "mutual sympathy and loyalties; of 'we-feeling,' trust, and consideration; of at least partial identification in terms of self-images and interests; of the ability to predict each other's behavior and ability to act in accordance of that prediction."[19] A security community constitutes a particular social structure

[15] For example, see Bruce Russett, *Grasping the Democratic Peace* (Princeton, N.J.: Princeton University Press 1993); John M. Owen, *Liberal Peace, Liberal War: American Politics and International Security* (Ithaca, N.Y.: Cornell University Press, 1997). For a review of most recent literature see Steve Chan, "In Search of Democratic Peace: Problems and Promise," *Mershon International Studies Review* 41, no. 1 (1997): 59–91; and Miriam Fendius Elman, "The Never-Ending Story: Democracy and Peace," *International Studies Review* 1, no. 3 (1999): 87–103.

[16] Most recently, Joanne Gowa, *Ballots and Bullets: The Elusive Democratic Peace* (Princeton, N.J.: Princeton University Press, 1999); see also Michael E. Brown, Sean M. Lynn-Jones, and Steven E. Miller, eds., *Debating the Democratic Peace* (Cambridge, Mass.: MIT Press, 1996).

[17] Spencer R. Weart, *Never at War: Why Democracies Will Not Fight One Another* (New Haven, Conn.: Yale University Press, 1998); James Lee Ray, *Democracy and International Conflict: An Evaluation of the Democratic Peace* (Columbia: University of South Carolina Press, 1995).

[18] John R. Oneal and Bruce Russett, "The Classical Liberals Were Right: Democracy, Interdependence, and Conflict, 1950–85," *International Studies Quarterly* 41, no. 2 (1997): 267–93; and Oneal and Russett, "The Kantian Peace: The Pacific Benefits of Democracy, Interdependence, and International Organizations, 1885–1992," *World Politics* 52, no. 1 (1999): 1–37; Russett, Oneal, and David R. Davis, "The Third Leg of the Kantian Tripod for Peace: Organizations and Militarized Disputes, 1950–85," *International Organization* 52, no. 3 (1998): 441–68; Russett, "A Neo-Kantian Perspective: Democracy, Interdependence, and International Organizations in Building Security Communities," in *Security Communities*, ed. Emanuel Adler and Michael Barnett (Cambridge: Cambridge University Press, 1998), 368–94.

[19] Karl W. Deutsch et al., *Political Community and the North Atlantic Area* (Princeton, N.J.: Princeton University Press, 1957), 5–6, 9.

of international relations, which then generates peaceful relations among the members.

A pluralistic security community[20] in which members retain their formal independence and sovereignty[21] is based on a collective identity among the members, on common institutions, and on habitualized practices that lead to "dependable expectations of peaceful change." Adler and Barnett define the latter as "neither the expectation of nor the preparation for organized violence as a means to settle interstate disputes."[22] In other words, we should not expect balancing behavior among the members of a security community.

One would add from a constructivist perspective that perceptions are all-important. Inside a stable security community, behavior will not be regarded as threatening that might be perceived as highly dangerous and worth a response if it came from states outside the community. The United States, for example, has never been concerned about British and French nuclear weapons even though they could inflict heavy damage on the U.S. mainland. Europeans and Japanese might strongly disagree with U.S. attempts to change the ABM Treaty, with the failure to ratify the Comprehensive Test Ban Treaty, to sign the international treaty banning landmines, or to join the regime against climate change. They might feel annoyed by American unilateralism and by legislation such as the Burton-Helms Act and seek remedy through the WTO dispute settlement system. But none of this is seen as a military security threat to the other democratic powers in the contemporary international system giving rise to balancing behavior or to building counteralliances.

But what explains the expectations of peaceful change among members of a security community? Three factors mutually reinforce each other and serve to account for the democratic peace in the contemporary security community of major powers:[23]

---

[20] In the following, I use the term "security community" routinely for *pluralistic* security communities, since not even the EU would qualify as an *amalgamated* security community in the strict Deutschian sense.

[21] As opposed to an "amalgamated" security community where states integrate their political systems; see also Bruce Cronin, *Community under Anarchy: Transnational Identity and the Evolution of Cooperation* (New York: Columbia University Press, 1999).

[22] Emanuel Adler and Michael Barnett, "A Framework for the Study of Security Communities," in *Security Communities*, ed. Adler and Barnett (Cambridge: Cambridge University Press, 1998), 29–65, 34.

[23] Ibid.; and Barnett and Adler, "Studying Security Communities in Theory, Comparison, and History," in *Security Communities*, 413–41.

1. Collective identity;
2. Stable and interdependent interactions across societies creating strong social interests in each other's well-being;
3. Strong institutionalization of relationships creating social order among the members of the community.

These three factors might vary, as a result of which we can distinguish comparatively strong from rather weak security communities. The EU, which scores rather high on all three aspects, constitutes one of the strongest expressions of the liberal security community in the contemporary international system, while the Organization for Security and Cooperation in Europe (OSCE) exhibits a rather weak sense of community.[24] The Asian efforts at building a security community based on the Association of Southeast Asian Nations (ASEAN) also have reached only intermediate levels of common identity, interdependence, and institutionalization.[25] Neither the OSCE nor ASEAN are composed of states with similar liberal internal orders.

Collective Identity

Among the three factors, collective identity is probably the most difficult to measure without getting into tautological reasoning.[26] However, John Owen's work shows the crucial significance of perceptions of the others as liberal or illiberal in diplomatic crises between the United States and foreign states.[27] My own work on transatlantic conflicts during the Cold War tried to show that a sense of community together with consultation norms and transgovernmental coalition-building indeed explain the disproportionate European influence on U.S. foreign policy during that period.[28]

To measure the strength of collective identities, we should distinguish them along two dimensions: the salience of the "self/other" or "in-group/out-group" distinction, on the one hand, and the price people are

[24] But see Adler, "Seeds of Peaceful Change: The OSCE's Security Community-Building Model," in *Security Communities*, 119–60; Gregory Flynn and Henry Farrell, "Piecing Together the Democratic Peace: The CSCE, Norms, and the 'Construction' of Security in Post–Cold War Europe," *International Organization* 53, no. 3 (1999): 505–35.

[25] Amitav Acharya, "Collective Identity and Conflict Management in Southeast Asia," in *Security Communities*, 198–227.

[26] Members of security communities do not fight each other; therefore, they must identify with each other, which explains their peacefulness.

[27] Owen, *Liberal Peace, Liberal War.*

[28] Thomas Risse-Kappen, *Cooperation among Democracies: The European Influence on U.S. Foreign Policy* (Princeton, N.J.: Princeton University Press, 1995).

prepared to pay for their sense of loyalty to the group, on the other. As to the "in-group/ out-group" distinction, democratic security communities usually score rather high in this regard. Liberal democracies hold what Giesen and Eisenstadt called a "sacred" identity construction.[29] We are the "shining city on the hill,"[30] but others can convert and become part of us, in other words, also become liberal democracies. Liberal security communities engage in rather strong boundary constructions along the "self/other" divide, which is a function of a country's internal order. Once states democratize, they are eligible as members of the security community.

The sharp "self/other" distinction explains, for instance, the missionary impulse in American foreign policy. It also explains why nondemocracies are often constructed as "empires or axes of evil," why autocratic leaders are often demonized,[31] why Western powers fought the Cold War as viciously as they did, and why the United States engaged in numerous unnecessary wars in the periphery such as Vietnam. The point is that perceived security threats emanate from a country's internal order and not just from its material capabilities. Liberal democracies only regard power capabilities as threatening and deserving a balancing response if autocratic regimes control them. As John Lewis Gaddis put it, "Whether in dealing with the Kaiser's Germany, Lenin's Russia, Nazi Germany, Imperial Japan, Stalinist Russia, Communist China, North Vietnam, Castro's Cuba, or even Nicaragua under the Sandinistas, the United States tended to equate internal forms with external behavior."[32]

If the sharp "self/other" distinction were the only feature in the collective identification process of the democratic security community, we would probably experience many more wars along the border between the community and its nondemocratic periphery than we actually do. Yet, the strong sense of community in terms of the "in-group/out-group" differentiation seems to be balanced by a comparatively weak sense of loyalty toward the community, at least as far as the ultimate price—to die for the community—is concerned. While ethno-nationalist, fundamentalist religious, and other primordialist identity constructions apparently mobilize followers rather easily to fight for the community up to what amounts to

[29] Shmuel N. Eisenstadt and Bernhard Giesen, "The Construction of Collective Identity," *European Journal of Sociology* 36 (1995): 72–102.

[30] To quote from the American collective mythology; similar self-descriptions can easily be found in French discourses.

[31] Cf. the comparisons of both Saddam Hussein and Slobodan Milosevic with Adolf Hitler as well as the description of Osama bin Laden as "personified evil."

[32] John L. Gaddis, *The United States and the End of the Cold War* (Oxford: Oxford University Press, 1992), 13.

suicide attacks, liberal identities come with notions of individualism which put severe constraints on the capacity of political leaders to mobilize for war fighting. The "no casualties" doctrine of the U.S. armed forces constitutes a case in point. Here, institutional constraints and collective identities work together to prevent the democratic security community from engaging in fruitless wars with nondemocracies, unless they win these wars.[33]

Still, there are sufficient examples to sustain the argument that the often-proclaimed "value community" of the Western alliance does not simply represent sheer rhetoric. After all, the United States—at least in its declaratory policies—was prepared to sacrifice New York for Berlin during the Cold War. The hot debates about the credibility of extended deterrence during the Cold War document that this was not regarded as an empty threat. And in the post–Cold War era, the Western security community did fight for its principles several times. For example, the Kosovo war and the transformation of most of ex-Yugoslavia into a Western protectorate can hardly be explained on material grounds. The liberal identity of the community and its commitment to humanitarian principles to a large extent account for the expenditure of substantial economic, military, and human resources by Western powers in the Balkans. Elite surveys in the United States and elsewhere show a continuing commitment and support of large majorities within the Western community toward cooperative internationalism, multilateral institutions, and more specifically, an identification with the democratic security community.[34] The enormous and spontaneous outpouring of solidarity with the American people in Europe after September 11, 2001, ("We are all New Yorkers!") confirms that the sense of community goes well beyond the political and business elites. While this solidarity does not necessarily translate into support for specific U.S. military action killing innocent civilians, it contradicts the widespread assumption that the two continents have been drifting apart. Even though European societies have been exposed to terrorist attacks and have been much more vulnerable to terrorism in the past than the United States, there is little sense in Europe that the current attacks are simply an American problem that Europe can safely ignore.

[33] David Lake, "Powerful Pacifists: Democratic States and War," *American Political Science Review* 20, no. 1 (1992): 24–37.

[34] Ole R. Holsti, *Public Opinion and American Foreign Policy* (Ann Arbor: University of Michigan Press, 1996); for mass public opinion data see for example John E. Rielly, ed., *American Public Opinion and United States Foreign Policy 1999* (Chicago: Chicago Council on Foreign Relations Press, 1999); Hans Rattinger, "Einstellungen zur europaeischen Integration in der Bundesrepublik: Ein Kausalmodell," *Zeitschrift fuer Internationale Beziehungen* 3, no. 1 (1996): 45–78; Holsti, "Public Opinion," in *Eagle Rules? Foreign Policy and American Primacy in the Twenty-First Century*, ed. Robert J. Lieber (Upper Saddle River, N.J.: Prentice Hall, 2002).

Transnational Interdependence

As to the second and third factors contributing to security communities, they can be measured more easily. Regarding transaction flows, the openness of liberal societies not only has an internal, but also an external component. In general, democratic governments are less eager to control transnational interactions among societies than their autocratic counterparts. As a result, we should expect interdependent relationships across democratic societies. The OECD world, which essentially comprises most countries belonging to the liberal security community, is characterized by what Keohane and Nye more than twenty years ago called "complex interdependence."[35] "Globalization" is largely confined to the OECD world.[36] The EU's single market constitutes the most integrated region economically if we use combined figures of trade, investment, and capital flows. The EU is followed by the transatlantic region, even though U.S. trade with Asia has now surpassed transatlantic trade. If we measure other transaction flows such as communications or tourism, the OECD region also comes out on top. Moreover, the trend toward regionalization in the international economy[37] and the overall increase in intraregional trade has not led to a substantial decline in interregional economic exchanges.[38] Finally, and this is the main difference to the economic interdependence of the nineteenth and early twentieth centuries, it takes place within the framework of a multilateral free trade regime (former GATT, now WTO).

One should not overemphasize the community-building impact of social interactions though. Barnett and Adler, for instance, argue that "political and economic transactions . . . are more than simply an exchange of goods and services but also potentially the cornerstone for trust and a sense of community."[39] At least, they should create mutual interests in maintaining the relationship and also in each other's political, economic, and social well-being. To a certain degree then, collective identities and material interests reinforce each other. Yet, interdependence based on

---

[35] Robert O. Keohane and Joseph S. Nye, *Power and Interdependence* (Boston: Little, Brown, 1977).

[36] Plus some democratizing states, particularly in East Asia and Latin America; cf. data in Marianne Beisheim, Sabine Dreher, Gregor Walter, Bernhard Zangl, and Michael Zürn, *Im Zeitalter der Globalisierung? Thesen und Daten zur gesellschaftlichen und politischen Denationalisierung* (Baden-Baden: Nomos, 1998); David Held, Anthony McGrew, David Goldblatt, and Jonathan Perraton, *Global Transformations: Politics, Economics, and Culture* (Stanford, Calif.: Stanford University Press, 1999).

[37] EU, NAFTA, Mercosur, and now ASEAN.

[38] Edward D. Mansfield and Helen V. Milner, "The New Wave of Regionalism," *International Organization* 53, no. 3 (1999): 589–627.

[39] Barnett and Adler, "Studying Security Communities," 416.

regular and frequent interactions does not necessarily lead to greater co-operation, it also instigates conflicts. In the absence of collective identification processes, frequent interactions might not at all increase trust among social groups, but also lead to increasing hostility, as social psychology experiments on stereotyping have shown.[40] If the interaction partner is perceived as member of an "out-group," frequent transactions can increase the "self/other" boundary. Moreover, the literature on economic interdependence has shown that sensitivity and vulnerability in interdependent relationships might actually increase rather than decrease conflicts among societies. Neoliberal institutionalism started from the assumption that international cooperation and regime-building are necessary to overcome trade conflicts resulting from increasing interdependence.[41]

Multilateral Institutions

This insight leads to the third factor constituting a security community, multilateral institution-building. While frequent transactions among states and societies might lead to disputes, they also increase the mutual interests in peaceful resolution of those conflicts through international institutions and regimes. The OECD world has given rise to an enormous variety of international regimes and organizations covering almost every aspect of international life. While some of these institutions such as the UN or the WTO extend beyond the security community, many international regimes and organizations are confined to the world of industrialized liberal democracies. However, the strength and density of these institutions vary quite a bit. Again and in parallel to the density of transnational interdependence, Europe and the transatlantic region constitute the most tightly coupled institutionalized settings within the larger security community.[42] This region of the world also hosts the two strongest political, economic, and security institutions in terms of robustness of norms, rules, and decision-making procedures, the EU and NATO.

In contrast, the East Asian and Oceanian part of the larger security com-

[40] For example see Michael A. Hogg and John C. Turner, "Intergroup Behavior, Self-Stereotyping and the Salience of Social Categories," *British Journal of Social Psychology* 26 (1987): 325–40; Penelope J. Oakes, S. Alexander Haslam, and John C. Turner, *Stereotyping and Social Reality* (Oxford: Oxford University Press, 1994).

[41] Robert O. Keohane, *International Institutions and State Power* (Boulder, Colo.: Westview, 1989).

[42] On loosely and tightly coupled security communities see Adler and Barnett, "A Framework for the Study of Security Communities," 30–31.

munity is less densely institutionalized. Moreover, some of the security institutions in the area, such as the U.S.–Japanese security relationship, are bilateral rather than multilateral. There are also less stable democracies and many more democratizing states such as South Korea, Taiwan, or—most recently—Indonesia in Southeast Asia than in Europe and the transatlantic area. As a result, East Asia constitutes a more loosely coupled part of the overall liberal security community than the transatlantic relationship and the EU.

As to the latter, the multilateral institutions of the transatlantic community serve to manage the inevitable conflicts inside a security community. Moreover, norms and decision-making procedures of the international institutions governing the relationship embody the collective identity and shared values of the security community. As I argued elsewhere, "democracies are then likely to form *democratic institutions* whose rules and procedures are oriented toward consensual and compromise-oriented decision-making respecting the equality of the participants."[43] Strong procedural norms of mutual consultation and policy coordination insure that the members of the community have regular input and influence on each other's policy-making processes. Other institutions such as the WTO exhibit dispute settlement procedures whereby conflicts are resolved by an independent judiciary. These procedural norms and regulations are among the major tools mitigating power asymmetries among community members. Of course, one cannot deny that these asymmetries exist, particularly between the United States on the one hand, and the rest of the community on the other, and that they affect outcomes. The United States has more clout inside NATO than everybody else, and Germany is more influential in the EU than, say, Portugal. However, procedural norms insure that superior material power does not necessarily carry the day and that the lesser states have a fair chance of being heard and of influencing decisions.

Such a norms-based argument explains similar effects as Ikenberry's "benign hegemony" thesis.[44] But the institutionalized rules exert their influence independently from the good will of a superior power. In particular, they can be used for remedies in cases of norm violation. While we would not expect that the United States never violates the norms of the security community, these rules set standards of appropriate behavior against which U.S. foreign policy can be judged. Allied complaints about "American arrogance and unilateralism" imply such common standards of

---

[43] Risse-Kappen, *Cooperation among Democracies,* 33.

[44] Ikenberry, "Institutions, Strategic Restraint, and the Persistence of American Postwar Order."

appropriateness against which the United States is held accountable. In a realist world of power balancing, Europeans and Japanese would not protest about American unilateralism, because they would not expect anything else. Rather, they would start reducing their ties with the hegemon, mind their own business, and gradually develop counteralliances.

If we assume a security community with its respective rules of appropriateness, however, complaints by Europeans and others make sense. Instead of ignoring the norms of the security community and developing a counterresponse, the typical response of European and other lesser members of the community to U.S. arrogance and unilateral impulses has been to tighten the norms of the community in the various institutional settings. In other words, the strategy has typically been one of binding rather than balancing. The European show of "unrestricted solidarity"[45] with the United States in the aftermath of September 11, 2001, constitutes another attempt at binding in order to prevent American unilateralism.

Binding strategies, however, can only be effective if one believes that institutions affect behavior and preferences. Binding constitutes an institutionalist response to perceived unilateralism. It is along these lines that European countries and Japan have dealt with crises in their relations with the United States for most of the post–World War II period. There is no reason to assume that this is about to change.

In sum, the dominant social structure of the post–Cold War era is a security community comprising all but one major power in the current international system, with Russia located on the community's periphery, both geopolitically and socially. The security community consists of highly industrialized liberal and capitalist democracies that tend to externalize their internal domestic structures, particularly the rule of law, embedded constraints on the (ab)use of power, and a political culture emphasizing the peaceful resolution of conflicts, when dealing which each other. Three dimensions are constitutive for the security community: a collective identity emphasizing shared liberal values and maintaining a strong "in-group/out-group" boundary, complex interdependence among the societies, and a high degree of international governance structures creating social order among the community members. While each of these three factors vary considerably inside the community, with some areas more tightly coupled than others, they result in mutual and dependable expectations of peaceful change, overcoming a "balance-of-power" world.

The existence of the liberal security community ultimately explains why the Europeans in particular have chosen not to balance against the United States, even though they have the material capacities to do so, at

---

[45] German chancellor Gerhard Schröder.

least when it comes to nuclear weapons. One could argue, though, that the reason for this reluctance to balance is German domestic politics rather than the existence of a security community.[46] German domestic politics would prevent an active European attempt to balance U.S. power militarily. It is true that German foreign policy in the post–World War II period has been one of a civilian power and that there is still a very strong domestic consensus in support of this stance.[47] Yet, it is impossible to separate out the domestic politics of German foreign policy from the security community in which it is embedded. The lessons learned from German history compelled a full embrace of the transatlantic relationship, European integration, and other multilateral institutions of the Western community in order to prevent another German *Sonderweg*. Thus, the German collective identity reinforces the sense of community, while at the same time being constituted by it.

The Security Community and Its Boundaries

The security community of liberal and capitalist democracies encompasses most of today's major powers, and some of its constitutive values and norms have assumed more or less hegemonic character in the contemporary world order. These include both human rights norms putting limits on state sovereignty[48] and rules governing an open international economic order. Being a recognized member of the international community "in good standing" implies an acceptance of human rights and an open world economy. Both sets of norms externalize constitutive principles of the internal order of capitalist democracies onto the international sphere. In this sense then, a liberal hegemony in a neo-Gramscian sense dominates the current world order.[49]

Yet, we do not live in a Kantian world of "perpetual peace" and justice.[50]

---

[46] I thank an anonymous reviewer for pointing this out to me.

[47] Andrew Markovits and Simon Reich, *The German Predicament* (Ithaca, N.Y.: Cornell University Press, 1997); Peter J. Katzenstein, ed., *Tamed Power: Germany in Europe* (Ithaca, N.Y.: Cornell University Press, 1997).

[48] Margret Keck and Kathryn Sikkink, *Activists beyond Borders: Transnational Advocacy Networks in International Politics* (Ithaca, N.Y.: Cornell University Press, 1998); Jack Donnelly, *International Human Rights: Dilemmas in World Politics* (Boulder, Colo.: Westview Press, 1993); David P. Forsythe, *The Internationalization of Human Rights* (Lexington, Mass.: Lexington Books, 1991).

[49] Robert W. Cox and Timothy J. Sinclair, *Approaches to World Order* (Cambridge: Cambridge University Press, 1996).

[50] Immanuel Kant, "Perpetual Peace: A Philosophical Sketch," in *Kant: Political Writings*, ed. Hans Reiss (Cambridge: Cambridge University Press, 1991).

While the liberal security community comprises most of today's major powers, it has clear boundaries and the strength of its institutions varies quite substantially. However, these boundaries as well as the variation in strength have little to do with the material distribution of power in the world system. Rather, the domestic structures of members, their mutual interdependence, and their embeddedness in international institutions constitute the features that define the geopolitical borders of the community. From this perspective, differences in social rather than material structures constitute the boundaries in the current world order.

The Kantian vision is most closely realized in the North Atlantic area, that is, North America and most of Europe, constituting the most tightly coupled security community in the current world system. While Japan and the other liberal democracies in Asia, Oceania, Latin America, and Africa all participate in the community of democratic states, there is quite some variation concerning collective identification, transnational interdependence, and institutionalization, the three defining characteristics of a security community. Then, there is the periphery of the security community, consisting largely of states in various stages of transition toward democracies and market economies. The defining characteristics of the liberal security community are largely absent. The fate of the democratizing world along the social and geopolitical periphery of the community remains unclear and will probably remain so for quite a while. The democratic transitions in many successor states of the Soviet Union are incomplete, with Russia only being the most obvious example. There are many examples of failed transitions in sub-Saharan Africa. In contrast, several Latin American and Southeast Asian states such as South Korea or Taiwan are in much better shape on their path to democracy and market economy.

So far, the OECD world has practiced restraint in its foreign policy toward these states. The EU went even further and has opened an accession perspective for all Eastern and Southeastern European states including the Balkans and Turkey. Membership in the union depends on three conditions: democracy and human rights, market economy, and willingness to implement the EU's *acquis communitaire*, that is, to make European law the law of the land. Western policies toward Russia have also shown quite some restraint so far, particularly in comparison with Cold War policies, even though Russia is a far cry from becoming member of the democratic club. Many have accused Western powers of employing a double standard toward Moscow with regard to its torched earth policy in Chechnya as compared to, for example, Belgrade under Milosevic. When former President Yeltsin issued nuclear threats against NATO and the United

States, nobody took him seriously. Just imagine the effects of a similar rhetoric during the Cold War. After September 11, 2001, a new strategic alliance has been formed with Putin's Russia.

While the democratizing states form the periphery of the liberal security community in the world system, those parts of the world governed by authoritarian rulers remain outside. Thus, the democracy-autocracy divide constitutes the boundary between the liberal community and the rest of the world, between "us" and "them." Many parts of the world, such as sub-Saharan Africa and half of Asia, China in particular, are decoupled from the security community. Moreover, transnational terrorist networks have emerged as a threat to the community "from the inside," since they exploit the infrastructure and the complex interdependence of the industrialized democracies. As a result, the security dilemma and traditional balance-of-power politics still govern parts of the world as well as relations between the liberal security community and authoritarian regimes. It is no wonder, therefore, that realist arguments such as is found in the chapter by Mastunduno in this book prevail in scholarly analysis of regional relations in East Asia, in sharp contrast to Europe and the transatlantic area.

Transatlantic Conflicts, U.S. Power, and the Liberal Security Community

Conceptualizing the dominant contemporary world order as a security community explains "big issues" such as the enduring absence of war and of power balancing among the community members. Social structures constitute actors as community members, but they do not determine behavior in a monocausal sense. The security community and its institutions exhibit certain norms of appropriate behavior, which influence definitions of interests and constraining behavior. But members still have choices about how to conduct their foreign policies and how to interpret the rules. Moreover, the shared values and norms of a security community are ultimately about the peaceful resolution of conflicts; they are not about their absence in a harmonious world. We need further insights from liberal and institutionalist theories of foreign policy[51] in order to account for concrete behavior among members of the community.

United States foreign policy, wavering between continued multilateralism and unilateralist impulses, is within the confines of the argument.

---

[51] For example, Andrew Moravcsik, "Taking Preferences Seriously: A Liberal Theory of International Politics," *International Organization* 51, no. 4 (1997): 513–53.

While Mastanduno sees a grand strategy here,[52] I find it more convincing to use liberal foreign policy theory as a toolbox to account for its inconsistencies.[53] From this perspective, there is not one single and coherent American foreign policy, but there are almost always several. "Divided government" largely characterizes U.S. policy-making, from the Clinton years with a Democratic executive and a Republican-dominated Congress to the current Bush administration with Congress practically in a stalemate between Republicans and Democrats.[54] This implies for defense and security matters that there are ongoing struggles between unilateral internationalists and multilateralists both inside the administration and inside Congress, leading to various cross-cutting coalitions between members of Congress and agencies of the executive. The wavering of U.S. foreign policy between multilateralism and unilateralism has been particularly pronounced after September 11, 2001. A split has emerged between the Pentagon and the vice presidency, dominated by unilateralists on the one hand and a more multilateralist orientation of the U.S. State Department on the other. President Bush and his national security team seem to follow a zigzag course between the two tendencies. As a result, U.S. allies and the coalition partners in the war against terrorism are faced with worrisome unilateralist rhetoric reminding them of the Reagan years ("axis of evil") and reassuring multilateralist statements at almost the same time. Yet, this hint concerning the Reagan years also demonstrates that wavering between unilateral behavior and multilateral practices does not constitute a novelty in U.S. foreign policy.

Concerning foreign economic policies, things are as complicated. International trade issues have become more politicized (on both sides of the Atlantic) than they used to be. The multilateral and free-trade orientation of the U.S. political elites from the center-right to the center-left is increasingly balanced by a strange coalition of isolationist right-wing Republicans with American labor and environmental activists who form the bedrock of support for the Democrats.[55] The struggle between the two groups is likely to continue, even though the Bush administration seems

[52] Mastanduno, "Preserving the Unipolar Moment."

[53] Moravcsik, "Taking Preferences Seriously"; Czempiel, *Amerikanische Außenpolitik;* Minkenberg and Dittgen, *The American Impasse.*

[54] For the original argument, see David R. Mayhew, *Divided We Govern: Party Control, Lawmaking, and Investigations, 1946–1990* (New Haven, Conn.: Yale University Press, 1991); also see Tobias Dürr, "From Divided Government to Post–Cold War Gridlock?" in *The American Impasse,* 76–95; Wilzewski, "Back to Unilateralism"; and Lieber, ed., *Eagle Adrift: American Foreign Policy at the End of the Century* (New York: Longman, 1997).

[55] For example, see Jay Mazur, "Globalization's Dark Side," *Foreign Affairs* 79, no. 1 (2000): 79–93.

to have shifted the balance once again a bit toward the multilateral free-trade orientation.

How does the argument about the security community come in here? First, conflicts per se do not contradict the logic of a security community. Inside the community, we often observe fierce bargaining over trade and security issues. However, these are temporary disputes and conflicts of interests to be expected in and among highly interdependent democratic societies that are unlikely to threaten the core of the community.

Second, the logic of the security community implies that we rarely observe traditional interstate conflicts between the United States and its European partners, which would pitch the United States against the Europeans. Rather, we observe changing and cross-cutting transnational, transgovernmental, and international coalitions on the various issues under dispute including various countervailing coalitions. Most current conflicts of interests do not pitch the United States against the rest, but societal interest groups and/or transnational coalitions against each other. Multinational corporations (MNC) on either side of the Atlantic share a preference toward a global open economy and against protectionist impulses in U.S. Congress or, say, in French and German societies. This is amply demonstrated by the rather harmonious relations inside the Transatlantic Business Dialogue (TABD), a transatlantic governance structure encompassing public and private actors, namely MNCs.[56] As far as the reform of the world financial institutions such as the International Monetary Fund (IMF) or the World Bank is concerned, a transnational neoliberal expert coalition is pitched against another alliance of center-left policymakers and experts who prefer maintaining a strong role of both institutions in poverty reduction and development policies.

Concerning international security, none of the controversies surrounding Western policies toward ex-Yugoslavia during the past decade put the United States against the Europeans. Rather, major European powers disagreed among themselves, to begin with. Transnational and transgovernmental alliances, with diverging preferences, formed across the Atlantic. In the transatlantic dispute over missile defense and the future of the ABM treaty, we can observe a similar transnational coalition between American Democrats and supporters of arms control on the one hand and their European counterparts including most European governments on the other. After September 11, 2001, a transatlantic coalition has formed between U.S. secretary of state Colin Powell and most European allies

---

[56] Maria Green Cowles, "Private Firms and US-EU Policymaking: The Transatlantic Business Dialogue," in *Policy-Making in the US–EU Relationship*, ed. Eric Philippart and Pascaline Winand (Manchester: Manchester University Press, 2000).

against the unilateralists in the Pentagon. This pattern of cross-cutting coalitions is precisely what one expects in a security community of open societies and democratic states.[57] While conflicts of interests are fairly common in the Western security community, they are usually transnational or transgovernmental rather than interstate in nature.

The third feature of security communities that is relevant for dispute resolution among the partners concerns norms of consultation and policy coordination. A constitutive aspect of the transatlantic security community concerns the fact that both sides consider each other as having legitimate input and access into one's own policy-making process. As a result, European governments and their diplomats are not considered foreigners in Washington, but as partners with a legitimate say in U.S. affairs. The same holds true in Brussels and in the European capitals. United States diplomats, for example, regularly and routinely participate in informal deliberations (the so-called "Quint") surrounding the European Security and Defense Policy (ESDP), thereby disconfirming the notion that the ESDP is being developed in opposition to U.S. security and defense policy or as an alternative to NATO.

In conclusion, two questions deserve further attention: first, if joint membership in a security community does not determine the participants' foreign policies how can one disconfirm the argument? To begin with, efforts at building a counterhegemonic alliance against the United States would falsify the proposition. Consistent movements from a tightly coupled security community (or parts thereof) toward a more loosely coupled one could also indicate that the community is weakening. If the United States, the EU, or Japan start to systematically reduce the ties of transnational interdependence with each other, this would serve as an indicator that the community is in trouble. If the major multilateral institutions that regulate social order start unraveling, this would also indicate a move toward more loosely coupled communities. The clearest indicator of such a development in the transatlantic area would probably be the development of the ESDP into a full-fledged alternative to NATO, particularly in the nuclear arena with Germany actively participating.

Finally, what is the role of U.S. power or power politics in general in the security community? Does it matter at all? Of course, one cannot ignore the overwhelming U.S. power in the current international system, both with regard to material and ideational resources, that is, "hard" and "soft" power. The question is not about capabilities, but the U.S. ability and willingness to use its material and ideational resources in order to exercise influence in world affairs. There are various ways in which the United States

---

[57] Risse-Kappen, *Cooperation among Democracies.*

can use its power to wield influence in the community, and not every use of power is inconsistent with its norms.

Let me consider instances in which the United States (ab)uses its power in the security community thereby violating its norms, in short American unilateralism and bullying. If American foreign policy were to consistently bully the European allies, one would indeed have to question whether the community norms have any effect at all on Washington's decisions. But how do we know whether U.S. unilateralism violates some community norms, or instead is an example of "normal" superpower behavior in an anarchic world? To begin with, norm violation should lead to apologetic behavior by the perpetrator and efforts should be undertaken to repair the relationship. Moreover, if there is a norm prohibiting bullying or co-ercing your partners, these partners should react to norm violation in peculiar ways. The allied impulse in response to U.S. unilateralism or bullying should be binding rather than balancing. This is exactly what the Europeans have done most of the time during the past fifty years, via the existing security institutions such as NATO and, more recently, through building up the institutional ties between the United States and the EU. The new transatlantic dialogue constitutes an emerging transatlantic governance structure that includes governments, the EU Commission, and private actors from both sides of the Atlantic.[58] We can observe similar developments in the security realm concerning the informal U.S. involvement in the new ESDP.

Community partners are expected to remind the United States of the norms and rules whenever they perceive American bullying or unilateralism. Thus the European partners are likely to be more outspoken in their criticism of U.S. foreign policy in the future. This has little to do with "fraying ties,"[59] but with a more mature security community. The current European social, political, and economic elites have by and large been socialized in the transatlantic security community. There is a growing sense that the U.S.–European relationship is stable and strong enough to survive transatlantic disputes, which are no longer dealt with only behind closed doors, as was largely the case during the Cold War. I take this as a healthy sign that the security community has grown up rather than a first step toward its disintegration.

But the United States can also use its influence on community members consistent with the norms of the security community. A multilateralist and

---

[58] Mark A. Pollack and Gregory C. Shaffer, eds., *The New Transatlantic Dialogue: Intergovernmental, Transgovernmental, and Transnational Perspectives* (Boulder, Colo.: Rowman & Littlefield, 2000).

[59] Walt, "The Ties That Fray."

cooperative foreign policy style that relies on "soft power," persuasion, and consensus-seeking might still lead to significant American influence inside the security community and—at the same time—does not contradict the basic values of the security community and the collective identity on which it is based.

The policy prescriptions of a security community argument coincide with the recommendations of the liberal "benign hegemony" concept.[60] This is understandable, because both arguments use liberal and institutionalist assumptions to make their claims. I would just submit that emphasis on a liberal security community yields additional explanatory leverage not only on U.S. foreign policy and its collective identity, but also on the reactions of European and Japanese community partners.

[60] Ikenberry, "Institutions, Strategic Restraint, and the Persistence of American Postwar Order."

Conclusion
American Unipolarity: The Sources of Persistence and Decline

G. John Ikenberry

How long will America's "unipolar moment" last? The chapters in this book provide answers to this question. They do so by grappling with a more specific question: why, despite the widening gulf in power between the United States and other major countries, has a counterbalancing coalition not yet been triggered? This question takes the debate to the heart of our understanding of modern international relations. One of the oldest and most enduring insights about world politics is that concentrated power tends to produce a balancing response. In a world of anarchy, a powerful state is threatening by its inherent potential to dominate, exploit, and abandon. The only sure check on that power is by arraying countervailing power against it. What is the status of this insight in the age of American unipolar power?

The decade since the end of the Cold War has been remarkable. The distribution of power took a dramatic turn. The Soviet Union collapsed and the bipolar structure of international relations disappeared. But the world did not return to a multipolar balance-of-power system. Instead, American power—military, political, economic, and cultural—grew even more overwhelming. Scholars and pundits who a decade ago were debating the prospects of cooperation and conflict in a post–Cold War and post-hegemonic world are now debating the character and future of world politics within an American unipolar order.

But disparities in material capabilities do not capture the full character of American unipolarity. It is not just a powerful state that can throw its weight around—although it is that as well. The United States also dominates world politics by providing the language, ideas, and institutional frameworks around which much of the world turns. The extended institutional connections that link the United States to the other regions of the world provide a sort of primitive governance system. The United States is a central hub through which the world's important military, political, economic, scientific, and cultural connections pass. No other great power— France, Germany, the United Kingdom, Japan, Russia, or China—has a global political or security presence. The European Union has a population and economic weight equal to the United States but it does not have a global geopolitical or strategic reach. It cannot project military power or pursue a unified foreign policy toward, for example, China. Japan, who many thought a decade ago might emerge as the next great world power, is struggling under the weight of political gridlock and economic malaise. America's far-flung network of political partnerships and security commitments—together with the array of global and regional institutions—provide what passes for global governance.

But how stable is this order? The answer depends on what the precise character of this order actually is. Some argue that behind the facade of democracy and institutional cooperation lies a predatory and imperial American state. Chalmers Johnson argues that the American "empire" is as coercive and exploitative as the Soviet empire and anticipates a backlash in which America's resentful junior partners will wreak their revenge and bring the entire imperial edifice down.[1] This is an echo of a revisionist tradition that sees American global dominance driven by expansionary and exploitative capitalists or a crusading national security state. American Cold War–era interventionism in Latin America and elsewhere around the world provides ample material to make this claim.[2] Taking the opposite view, several of the chapters in this book argue that American power is fundamentally different from other dominant states in history. The structure of democracy, multilateral institutions, and liberal values— manifest across the advanced industrial world—shape and limit the way

---

[1] Chalmers Johnson, *Blowback: The Costs and Consequences of American Empire* (New York: Metropolian Books, 2000).

[2] See, for example, Noam Chomsky, *Turning the Tide: U.S. Intervention in Latin America and the Struggle for Peace* (Boston: South End Books, 1986).

American power is exercised and experienced. Advancing a realist view, Kenneth Waltz argues in chapter 1 of this book that the American unipolar order is inherently unstable not because of any special malign American characteristics but because of the inherent insecurity that unequal power confers on weaker states. In anarchic orders, weaker states are threatened by extreme concentrations of power and will seek protection in counterhegemonic groupings. The balance of power will reassert itself.

As the chapters in this book reveal, the issue of a coming backlash begs the question: what is the character of American unipolar order as a political formation? Is it built simply on a momentary and evolving distribution of power that will soon yield to a different and more traditional multipolar system of relations? Or is American unipolarity evolving into a more robust political order with a distinct logic and a long future? In short, is the current "unipolar moment" a transitional phase in world history or a new and enduring type of international order?

In grappling with the issue of unipolar stability, the authors in this book focus on three questions. First, is American power less threatening than that of other major states in the past? Is the United States simply the latest in a long line of powerful states that have risen up, triggered balancing reactions, and grudgingly endured the return to multipolar order? Or is the United States a different kind of superpower? Is the distribution of power a brute reality that creates its own logic, or is power something that can be modified, muted, and restrained? Kenneth Waltz and William Wohlforth both see material power capabilities and distributions as the primary determinants of order—even as they disagree on the logic and implications of concentrated American power. I argue that the open and penetrated character of American hegemony makes that power easier for other states to influence, shape, and work around. Thomas Risse provides the strongest statement on this side of the debate, arguing that the United States and the other advanced democratic countries have evolved into a security community that radically depreciates the role of power in the security policies and thinking of these states.

A second question asks whether American power solves problems for other states, thereby altering the costs and incentives for balancing against the United States. Josef Joffe and Michael Mastanduno argue that American power—manifest in an extended military presence around the world—is useful in solving regional security dilemmas in Europe and East Asia. Allies in these regions have benefited from security protection and the wider bundle of market and political partnerships that comes with American hegemony. The costs and benefits of unipolarity must be weighed in relation to alternative security orders—and those alternatives that are feasible are less attractive and those that might be more attractive are not feasible. Stephen Walt argues that the United States can manipulate the threat characteristics of American power. Charles Kupchan argues that in Western Europe—and perhaps even in East Asia—small steps are nonetheless being taken to develop alternatives to the extended American security presence. But ultimately, according to Kupchan, it will be the reluctance of the United States to pay the price of sustaining this security empire that will trigger its unraveling.

Finally, there is the question: what does balancing really mean in the twenty-first century? If nuclear weapons make war among the great powers less likely and if economic interdependence is a vital source of national wealth and power, what will propel states to engage in full-scale, countercoalition balancing? This question becomes particularly critical because the character of American dominance is not simply based on military—or even economic—capabilities. It is also political, scientific, linguistic, and cultural. It is rooted in the deep infrastructure of the modern world and manifest, to use Joseph Nye's apt term, as "soft power." If this is true, how do you balance against soft power? Joffe and other authors in this volume raise this question. There may indeed be some form of "balancing" emerging today but it will not take the traditional counteralliance form. Indeed, an important task for future investigation is to identify more fully the strategies and tactics that states are developing to cope with American unipolar power. But the larger issue concerns the future stability of American unipolarity. In the rest of this conclusion, I attempt to identify the factors that are both reinforcing and undermining American unipolar order.

Sources of Durability and Persistence

There are four major facets of the American unipolar order that make it durable—indeed even expansive.[3] Realist theorists of hegemony, such as Robert Gilpin, who focus on power as the essential glue, identify one dimension. This is power manifest in American security protection, technological superiority, and market dominance. A second dimension is found in the special circumstances of American geography and historical staging. American power is offshore—geographically isolated from the other

---

[3] The following section draws on G. John Ikenberry, "American Power and the Empire of Democratic Capitalism," *Review of International Studies* 27 (winter 2001–2): 191–212.

major powers—making that power less threatening and more useful in stabilizing regional relations. The timing of America's rise to dominance—after the colonial and imperial eras—has also allowed it to articulate universal principles of order that are congruent with the strategic interests of other states. A third dimension is the distinctive way in which democracy and institutions have provided the United States with mechanisms to make itself less threatening to the rest of the word. Finally, the deep forces of modernization and the distinctive principles of the American polity—civic nationalism and multicultural identity—also give the United States unusual influence and political compatibility with world political development.

Security Protection, Nuclear Weapons, and Markets

American power—military, political, economic—is the not-so-hidden hand that built and sustains American unipolar order. The realist narrative is straightforward. The United States emerged from World War II as the leading global power and it proceeded to organize the postwar system in a way that accorded with its interests. America's allies and the defeated axis states were battered and diminished by the war, whereas the United States grew more powerful through mobilization for war. America's position was also enhanced because the war had ratified the destruction of the old order of the 1930s, eliminated the alternative regional hegemonic ambitions of Germany and Japan, and diminished the viability of the British imperial order. The stage was set for the United States to shape the postwar order.

The importance of American power in postwar order building was most evident in the occupation and security binding of Germany and Japan. American troops began as occupiers of the two defeated axis states and never left. They eventually became protectors but also a palpable symbol of America's superordinate position. Host agreements were negotiated that created a legal basis for the American military presence—effectively circumscribing Japanese and West German sovereignty. West German rearmament and restoration of its political sovereignty—made necessary in the early 1950s by a growing Cold War—could only be achieved by binding Germany to Europe, which in turn required a binding American security commitment to Europe. Complex and protracted negotiations ultimately created an integrated European military force within NATO and legal agreements over the character and limits of West German sovereignty and military power.[4] A reciprocal process of security binding lay at the heart of the emerging American-led order. John McCloy identified the "fundamental principle" of American policy in the early 1950s: that "whatever German contribution to defense is made may only take the form of a force which is an integral part of a larger international organization. . . . There is no real solution of the German problem inside Germany alone. There is a solution inside the European-Atlantic-World Community."[5]

Japan was also brought into the American security and economic orbit during the 1950s. The United States took the lead in helping Japan find new commercial relations and raw material sources in Southeast Asia to substitute for the loss of Chinese and Korean markets.[6] Japan and Germany were now twin junior partners of the United States—stripped of their military capacities and reorganized as engines of world economic growth. Containment in Asia would be based on the growth and integration of Japan in the wider noncommunist Asian regional economy—what Secretary of State Dean Acheson called the "great crescent" in referring to the countries arrayed from Japan through Southeast Asia to India. Bruce Cumings captures the logic: "In East Asia, American planners envisioned a regional economy driven by revived Japanese industry, with assured continental access to markets and raw materials for its exports."[7] This strategy would link together threatened noncommunist states along the crescent, create strong economic links between the United States and Japan, and lessen the importance of European colonial holdings in the area. The United States would actively aid Japan in reestablishing a regional economic sphere in Asia, allowing it to prosper and play a regional leadership role within the larger American postwar order. Japanese economic growth, the expansion of regional and world markets, and the fighting of the Cold War went together.

Behind the scenes, America's hegemonic position has been backed by the reserve and transaction-currency role of the dollar. The dollar's special status gives the United States the rights of "seigniorage": it could print extra money to fight foreign wars, increase domestic spending, and go deeply into debt without fearing the pain that other states would experi-

[4] See Mark Trachtenberg, *A Constructed Peace: The Making of the European Settlement, 1945–1963* (Princeton, N.J.: Princeton University Press, 2000).
[5] Quoted in Thomas Schwartz, *America's Germany: John J. McCloy and the Federal Republic of Germany* (Cambridge, Mass.: Harvard University Press, 1991), 228.
[6] Michael Schaller, "Securing the Great Crescent: Occupied Japan and the Origins of Containment in Southeast Asia," *Journal of American History* 69 (September 1982): 392–414.
[7] Bruce Cumings, "Japan's Position in the World System," in *Postwar Japan as History,* ed. Andrew Gordon (Berkeley: University of California Press), 38.

ence. Other countries would have to adjust their currencies, which were linked to the dollar, when Washington pursued an inflationary course to meet its foreign and domestic policy agendas. Because of its dominance, the United States did not have to raise interest rates to defend its currency, taking pressure off its chronic trade imbalances. In the 1960s, French President Charles de Gaulle understood this hidden source of American hegemony all too well and complained bitterly. But most of America's Cold War allies were willing to hold dollars for fear that a currency collapse might lead the United States to withdraw its forces overseas and retreat into isolationism.

In this "realist" postwar bargain, American security protection, its domestic market, and the dollar have bound the allies together and created the institutional supports of the stable political order and open world economy. Because the U.S. economy dwarfed other industrial countries, it did not need to worry about controlling the distribution of gains from trade between itself and its allies. The United States has provided its partners with security guarantees and access to American markets, technology, and supplies within an open world economy. In return, East Asian and European allies have become stable partners who provide diplomatic, economic, and logistical support for the United States as it leads the wider American-centered postwar order.

Also behind the scene, the America order has been made more stable by nuclear weapons.[8] Even if the other major powers were to lose interest in the postwar bargain, the possibility of seeking a wholesale reorganization of the system through great-power war is no longer available. The costs are too steep. As Robert Gilpin has noted, great-power war is precisely the mechanism of change that has been used throughout history to redraw the international order. Rising states depose the reigning—but declining—state and impose a new order.[9] But nuclear weapons make this historical dynamic profoundly problematic. On the one hand, American power is rendered more tolerable because in the age of nuclear deterrence American military power cannot now be used for conquest against other great powers. Deterrence replaces alliance counterbalancing. On the other hand, the status quo international order led by the United States is rendered less easily replaced. War-driven change is removed as an historical process, and the United States was lucky enough to be on top when this happened.

[8] See Robert Jervis, "America and the Twentieth Century: Continuity and Change," in *The Ambiguous Legacy: U.S. Foreign Relations in the "American Century,"* ed. Michael J. Hogan (New York: Cambridge University Press, 1999).

[9] Robert Gilpin, *War and Change in World Politics* (New York: Cambridge University Press, 1981).

Geography and Historical Setting

The geographic setting and historical timing of America's rise in power have also shaped the way American primacy has been manifest. The United States is the only great power that is not neighbored by other great powers. This geographical remoteness made the power ascent of the United States less threatening to the rest of the world and it reinforced the disinclination of American leaders to directly dominate or manage great-power relations. In the twentieth century, the United States became the world's preeminent power but the location and historical entry point of that power helped shaped how this arrival was greeted.

In the 1870s, the United States surpassed Britain as the largest and most advanced economy but because of its geographical remoteness this development—and its continued growth—did not destabilize great-power relations.[10] America's era of territorial expansion took place without directly threatening other major states. The European powers had stakes in the New World but not fundamental interests or even—at least by the mid nineteenth century—a direct presence. The United States purchased territory from France rather than acquiring it by conquest. Indigenous peoples were the main losers in the American pursuit of manifest destiny. Later in the nineteenth century, the United States became the leading industrial power without triggering new interstate rivalries. Germany, of course, was not as geographically lucky and the expansion and unification of Germany unleashed nationalist rivalries, territorial ambitions, arms races, and ultimately world war.[11] More generally, power transitions—with rising powers overtaking status quo powers—are dangerous and conflict-prone moments in world history.[12] As European great powers grew in strength, they tended to trigger security-dilemma-driven conflict and balancing reactions in their regional neighborhood. But America's remoteness lessened the destabilizing impact of its transition to global preeminence.

When the United States was drawn into European power struggles, it did so primarily as an offshore balancer.[13] This was an echo of Britain's continental strategy, which for several centuries was based on aloofness for European power struggles, intervening at critical moments to tip and

[10] As A. J. P. Taylor notes, for the perspective of Europe during this period, "The United States seemed ... not merely in another continent, but on another planet." Taylor, *The Struggle for the Mastery of Europe, 1848–1918* (Oxford: Oxford University Press, 1957), xxxiii.

[11] A. J. P. Taylor, *The Course of German History* (London: Hamish Hamilton, 1945).

[12] On power transitions and hegemonic wars, see Gilpin, *War and Change in World Politics.*

[13] On the notion of offshore balancing, see Christopher Layne, "From Preponderance to Offshore Balancing," *International Security* 22, no. 1 (summer 1997): 86–124.

restore the balance among the other states.[14] This offshore balancing role was played out by the United States in the two world wars. America entered each war relatively late and tipped the balance in favor of the allies. After World War II, the United States emerged as an equally important presence in Europe, Asia, and the Middle East as an offshore military force that each region found useful in solving its local security dilemmas. In Europe, the reintegration of West Germany into the West was only possible with the American security commitment. The Franco-German settlement was explicitly and necessarily embedded in an American-guaranteed Atlantic settlement. In Josef Joffe's apt phrase, the United States became "Europe's pacifier."[15] In East Asia, the American security pact with Japan also solved regional security dilemmas by creating restraints on the resurgence of Japanese military power. In the Middle East a similar dynamic drew the United States into an active role in mediating between Israel and the Arab states. In each region, American power is seen less as a source of domination and more as a useful tool.

Because the United States is geographically remote, abandonment rather than domination has been seen as the greater risk by many states. As a result, the United States has found itself constantly courted by governments in Europe, Asia, and elsewhere. When Winston Churchill advanced ideas about postwar order he was concerned above all in finding a way to tie the United States to Europe.[16] As Geir Lundestad has observed, the expanding American political order in the half century after World War II has been in important respects an "empire by invitation."[17] The remarkable global reach of American postwar hegemony has been at least in part driven by the efforts of European and Asian governments to harness American power, render that power more predictable, and use it to overcome their own regional insecurities. The result has been a durable system of America-centered economic and security partnerships.

Finally, the historical timing of America's rise in power also left a mark. The United States came relatively late to the great-power arena, after the colonial and imperial eras had run their course. This meant that the pursuit of America's strategic interests was not primarily based on territorial control but on championing more principled ways of organizing great-

---

[14] See Paul Kennedy, *The Rise and Fall of the Great Powers: Economic Change and Military Conflict from 1500 to 2000* (New York: Vintage Books, 1989).

[15] Josef Joffe, "Europe's American Pacifier," *Foreign Policy* 54 (spring 1984): 64–82. See also Robert Art, "Why Western Europe Needs the United States and NATO," *Political Science Quarterly* 111 (1996): 1–39.

[16] See G. John Ikenberry, *After Victory: Institutions, Strategic Restraint, and the Rebuilding of Order after Major War* (Princeton, N.J.: Princeton University Press, 2001), chap. 6.

[17] Geir Lundestad, "Empire by Invitation? The United States and Western Europe, 1945–1952," *The Journal of Peace Research* 23 (September 1986): 263–77.

power relations. The world had already been carved up by Japan and the European states. As a late-developing great power the United States needed openness and access to the regions of the world rather than recognition of its territorial claims. The American issuance of its Open Door policy toward China reflected this orientation. Woodrow Wilson's championing at Versailles of democracy and self-determination and FDR's support of decolonialization several decades later were also statements of American strategic interests issued as principled appeals.[18] American officials were never fully consistent in wielding such principled claims about order, and they were often a source of conflict with the other major states. But the overall effect of this alignment of American geostrategic interests with enlightened normative principles of order reinforced the image of the United States as a relatively noncoercive and nonimperial hegemonic power.

Democracy and Institutional Restraint

The American unipolar order is also organized around democratic polities and a complex web of intergovernmental institutions—and these features of the American system alter and mute the way in which hegemonic power is manifest. The calculations of smaller and weaker states as they confront a democratic hegemon are altered. Fundamentally, power asymmetries are less threatening or destabilizing when they exist between democracies. American power is "institutionalized"—not entirely, of course, but more so than in the case of previous world-dominating states. This institutionalized hegemonic strategy serves the interest of the United States by making its power more legitimate, expansive, and durable. But the price is that some restraints are indeed placed on the exercise of power.

In this view, which can be found in detail in chapter 7 of this book, three elements matter most in making American power more stable, engaged, and restrained. First, America's mature political institutions organized around the rule of law have made it a relatively predictable and cooperative hegemon. The pluralistic and regularized way in which American foreign and security policy is made reduces surprises and allows other states to build long-term cooperative relations. The governmental separation of powers creates a shared decision-making system that opens up the process and reduces the ability of any one leader to make abrupt or aggressive moves toward other states. An active press and competitive

---

[18] See Tony Smith, *America's Mission: The United States and the Worldwide Struggle for Democracy in the Twentieth Century* (Princeton, N.J.: Princeton University Press, 1994).

party system also are helpful to outside states by generating information about American policy and determining its seriousness of purpose. The openness of a democracy can, indeed, frustrate American diplomats and confuse foreign observers. But over the long term, democratic institutions produce more consistent and credible policies—policies that do not reflect the capricious and idiosyncratic whims of an autocrat.

Think of the United States as a giant corporation that seeks foreign investors. It is more likely to attract investors if it can demonstrate that it operates according to accepted accounting and fiduciary principles. The rule of law and the institutions of policy making in a democracy are the political equivalent of corporate transparency and accountability. Sharp shifts in policy must ultimately be vetted within the policy process and pass muster by an array of investigatory and decision-making bodies. Because it is a constitutional, rule-based democracy, outside states are more willing to work with the United States—or, to return to the corporate metaphor, to invest in ongoing partnerships.

This open and decentralized political process works in a second way to reduce foreign worries about American power.[19] It creates what might be called "voice opportunities"—it offers opportunities for political access and, with it, the means for foreign governments and groups to influence the way Washington's power is exercised. Foreign governments and corporations may not have elected officials in Washington but they do have representatives. Looked at from the perspective of the stable functioning of America's hegemonic order, this is one of the most functional aspects of the United States as a global power. By providing other states opportunities to play the game in Washington, the United States draws them into active, ongoing partnerships that serve its long-term strategic interests. This interactive character of the unipolar order was evident in the post-September 11 actions of America's allies. European and other world leaders trooped into Washington in the weeks following the terrorist attacks. Each offered its support but also weighed in on how best to wage the coming campaign. Prime Minister Tony Blair is the best example of this strategy of engaging America. The British leader tied himself to the American antiterrorist plan, but in doing so he has made it a Anglo-American—and even alliance-based—campaign. By binding itself to the

---

[19] The openness of American hegemony provides opportunities for others to advance their interests within the order, and that gives the system a measure of stability. But at the events of September 11 make clear, this political openness also makes the United States even as a hegemon vulnerable to penetration of a far more destructive sort by its enemies.

superpower, Britain gained a stake in the struggle but also—it hopes—a voice in the policy.

A final element of the American order that reduces worry about power asymmetries is the web of multilateral institutions that mark the postwar world. After World War II, the United States launched history's most ambitious era of institution building. The UN, IMF, World Bank, NATO, GATT, and other institutions that emerged provided the most rule-based structure for political and economic relations in history. The United States was deeply ambivalent about making permanent security commitments to other states or allowing its political and economic policies to be dictated by intergovernmental bodies. The Soviet menace was critical in overcoming these doubts. Networks and political relationships were built that—paradoxically—both made American power more far-reaching and durable but also more predictable and malleable.

In effect, the United States has spun a web of institutions that connected other states to an emerging American-dominated economic and security order. But in doing so, these institutions also bind the United States to other states and reduce—at least to some extent—Washington's ability to engage in the arbitrary and indiscriminate exercise of power. Call it an institutional bargain. The United States has gotten other states to join in a Western political order built around economic openness, multilateral management of trade and monetary relations, and collective security. The price for the United States is a reduction in Washington's policy autonomy. Institutional rules and joint decision making reduce American unilateralist capacities. But what Washington gets in return is worth the price. America's partners also have their autonomy constrained but in return are able to operate in a world where American power—channeled through institutions—is more restrained and reliable.

This embrace of multilateralism does not mean that the United States submits itself fully to a rule-based order on an equilateral basis. In the American unipolar order, the United States accepts restraints on its power, but this is not the same as the absolute and across-the-board acceptance of formally binding rules. The restraint is manifest in more subtle ways that entail conducting foreign policy in a way that is sensitive to norms and processes of multilateral cooperation. In effect, the United States builds an institutionalized coalition of partners and reinforces the stability of these long-term relations by making itself more "user-friendly"—that is, by playing by the rules and creating ongoing political processes with these other states that facilitate consultation and joint decision-making. The United States makes its power safe for the world and in return the world agrees to live within the American-led international order.

Modernization and Civic Identity

American power has been rendered more acceptable to the rest of the world because the United States' "project" is congruent with the deeper forces of modernization. The point here is not that the United States has pushed other states to embrace its goals and purposes but that all states are operating within a transforming global system—driven by modernization, industrialization, and social mobilization. The synchronicity between the rise of the United States as a liberal global power and the system-wide imperatives of modernization create a sort of functional "fit" between the United States and the wider world order. If the United States were attempting to project state socialist economic ideas or autocratic political values, its fit with the deep forces of modernization would be poor. Its purposes would be resisted around the world and trigger resistance to American power. But the deep congruence between the American model and the functional demands of modernization boost the power of the United States and make its relationship with the rest of the world more harmonious.

Industrialization is a constantly evolving process and the social and political characteristics within countries that it encourages and rewards—and that promote or impede industrial advancement—change over time and as countries move through developmental stages.[20] In this sense, the fit between a polity and modernization is never absolute or permanent, as the changing virtues and liabilities of the Japanese developmental state makes clear.[21] Industrialism in advanced societies tends to feature highly educated workforces, rapid flows of information, and progressively more specialized and complex systems of social and industrial organization. These features of industrial society—sometimes called late industrialism—tend to foster a citizenry that is heterogeneous, well educated, and

[20] Modernization is a slippery notion that is difficult to specify but generally refers to the processes whereby historically evolved institutions are adapted to the changing demands and opportunities created by ongoing scientific, technological, and industrial revolutions. See C. E. Black, *The Dynamics of Modernization: A Study in Comparative History* (New York: Harper and Row, 1966); and Edward L. Morse, *Modernization and the Transformation of International Relations* (New York: Free Press, 1976).

[21] See Meredith Woo-Cumings, ed., *The Developmental State* (Ithaca, N.Y.: Cornell University Press, 1999).

difficult to coerce.[22] From this perspective it is possible to see why various state socialist and authoritarian countries—including the Soviet Union—ran into trouble as the twentieth century proceeded. The old command order impeded industrial modernization while, at the same time, industrial modernization undercut the old command order.[23] In contrast, the American polity has tended to have a relatively good fit with the demands and opportunities of industrial modernization. European and Asian forms of capitalist democracy have also exhibited features that seem in various ways to be quite congruent with the leading edge of advanced industrial development.[24] The success of the American model is partly due to the fact that it used its postwar power to build an international order that worked to the benefit of the American style of industrial capitalism. But the success of the American model—and the enhanced global influence and appeal that the United States has experienced in recent decades—is also due to the deep congruence between the logic of modernization and the American system.

The functionality between the United States polity and wider evolutionary developments in the international system can also traced to the American political identity—which is rooted in civic nationalism and multiculturalism. The basic distinction between civil and ethnic nationalism is useful in locating this feature. Civic nationalism is group identity that is composed of commitments to the nation's political creed. Race, religion, gender, language, or ethnicity are not relevant in defining a citizens rights and inclusion within the polity. Shared belief in the country's principles and values embedded in the rule of law is the organizing basis for political order, and citizens are understood to be equal and rights-bearing individuals. Ethnic nationalism, in contrast, maintains that individual rights and participation within the polity are inherited—based on ethnic or racial ties.[25]

Civic national identity has four sorts of implications for the orientation—and acceptability—of American hegemonic order. First, civic

[22] See Daniel Dell, *The Coming of Post-industrial Society* (New York: Basic Books, 1973).

[23] See Daniel Deudney and G. John Ikenberry, "Soviet Reform and the End of the Cold War: Explaining Large-Scale Historical Change," *Review of International Studies* 17 (1991): 225–50.

[24] For a discussion of the variety of advanced industrial democratic forms, see Herbert Kitschelt, Peter Lange, Gary Marks, and John D. Stephens, "Convergence and Divergence in Advanced Capitalist Democracies," in *Continuity and Change in Contemporary Capitalism*, ed. Kitschelt, Lange, Marks, and Stephens (Cambridge: Cambridge University Press, 1999).

[25] This distinction is made by Anthony D. Smith, *The Ethnic Origins of Nations* (Oxford: Blackwell, 1986). For an important reconceptualization of nationalism—emphasizing the strategic use of national identity by elites—see Michael Hechter, *Containing Nationalism* (Oxford: Oxford University Press, 2000).

identity has tended to encourage the American projection outward of domestic principles of inclusive and rule-based international political organization. The American national identity is not based on ethnic or religious particularism but on a more general set of agreed-upon and
normatively appealing principles. Ethnic and religious identities and disputes are pushed downward into civil society and removed from the political arena. When the United States gets involved in political conflicts
around the world it tends to look for the establishment of agreed upon political principles and rules to guide the rebuilding of order. Likewise,
when the United States promotes rule-based solutions to problems it is
strengthening the normative and principled basis for the exercise of its
own power—and thereby making disparities in power more acceptable.

Second, because civic nationalism is shared with other Western states it
tends to be a source of cohesion and cooperation. Throughout the industrial democratic world, the dominant form of political identity is based on
a set of abstract and juridical rights and responsibilities that coexist with
private ethnic and religious associations. Just as warring states and nationalism tend to reinforce each other, so too do Western civic identity and cooperative political relations reinforce each other. Political order—domestic and international—is strengthened when there exists a substantial
sense of community and shared identity. It matters that the leaders of
today's advanced industrial states are not seeking to legitimate their power
by making racial or imperialist appeals. Civic nationalism, rooted in
shared commitment to democracy and the rule of law, provides a widely
embraced identity across most of the American hegemonic order. At the
same time, potentially divisive identity conflicts—rooted in antagonistic
ethnic, religious, or class divisions—are dampened by relegating them to
secondary status within civil society.[26]

Third, the multicultural character of the American political identity
also reinforces internationalist—and ultimately multilateral—foreign policy. John Ruggie notes that culture wars continue in the United States between a pluralistic and multicultural identity and nativist and parochial alternatives but that the core identity is still "cosmopolitan liberal"—an
identity that tends to support instrumental multilateralism. "The evocative significance of multilateral world order principles—a bias against ex-
clusive bilateralist alliances, the rejection of discriminatory economic
blocs, and facilitating means to bridge gaps of ethos, race, and religion—
should resonate still for the American public, insofar as they continue to

---

[26] See Daniel Deudney and G. John Ikenberry, "The Nature and Sources of Liberal International Order," *Review of International Studies* 25, no. 2 (April 1999): 179–96.

reflect its own sense of national identity."[27] The American society is increasingly heterogeneous in race, ethnicity, and religion. This tends to reinforce an activist and inclusive foreign policy orientation and a bias in favor of rule-based and multilateral approaches to the organization of hegemonic power.[28]

Finally, the American civic identity has tended to give the United States an unusual ability to absorb and integrate immigrants within a stable yet diverse political system.[29] This integrative capacity will grow in importance. The mature industrial democracies are all experiencing a decline in their birth rates and a gradual population aging. In the decades ahead, many of these countries—most notably Japan and Italy—will see their populations actually shrink with a smaller work force unable to support an aging demographic bubble. Immigration is increasingly a necessary aspect of economic growth. If Japan and other industrial societies are to maintain their population size and social security provisions they will need to open the door wide to immigration—but these imperatives are fiercely resisted.[30] The American willingness and ability to accept immigrants—putting it on the receiving end of the brain drain—already gives it an edge in knowledge and service industries. These advantages will only grow in the future and keep the United States at the dynamic center of the world economy. Multinational and multiethnic empires of the nineteenth century ultimately failed and were broken apart in the twentieth century. Built on a civic national base, the United States has pioneered a new form of multicultural and multiethnic political order that appears to be stable and increasingly functional with the demands of global modernization.

Sources of Breakdown and Decline

Other forces can be identified that could lead to breakdown or decay in the American unipolar order. First, there are dynamics associated with material power capabilities that might trigger a balancing response to

[27] John Gerard Ruggie, *Winning the Peace: America and World Order in the New Era* (New York: Columbia University Press, 1996), 170.

[28] On the ways in which American ethnic groups encourage foreign policy activism, see Tony Smith, *Foreign Attachments: The Power of Ethnic Groups in the Making of American Foreign Policy* (Cambridge, Mass.: Harvard University Press, 2000).

[29] For a discussion of America's advantages in absorbing high-tech trained immigrants compared to Japan and Europe, see David Ignatius, "Europe's 'Diversity Envy,' " *The Washington Post,* June 24, 2001.

[30] See Christian Joppke, *Immigration and the Nation-State* (New York: Oxford University Press, 1999).

American power. This expectation follows from realist balance-of-power theory. Unipolar order might also unravel if the United States itself withdraws from its alliance and other multilateral commitments to the existing order—withdrawal that might follow from shifting cost and benefit calculations made by American officials or declining domestic public support for such commitments. A third source of breakdown or decline might follow from a collapse in the world trade or financial system, fueling national or regional protectionism. Finally, unipolar order might unravel in less traditional ways, by the chaos and instability created by global terrorism.

Power Balancing among the Major Powers

The sheer disparities in power give states reason to worry about their status as willing partners within the American unipolar order. In order to protect themselves from the arbitrary and indiscriminate exercise of American power, this view argues, these states will loosen their security and economic ties to United States and ultimately organize a counterbalancing coalition. As noted throughout this book, Kenneth Waltz provides the logic of this expectation, which is rooted in the structural insecurities of the anarchic international system. Waltz argues that in domestic orders, organized around hierarchical authority, "bandwagoning" is the logical response to the emergence of a dominant political party or faction. The rule of law puts limits on what the power holder can do with its new capabilities. It is possible for weaker or losing groups to join the coalition and realize gains. The fear of domination or exploitation is low so the risks of joining the dominant party or faction are low. But in anarchical orders the power of the leading state is not capable of being checked by the rule of law or other institutional restraints. This leaves balancing as the chief strategy for coping with the dangers of concentrated power.

From this view, the gross disparities in power render weaker and secondary states in the unipolar order vulnerable and insecure. In practical terms, this vulnerability and insecurity is manifest in several ways. One way is simply that the United States needs the outside world less than it needs the United States. Power is manifest in the differential costs of nonagreement. On a wide range of economic, environmental, and arms control issues, the unipolar state finds it easier to walk away from agreements than do other states.[31] This might be because it has the military capacity to protect itself while other states do not or because it has a large internal mar-

---

[31] John S. Odell, *Negotiating the World Economy* (Ithaca, N.Y.: Cornell University Press, 2000).

ket that makes nonagreement less economically costly. Subordinate states are constantly worried that their goals will be thwarted or disrupted by the United States. In turn, such chronic and inherent worries lead secondary and weak states to seek alternatives. They loosen their ties to the unipolar state and seek refugee in cooperation within their own regions. Another way in which vulnerability and insecurity is manifest is more directly in the realm of security protection. Weaker and secondary states rely on the unipolar state for security. The unipolar state may realize some gains from alliance cooperation with its junior partners but, ultimately, its security is guaranteed by its own power capabilities. Subordinate states must always worry if this security protection will be forthcoming. These security asymmetries, as a result, create incentives for weaker and secondary states to seek alternative ways to protect themselves—loosening their security ties to the unipolar state and fostering regional alternatives.

In this context, there are several ways that realists have depicted the logic of "the return to balance." One is simply the formation of a counter-coalition by those great powers that reside outside the advanced industrial core, namely China and Russia. These great powers might trigger balancing by moving toward a more formal military countercoalition. When Chinese and Russian leaders meet, they do typically speak about the dangers of American "hegemonism." Moscow and Beijing also recently signed their first friendship treaty in several decades.[32] Obviously, these two countries are competitors in many areas and share a long international border that is fraught with economic and demographic tensions and instabilities. But global balancing might nonetheless emerge out of an alliance among outsiders. Various considerations other than the distribution of power itself might reinforce this coalition. Unlike the other great powers, neither of these countries has formal security ties with the United States. Neither of these countries has fully embraced Western style capitalism and democracy. An anticapitalist or antidemocratic ideology has not yet been articulated by these countries or by others. But insecurities and hostilities created by their deep ambivalence to the American or Western model could give some impetus to a Sino-Russian counterbalancing alliance.

Another return to balance sequence could be triggered from inside the Western core. In this case, Western Europe and Japan might increasingly bridle at American domineering and unilateral tendencies. On economic, security, and environmental issues, the American pursuit of its narrow national interest could well increasingly clash with European and Japanese

[32] Michael Wines, "A World Seeking Security Is Told There's Just One Shield," *The New York Times,* July 22, 2001; and Patrick E. Tyler, "Behind the Shield, a 3-Sided Rivalry," *The New York Times,* May 6, 2001.

agendas.[33] This rising discord might in turn lead to small steps toward greater independence across the board. These small steps probably would not be made with a goal of moving toward a dramatic break with the United States or the development of a countervailing security alliance. European and Japanese officials might only be attempting to create a buffer against American unilateralism. But these small steps over a decade or so—toward more independent regional economic and security arrangements—could lay the groundwork for a more decisive break later on.

In the first months of 2001, the Bush administration hinted at a general foreign policy of unilateralism and selective engagement and exposed some of these deep tensions with Europe and Japan. "It is not isolationist but unilateralist, unashamed of using military power," one reporter noted.[34] The most visible sign of this skepticism about multilateralism and institutional commitments in the Bush administration was the dramatic sequence of rejections of pending international agreements—including the Kyoto Protocol, the International Criminal Court, the Germ Weapons Ban, and the Trade in Light Arms Treaty. In pushing national missile defense, the administration also took steps to unilaterally withdraw from the 1972 Anti-Ballistic Missile Defense Treaty, which many regard as the cornerstone of modern arms control agreements. Together the chorus of rejections underscore the misgivings the Bush administration has had about the entire enterprise of multilateral and rule-based cooperation.[35] This unilateralist tendency was not lost on European public opinion, which has evinced deep misgivings about living under the shadow of American power.[36] It is unclear whether the American-led coalition against terrorism, launched after the September 11 attacks, will reverse this deterioration in relations or simply delay it.

The key turning point would probably be in security ties. The current thinking in Europe and Japan is that they can remain subordinate alliance partners with the United States and still realize their policy goals. But this thinking could change: security partnership could be seen as a net cost to these states because it denies them the capacity to be the masters of their own fate. Again, this possible breakdown in the unipolar order is not driven by an explicit goal by these advanced industrial states to balance

[33] See Stephen M. Walt, "The Ties That Fray: Why Europe and America Are Drifting Apart," *The National Interest* 54 (winter 1998/99): 3–11.

[34] Stephen Fidler, "Between Two Camps," *Financial Times*, February 14, 2001.

[35] See Gerard Baker, "Bush Heralds Era of U.S. Self-Interest," *International Herald Tribune*, April 24, 2001.

[36] See, for example, Roger Cohen, "News Analysis: To European Eyes, It's America the Ugly," *The New York Times*, May 7, 2001; Alan Beattie, "Europe Assails U.S. on Co-operation," *The Financial Times*, May 17, 2001; and Norman Kempster, "Europeans Dislike Bush's Foreign Policy, Poll Finds," *Los Angeles Times*, August 16, 2001.

against the United States, but small steps away from unipolarity would lay the foundation for a more dramatic break later on.

A third sequence that could lead to a return to the balance of power centers on Germany and Japan. Some realists have emphasized the deep logic of great-power status. Great powers may rise and decline but they do not fade away—and they certainly always look for ways to increase their power and status.[37] For half a century, Japan and Germany have remained "civilian" great powers, marked by constitutional and treaty-based limits on their military capacity and autonomy, including a prohibition on possession of nuclear weapons. The United States and the other allies initially imposed these limits on Japanese and German military status after World War II. During the Cold War decades, the Soviet threat and the imperatives of alliance solidarity made this subordinate position useful to all parties. But in the post–Cold War environment, these restrictions appear to many Japanese and Germans as artificial and outdated. Even to Japanese and Germans who embrace a security partnership with the United States, it is still seen as odd that the United States should—fifty years after the war—still have its troops stationed in these two countries, the second and third largest economies in the world.

Accordingly, Germany and Japan will eventually want to return to more "normal" great-power status. This move—signaled perhaps most importantly by their acquisition of nuclear weapons but also by a movement away from subordinate security partnership with the United States and toward the development of autonomous military capabilities—could spiral into a more general fragmentation and estrangement of relations within the American unipolar order. As in the other scenarios, such steps need not be taken with the direct aim of balancing against the United States but security separation and the redrawing of the distribution of military capabilities could pave the way for later crises and tensions to push the countries toward outright strategic rivalry.

American Disengagement and Collapse

Another pathway from unipolarity to the balance of power might be triggered by the United States itself. In this scenario the great powers arrayed around the United States are not seeking to balance American power or

[37] This argument is emphasized in Christopher Laye, "The Unipolar Illusion: Why New Great Powers Will Arise," *International Security* 17, no. 4 (spring 1993): 5–51. See also John J. Mearsheimer, "Back to the Future: Instability of Europe after the Cold War," *International Security* 15 (summer 1990): 5–57; and Mearsheimer, *The Tragedy of Great Power Politics* (New York: W. W. Norton, 2001).

even to alter the security and economic bargains of the unipolar order. Rather, the unraveling happens when the United States makes choices to reduce or withdraw from the order itself. This disengagement might take the form of the withdrawal of overseas troops and the weakening or abandonment of security commitments to Europe and East Asia. Or it might take the form of withdrawal from the world's multilateral economic institutions, such as the IMF and the WTO. These provocative steps could trigger a spiral downward in cooperation and economic openness, which in turn might lead to the fragmentation of security alliances and ultimately to a multipolar balance-of-power system.

Why would the United States "pull the plug" on its own unipolar order? Two sorts of answers are possible. One focuses on the actual costs and benefits to the United States in playing a system-supporting role. Paul Kennedy and Robert Gilpin have explored this logic.[38] In the mature phase of an imperial or hegemonic order, the lead state is forced to spend more resources on supporting the order than is sustainable over the long run. Resources and productive capacities are diminished and diverted from their most productive uses thereby reducing the long-term ability of the state to play this extended imperial or hegemonic role. The American imperial burden is manifest in its extended military presence around the world. Roughly one hundred thousand American troops are stationed in both Western Europe and East Asia. Defense spending in the United States is much greater as a share of GNP than it is in the other advanced industrial countries. The drag that these commitments and expenditures put on the American economy is difficult to calculate and debate.[39] Allied countries do cover some of the costs entailed in the forward deployment of American troops. Military research and development spending also has some positive spin-offs for the civilian economy. But the costs are nonetheless real. Paul Kennedy's vision of imperial or hegemonic decline anticipates the actual relative decline of the lead state—burdened and overextended by its military commitments—and the rise of new great powers. But it might be that the United States would actually recognize the rising costs and declining benefits of its global military presence and cut back. This in turn could lead to new insecurities in Europe, Asia, and elsewhere and the spiral of security competition begins.

The souring of public opinion could also spark the disengagement of the United States from its own unipolar order. Charles Kupchan's chapter

[38] Paul Kennedy, *The Rise and Decline of the Great Powers: Economic Change and Military Conflict, 1500 to 2000* (New York: Random House, 1987); and Gilpin, *War and Change in World Politics.*

[39] For a survey of these issues, see Todd Sandler and Keith Hartley, *The Economics of Defense* (New York: Cambridge University Press, 1995).

explores this possibility. A growing mismatch between America's foreign commitments and the willingness of the American public to support these commitments could lead to a dramatic downsizing of American internationalism and global leadership. This is true even if the foreign policy elite remains committed to leadership. The stark asymmetries in military capacities puts the United States in a unique position of responsibility to respond to civil wars, humanitarian crises, rogue states, and other troubling developments that threaten the core interests of the major industrial states. A sort of post–Cold War division of labor has emerged that leaves the United States "indispensable" in responding to threats and the management of instability around the world, particularly where the use of force is necessary. This "system maintenance function" that the United States plays, however, is built on a soft domestic foundation. The American public does not fully recognize this role or appreciate its importance. Without the Cold War and a serious global peer competitor, as Kupchan argues, the American people will not be willing to bear the burdens of an American empire. In the past decade, this unipolar provision of a global security guarantee has not exacted a high price within American society. The "wars" have been relatively free of American casualties and economic pain. But it is possible to imagine the next war—perhaps involving Korea or Taiwan—exposing the gross asymmetries in burden between the United States and its allies. Calls would emerge in Congress to redress these imbalances in burdens. This in turn could lead to a quick unraveling of America's unipolar military commitments.

Global Economic Collapse

The route to unipolar collapse could also start with a global trade or financial meltdown. This is the vision of a return to the 1930s where depression led to protectionism and beggar-thy-neighbor policies, which led to regional blocs, geopolitical conflict, and war. Economic relations between the major powers could quickly deteriorate if global markets collapse or even experience simply a prolonged era of contraction. During the best of economic times, such as the 1990s, economic relations among the great powers are complicated and laced with conflict.[40] In bad economic times, they can quickly worsen. The end of the Cold War removed a source of cohesion among the advanced industrial countries and rendered more fragile the political consensus among the major countries in

[40] See C. Fred Bergsten, "America's Two-Front Economic Conflict," *Foreign Affairs* 80, no. 2 (March/April 2001): 2–8.

favor of multilateral economic openness. The deregulation of financial markets and the vast movements of capital around the world threaten to make future crises more severe and widespread.[41] Ironically, American unipolar power has been put in the service of creating a global economic system—unprecedented in scope and integration—that could in due course lead to instability, collapse, backlash, and the shattering of that unipolar order.

In this scenario, crisis and a prolonged economic downturn in the world economy would lead Europe and East Asia to pull away from the United States and pursue their own visions of regional economic order. Markets would become more political, trade conflict would rise, and the three major regions would compete for supremacy.[42] In the view of some, the severity of these regional clashes would be intensified because of deep differences in the character of modern capitalism that each region embraces. Continental Europe, Anglo-America, and East Asia each has its own values and institutions that gives each a distinctive approach to state, society, and market. Chalmers Johnson, for example, has argued that with the end of artificial Cold War constraints, Japan will eventually reassert its economic independence from the United States, triggering greater conflict across the Pacific.[43] At the global level, the decline in a consensus over the merits of American-led globalization—most dramatically exhibited in the increasingly frequent protests at meetings of the IMF, World Bank, WTO, and the Group of Eight—also reinforces national and regional economic priorities at the expense of the open global economy.

The United States is today committed to using its global position to stabilize and promote economic openness but it is possible that the asymmetries in its burdens could trigger a domestic backlash. The United States has taken a lead over the decades in building and running the multilateral world economy. The creation of the WTO is a major accomplishment of post–Cold War cooperation among the advanced industrial countries. So too is the agreement reached in November 2001 by WTO members to launch a new multilateral trade round. But it is imaginable that if the American economy were to take a dramatic downturn and the European and Japanese economies were to rebound, the costs of American leader-

---

[41] John Eatwell and Lance Taylor, *Global Finance at Risk: The Case for International Regulation* (New York: New Press, 2000).

[42] For one version of coming regional economic conflict, see Lester Thurow, *Head to Head: The Coming Economic Battle among Japan, Europe, and America* (New York: William Morrow, 1992).

[43] Chalmers Johnson, "History Restarted: Japanese-American Relations at the End of the Century," in *Japan: Who Governs? The Rise of the Developmental State*, ed. Johnson (New York: Norton, 1995).

ship in these institutions could become a domestic political issue. Politicians are only too eager to exploit such situations. Currently, the protectionist interests in the United States are divided—located on the outer fringes of the two major political parties. But an extended economic recession—or certainly a global depression—could bring these groups into the mainstream and push national policy in a protectionist direction. Again, this scenario would anticipate a spiral of protectionist reactions, fissures in alliances and multilateral economic regimes, and a breakdown of unipolarity.

Terrorism and Global Crisis

The terrorist events of September 11, 2001, remind the world that attacks on American unipolarity need not only come from the great powers. Even if the major states do not have incentives to challenge or balance against the United States, terrorist groups certainly do. Although the open and penetrated character of American hegemony has made unipolarity less threatening to other states, it has also made the United States more vulnerable to terrorism. The challenge of global terrorism is not likely to threaten the global power structure over the long term—at least not directly. Even if terrorists kills thousands of people, those that commit these acts will not conquer territory or overthrow governments. The consequences of global terrorism are likely to be less direct and, depending how the responses unfold, the result could either reinforce or diminish American unipolarity.[44]

In one scenario, the fight against global terrorism could encourage cooperative great-power relations—and thereby reinforce unipolarity. To conduct an effective campaign, the United States will discover incentives to pursue a multilateral strategy and make bargains with other countries in order to gain their support. The United States needs partners: the military and logistical support of allies, intelligence sharing, and the practical cooperation of front-line states. The transnational character of terrorism makes a national strategy impotent. Fighting terrorism entails tracing bank accounts, sharing criminal information, and other basic tasks of international law enforcement. As Fareed Zakaria has indicated, "the crucial dimensions of the struggle are covert operations, intelligence gathering and police work. All of this requires the active cooperation of many other governments. U.S. Marines cannot go into Hamburg and arrest suspects.

---

[44] For a discussion of these issues, see G. John Ikenberry, "American Grand Strategy in the Age of Terror," *Survival* 43, no. 4 (winter 2001–2): 19–34.

We cannot shut down banks in the United Arab Emirates. We cannot get intelligence from Russia except if the Russians share it with us."[45] The United States now needs lots of things from lots of governments. This is a potential boon to cooperation between the United States and other states.

The Bush administration's response to the terrorist attacks of September 11 illuminate this cooperative logic. In seeking partners in its struggle, the United States does appear to be rediscovering that the strategic partnerships it has built over the decades still exist and are useful. After NATO voted its support of the American campaign, Secretary of State Powell remarked that fifty years of steady investment in the alliance had paid off.[46] When the United States ties itself to a wider grouping of states it is more effective. But to do so requires some compromise of national autonomy. It must both restrain and commit its power. The Bush administration showed an impulse toward unilateralism in early 2001 in its dramatic rejection of a sequence of multilateral treaties and agreements. But the administration's subsequent ambition to lead a global coalition against terrorism would seem to make unilateralism more problematic. Much as leadership of the free world coalition during the Cold War forced the United States reluctantly to make policy compromises and commitments, so too will its leadership of an antiterrorist coalition.

The American campaign against terrorism could also change the wider terms of great-power cooperation. Russian President Vladimir Putin is the best example of a leader seeking to exploit this new opportunity to make bargains. By throwing his support to the American cause, he is opening the way for support and accommodation by the United States on a range of issues crucial to the Russian agenda—such as economic aid, Chechnya, NATO expansion, and missile defense. Even before September 11, the United States had been seeking to recast the strategic relationship with Russia. While the Bush strategy was to offer that strategic relationship in exchange for accommodation on missile defense, the ultimate result might be some more expansive form of cooperative security between Russia and the West. Indeed, Russian cooperation on terrorism may in the long run strengthen the argument that Russia should be brought fully into the Western security framework.[47] China's response to the U.S. antiterror campaign is more restrained, but it too may find ways to exchange its support of the American antiterrorist campaign for a stable policy of engagement by the United States. This was the first great call to arms by

---

[45] Fareed Zakaria, "Back to the Real World," *The Washington Post*, October 2, 2001.

[46] Secretary of State Powell, public statement, October 10, 2001.

[47] See Quentin Peel, "Washington's Balancing Act," *Financial Times*, October 1, 2001; and Timothy Garton Ash, "A New War Reshapes Old Alliances," *The New York Times*, October 12, 2001.

an American president where the enemy was not another great power. In the past the enemy was totalitarianism, fascism, and Nazism—all of which followed the path, in the words of President Bush, to "history's unmarked grave of discarded lies"—but this new transnational threat offers incentives to deepen strategic cooperation among all the great powers.

But the American struggle with terrorism could also make the unipolar order more vulnerable. The United States could decide that its desire to oppose terrorist regimes such as Iraq is more important than maintaining the coalition. In this instance it might use force that split the allies into fragmented groups each seeking a separate settlement. The United States could also return to its unilateral ways on other issues, allowing the deep disagreements and latent antagonisms between America and Europe—currently not visible because of the temporary united front against terrorism—to break into the open. The deals that the United States and its allies make with repressive regimes in the Middle East and South Asia could also come back to haunt the Western democracies by undercutting the credibility of the West's commitment to democracy and human rights and creating locales for breeding the next generation of terrorists. If a terrorist group did gain access to nuclear weapons and exploded a device in Europe or the United States, the political consequences could be catastrophic. The borders of the advanced countries would probably be shut down. Trade and financial interdependence would likely be rolled back ending the current era of globalization. What sort of global political order would emerge in the wake of this disaster is unknowable.

Conclusion

The world has seen many great powers rise up to dominate the international system. Charles V, Louis XIV, Napoleon I, Wilhelmine and Nazi Germany—each became a hegemonic threat to Europe and triggered a backlash that rearranged the geopolitical landscape. Today it is the United States that looms above all other states and the question that many observers pose is: will the United States suffer a similar fate? Resistance has in fact appeared and may be growing. But it is remarkable that despite the sharp shifts in the distribution of power, the other great powers have not yet responded in a way anticipated by balance-of-power theory.

There is some evidence that American power—and the American unipolar order—is different and less threatening to other states than that which is envisaged in theoretical and historical claims about the balance of power. A variety of features associated with American hegemony—rooted in geography, history, ideology, democracy, institutional structures, and modernization itself—make it different than past great powers. These characteristics of American power mute and restrain that power and alter the risk calculations of weaker and secondary states. It also matters that these restraining characteristics are deeply rooted in the American polity. Situated offshore from the other great powers, the United States is removed from regional antagonisms and rivalries. The United States is also able to deploy its power to solve problems for other states— particularly regional security dilemmas—and this weakens the incentives other states might have to engage in counterbalancing.

The United States used its power in the 1940s and afterward to build a world order. An entire system of alliances, multilateral institutions, and entangling relations have emerged such that it is possible to talk about American unipolarity as a distinctive political formation. Pax Americana is not just a powerful country throwing its weight around. It is a political formation with its own logic and laws of motion. It is an order that was created and sustained by American power but it is not simply a reflection of that power. Indeed, it is the ability of this order to mute the impact of power symmetries that give it its durability. The deep congruence between the internal American political system—and its civic and multicultural identity—and the long-term project of modernity also gives the unipolar order robustness. The United States remains at the core of this order but it is an order that now has a life of its own.

But no political orders have yet been immutable. Most of the authors in this book argue that the underlying concentration of American power is itself the most vital ingredient in the unipolar order. History speaks very loudly that power distributions are always in motion. American power will decline just as the power of other hegemonic states in past eras has eroded. It is possible to imagine a variety of crises and breakdowns in the current world order that could speed the process of rise and decline and usher in an entirely new set of principles and institutions of order. It remains an intriguing question whether today's unipolar order is primarily an artifact of American power and will be swept away when that power declines or whether the political features of unipolarity are actually more deeply embedded in modernity and the international features of democracy and capitalism.

Index

Cornell Studies in Security Affairs

A series edited by ROBERT J. ART
ROBERT JERVIS
STEPHEN M. WALT

The Ideology of the Offensive: Military Decision Making and the Disasters of 1914
   by Jack Snyder
Myths of Empire: Domestic Politics and International Ambition by Jack Snyder
The Militarization of Space: U.S. Policy, 1945–1984 by Paul B. Stares
The Nixon Administration and the Making of U.S. Nuclear Strategy
   by Terry Terriff
The Ethics of Destruction: Norms and Force in International Relations
   by Ward Thomas
Causes of War: Power and the Roots of Conflict by Stephen Van Evera
Mortal Friends, Best Enemies: German-Russian Cooperation after the Cold War
   by Celeste A. Wallander
The Origins of Alliances by Stephen M. Walt
Revolution and War by Stephen M. Walt
The Tet Offensive: Intelligence Failure in War by James J. Wirtz
The Elusive Balance: Power and Perceptions during the Cold War
   by William Curti Wohlforth
Deterrence and Strategic Culture: Chinese-American Confrontations, 1949–1958
   by Shu Guang Zhang